JAN LIBICH

REAL–WORLD ECONOMIC POLICY

INSIGHTS FROM LEADING AUSTRALIAN ECONOMISTS

To all my students, colleagues, family and friends for inspiring me to search for answers.

JAN LIBICH

REAL–WORLD ECONOMIC POLICY

INSIGHTS FROM LEADING AUSTRALIAN ECONOMISTS

Real-World Economic Policy: Insights from Leading Australian Economists
1st Edition
Jan Libich

Publishing manager: Dorothy Chiu
Publishing editor: Michelle Aarons
Publishing assistant: Stephanie Heriot
Project editor: Natalie Orr
Text designer: Danielle Maccarone
Permissions/Photo researcher: QBS Learning
Editor: Greg Alford
Proofreader: Paul Smitz
Indexer: Russell Brooks
Cover: Illustration by Veronika Mojžišová and full colour
    application by Gregory Baldwin
Typeset by Cenveo Publisher Services

Any URLs contained in this publication were checked for
currency during the production process. Note, however,
that the publisher cannot vouch for the ongoing currency of
URLs.

For product information and technology assistance,
    in Australia call **1300 790 853**;
    in New Zealand call **0800 449 725**

For permission to use material from this text or product, please email
aust.permissions@cengage.com

National Library of Australia Cataloguing-in-Publication Data
Creator: Libich, Jan, author.
Title: Real-world economic policy : insights from leading
             Australian economists / Jan Libich.
ISBN: 9780170364386 (paperback)
Subjects: International trade--Case studies.
             Economics--Case studies.
             Economic policy--Case studies.
Dewey Number: 382.1

Cengage Learning Australia
Level 7, 80 Dorcas Street
South Melbourne, Victoria Australia 3205

Cengage Learning New Zealand
Unit 4B Rosedale Office Park
331 Rosedale Road, Albany, North Shore 0632, NZ

For learning solutions, visit **cengage.com.au**

Printed in China by 1010 Printing International Limited.
1 2 3 4 5 6 7 19 18 17 16 15

Contents

Preface: why economic policy? Why real-world?

Imagine you are in charge of a country; a policymaker responsible for designing all of the country's economic policies. How would you go about this important job? You are obviously not a self-imposed despot; you are a democratically elected leader who genuinely cares about the wellbeing of your nation.

But while you are trying very hard, your citizens are not happy. Retirees believe they deserve greater respect and a higher pension. Young families expect more support with the challenging task of raising the next generation. University students argue for more financial assistance for their key mission of acquiring human capital to drive future technological progress and economic growth. New entrants into the housing market expect the 'first home owner grant' to help them buy their dream home, the way their parents were able to. Employees feel entitled to longer annual leave and a fair minimum wage for all their hard work. People without a job hope that you will help them find one, and that you will assist them financially in the meantime.

The businesses in your country do not seem happy either. They present arguments for enhanced government support of their research and development efforts, as well as for lower interest rates and taxes – to help them innovate, invest and create jobs.

They also feel entitled to patent protection of their inventions enforced by a well-functioning legal system. Financial companies expect to be bailed out when they get into trouble. Domestic firms strongly lobby for imposing tariffs and quotas on foreign imports to protect them from unfair competition from low-wage countries. Exporting companies argue for weakening the exchange rate to make them more successful overseas.

After a few days in office you are starting to feel a headache from all these reasonable-sounding demands. The adrenaline of the election campaign has subsided and you are now back to reality, fully aware that due to the scarcity of resources you cannot possibly satisfy every person's myriad wishes. You feel that the best you can possibly do is to design policies that maximise the wellbeing of the society as a whole. And you realise that it should be done in a way that is sensitive to the needs of the less fortunate in the society. But you also realise that it needs to be done in a way that does not create strong work disincentives and does not lead to people giving up responsibility for their own destiny. Put differently, from the failures of centrally planned economies of the past century you realise that you will need to largely rely on the markets. On the other hand, from the many economic downturns, including the recent Global Financial Crisis, you realise that markets need clear rules and competently designed regulation to function effectively.

In the jargon of economics, you want your policies to strike the right balance between efficiency and equity. This book will assist you in achieving that goal. It will help you identify welfare-improving policies in many areas such as healthcare, education, retirement financing, monetary and fiscal policies, banking regulation and climate change. But what is even more important, the book strives to teach you 'by example' about the decision-making process behind optimal actions. It reveals how esteemed

Australian economists and policymakers, including four former central bank Governors and Board members, an ACCC Commissioner, and a current member of the federal parliament and Shadow Minister go about economic policy. It demonstrates how they think through the effect of policy actions on people's behaviour, and how this influences their decisions. Needless to say that such 'strategic' thinking is useful not only in the policymaking arena but also in one's personal life.

You may wonder why you should be interested in what Australian economists and policymakers have to say. Their insights are worth listening to since they seem to have juggled the efficiency and equity trade-off more skilfully than most of their foreign counterparts; Australians seem to be good at finding the right balance. This is evident in the fact that a number of key policies in Australia, some designed by the economists featured in this book, are used as a role model by policymakers in the rest of the world and are widely imitated.

So is it not true that economics is divorced from the real world? This book demonstrates that the depiction of 'ivory tower' (dinosaur-like) academic economists building useless, unrealistic mathematical models is not quite accurate. It does so by highlighting the applicability of economics in real-world policymaking. The 14 chapters show that economics is not about boring curve-shifting, equations and heartless definitions, but about helping people to make better decisions and thus improve their prosperity. This is depicted in the cartoon below featuring Reserve Bank of Australia Governor Glenn Stevens.

Concept by Jan Libich © 2015, drawing by Veronika Mojžišová. Used by permission.

About the author

Jan Libich has taught and done research at La Trobe University in Melbourne since 2005, and more recently also at VŠB-Technical University Ostrava, Czech Republic. He holds a PhD from the University of New South Wales and earlier degrees from the University of Economics, Prague.

Jan's research focuses on macroeconomic topics, primarily monetary and fiscal policies, as well as the microeconomic areas of game theory and sports economics. He has published two dozen papers in academic journals including *Macroeconomic Dynamics*, *Journal of Institutional and Theoretical Economics*, *Economic Modelling*, *Journal of Macroeconomics*, *Economics Letters* and *Journal of Sports Economics*. Over the past decade, Jan has presented his research at nearly a hundred seminars and conferences, including invited talks at high-profile policy institutions such as the International Monetary Fund and nine central banks (e.g. the European Central Bank, the US Federal Reserve and the Reserve Bank of Australia).

Jan is also a dedicated teacher who has received a number of awards for his contributions to students' learning. For example, he was awarded a 2012 Citation by the Australian government; and, based on student nominations, reached the top spot for La Trobe University in the UniJobs 'Lecturer of the Year' poll four years in a row (2009–12).

About the contributors

Chapter	Contributor	Current affiliation	Current and past policy involvement
1	**Prof. Paul Frijters**	University of Queensland	Consultancy for various Australian and Dutch governments
2	**Prof. Robert Gregory, AO**	Australian National University	RBA Board member, Australian Sciences and Technology Council, Commonwealth Committee on Higher Education, Commonwealth Taskforce on Employment Opportunities
3	**Dr Andrew Leigh, MP**	Australian House of Representatives	Shadow Minister for Competition, Shadow Assistant Treasurer
4	**Prof. Stephen King**	Monash University	Commissioner of the Australian Competition and Consumer Commission, expert witness in public inquiries (Senate and Australian Federal Court)
5	**Prof. Bruce Chapman**	Australian National University	Architect of the Australian Higher Education Contributions Scheme, consultancy for many governments on tertiary education
6	**Dr Stephen Kirchner**	Australian Financial Markets Association	Adviser to members of the Australian House of Representatives and Senate
7	**Prof. John Piggott**	University of New South Wales	Consultancy for Australian, Indonesian, Japanese and Russian governments

Chapter	Contributor	Current affiliation	Current and past policy involvement
8	**A/Prof. Frank Jotzo**	Australian National University	Lead author of the 2014 Intergovernmental Panel on Climate Change, advising on the 2008 Garnaut Climate Change Review for Australia
9	**Prof. Adrian Pagan**	University of Sydney	RBA Board member, review of modelling and forecasting at the Bank of England
10	**Michael Knox**	RBS Morgans	Australian Trade Commissioner in Saudi Arabia and Indonesia, Chairman of the Queensland Food Industry Strategy Committee, Ministerial Advisory Committee on Economic Development
11	**Prof. Warwick McKibbin**	Australian National University	RBA Board member, The Brookings Institution, Congressional Budget Office, Australian Prime Minister's Science, Engineering and Innovation Council
12	**Dr Don Brash**	Company director and consultant	RBNZ Governor, The World Bank, leader of the New Zealand National Party
13 & 14	**Dr Jan Libich**	La Trobe University	Many invited research presentations at policy institutions such as the International Monetary Fund, the Treasury and nine central banks (with visiting appointment at two of them). Proposal to the International Football Association (FIFA) regarding penalty shootouts

Introduction: learning economics by applying it to policy

The book is based on a series of video-interviews with leading Australian economists and policymakers that I recorded for my students during the 2011–14 period (the full-length videos, mostly of one-hour duration, are available together with those not included in the book at www.youtube.com/c/JanLibich). Following the Global Financial Crisis, this period provided economists with a lot of stimulating new material, and policymakers with a number of challenges. While the Australian economy went through the crisis with only minor bruises, most other high-income countries suffered major 'injuries'. Jokes such as 'The economy is so bad, parents in Beverly Hills fired their nannies and learned their children's names' have probably been arriving in your inbox on a regular basis.

Are you still sceptical about moving from the calm waters of economic theories to the turbulent ocean of real-world policy? That's a good thing. Scepticism makes one dig deeper, question conventional wisdom and attempt to square it with facts. That's what real-world economics is about! The following cartoon, featuring former US Federal Reserve Chairman Alan Greenspan and former US President George W. Bush, points to the possible clash between (misunderstood) economic theory and real-world policy in the lead-up to the 2008 Global Financial Crisis.

Concept by Jan Libich © 2015, drawing by Veronika Mojžišová. Used by permission.

In order to bring economics to life, each chapter will feature a cartoon related to the discussion topic. This is in line with the book's main aim: to enable the reader to 'learn economics by applying it' within the real-world context rather than wasting time by memorising definitions and diagrams. This can be compared to learning to swim by jumping in the pool as opposed to reading manuals about the perfect stroke.[1]

Educational research reveals that students who apply the material to real-life learn much more effectively. For example, in their 1992 book titled *Accelerate Your Learning*, Rose and Goll showed in an experiment that after 48 hours students on average retain only 10 per cent of what they have read, 20 per cent of what they have heard, and 30 per cent of what they have seen. In contrast, they remember a whopping 80 per cent of what they have used in real life!

In embracing the real-world policy approach to economics, one should be prepared to encounter plurality of views and potentially conflicting opinions. It is rightly said that economics is the only field in which two people can get a Nobel Prize for saying the opposite thing, and in fact this happened as recently as 2013. Why is that? Does economic science not fit Albert Einstein's description that: 'The whole of science is nothing more than a refinement of everyday thinking?'

Yes, it does, but economics, like other social sciences, has a notable disadvantage compared to natural sciences. It is because it studies human behaviour rather than natural (non-human) phenomena. Given the complexity of the human psyche and human systems, it should be no surprise that the success of social sciences in predicting the outcomes of millions of decisions and interactions between people is lower than in physics or chemistry. This implies that it is impossible to have a 100 per cent correct economic model capturing the full details of complex human systems. Despite this, even imperfect models featuring simplifying assumptions may still teach us important insights about how people behave and help us make better decisions. As George Box once put it: 'All models are wrong but some are useful.'[2]

The 2008 crisis, as well as the subsequent period over which the book's interviews were conducted, has once again highlighted the fact that a good economist should be humble and open about the things economics can and cannot do. For example, it will be apparent below that economics is incapable of making accurate predictions about short-term movements in exchange rates or stock prices (which inspired a plethora of jokes about God creating economists to make weather forecasters look good).

On the positive side, economics can explain quite well why this is the case (i.e. why some asset markets tend to follow a 'random walk'), and why economists are much more successful in understanding longer-term economic outcomes. Economics can provide, based on theoretical models and state-of-the-art data analysis, convincing answers to questions such as: 'What drives economic growth and living standards?', 'What happens to prices over time when too much money is injected into the economy?',

---

1 Accept my apologies if you do find the cartoons neither funny nor informative. It may not be a good idea for someone without a sense of humour to be coming up with jokes (one of my students once wrote on the official teaching feedback form in relation to my joke attempts that 'Jan sometimes does not realise that students are laughing at him rather than with him').

2 See George E. P. Box and Norman R. Draper (1986), *Empirical Model-Building and Response Surfaces*, John Wiley & Sons, Inc.

or 'What are the various causes and effects of unemployment?' As economics Nobel laureate Robert Shiller put it:

> Yes, most economists fail to predict financial crises – just as doctors fail to predict disease. But, like doctors, they have made life manifestly better for everyone.

Project Syndicate (2015), *What Good are Economists?*, www.project-syndicate.org/
commentary/are-economists-good-by-robert-j--shiller-2015-01

The future may not take you down the path of economic policy in the end. But economics will still provide you with knowledge that may be useful in whatever you choose to do in the future. It certainly did that for body-builder/actor/politician Arnold Schwarzenegger, the Rolling Stones singer Mick Jagger and golfer Tiger Woods, who all studied economics. I sincerely hope that the real-world policy approach presented in this book can help you too in developing valuable skills and ultimately achieving your goals, whatever they may be.

Notes for the reader: coverage and chapter map

The book attempts to give you a deeper understanding of topical policy areas in both macroeconomics (about two-thirds of the chapters) and microeconomics (about one-third). While the level of the debate is accessible to first-year economics students (even to a complete novice in the econ swimming pool), the discussions may be of interest to a much wider audience ranging from more advanced students to private-sector economists to practitioners in public institutions.

The interviews in the first four chapters offer brief *overviews* of the main economics themes from the perspective of policymakers. They attempt to provide you with a refresher, a 'big picture' foundation on which you can build your understanding of specific areas of economic policymaking. In particular, Chapters 1 and 2 focus on macroeconomics – the former on the long-term and the latter on the short-term perspective. Chapters 3 and 4 then summarise the key microeconomic policy areas.

Following these summaries, Chapters 5 to 14 explore the main themes in more detail. The first four discuss important long-term topics, namely education and its financing (Chapter 5), fiscal policy sustainability (Chapter 6), populating ageing and pension systems (Chapter 7), and climate change (Chapter 8). Chapters 9 to 13 then examine economic policy themes of a short- and medium-term nature. Specifically, these are monetary policy (Chapter 9), banking, financial markets and crises (Chapter 10), the causes, consequences and policy responses to the economic turmoil of 2008 (Chapter 11), the interaction of the central bank and government (Chapter 12), and the desirability of currency unions such as the Eurozone (Chapter 13). Finally, Chapter 14 offers advice on managing personal finances. In the latter two chapters I am no longer the interviewer but take on the role of the interviewee (which means that the 'leading' pronoun in the title of the book does not apply …).

You will see that some topics are touched on in several chapters; for example, the demographic trend of ageing populations, public debt problems, the unconventional monetary policy of quantitative easing and its possible inflationary consequences, tertiary education financing, the impact of minimum wages on unemployment, and the effect of human capital on economic growth and prosperity. This is in order to give you a broader perspective on these topical policy issues by each interviewee offering his unique view.

Each chapter has the following structure. It starts with a list of the main economic concepts discussed. Section 1 of each chapter then offers the motivation of the covered topic, as well as an introduction of the economist/policymaker sharing his insights in the chapter. It also provides an overview of the debate and more broadly a summary of the relevant policy area.

Section 2 contains the interview itself. It is somewhat shortened and edited to make it more accessible to the reader. At various instances statistics have been added to make the discussion more informative, but no important messages or predictions have been changed, to maintain the authenticity of the interviewee's narrative. Due to the real-world policy focus, a discussion has been added to each chapter regarding policies that economics shows would improve people's wellbeing, but which politicians have shied away from.

Section 3 contains a summary of the chapter's key economic insights and implied policy lessons. Their normative prescription 'Policymakers should …' obviously relates to benevolent policymakers in government, central banks and other public agencies who attempt to maximise society's welfare. And as such, it will be apparent that some of the prescriptions may not be 'incentive compatible', in the sense that short-sighted politicians seeking re-election are unlikely to implement them. In fact, politicians may be tempted to do the exact opposite. This implies that the policy lessons are aimed at the general public as well; it is imperative that voters put pressure on the political leadership to institutionalise sound, long-term oriented policies.

Section 4 of each chapter then offers questions for further discussion of the topic, relating to both the speaker's views and your own. Such discussion is essential – it is a great way not only to remember the themes but also to expand your understanding. Scientific research shows that when we talk, our brain does a different – much deeper – type of thinking compared to when we are reading or listening. This includes the practice of asking good questions, which is often more important than being able to answer them. As Paulo Freire has argued: 'Human existence … came into being through asking questions.'[3]

Section 5 concludes each chapter by reporting references mentioned in the interview and by making suggestions for further reading for interested readers.

The glossary at the end of the book also offers short descriptions of the main (approximately 250) economic terms covered in the book, which have been **highlighted** in the text. This is to enable readers without prior economics knowledge to quickly find any relevant information and engage with the debates on economic policy more effectively.

---

3 See Paulo Freire and Antonio Faundez (1989), *Learning to Question: A Pedagogy of Liberation*, Continuum International Publishing Group.

Acknowledgements

I would like to express my gratitude to my lovely wife Simona for her support while I was working on this book (including the crucial choice of which tie to wear for each interview). Our sons Adam and Dan helped to keep me grounded throughout the process, I hope you will enjoy reading the book one day.

A special thank you goes to the interviewees for providing their time and wisdom. You have been my role models; through your ongoing contributions to economic policy you have convinced me that it is important to bridge the gap between academic economists, policymakers, students and the general public.

I am indebted to my research assistants who have contributed to various aspects of the book. Laura Moate and Zoe Roland provided the interview transcripts; Zoe also put together most of the student discussion questions, and made suggestions for improvement of the text. Karla Jurásková tracked down the details for the quotes at the start of each chapter, Nick Vecci drafted most of the economic concepts at the end of the book, and Dat Nguyen helped with the references at the end of each chapter.

I am thankful to Veronika Mojžišová, arguably the world's most talented artist with a (almost completed) PhD in law, for her patience in the process of converting my cartoon ideas into beautiful drawings. Let me also thank Eric Hanushek from Stanford University, Przemyslaw Kowalski from the OECD, Grégory Claeys from Bruegel and Bruno Albuquerque from the European Central Bank for sharing their data. I would also like to acknowledge the work of a number of incredibly competent and nice people at Cengage who have helped with the book along the way.

I would like to thank the Australian Research Council and the Neuron Foundation for financial support of my research; and the Australian government's Office for Learning and Teaching for their award, which helped finance this book. I would also like to acknowledge the great work and professionalism of the staff at the La Trobe University media studio, where most of the interviews were recorded.

Most of all, I am grateful to all my students and colleagues for showing me every day that asking questions and attempting to answer them can be both enjoyable and worthwhile.

1   An exploration of long-term macroeconomic trends

When learning is purposeful, creativity blossoms. When creativity blossoms, thinking emanates. When thinking emanates, knowledge is fully lit. When knowledge is lit, economy flourishes.

A. P. J. Abdul Kalam, scientist and former President of India, *Indomitable Spirit*, Rajpal & Sons, 2006.

Economic concepts discussed

Easy-to-understand explanations of all the concepts listed below appear in the glossary at the end of this book.

- Beggar-thy-neighbour
- Creative destruction
- Diminishing returns
- Economic growth
- Fiscal policy
- Global warming
- Grease effects

- Great Depression
- Gross domestic product (GDP)
- Happiness
- Human capital
- Inflation
- Money

- Opportunity cost
- Pay-as-you-go financing
- Poverty
- Prisoner's dilemma
- Productivity
- Technological progress
- Wage rigidity

1.1 Motivation and overview

Macroeconomics deals with many important 'big picture' topics, and this chapter is devoted to a long-term perspective on macroeconomic outcomes and policies. For example, 'Will **technological progress** continue at a fast pace or is the funeral of **economic growth** on the horizon?', 'What role should economic policies play in the long term?', 'Is **inflation** always harmful or can it sometimes be useful?', 'Should we take action regarding the warming of the planet?', 'Is **money** neutral in the long run or does it still affect economic activity?'.

Questions like these have been at the forefront of the interest of economists and policymakers around the globe as they can have an enormous impact on people's prosperity and wellbeing. In this chapter, Professor Paul Frijters from the University of Queensland shares his answers to these and many other questions in an interview with me recorded on 19 September 2012.

Recipient of the 2009 'Best Australian Economists under the Age of 40' award, Prof. Frijters is not an ordinary economist. As suggested by his ever-present hat and the title of his bestselling book *An Economic Theory of Greed, Love, Groups and Networks*, Prof. Frijters likes to think outside the box. His self-proclaimed interest 'in how socioeconomic variables affect the human life experience and the unanswerable economic mysteries in life' is apparent in his research, ranging from **happiness** in Russia to migration within China and Indonesia, expectations in East Germany after the fall of communism, and exploring the relationship between macroeconomic conditions and problem drinking in the United States as captured by Google searches.[1]

Reading the chapter is recommended to all those who would like an unconventional crash course in long-term macroeconomic trends, and who do not share the belief of John Maynard Keynes that 'in the long run we are all dead' (see the cartoon below, in which Keynes chats to another influential economist, Milton Friedman).

Concept by Jan Libich © 2015, drawing by Veronika Mojžišová. Used by permission.

Prof. Frijters starts by outlining the scope of macroeconomics (compared to microeconomics) and highlighting its applicability in real-world policymaking. Based on his wealth of experience advising various Dutch and Australian government bodies, he argues that macroeconomics 'is one of those areas in economics where politicians defer to economic expertise'.

The discussion moves onto the topic of economic growth, outlining its main drivers as well as its consequences on people's lives. Did you know widespread economic growth is a fairly recent phenomenon, only observed over the past two and a half centuries? There were no sustained increases in the income of the average person prior to that. Prof. Frijters explains the role of education and **human capital** in driving increases in

---

1 The full video-interview is available at **https://youtu.be/jvZpRwTn_94**. For more details regarding Prof. Frijters and his research see **www.paulfrijters.com**

wealth and prosperity. The discussion mentions the stunning fact that most of the cross-country differences in economic growth since the mid-twentieth century can be explained by differences in the quality of human capital and education; see Figure 1.1.

Figure 1.1: Human capital and economic growth: a plot of a regression of the average annual rate of GDP per capita growth (%) 1960–2000 on average test scores on international student achievement tests (conditioned on average years of schooling in 1960 and real GDP per capita in 1960)

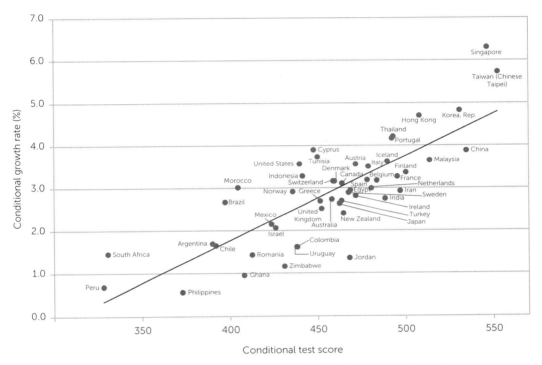

Source: Hanushek (2014); Hanushek and Woessmann (2015).

Prof. Frijters further notes that economic growth has lifted a huge amount of people out of **poverty**. For example, *The Economist* (2013) reports that in the two decades between 1990 and 2010, the number of people living in extreme poverty:

> *fell by half as a share of the total population in developing countries, from 43 per cent to 21 per cent – a reduction of almost 1 billion people.*

The debate then proceeds to the relevance of standard economic production indicators as measures of society's wellbeing. The criticisms were beautifully captured by US politician Robert Kennedy in 1968:

> *Our gross national product … counts air pollution and cigarette advertising … it counts special locks for our doors*

*and the jails for those who break them. It counts the
destruction of our redwoods and the loss of our natural
wonder in chaotic sprawl … Yet the gross national product
does not allow for the health of our children, the quality of
their education, or the joy of their play. It does not include the
beauty of our poetry or the strength of our marriages … It
measures everything, in short, except that which makes life
worthwhile.*

Prof. Frijters discusses the appropriateness of **gross domestic product (GDP)** in light of
Kennedy's criticism. The debate implies that while GDP is certainly not a perfect
measure of wellbeing, and should be used with caution, data show that it is still very
strongly linked to people's happiness. Figure 1.2 demonstrates that higher GDP per
capita tends to be associated with greater life satisfaction. This is true both across
countries (the apparent positive relationship in the figure) and within a country
(indicated by the upward-sloping line for most individual countries).

Figure 1.2: The relationship between gross domestic product per capita and people's life
satisfaction across and within countries

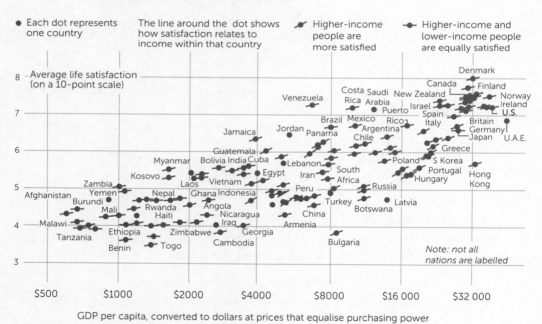

An interesting discussion centres on the future prospects for economic growth.
Prof. Frijters disagrees with the pessimistic analysis of Prof. Robert Gordon of
Northwestern University, who believes that:

*the rapid progress made over the past 250 years could well
turn out to be a unique episode in human history.*

This is followed by a debate about the physical limits of economic growth due to the warming of the planet, and the desirable course of action by policymakers to tackle climate change.

The interview then discusses inflation and its role in the economy. You may be surprised to learn that mild inflation (0–4 per cent) may actually be beneficial as it may 'grease the wheels' of the economy in which wages do not adjust flexibly to economic conditions (for more, see Groshen and Schweitzer, 1997). Such mild inflation can thus contribute to lower unemployment and faster recovery following an economic downturn. On the other hand, inflation above approximately 4 per cent has a tendency to 'add sand' to the price- and wage-setting processes, and therefore drag the economy down.

Many other topics are touched on in the interview. For example, Prof. Frijters discusses some lessons from the 1930s' **Great Depression** that were useful during the 2008 Global Financial Crisis; the demographic trend of population ageing and its implications for public policy; the economic future of Southern Europe; urbanisation in China; and the concept of money. He also proposes three long-term policies that economic research suggests would improve the welfare of society, but which politicians have been reluctant to adopt for various reasons.

1.2 The debate

Dr Jan Libich (JL): Let's start with the big picture of what macroeconomics is about. There is this perception that it is really dry and boring, that it is all about curve-shifting and definitions. Is this accurate?

© Paul Frijters. Used by permission.

< Prof. Paul Frijters (PF): I think not, I think that macro is one of the most exciting areas because it's where economics has so much power. Economic thinking about inflation drives interest rates, it drives what everybody pays for their mortgage, it drives money creation. When it comes to the whole debate about how rich we are, long-term investments, or the role of the government in the economy, macroeconomists are basically driving the agenda. So macroeconomics is one of those areas in economics where politicians defer to economic expertise.

JL: Are you saying economics is not about abstract equations and curves, but about how people decide and the implications of their decisions for the economy and their lives?

PF: Sure, but it is also an area where you see the results of abstract thinking. The ideas in macro, as with the ideas in any social science, will sound a little bit dry and abstract to the outside world, but those ideas drive what is generally thought in the population about how societies should be organised, how we should run our economy.

JL: I take your support of abstract thinking to imply that no curves and definitions will be harmed while we are recording this interview … Let us consider the two main areas of economics, how does macro actually differ from microeconomics?

PF: Macroeconomics differs from microeconomics mainly in that it deals with big picture questions. 'What is the optimal rate of interest?', 'Should governments spend more, should governments spend less?', 'Should governments be worried about housing bubbles?'. Macroeconomics does not deal with specific questions such as 'What does Jan Libich pay in the supermarket for his goods?', but such a microeconomic question will nevertheless link to macroeconomic concepts. For example: Jan now pays more than he did last year which implies that the price level has risen and we have some inflation. So at its core, macroeconomics is not really about individual behaviour, it is about trying to understand what all the decisions and interactions between millions of people lead to at the aggregate level.

JL: Yoram Bauman from the University of Washington, the world's leading (and only) stand-up economist, summarised the difference between microeconomics and macroeconomics when commenting on Greg Mankiw's *Ten Principles of Economics*: 'Microeconomists are wrong about specific things, and macroeconomists are wrong about things in general.' Is he right or is this too pessimistic about economics?

PF: Well, as the old joke goes, economists have predicted nine out of the last four recessions … I think it is very true about economics in general that we are not so great at predicting what is going to happen next. And our theories are, at every level, slightly wrong. There are those who belittle economics for that, who say: 'Now look, it is not exact. You cannot tell me what interest rates will be. You cannot prove that this is what we should do.' All you can give is a vague argument that on the basis of historical analysis roughly this and that may be the best thing to do. But it may not. And many people put economics down for that – because they are looking for something that economics can never be.

JL: People often criticise the advice some economists gave before the 2008 Global Financial Crisis …

PF: Yes, but some advice during the crisis was actually beneficial. Let me give you an example of great advice which really swayed the day. One of the mistakes made during the Great Depression of the 1930s was to cut trade ties with other countries. Countries reneged on their promises to other countries in two ways. They reneged on the bonds that they held of each other, the amount of money they owed each other. But they also started to actively put up more and more trade barriers, making it harder for countries to export towards them. And this was a 'beggar-thy-neighbour' policy.

It led to an enormous collapse in trade which greatly aggravated the economic downturn. The same reflex was there in the Global Financial Crisis, you had unions saying 'We must protect local jobs', you had local industry shouting for trade barriers to be imposed.

JL: A lot of voices like that can now be heard in the United States.

PF: The United States put up huge import barriers for solar panels, right. If you think about something funny, the whole **global warming** debate is predicated on trying to find the cheapest solar panels. And the Americans just stopped them from getting there.

JL: I wish I could laugh at this ...

PF: But by and large, politicians avoided putting up trade barriers because mainstream economic thinking firmly says this is a bad thing to do. They have resisted the temptation to do this to the same degree as in the Great Depression and this is where economics has come to the fore; in the World Trade Organization, the International Monetary Fund, the World Bank. They all said: 'Oh no, don't do this again. This would be a big mistake.' And we didn't make the mistake, which is why Australian GDP has gone up in the Global Financial Crisis; we are the big winners of global trade flows. So Australia is one of the beneficiaries of mainstream macroeconomic thinking.

JL: Let us advance our long-term perspective on the economy by mentioning the major long-term macro concepts.

PF: Well, the major thought in economics about the long term is that you are as rich as you produce. So the whole economic debate about what makes us well-off in the long term is how many production factors you build up. We pretend that in the long run the economy is a little bit like a farm, or a little bit like a group of businesses, and it is just a matter of how productive they manage to become. So it is all about long-term investments. Long-term investment into how much we know, which is human capital. Long-term investments into how big these farms are, how many buildings, how good the machines are, which is captured in the notion of physical capital and in the notion of technology. It is also about the interaction between everybody, namely all suppliers, all the clients, the overseas people, all of which allows us to coordinate. This comes forth in the notion of networks.

Combining all this, the long-term perspective in macroeconomics is that we are as prosperous as we are productive. And we have got pretty good ideas as to what makes us productive. The mainstream advice how to become richer as a country is exactly the policies that countries now becoming richer are enacting. So you look at China and India today, the two big emerging powerhouses, they are making huge long-term investments in education. The number of years of education amongst the Chinese has risen about three to four years in the last generation or so. And similarly in India, primary school education is really spreading, secondary school education too. Capital investments are shooting off the planet in China.

JL: There is a lot of research showing the importance of education and human capital for economic growth and prosperity. For example, Professor Eric Hanushek from Stanford University shows that virtually all cross-country differences in economic growth rates post-WW2 can be explained by the quality of their education. Is that an argument for providing free public education, even at the tertiary level?

PF: Well, there comes a point, of course, at which more education is no longer useful because you are spending more years in education and less years being productive. There is always an **opportunity cost** to being educated. And the jury is out as to whether we have reached that point in a place like Australia and the US. But it is clear that they have not yet reached that point in a place like China and India. So for them there is a clear benefit to the government investing in education because individuals don't have enough money to spend on it, they just can't afford to wait so long for the benefits of education to come around. But in a place like Australia, most investments are, of course, made by parents and students. Students make the major investment in their education by spending time learning economics, rather than having extra hours in their jobs.

JL: One of the facts that surprises many people is that economic growth, which they take for granted, is a fairly recent phenomenon. It basically started 250 years ago with the industrial revolution; prior to that we had had thousands of years of virtually no growth in an average person's income. But has this growth actually benefited everyone, or at least the majority of people? Or has it been the selected few as the '99 per cent movement' in the US argues? What happened to poverty over this period?

PF: I am in the camp of people who sing the praises of economic growth. As you say, continued economic growth decade after decade was an unheard-of phenomenon before. You had growth in particular regions for a while, and a very slow incremental growth over a long time, but now we have been growing 2 per cent for more than a century. And if you go back two and a half centuries, we have, sort of, been on the steady 1 to 2 per cent growth path. This has been associated with tremendous improvements in living standards for the whole population. Life expectancy has gone up, because we can pay for sewerage for everybody, vaccination for everybody, blood thinners for almost everybody. Hygiene has improved off the scale. Our local environment has improved, which has helped both the quality of life, and health again. Literacy rates have gone up, everybody gets a chance at reading and writing in our societies.

People no longer die of poverty, not just in our country but throughout the West, and throughout most of Asia and Latin America. Dire poverty to the degree that you are threatened by dying of starvation is almost a thing of the past. And you see the same phenomena in the up-and-coming economies, so at a world level dire poverty has reduced a lot. Infant mortality has basically been wiped out in China, it is reducing very rapidly in India, in the last pockets of Latin America, and even in places in Africa that are growing. So economic growth has really risen humanity from the dregs to a much better place. We now all live longer, we are happier, we don't have to fear as much crime for our kids because violence has also gone down. We trade with each other instead of killing each other. And I would causally link all of those things together.

JL: But what does the future hold? You mentioned China a few times, and there are some very good economic reasons and theories that predict that the Chinese 'miracle' growth we have seen over the past three decades cannot last. They imply that the gradual slowdown of economic growth that occurred in Japan and other high-income economies will occur in China too. Can you outline what economics says about the future of economic growth, and whether you subscribe to it?

PF: One of the theories of Chinese growth is that they will not be able to be that much more productive than other countries that have made all the investments into education and factories already. The main theory saying that Chinese economic growth must slow down at some point is a notion of a technological frontier. It says that things can only get as good as they are in the richest countries at the moment, and after that, growth of 10 per cent, which the Chinese have had for almost 30 years, must come to an end. And I certainly subscribe to that.

But China still has a lot of growth left. If you look at their education investments, they can still increase a lot. The road network can improve a lot. There is a lot more population which is not yet used in the modern sector. So I am one of the people who would say growth in China can keep on going for another 15 to 20 years, easily. But after that I do expect it to level out, just as other Asian countries have levelled out, and they have historically levelled out at about two-thirds to 70 per cent of US per capita GDP. So they are not quite as rich as the Americans, because their economies have some structural problems. And that is also true in China, so I don't expect them to be as rich as the Americans per person. But at two-thirds per capita GDP of the Americans, the Chinese economy will be three times bigger than that of the US. So, it is a clear expectation that China will become the world superpower this century. And it probably won't be overtaken by India until the end of the century – if India can stay together.

JL: What you were talking about in terms of the technological frontier is linked to the concept of **diminishing returns** to capital. It is the idea that when a country invests heavily into physical capital, its total product grows at a decreasing rate, because the marginal contribution of each additional machine becomes smaller and smaller. Apart from these economic constraints, there are naturally various political constraints facing China. For those interested, Paul runs a research group on China, and has a series of posts on the Core Economics and Club Troppo blogs on the politics of China and what the future holds.

PF: Thank you for that advertisement ...

JL: But going back to the future of economic growth, it is not only China. There are a lot of voices saying that the growth in countries like the United States is over, or at least it is going to slow down. And it is for reasons other than the Global Financial Crisis. For example, Professor Robert Gordon from Northwestern University provides arguments for his conjecture that 'the rapid progress made over the past 250 years could well turn out to be a unique episode in human history'. What do you think about this view?

PF: It is very hard to predict the future of economic growth in general if we are talking about centuries to come because of unknown technological improvements. What we can say is that historically speaking the last 50 years has had higher growth than the one and a half centuries before that. So what we do know, in a very long timescale horizon of the last two centuries, is that growth overall has actually been increasing.

If one just thinks of it as going on the trend line, then one would say that growth probably won't come to an end because there are still huge technological areas to go. Medicine can still improve beyond all recognition, we can become half robots, and maybe live a lot longer. ICT improvements are happening all the time, automation is likely to happen all the time, the use of robots in everyday life has a huge potential future. So there are clear areas where we all expect economic growth to come from technological improvements.

JL: But Prof. Gordon argues that the kind of technological advances that we saw in the late nineteenth century, like running water in the house, sewerage, electricity and antibiotics, were more important for prosperity than the current inventions. He points out that all the recent technological progress on the ICT front hasn't really been that satisfactory in terms of raising our **productivity**. Whether you have iPhone 4 or iPhone 5, does that make such a big difference in terms of our productivity?

PF: I think that is a little bit short-sighted, as to the notion of what productivity is. If we think of productivity as improving people's lives, as building things that we want more than the things we already have, then the slope of human improvement is still almost linear. We are still, in the last 10–20 years, increasing our life expectancy at an almost linear rate. It is quite amazing, but it is truly happening. There are still huge advances to be made, and I do not see real evidence whatsoever for the notion that the end of the nineteenth century was the real era of progress. Our ability to build cars quicker has gone up and up and up. The cost of computers has gone down and down and down.

Just think of the technological marvel that people use every day, in terms of the little smart phones. If you go back 20 years, when supposedly technological development would have been finished, that same smart phone would have needed a whole truck full of stuff, and now it is in this teeny-weeny little thing. And so what does Gordon mean that there haven't been valuable technological improvements? You can hold the technological improvement in your hand, and just reflect – would this thing have been possible five years ago? What would I have needed five years ago to get the same thing? It is just beyond recognition how much we have advanced.

JL: Okay, but even if we accept that the long-term technological drivers of economic growth are alive and well, some people would argue that all this growth, and all these increases in prosperity, haven't actually made people happier. You have done a lot of research on happiness so what can you say about that?

PF: It is definitely a stylised fact within the happiness literature that in a country that is rich, like Australia, the United States or much of Europe, there has not been an improvement in how happy we are from year to year. In Australia we are close to an eight on the zero-to-10 scale, and we have been close to an eight for a very long time. We are expected to be close to an eight for a long time still. But there are two things to say about that for the long-term future. One is, of course, that if you live longer you are an eight for an extra few years. So even if you accept the argument that there is unlikely to be an improvement in happiness per year, just the fact that you enjoy happiness for more years is a direct improvement from a happiness point of view.

JL: Well, unless the added years are spent lying in bed with the doctors artificially keeping you alive.

PF: Yeah, but data show that's not the case. And so the stylised fact that happiness levels are constant beyond a certain GDP per capita level also includes these happiness levels at older years. In fact, the group which is almost happiest in Australia are the people between 60 and 75. It is not that they are happy when they are young and they are miserable as death approaches; that is only true for the last 10 years. Retirement is almost the happiest period in people's lives, particularly in Australia.

JL: The elderly have some reasons to be happy. Data show that in most countries they have been receiving more from the public purse than they have put into it in terms of pensions and healthcare, and the real estate market has also moved in their favour. Importantly, the demographic trend towards an ageing population means that we are going to have fewer people paying taxes in the future, and a lot more people receiving pensions and healthcare, which is going to burden the younger generations and lead to some major fiscal problems. In fact, some countries in Europe are already feeling the debt pressures. Is it something that you think may threaten future growth and prosperity?

PF: One of the great things about economics is that every problem is also an opportunity. So let me turn this around, and let me talk about it in entirely different ways. One of the ways you can interpret the notion that there will be fewer young people and more old people is that there are going to be more jobs for young people. And particularly in Europe, unemployment amongst young people is quite high. So you are now talking about a demographic shift which will improve their chances in the labour market. Should we be worried about this? Clearly not.

So from a long-term perspective, this in fact is going to be a good thing for the junior generations. And it is not really a problem on the world scale either because there are plenty of young people being born, but not necessarily in the richest countries. That just means that services and products made by young people in low-income countries will be bought by old people in high-income countries. And this is already starting to happen. We are starting to farm out health services to India, and we are starting to buy in all kinds of holidays, which are offered by young people for older people.

JL: Don't get me wrong, I don't think the demographic change poses a problem for the market economy as such. The problem is that the setting of **fiscal policies** in most countries, especially European countries, is based on a 'pay-as-you-go' system, where governments take money from the currently working and give it to the current retirees. And if the ratio of retirees to workers increases two-fold or three-fold, as it is predicted to, public finances become unsustainable and a public debt crisis may occur. We see in Greece what happens when a country hits the fiscal wall – a government-induced economic collapse and social unrest ensue. So this is what worries many economists. I am not seeing enough of a change in Europe addressing these long-term fiscal imbalances; policies are all about the current problems in the banking sector, all about balancing the budget in the short-term …

PF: Sure, I agree with you that there is a transition path, as economies get used to the fact that there are fewer young people. And hence, the systems which were predicated on there being many young people you could tax a little bit to fund a few old people have to go, because there are now many older people, and fewer younger people. But you can see the adjustments within Europe taking place, there are countries which don't have a 'pay-as-you-go' system but a prepaid system. This is true for the Netherlands, for instance, where there are huge investments on behalf of the elderly via general pools. This is also true for Australia, which is why Australia doesn't have to worry so much about this. But in all the European countries, you see for instance shifts in the pension age. If you are going to live for longer you have got to work for a little bit longer as well.

And you see tremendous changes within the pension system in southern Europe. In Italy there has been an enormous pension reform, which to a certain extent cheats a generation. There will be a generation of people who grew up, and who are now in the 25 to 40 range, who are royally stuffed in southern Europe. It is a technical term, 'stuffed'. They truly will be the losers of this, because they will not enjoy the benefits that their parents will have enjoyed. And you see major adjustment problems, really good people are leaving southern Europe because they don't want to pay for the next generation, and then pay for themselves as well. This is a very difficult problem. And the obvious solution is not pretty, but it is being taken in most of southern Europe, which is to sort of cheat the elderly. They were promised they were going to have a high pension and their pension is being cut all over the place, particularly in Greece.

JL: As for the pension system, I agree that we have a good template of how to reform it. Australia did a pension reform more than two decades ago and it has been working well. Sweden and a handful of other countries have made good reforms. But healthcare seems to be the bigger problem in an ageing population, because a large part of public health expenditures goes to the elderly. And no one really knows how to reform the healthcare system. We see from the US – which basically spends double the amount of GDP on healthcare compared to other countries – that relying primarily on private sector health insurance may not be the solution.

PF: Yes, traditionally the US healthcare system has been a shining example of what *not* to do.

JL: But let us go back to the concept of GDP, and whether it actually is a good measure of happiness. We can't go past Bob Kennedy's famous quote from 1968:

> Our gross national product ... counts air pollution and
> cigarette advertising ... It counts the destruction of our
> redwoods and the loss of our natural wonder in
> chaotic sprawl ...

Like him, many people think that past economic growth has been enabled by abusing the environment. Is destroying nature a necessary condition of economic growth?

PF: Well, there are two distinct points here. One of your questions is: 'is GDP a great measure of how a country is doing?' And I would say no, it is not the best measure. I am definitely one of the people who think that happiness is a more important outcome than money. Money just goes into happiness.

JL: You are writing a book along these lines ...

PF: Yes. It is *An Economic Theory of Greed, Love, Groups and Networks*. It does have the notion in it that GDP is not the only measure of how well we have been doing. But as an economist I would say that the pursuit of more GDP has been good for the world as a whole, it has helped us overcome many of the previous problems we had. For example, with violence, people dying young, of starvation, it has helped us with overcoming illiteracy and dire poverty. But amongst economists it has been recognised for a long time that GDP doesn't measure everything. It has for instance never measured the hugs that parents give each other, or the smiles that they get from their children, or the sunshine that shines on their backs. And nevertheless, these are things which are worth something to us. We would be willing to pay for them if we didn't get them for free.

Hence, there have been long debates about what else to measure. And I am one of the people who would say that we should have a gross national happiness indicator that our policy should be about. I think it would be difficult, because our societies are used to thinking in terms of more goods as the thing to have, but there is a constituency for at least also measuring how well we are doing with happiness. So that is the measurement thing. Then your second question was whether we as humans are using the environment, and we definitely are. There is no denying that more and more of the world's natural resources are being used for us.

JL: Is it done in a sustainable way?

PF: Well some things are clearly not sustainable. We are going to run out of coal and gas and oil eventually. It is always a bit of an empirical question as to when, but the 'peak-oil' and the 'peak-gas' people tell me that we might have reached the peak already, and that from now on it is all downhill.

JL: Beware, the lights are going to be turned off any minute now, and we will go back to the dark ages …

PF: Well, it is an empirical question as to how quickly this will happen. But it is clear that we have been living off the Earth's resources, and will continue to do so because it is just the road of least resistance. But it is important to recognise that our interaction with the environment has not been all bad. In many ways the environment, in terms of whether it is sustainable, has actually benefited in the last 20 to 30 years. Local rivers have been cleaned up almost throughout the Western and Asian worlds now. Salmon has been reintroduced in many European rivers, whereas they were too dirty 30–40 years ago. Smog is an unheard-of phenomenon in most places. Asthmatic-type things are no longer brought on so much by the dirt in the air which used to be a lot more normal.

We are getting better and better at preserving the things of nature which we think are valuable. And hence the capacity of nature to provide things for us doesn't really seem to have been affected that much. If you want an empirical measure, biomass, which is, sort of, the total production of new stuff, it has in fact not declined. So yes, it is true that we are raping the Earth in the sense that it is all now for us. We have now got cows instead of endangered species, but it is still an animal, there is still nature in some degree.

JL: You described the micro level, and I would agree with that. But at the global level, there are major environmental challenges related to the unprecedented speed of human-caused warming of the planet. Over the last century energy consumption on Earth has been increasing at a very linear rate, almost 3 per cent per year, which means doubling of global energy consumption every 23 years. And the laws of thermodynamics imply that this obviously cannot continue. Even if we did only use clean energy and greenhouse gases stabilised at today's levels, thermodynamic laws imply that we would boil ourselves with such energy consumption growth.

PF: I would say that in the coming hundred years or so, the world as a whole, and this is not a statement of how things should be, but how I think they will be, won't be bothered too much by climate change, I am afraid. And the reason for that is really simple – most of the decisions that are taken towards greater economic growth, and greater wealth, are not taken at a world level. They are not even taken by national politicians. They are taken by households, small regions, local politicians. People who want a second car or who want their first car, people who want to build lives for their kids. And that is a tremendous force, that wish to amass more goods, particularly on the side of people who don't have much …

JL: Is this the greed part in your book?

PF: It is, it is a large part in the book yes, that there is no real way in which we can coordinate at the world level to undo this. Poor people wanting to get richer, rich people wanting to stay rich. And every election in the last 100 years has almost been fought on the platform of more economic growth. So when push comes to shove, I am sure all of us in this room still want economic growth. And against that reality, I don't think that there is truly a constituency at the world level to countervail this, and have less energy consumed.

But there is a lot to say about the trend you mention, let me give you some counter figures. At the moment we only use about as much energy as 1/7000th of what the Sun hits us with every year, and hence there are also clear alternatives on the table. We already know that the thermal from solar is cheap enough that we can in fact switch from fossil fuels to solar. We don't want to because it is more expensive; read: more jobs involved in generating it. But we will, once we run out of cheap fossil fuels. There is a natural progression from the cheaper fuels to the more expensive fuels, hence we have got alternatives already in line which will keep us going for a long, long time. We can keep going for at least 100 years in just building more and more solar panels which will get us to maybe 1/700th, 10 times the amount of energy we know now without any problems. So there is no real bottleneck yet.

JL: True, but with a continued 3 per cent growth in global energy consumption, we would get a 7000-fold increase in as little as 300 years. Within this timeframe we would be consuming energy equalling all the energy arriving to us from the Sun, so even covering every centimetre of Earth's surface with solar panels would not be enough. I encourage everyone to check out the blog of American physics Professor Thomas Murphy devoted to these issues. But I am sure you will argue that the 3 per cent energy growth will not continue; for example, because of declines in fertility and technological improvements, and I agree. So let us get back to the prospects for global climate change action, which you are pessimistic about.

PF: My proposition is that the politics of organising a counter-movement to all these micro people, and all the politicians elected on the basis of getting more growth for people, are so hard, so intractable, and so easy to circumvent that I would only place my hope in engineers. I would tend to place my hope in asking a physicist, 'Well, if I give you a budget of $1000 billion, could you undo this warming somehow? Could you throw something in the air which would do it? Could you put something up in the skies? Can you make more clouds? Can you give me a filter? Can you bury the charcoal in the ground?'

JL: You are referring to geo-engineering ...

PF: Yes. I would say there is more chance that it will work than some magic revelation of a political solution at the world level, and we will all storm forwards and forget that we are going to vote for growth next election again. In the last 20 years we have pretended that we are going to do something, but on the ground almost none of us are doing something. So the pretence is so far from the reality that if you are an intellectual, and care about what actually happens, you have got to put your hope in something realistic.

And these international treaties, I'm afraid, they are just dead ducks. These are circuses made for our amusement, but they are not serious attempts to do something, and the serious attempts that do something are on the way. There are now large research units trying to look at how we can geo-engineer our way out of climate change, and people laugh at them not realising that this is our only chance. But there are also whole government departments now who see this as our only chance, and I'm with them.

JL: I share your scepticism about what can be done at the global level, it is a classic **prisoner's dilemma**, but I am worried about the major environmental risks associated with geo-engineering. Anyway, let's move onto another macroeconomic topic, inflation. Some people believe that we need money printing and inflation to fuel economic growth. What would you say to that?

PF: For me, this is an entirely empirical question. Theoretically speaking, economists have great difficulty working out why you would need inflation. In most of the ways in which we view an economy, it is in fact not so hard for some prices to go up, and some prices to go down. And so, it is more a question of looking at reality. Is it possible to have growth and no inflation? And I would say that the empirical reality has been that it is hard to have growth, especially following an economic downturn, if you don't have a bit of inflation. And the real usefulness of inflation is that it makes it easier to change relative prices, it makes it easier for some people to earn less without them noticing too much that they earn less. If you don't have inflation, if prices on average remain the same, then people notice much quicker whether or not they go down in their wages because their nominal wages drop. They see their take-home pay drop.

JL: You are talking about adjustment of real wages in the presence of **wage rigidity** ...

PF: Yes, it is about nominal wage rigidity and the money illusion that is associated with it. You can see this phenomenon inside enterprises. One of the stylised facts is that virtually no one, I mean less than something like 1 per cent of people, take an hourly pay cut from one year to the next. The only way to do it is to fire them, because they get so upset if they realise that their nominal wage is going down. But if inflation is 10 per cent, and people have the same nominal wage, implying a 10 per cent reduction in real wage, they don't complain so much. So the same cut in real wage is organisable via an inflation level that you can't organise by having actual take-home nominal wage go down. So I would say a bit of inflation is a good thing.

JL: You just described the so-called 'grease effects', as inflation can grease the wheels of the economy by adjusting the real wage. That is why most central banks have an inflation target around 2 per cent rather than 0 per cent. But what about higher inflation – in the double or triple digits?

PF: High inflation or even hyperinflation is empirically noticeable to be very, very bad. So you don't want inflation in the hundreds of per cent, but if you have got a couple of years of higher inflation, just below the two digits say, that is not generally a problem, that can in fact be healthy. And particularly in Europe now, there are lots of voices, and I would be amongst them, who say that we need a bit of inflation to get rid of all these debts.

JL: Let me ask one last question before we turn to the audience. Can you briefly mention long-term policies that economics implies would improve overall wellbeing, but politicians have shied away from?

PF: I can think of three policies that are too hard politically. The first is a classic – freer movement of people between countries. At present the professional elites are able to move around the world, but the poor have to stay where they are. Whilst it is probably optimal for each individual country to refuse to take in the poor of others, it is probably detrimental to the productivity and wellbeing of the world.

The second is the tackling of vested interests that get private political favours at the expense of others in their own countries and others in other countries. This problem is becoming bigger and bigger, ranging from patents on medicines and movies that are far too easy to get and last far too long, to implicit public guarantees to big banks, to property market licences given to political insiders. The solutions that economists provide are relatively simple, which is to price political favours and make market participants bid up for them so as to benefit the community as a whole and to get proper incentives. But politicians, both central and local, understandably do not want to give up their 'rights' to give lucrative favours to friends that reciprocate the favour. Yet it clearly is in the interest of the public to move towards democratic systems that explicitly price political favours.

Lastly, it is clear that there is a benefit to having a public bank with which each citizen has an account, via which basic deposit transactions and secure mortgages can be arranged. Such a public bank would put pressure on the private providers to reduce their fees and to concentrate on the risky part of banking (investments). Having the public bank do deposits negates the need for bailouts during financial crises, which come from the bundling of deposit banking and investment banking. An additional benefit from having a public bank is that it can be the vehicle for printing money in times of crises, whereby the public bank for instance increases the deposits of everyone by 10 000 dollars during a large financial crisis, thereby reducing the debt burdens and facilitating retail investments.

At the moment, money printing happens by essentially giving money to bank managers in the vain hope that they will do something with that money. Having a public bank would offer a much more efficient channel for money printing that reaches the right people much quicker. Politically, the difficulty with a public bank (such as what the Commonwealth Bank in Australia used to be) is that there is always the temptation to sell it off and make a quick buck. However, in a place like Europe that would be hard so they should just do it.

Audience member 1: Going back to what you said about the global warming situation, do you feel that if we were to have a bureaucracy of a world order a solution would be possible politically?

PF: Could a bureaucracy succeed where coordination between countries can't? Yes, it could. In a world empire if you like, the ability to reduce economic growth and to push at all levels would be a lot easier. Because one of the reasons that economic growth is so sacred in our societies is that we are status seekers. We want our country to do well relative to other countries. We don't want to be the schmucks who have a losing economy and other places doing well. If we find that, then we move abroad. But solutions to global problems featuring externalities are just not possible to organise at the decentralised level.

Can I see a worldwide government happen though? Not easily. I have tried for many years to think of a scenario in which we would get a world government. But I can't realistically see anybody giving up their own sovereign power for this world government. Because in order to implement something as big as climate change regulation, you have to have an international police. You have to have people actually going into factories everywhere, and putting in heavy fines in other countries. I can't see countries agreeing to that, they just don't care enough about global warming.

Audience member 2: You talked about the future of the Chinese economy, are there any foreseeable obstacles you see the Chinese economy having? Whether they be an ageing population, inflation, or even the environmental problems that have been created by their recent surge in growth?

PF: Well, I have been to China a couple of times, and the thing that struck me is just how real their growth is. For a long time there were development economists pretending that it didn't happen, that somehow the Chinese were inventing their growing economy in the books. But it really is happening. You can see the buildings going up, you can see the bullet trains being made. You can see the new schools in effect, you can see the degree to which the whole population is learning more English. You can see the growth of the cities, you can see the emptying of the countryside, the production boom. You can just look at the imports and exports. So it is really happening, and there are no major obstacles that I can see for at least the next 10 years. Because everything you would want to put in their growth are still areas where they can improve a lot. Their education can improve leaps and bounds, they have a small proportion of university-educated people. But they have, just in the last 10 years or so, started building lots more universities. Now these still have to fill up.

JL: The same applies to the ghost cities scattered around China …

PF: The ghost cities, yes, there are lots and lots of regional cities yet to go. There is only 50 per cent urbanisation in China, whereas a country like Australia is about 80 per cent urbanised. There is growth to come from all the people from the countryside who are yet to go into the cities to provide the manpower there. The electricity clearly can be generated. China is building several coal-powered stations a week which tells you how serious they are about global warming. If you just look at their actions rather than their words, they are just like us. They vote for growth too.

JL: But from the analysis I have seen they will be more negatively affected by climate change than most other countries.

PF: Well that is not clear, I've seen some food projections which say that they in fact will see their agricultural production go up. So it is not clear at all that China will lose out, it is more the cities on the coast side which may have to put up more dykes. That is a discussion for another day. But in terms of the electricity barriers, the energy barriers, they don't seem to be there population-wise. Technologically also, a lot of their manufacturing is 1960s, 70s, 80s-type manufacturing, and that can still improve beyond bounds. They have not yet become as IT dense as the US is. They have not really started yet with the innovation sector, and I think that the Chinese could actually be pretty good at that once they get their minds to it. Politically, too, China seems very stable. There are no real problems on the horizon yet. So I can't see the barrier, I am very optimistic about Chinese growth for the next 20 years; then I think it is over. Then they will be at the level at which their GDP per capita will flatten out.

Audience member 3: In summarising long-term macroeconomics, what are the main threshold concepts you think should be in every first-year macroeconomics course?

PF: I would say that there are three main things that students have to get their heads around to really be able to grasp macro. The first is the notion of equilibrium, which is the central economic concept via which economists look at the whole macro economy. It is this notion that we are going towards a place in which all opportunities are taken at any given time. We will never get there, but it is a place we are moving towards.

I would say 'creative destruction' is also a very important concept. It says that new things come along all the time which require you to adapt to change, and to find more information, to find new trading partners. And the notion that at every level there are shocks to the system which create a new equilibrium is very important to understand. This is because it explains everything to do with information, why there are entrepreneurs. It explains everything to do with unemployment. Unemployed people are basically people who are not matched in the labour market, who have had a productive match before but who now need to be connected to other people.

The third thing, and probably the hardest thing you have got to get your head around, is money. Money is an invention, money is this weird piece of paper we give each other, or a bank account, and we trust that somehow this will be worth something if we go to another person. And as soon as there is money there is abuse of money, because someone can print that piece of paper. And they can print lots more of it, and hence cheat us. But also, if you are a bank and there is lots of money flowing through that is not yours, you can in various ways steal from that bit of money.

And the whole Global Financial Crisis can best be understood as people abusing their positions of power inside financial institutions. They have got all these hundreds of billions of dollars flowing through their institutions that are not theirs. But they can use the money, they can borrow against it, they can gamble with it. If they win big on the stock market they get part of the benefits. If they lose, it is not their money, someone else loses. So the whole financial system hangs on an understanding of money, and that is the toughest one to get your head around. And if I had to be self-critical about economics, money is the one we understand the least, because it is too hard to model. We don't have useful micro models of money.

JL: Well, from the answer you actually see that Prof. Frijters' take on economics is different from the standard line. I noticed on your website that you are 'interested in the unanswerable economic mysteries in life'. On behalf of our audience, I would like to thank you for sharing some of your insights into these economic mysteries with us!

1.3 Key economic insights and policy lessons

Economic insights	Implied policy lessons (for public officials and voters)
Economics is not about abstract definitions and curve-shifting, but about helping us understand our decisions and improve our wellbeing.	Policymakers should not ignore the recommendations of economic analysis in designing and implementing policies.
Given the focus on people's behaviour and complex human systems, all economic models are simplifications of reality and thus partly wrong.	Policymakers should be cautious and not rely on one particular economic model or doctrine.
Economics is incapable of correctly predicting short-term economic movements, but it is fairly successful in identifying the drivers of long-term trends.	Policymakers should beware of 'expert' advice regarding short-term developments, and adopt a long-term perspective in designing quality institutions and policies.
A country's prosperity is largely determined by its productivity.	Policymakers should help the society use its natural and human resources efficiently, especially by long-term investments in education, research and innovation.
While not a perfect measure, real gross domestic product (GDP) per capita is a strong predictor of people's life satisfaction.	Policymakers should pay attention to GDP as well as to alternative measures of wellbeing that capture its non-monetary aspects.
Widespread economic growth is a fairly recent phenomenon, initiated by the industrial revolution of the mid-eighteenth century.	Policymakers should not take ever-rising prosperity for granted and monitor the changing circumstances to be able to adjust policies accordingly.
Economies feature 'diminishing returns' to physical capital, which means that, other things equal, less-industrialised countries tend to grow faster. But once they catch up their growth slows down.	Policymakers should not overemphasise high short-term economic growth numbers, and prepare for their eventual decrease when the convergence process is complete.
Per capita economic indicators do not reveal the (un)evenness with which income and wealth are distributed in society.	Policymakers should keep trends in inequality in check and consider policies that prevent it from becoming excessive.
Poverty has decreased substantially around the globe over the past several decades.	Policymakers should continue their efforts to alleviate poverty as past experience shows that these can be successful.
Like trade within a country, foreign trade is generally beneficial because it enables specialisation and reaping economies of scale.	Policymakers should promote the idea of free trade. But they should carefully consider the pros and cons of new-generation agreements, such as the proposed Transatlantic Trade and Investment Partnership, which tend to be more about corporations attempting to bypass government regulation and courts.
Trade barriers such as import tariffs are beneficial to a limited group of economic subjects, but they increase import prices and thus reduce society's overall wellbeing.	Policymakers should implement mechanisms that help them resist the temptation to impose protectionist policies, especially in an economic downturn.
Every economic problem poses an opportunity.	Policymakers should identify the lessons of past economic failures in order to improve policies and future outcomes.
Global economic problems (such as climate change) are difficult to solve, because the relevant decisions are not taken at the global level and negative externalities exist.	Policymakers should attempt to design functional international cooperation platforms.

Economic insights	Implied policy lessons (for public officials and voters)
If wage setting is inflexible, higher unemployment can arise, especially in a downturn. Then mild inflation can be beneficial and 'grease the wheels' of the economy.	Policymakers should promote flexibility of the labour market, hand in hand with supporting education approaches that make (current and future) workers well prepared for this flexibility.
Very high inflation is always a result of excessive money printing, and it is detrimental to the economy and people's wellbeing.	Policymakers should never abuse their monopoly to print money for their political agenda.

1.4 Discussion questions

1 Using your own words, summarise the debate of Section 1.2 in three to five sentences.
2 Write down one idea discussed in the interview that you found new or interesting, or that you disagree with, and briefly explain why.
3 Write down one question on any topic covered in the interview that you would ask the speaker if you had a chance.
4 Consider the cartoon in Section 1.1 and explain the point to someone who has not read the section and does not have any knowledge of economics.
5 Examine Figure 1.1 from the perspective of a policymaker. Describe its key message to the public and explain what kind of policy improvement is implied by the data. Do the same for Figure 1.2.
6 Suppose you take part in a debating contest, in which the topic is the opening quote of the chapter by Abdul Kalam:

> When learning is purposeful, creativity blossoms. When creativity blossoms, thinking emanates. When thinking emanates, knowledge is fully lit. When knowledge is lit, economy flourishes.

Prepare a speech you would give for the affirmative side. Then (you or your classmate) prepare a speech for the negative side. If possible, organise an audience and perform the debate.
7 What is the scope of macroeconomics and microeconomics, and what is their relationship?
8 Prof. Frijters talks about the limitations of economics and argues that it is not very good at predicting the near-term future. Why do you think this is the case?
9 In the discussion Prof. Frijters points to some errors made during the 1930s Great Depression that were not repeated during the Global Financial Crisis of 2008. What were they? Can you think of any more differences in economic outcomes and policy actions during the two major downturns? Support your views with statistics.

10 In Prof. Frijters' view, what determines the level of prosperity of a country in the long term? What is your view on this? Attempt to support your arguments with publicly available data.

11 The history of economic growth and its effect on human development and poverty are discussed in the chapter. Summarise Prof. Frijters' observations and relate them to your own. Report some data on the changes in poverty over time and countries.

12 Prof. Frijters discusses the future of economic growth in China. In his opinion, will the rapid growth last? Write down some supporting arguments as well as counter-arguments.

13 Regarding the prospects of economic growth in high-income countries, Prof. Frijters discusses research by Gordon (2012), who predicts a decline and possible demise of economic growth. Outline Gordon's arguments, summarise Prof. Frijters' view on this issue, and then offer your own views on the future of technological progress and economic growth.

14 Critics argue that the concept of GDP is flawed and it is not a good indicator of people's wellbeing. What is Prof. Frijters' view on that? What is your own view? Find information on alternative indicators and discuss their relevance.

15 Some people believe that economic growth has been conditioned on exploitation of the environment. Does Prof. Frijters agree with this? Do you think destroying the environment is necessary for economic growth to continue? Why?

16 What does Prof. Frijters think about global warming and the desirable action regarding climate change? Is he optimistic about international cooperation? What are your views on these themes?

17 Summarise Prof. Frijters' view on the respective desirability of mild inflation and hyperinflation. Find data on two major hyperinflations and compare their magnitude as well as the resulting economic effects.

18 What are Prof. Frijters' beliefs regarding a worldwide government? What do you think about its feasibility and desirability?

19 What are the main threshold concepts in macroeconomics according to Prof. Frijters? Briefly explain why they are important to grasp.

20 Propose a set of policies that you think best promote long-term economic growth and ultimately people's wellbeing.

1.5 Where to find out more

Club Troppo blog, www.clubtroppo.com.au

Core Economics blog, www.economics.com.au

Frijters, P. (2013), *An Economic Theory of Greed, Love, Groups and Networks*, Cambridge University Press.

Frijters, P., I. Geishecker, J. P. Haisken-DeNew and M. A. Shields (2006), 'Can the Large Swings in Russian Life Satisfaction be Explained by Ups and Downs in Real Incomes?', *Scandinavian Journal of Economics*, 108(3), pp. 433–458.

Frijters, P., J. P. Haisken-DeNew and M. A. Shields (2004), 'Money Does Matter! Evidence from Increasing Real Income and Life Satisfaction in East Germany Following Reunification', *American Economic Review*, 94(3), pp. 730–740.

Frijters, P., D. Johnston, G. Lordan and M. A. Shields (2004), 'Exploring the Relationship Between Macroeconomic Conditions and Problem Drinking as Captured by Google

Searches in the US', *Social Science & Medicine*, 84(C), pp. 61–68.

Gordon, R. (2012), 'Is U.S. Economic Growth Over? Faltering Innovation Confronts the Six Headwinds', National Bureau of Economic Research, Working Paper No. 18315.

Groshen, E. and M. Schweitzer (1997), 'Identifying Inflation's Grease and Sand Effects in the Labor Market', National Bureau of Economic Research, Working Papers No. 6061.

Hanushek, E. (2014), 'The Economics Returns to a Good Teacher', public lecture at CERGE-EI, 18 September 2013, video and summary available at https://blog.cerge-ei.cz/?p=2586

Hanushek, E. A. and L. Woessmann (2015), *The Knowledge Capital of Nations: Education and the Economics of Growth*, Cambridge, MA: MIT Press.

Kennedy, R. (1968), Remarks at the University of Kansas, 18 March, available at www.jfklibrary.org/Research/Research-Aids/Ready-Reference/RFK-Speeches/Remarks-of-Robert-F-Kennedy-at-the-University-of-Kansas-March-18-1968.aspx

Krugman, P. (2015), TPP at the NABE, blog post from 11 March 2005, available at http://krugman.blogs.nytimes.com/2015/03/11/tpp-at-the-nabe/

Leonhardt, D. (2008), 'Maybe Money Does Buy Happiness After All', *The New York Times*, 16 April, available at http://www.nytimes.com/2008/04/16/business/16leonhardt.html?_r%C2%BC0

Monbiot, G. (2013), 'The lies behind this transatlantic trade deal', *The Guardian*, 3 December, available at www.theguardian.com/commentisfree/2013/dec/02/transatlantic-free-trade-deal-regulation-by-lawyers-eu-us

Murphy, T. (2011), 'Galactic-Scale Energy', blog post 12 July, available at http://physics.ucsd.edu/do-the-math/2011/07/galactic-scale-energy

Murphy, T. (2011), 'Can Economic Growth Last?', blog post 14 July, available at http://physics.ucsd.edu/do-the-math/2011/07/can-economic-growth-last

Peterson, P. and E. Hanushek (2013), 'The Vital Link of Education and Prosperity', *The Wall Street Journal*, 11 September, available at http://hanushek.stanford.edu/publications/vital-link-education-and-prosperity

Stevenson, B. and J. Wolfers (2008), 'Economic Growth and Subjective Well-Being: Reassessing the Easterlin Paradox', Brookings Papers on Economic Activity, Economic Studies Program, The Brookings Institution, 39(1), pp. 1–102.

Stonecash, R., J. Libich, J. Gans, S. King, M. Byford and G. Mankiw (2014), *Principles of Macroeconomics: Australian Edition*, 6th edition, Cengage Learning Australia.

The Economist (2013), 'Towards the End of Poverty', 1 June, available at www.economist.com/news/leaders/21578665-nearly-1-billion-people-have-been-taken-out-extreme-poverty-20-years-world-should-aim

2 Musings on short- and medium-run macroeconomic topics

Unemployment is like a headache or a high temperature – unpleasant and exhausting but not carrying in itself any explanation of its cause.

William H. Beveridge, British economist, *Causes and Cures of Unemployment*, Longmans, Green and Company, 1931.

Economic concepts discussed

Easy-to-understand explanations of all the concepts listed below appear in the glossary at the end of this book.

- Aggregate demand
- Appreciation/depreciation of the exchange rate
- Business cycle fluctuations
- Comparative advantage
- Data aggregation problem
- Discouraged workers
- Dutch Disease
- Fiscal policy
- Fixed/floating exchange rate
- Foreign exchange market
- HECS
- Hysteresis
- Inequality
- Labour force participation rate
- Labour market
- Liquidity
- Minimum wage
- Mining boom
- Monetary policy
- Resource Rent Tax
- Skill mismatch
- Tariff
- Trade balance/surplus/deficit
- Unemployment

2.1 Motivation and overview

Economies experience incessant change at the micro level – driven by the actions of households, firms and policymakers. These manifest at the macroeconomic level as fluctuations in a number of variables such as gross domestic product (GDP), **unemployment**, investment and exchange rates. We can therefore see, at any point in time, countries that grow fast, countries that develop at a somewhat slower pace, and countries that struggle in a recession. Importantly, at another point in time the list of countries in each category may be very different.

This chapter sheds light on some of the causes and consequences of medium- and short-term macroeconomic swings, and identifies appropriate policy responses that reduce the magnitude of 'business cycle fluctuations'. It is based on an interview with Professor Bob Gregory from the Australian National University recorded on 6 November 2012. Prof. Gregory is a recipient of the Order of Australia medal for his contributions to economic research and public policy; for example, as a member of the Reserve Bank of Australia Board and the committee that introduced the world's pioneering Higher Education Contribution Scheme (**HECS**).[1]

The discussion deals with a number of policy-relevant questions such as: 'Can a resource boom, while beneficial in the short term, turn out to be harmful?', 'Should countries run trade surpluses (like China) or trade deficits (like Australia)?', 'Is it a good idea to buy or sell currencies for speculation purposes?', 'Should countries have a fixed or a flexible exchange rate?', 'What are the main determinants of unemployment?', and 'Do we need to worry about the inflationary consequences of money printing in the aftermath of the Global Financial Crisis (GFC)?'. In contrast to the previous chapter, which adopted a long-term perspective on macroeconomics, this chapter emphasises the short-term horizon (as depicted in the cartoon below).

Concept by Jan Libich © 2015, drawing by Veronika Mojžišová. Used by permission.

The interview starts with 'the **Dutch Disease**'. Don't worry, it is not that economists reach for the stethoscope all of a sudden. The name simply suggests that they are sometimes able to identify a malaise in the economy, and propose an appropriate policy treatment. While the term 'Dutch Disease' itself was coined by *The Economist* magazine, the important insight behind it was a product of Prof. Gregory's research and is often called 'the Gregory thesis' (for more details, see Corden and Neary, 1982).

---

1 The full video-interview is available at https://youtu.be/Ww6gn-KZoyw. For more details regarding Prof. Gregory and his research, see **www.cbe.anu.edu.au/about-us/about-us/people/?profile=Bob-Gregory**

In a nutshell, an economy rich in natural resources may benefit from exporting them, but it tends to have a downside because it leads to strengthening of the country's currency, making its manufacturing sector less competitive internationally. Therefore, a large endowment of natural resources may lead to 'de-industrialisation'; see Figure 2.1, which shows a drop in investment in the manufacturing (as well as service) sector in Australia since around 2005, caused by increased investment in the mining sector.

Figure 2.1: Industry share of business investment (in nominal terms) in Australia

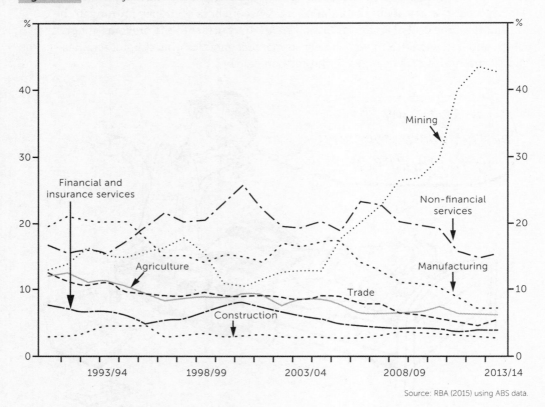

Source: RBA (2015) using ABS data.

This may turn out to be harmful for longer-term economic performance, and makes the economy more susceptible to swings in the prices of minerals. Some economists worry that this is currently the case in Australia, and talk about its 'two-speed' economy, with the states experiencing a **mining boom** growing but other states underperforming. Countries rich in oil (e.g. in the Middle East, Russia) are also used as an example – while their average income may be fairly high, they feature a very unequal distribution of wealth and face a number of challenges going forward.

An intuitive analogy for the Gregory effect would be children born to very wealthy parents. Should we dream of being one of them? The answer is not as obvious as it may seem. While such a child enjoys a number of advantages, wealth may reduce the child's motivation to study hard, and it may take away the usual challenges and obstacles that are essential for personal growth. To demonstrate, a member of the wealthy family that founded Georgia-Pacific Corporation reflected in *Forbes* (2013):

*The biggest curse of intergenerational wealth for me and
many other people is the illusion that you don't have to do
much with your life … you don't have the same pressure to
earn enough to live on. And that takes away a lot of the
incentive to find meaningful work.*

And incentives are for economics what gravity is for physics – one of the building
blocks. Incentives also play a major role in the next topic of the interview, which regards
the politicians' response to a resource boom. Prof. Gregory discusses the **Resource Rent
Tax** legislation in Australia and appropriate fiscal actions, arguing: 'That's now a
complete disaster area. They should have tried to run budget surpluses a little earlier,
and they should not have cut taxes quite as much as they did …' Naturally, the
incentives here are political in nature rather than economic. As Prof. Gregory stresses:
'There are always two games to be played when designing policy: a political game and an
economic game. Both affect the final result.'

The debate then moves onto **foreign exchange markets**. Prof. Gregory explains why
short-term currency speculation is like buying a lottery ticket:

*The exchange rate is very hard to predict for an obvious reason:
everybody is trying to predict it … So by buying a future
exchange rate contract, you are saying: 'My prediction is better
than the average'. And you know what happens, generally
speaking, half the predictions are better than average and half the
predictions are worse than average. So buying future currency
contracts is a gamble, and it should be thought of as a gamble.*

A core focus of the interview is the **labour market**, Prof. Gregory's prime research area. He
discusses the issue of unemployment and points to the dramatic change over the past decades:

*In 1970 there were 8000 unemployed men in this country
receiving unemployment benefits. So with a bit of luck, I could
probably remember everybody's name!*

Needless to say that such an unemployment rate of below 1 per cent can no longer be
found (virtually) anywhere in the world, and values between 5 and 15 per cent,
sometimes significantly higher, have become the norm.

However, Prof. Gregory highlights the fact that we need to look beyond the headline
unemployment figures. Policymakers must also consider the major changes in the male/
female composition of the labour force (see Gregory, 2012), the proportion of part-time
workers (which has grown rapidly in Australia) and the shifts in the **labour force
participation rate**. The latter may be driven by demographic trends as well as changes in
the number of '**discouraged workers**', and seem to have resulted in hidden
unemployment, as Figure 2.2 shows using US data (for the same argument regarding
Australia, see Mitchell, 2013).

Figure 2.2: Civilian labour force participation rate (left panel) and the unemployment rate (right panel) in the United States. The top lines show what the rates would have been if all the 'discouraged workers' from October 2007 onwards came back into the labour force.

Source: Boesler (2015), *Business Insider, Inc.,* 117475:0515DS. Used by permission.

Prof. Gregory's attention to the finer details comes from his focus on economic statistics and trends – he describes himself as a 'data man'. And as he points out: '… most of my applied ideas come from being closely involved in government'. The discussion then centres on two main macroeconomic policies for reducing medium- and short-term fluctuations in the economy. Prof. Gregory tracks how the views on the use of monetary and fiscal policies for the stabilisation of the business cycle have changed over time, building on his rich real-world expertise with both; for example, as a Reserve Bank of Australia (RBA) Board member. He also assesses the policies in the aftermath of the GFC, and is concerned about the inflationary consequences of 'money printing' that many central banks have engaged in since 2008 (more details follow in Chapters 9 – 11 of this book).

The role of the government is also discussed more broadly. Prof. Gregory reveals that:

> … on industry policy I'm very right-wing … On social issues,
> however, I'm sort of left-wing. And I don't find any real
> problem with my lack of left-wing right-wing consistency
> because, as I keep saying: 'When things are different, you
> should and will behave differently.'

Unfortunately, the situation in many high-income countries seems the opposite; it can for example be argued that the United States is fairly left-wing on industry policy and more right-wing on social issues.

Several other topics are touched on in the interview. For example, while the issue of fixed versus flexible exchange rates was once hotly debated, Prof. Gregory notes that: '… in Australia there's hardly an economist that would vote for a fixed rate'. He also discusses the common European currency (the topic of Chapter 13), and explains why he was against it when it was being put together and why he still thinks it is a bad idea. Prof. Gregory further offers a fascinating 'insider view' of the HECS adoption (a topic covered in detail in Chapter 5).

2.2 The debate

Dr Jan Libich (JL): Let's start with your influential 1976 paper, in which you invented a whole new economic topic – later called the 'Dutch Disease' by *The Economist* magazine. It's about a resource boom possibly being a blessing in disguise and having some undesirable effects in the rest of the economy. Can you tell us more about it?

© Robert Gregory. Used by permission.

< Prof. Bob Gregory (BG): I was working in the government at the time. In fact, most of my applied ideas come from being closely involved in government. Australia was about to be subject to a 25 per cent across-the-board **tariff** cut in 1973. The key issue was: 'When Australia has never been subject to such a large tariff change, how can we guess what effect it might have?' So I was looking around for something that had occurred in the past which would provide some indication of the likely tariff change outcomes.

And then I got the idea: 'Something that would have a similar effect as a large tariff change on import-competing industries in the short run is an exchange rate change.' But nobody knew very much about exchange rate changes in those days because the exchange rate was more-or-less fixed. And then I thought: 'What would alter an exchange rate a lot?' And I got the answer: a large increase in mineral exports. So then I thought: 'Well, if a large increase in mineral exports can change the exchange rate a lot, and a change in the exchange rate is similar to a tariff change, then development of the minerals sector has a similar effect as a tariff cut.' Of course, an exchange rate change is not exactly the same as a tariff change, but for the question I was posing there are important similarities.

So this was the idea: if Australia developed large mineral exports from, say, the Northern Territory, then the clothing industry in Fitzroy, Melbourne, which competes with imports, suffers because the exchange rate strengthens. But nobody in Fitzroy understands that the suffering of the clothing industry from increased import competition is the result of the Northern Territory development of minerals. The import-competing sector also finds it tougher because the appreciated exchange rate leads to import price falls. These ideas took off dramatically because the political timing was right. There were lots of political fights and worries at the time about the appropriate level of Australian tariffs and what Australia should do about mineral development.

JL: Given that a resource boom may be a curse in some way, a large endowment of oil and other natural resources may lead to 'de-industrialisation' with the economy devoting most of its productive capacity to the resource sector and neglecting other sectors including manufacturing. This may hold the economy back in the long term, right?

BG: Yes, but I didn't use and I don't like the word 'curse'. What I tried to stress was that when a country has a mineral boom focused on exports, lots of things happen in terms of structural changes. Import-competing manufacturing industries and pre-existing old export industries go into decline as a result of the exchange rate **appreciation**.

These structural changes have implications for the type of labour the economy needs, where workers are located and whether the adjustment costs are worth the economic growth in the short term. Mineral exports cause a country to grow just like any other new and profitable discovery causes a country to grow; it's just that this particular development causes the country to grow in a particular way. The new mineral export industry has low labour content for example, and is concentrated in particular states – Western Australia and Queensland – and not in others – Tasmania and South Australia. Also, as you pointed out, as the country becomes more export-intensive and focused on minerals, the economy becomes more sensitive to trade shocks, because mineral prices have a higher variance over time than manufacturing prices.

JL: If we take your insight one step further and look at countries that have a lot of oil, it may be hurting them in the long term. Middle Eastern countries might be rich but they're certainly not at the frontier in terms of the key productivity-enhancing inputs, human capital and technology. So once they run out of oil they are unlikely to sustain their current income levels.

BG: Well, that's true. First of all, these countries are rich. If you compare the Middle East now to what it used to be, it is rich, so the Middle East has gained a lot from oil. An important question of course is: 'Who gained?' It is whoever owns the oil, and whoever taxes the oil. And, in line with the predictions of the theory, oil has made it much harder for other export industries, such as tourism or the manufacturing sector, to develop. Oil has affected the structure of the economy and there have been winners and losers.

If we bring the 1970s discussion forward to today, there is no doubt in my mind that if Australia did not have the mineral expansion of the last 10 years, and especially the big investment boom, Australia would be going through more of a European and US-style crisis. Not as bad, because Australia did not have the banking crisis, but the unemployment rate might be 7 or 8 or 9 per cent rather than where it is now, just above 5 per cent. So this time around Australia has gained a lot from minerals. Down the track, when the mining investment stops and when the price of minerals falls, then those gains will not be there anymore, and then Australia will have to adjust. I think the downside adjustment will occur over the next two or three years and then may continue for some time.

I have a recent paper on this in the same journal in which I published the original Gregory thesis paper just over 35 years ago.

JL: So how should Australian policymakers respond and alleviate the 'two-speed economy' problem in which the mineral sector is booming and the rest of the economy is faltering? Should they be, at a minimum, running budget surpluses to save up much of the benefit of the resource boom for bad times?

BG: Well, governments should have responded more-or-less in the way they did, but better. They should, for example, have had in place a Resource Rent Tax. The taxing of mineral developments is now a complete disaster area. They should have tried to run budget surpluses a little earlier, and they should not have cut taxes quite as much as they did four or five years ago. So, they mucked it up a bit.

But what people don't really understand is that policymakers can never quite know what exactly is going on in the economy. It takes a while to figure it out. So it is explainable that all the sensible policies were a bit late coming and did not go far enough. Ignorance as to what is happening in the economy and what will happen in the future cannot be over-emphasised as an explanation for policy responses and their timing. Mining companies, believe it or not, did not even pick the price increases before they occurred. It seems unbelievable that in 2002 none of the mining forecasters stressed that China would force up the iron ore and coal prices so much and for so long. Government forecasts were similar.

If you are interested in policy, there are two important lessons to be learnt from this boom. One lesson is that policy, as a general rule, is always late in responding. Partly because policymakers are late in recognising what is happening in the economy and partly because policymakers are frightened to make large policy changes before the need is absolutely clear. Another lesson is that it is impossible to introduce perfect policies. Use the Resource Rent Tax as an example. Economic policy can be designed on paper and look very sensible, but introducing it is about politics as well as economics. So policymakers never end up with exactly what they initially want. That means that, when designing a policy, it is important to make judgements about what the introduced policy will finally look like after the political process is completed. It is just as important to account for the politics as it is to get the plan of what policy you would like. There are always two games to be played when designing policy: a political game and an economic game. Both affect the final result.

JL: And one needs to make sure the resulting hybrid policy is not worse than no policy intervention in the first place …

BG: Yes, that's right. When I say the mineral tax was a disaster, I mean if a classroom lecturer explained to students what actually happened, few would believe him. Suppose, for example, the following was the government plan: 'The federal government will effectively take most royalties away from the states and collect most of the tax itself and at the end of the process collect more mining tax in aggregate.' But where did government end up (before the tax was repealed)?

Australia arrived at a situation in which if the states increased their royalties the federal government would reduce the mining tax for companies. So this hybrid policy encouraged states to increase their royalties since mining companies knew they would not pay any extra tax due to the federal government's offset. Australia thus ended up where nobody wanted to be (except perhaps the states). This history provides an important lesson: the plan to develop and introduce a mining tax was all done too quickly and the politics weren't adequately thought through. Of course, in the end Australia never even put in place a permanent new federal mining tax.

JL: Moving onto other open economy topics, students often ask whether countries should run a **trade surplus** or a **trade deficit**, or **balance** their trade. What's your answer to that?

BG: Well, the economic answer to that is fairly straightforward and has been in place for a long time. Whether a country is running a trade surplus or deficit doesn't, by itself, provide any guide as to what is a sensible policy. You must look at why the trade outcome occurs. If a country is running a trade deficit because it wants foreign investment with high rates of return, that's good. If the country is running a trade deficit because it wants to spend lots of money on consumption and borrows from the rest of the world so that consumers can buy imported TV sets, that may or may not be good. It depends on the judgement as to the appropriateness of the country's savings rate and how much international debt the country can manage. Finally, if the trade deficit is the counterpart to a large government deficit, then that may not be good.

So it's a tricky question in practice and there is no rule. Australia, for example, has practically always run trade deficits, and by-and-large young countries which are growing do that because they need foreign investment and the rate of return to the investment is high. These countries believe that they will be richer in the future as a result of the investment so they want to borrow now and pay off the debt later.

JL: But could there be any long-term negative implications of having a persistent trade deficit?

BG: Well, the trade deficit means that the country is running up foreign debt, one way or another; foreign equity or debt which has to be paid for. So what the policymakers should do is compare what the country is paying in terms of foreign equity obligations and interest rates with the economy's growth rate. And providing that the economy growth rate is equal or above that of the servicing obligations, then the country is usually more-or-less okay. Now the US, for example, is not okay. They have been running up government debts along with their trade deficit and it seems that the government's fiscal situation is unsustainable in the long run. So for them the trade deficit poses problems, but for us there is no real problem. Of course, some economists have argued that the trade deficit can never be a problem, especially in a world of flexible exchange rates.

JL: One of the possible consequences of a trade deficit might be a **depreciation** (weakening) in the exchange rate. This points to another question students often ask: 'Which way is the exchange rate going to go?' Can you talk a little about the determinants of exchange rates, both long term and short term, and whether we can actually predict short-term exchange rate fluctuations?

BG: This answer may sound a bit ridiculous but if you feel lucky at buying a lottery ticket then buy a future exchange rate contract – do whatever you're lucky at! The exchange rate is very hard to predict for an obvious reason: everybody is trying to predict it and this process affects the current price. So by buying a future exchange rate contract you are saying: 'My prediction is better than the average.' And you know what happens, generally speaking, half the predictions are better than average and half the predictions are worse than average. So buying future currency contracts is a gamble, and it should be thought of as a gamble. If you are spreading exchange rate risks by buying future contracts, that may be okay, just as laying-off bets on horse races is not a bad idea for bookmakers.

JL: I think the analogy with the casino and gambling is spot on. The transaction cost associated with exchange rate trading is like the zero in roulette, so on average you're actually in the red compared to the no-gamble alternative.

BG: Well, all gambles have transactions costs and the money you lose on average to buy a future exchange rate contract is the equivalent to the average gambling loss to pay for the casino. But exchange rates are interesting because of people's attitude towards them. This goes back to an issue which I would like to stress – economics alone does not tell you what should be done. Economics hopefully explains how things work and what impact policy will have. Then what to do turns on politics, value judgements, the cost of action and so on.

When I began as an economist, most policy advisors felt that countries needed **fixed exchange rates**. They believed that fixed exchange rates were good because **floating (flexible) exchange rates**, in their minds, meant that devaluations would occur and produce higher inflation rates, on average. The support for fixed rates flowed from the belief that they gave discipline to governments – because of the political costs associated with a devaluation that would follow loose monetary and fiscal policies.

By the 1970s this view had changed in Australia. Australia started introducing a more flexible exchange rate in the 1970s and began by changing the fixed rate often as part of the process of moving towards a more flexible system, but the Treasury opposed flexible exchange rates at the time. They said: 'If we have a flexible exchange rate this will remove discipline from government who will spend too much and tax too little.' The result would be devaluations on average and higher inflation rates. Now, 40 years later, in Australia at least, nobody talks about the exchange rate in terms of imposing discipline on government. Economists emphasise that it is better to have a flexible exchange rate responding quickly to changing circumstances than to wait and take the necessary adjustments by domestic price level variations.

Suppose the Australian dollar needed to appreciate but did not, then domestic prices would begin to increase. Then, if price inflation has a **hysteresis** component, it may be difficult to stop the inflation process without substantial cost. Advisors now believe that exchange rate changes are better because they're more flexible than taking necessary adjustments in terms of domestic prices. A flexible exchange rate is certainly better for Australia because when export prices fluctuate, exchange rate changes are needed to partially offset these swings. In Australia there's hardly an economist that would vote for a fixed exchange rate today.

JL: Well, in Europe they voted for it big time by tying the currencies together into the Euro, and it's an interesting natural experiment. But there is a downside to having a common currency ...

BG: When the Euro was being put together I was against that. Me, and lots of economists – not that anybody listened to us at the time. If a fixed exchange rate is imposed across countries subject to very different economic fluctuations, then fixing the exchange rate takes out an adjustment mechanism across these countries. It forces the adjustment back onto the price level of each country and we know that prices and wages are not very flexible, at least in a downward direction. Wages can increase fairly easily if required, but it is not easy for wages to fall. So I thought the Euro was not going to work in the longer term. But it has lasted longer than I thought and of course there was considerable early economic growth for lower-income members which was clearly a part of the European integration process.

The reason why people didn't listen to me was the old discipline argument. Many countries said: 'If we have fixed rates we buy the German inflation rate and their monetary discipline. The German inflation rate is low; and Germany will give the discipline our government needs.' So the EU members accepted fixed rates but in fact they did not accept the discipline that was required. Governments behaved much the same as they would have without the fixed rates. And now you can see what a disaster the fixed rates have been over the last decade. But the Euro became so identified with the meaning of a united Europe that it will be very hard to change the current situation.

JL: True, unemployment in some European countries is very high, especially among the youth. This leads us onto your most favourite topic, the labour market. At its centre stage there is always the question of the main drivers of unemployment. Can you talk a little bit about why it is that not everyone actually has a job and what determines the level of unemployment?

BG: Well, this is one of the many interesting issues in economics. In the classroom, the answers to your questions seem obvious. The lecturer draws a demand and supply curve for labour and puts the wage on the diagram. If the wage is too high, there is unemployment. If the wage is too low, there are jobs unfilled. The free market system, if it is working efficiently, will produce just the right wage consistent with the demand and supply of employment. And then occasionally, somebody in the classroom might talk about shifting demand for labour because of technological reasons and that will create unemployment if the wage is not flexible. Some other person might occasionally talk about shifting the supply of labour; for example, the introduction of a generous welfare state encouraging people not to work. This will also create measured unemployment.

But unemployment is not as simple as this. There is controversy about the causes of unemployment in the 'real' economy. Should we think of unemployment as a wage flexibility problem? Should we think of unemployment as a demand for labour problem? Should we think of it as a supply of labour problem? The building blocks of the basic analysis have not changed very much over the last century but how to think about aggregate labour markets and unemployment has changed. When I began economics the aggregate unemployment rate was under 1 per cent and unemployment was clearly seen as an inadequate demand for labour problem. Today it seems more complicated.

In 1970 there were 8000 unemployed men in this country receiving unemployment benefits. So with a bit of luck, I could probably remember everybody's name! Today, there are 200 000–300 000 men receiving unemployment benefits, plus another 300 000 on disability pensions. If you add all the men receiving some income support there are about 700 000 or

800 000 thousand not working. So this is a very different environment from the 1960s and early 1970s.

One of the most important unresolved issues in Australia, in my opinion, is why these labour market outcomes have changed so much. I have worked on these issues for ages and I don't really know the answer, I can only tell you bits and pieces of an answer. For example, technology has changed so that if a worker does not have skills – education skills or personality skills – it is much harder to get a job today. This seems to be part of the story. Competition has also changed in the market place, so firms have to be more efficient and they rarely hire people who do not contribute. Whereas when I was a kid, firms often employed people who didn't contribute a great deal. Often the firm hired them by mistake, but they didn't really want to sack anybody, so there was considerable 'unemployment' inside the firms. That has changed, the scope and level of welfare payments has changed and 'welfare' is now more a responsibility of the state than the firm.

JL: You have touched on several interesting labour market issues, which you developed in your research. I recall your 2012 paper called 'Dark Corners in a Bright Economy', which is about the male unemployment problem and the **skill mismatch**. Can you tell us about that?

BG: Well, I cannot stress enough how much of this large change in the labour market over the decades has been a big surprise to me. When unemployment started to increase in 1975–76, I primarily thought of it as a demand-side development – a macro cause and a lack of **aggregate demand**. The way to fix unemployment was to get growth going again. All that was needed, I thought, was an expansion of aggregate demand, stimulated by government. The opponents of that view were the real wage cut advocates. They believed that what was needed was a large real wage cut – just like the demand and supply model in first-year economics; if there is unemployment the wage must be too high. There had been large increases in the real wage in the early to mid-1970s, but after 1975 real wages did not grow for almost a decade, which should have provided the real wage adjustment the economy needed.

Yet four decades later Australia still has large-scale unemployment and under-utilisation of labour. A large fraction of the unemployed are unskilled men. If a man is unskilled and unmarried, for example, the probability of a full-time job is only about 50 per cent, whereas 40 years ago, it used to be 80–90 per cent. Unskilled men are finding it hard going in the modern labour market. And that has its counterpart in the female labour market because if the unskilled men can't get jobs they tend not to marry and tend not to form partnerships. Whether this is because the women won't have them or what, I don't know. So the poor economic prospects for unskilled men affect women who end up being sole parents and reliant on income support.

The problem of unemployment among the unskilled has not gone away. It really is quite surprising that the unemployment rate of unskilled men is much the same as it was 20 to 30 years ago in the depths of the early 1990s recession. The number of unskilled men and women has shrunk as education has been expanded. But amongst the unskilled, despite the reduction in supply, job prospects have not improved. What this means is that the obvious policy solutions to the lack of unskilled jobs – increasing education levels, being more careful who our migrants are, more flexibility in labour markets – have hardly impacted on the job prospects for the unskilled group.

So policy advisors are now coming around, I think, to putting more emphasis on the welfare system and the financial contributions that government makes to the unemployed. The economics profession is moving to what we might think as a 'right-wing' position on the unemployment issue. Thirty or so years ago there were lots of people (including me) saying: 'We just need more government expenditure'. Today, you don't hear this recommendation so often because the unemployment problem has been very, very persistent, especially among older unskilled men. So Australia is a bright economy with economic and real wage growth but not much improvement in the dark corner where unemployed, unskilled men are found.

JL: Professor Warwick McKibbin, your colleague at ANU and successor on the RBA Board [see Chapter 11], believes that this structural educational and skill mismatch, especially with males in the United States, was one of the driving forces of international capital flows that contributed to the Global Financial Crisis (GFC). He argues that governments have been trying to sweep the problem under the carpet by providing subsidies to the automobile and other industries, rather than deal with the low skills of some males.

BG: Well, it's certainly true in the US that there is a skill mismatch; just like the one I was describing in Australia. Unskilled men, primarily, find it very difficult to find full-time jobs. And that's been true, more-or-less, since the mid-1970s. You can see the problem clearly in the wage distribution in the US. For unskilled men the real wage may not be that different from 30 or 40 years ago. Whereas, in Australia, the real wage has increased but unskilled employment has not grown sufficiently. The lack of unskilled male employment has not been solved in either country.

But, unlike Warwick, I don't buy at all that the unskilled problem has anything to do with the creation of the GFC. In my view it was primarily a banking crisis. And then, once the crisis occurs, all the long-standing labour market problems I have been discussing suddenly begin to become obvious. So, if you could magically take every unskilled person in America and give them two years additional education instantly, that would not solve the GFC. After a macro crisis most costs are increasingly borne by the least skilled after the first few years. At the beginning of the crisis, lots of people lose jobs, including the skilled and well-paid. But, within a year or so, the skilled and well-paid have found new jobs and as time goes by, the unskilled bear more and more of the cost. The concentration of job loss among the unskilled is the effect of the GFC, not its cause. I think the effects of the crisis on the unskilled in Europe and the US will last a long, long time. I am talking about a decade. Stock markets may recover, GDP growth rates may pick up, but the unskilled will still find it hard to become employed.

JL: We'll certainly talk more about the 2008 crisis, but you mentioned the data and one of your contributions was always to look at economic data in some novel way and see interesting trends. You mentioned the wages in the United States and one thing that I find really concerning is how people misread the data, e.g. how they ignore the 'aggregation problem'.

People generally look at the median real wage for both males and females combined and say: 'Over the last 30 years, inflation adjusted wage has been virtually flat in the US.' But when you disaggregate it, what you find is that for females the real wage has actually increased by more than 60 per cent – for both white and non-white women. And for males it's increased by more than 15 per cent. But when you put them together, you can't see these large increases because of a combination of two things: convergence in the labour participation rate – women work more and men less – and the wage gap between the two genders. Can you talk a bit about that?

BG: I agree with this general point. I am a data man. I really do believe in integrating the analysis of data and the understanding of data more into economics. I don't know when that belief started for me but I increasingly believe that once you have an economics degree and want to find out about the world, it is better to go and look at the data. There are diminishing returns to learning economic theory alone, which come about at roughly the PhD level. So I'm very keen on trying to make more economists data sensitive, and the labour market data were always of special interest.

You are absolutely right about the US and the change in the real wage distribution. It is quite shocking what's happened. The way I begin to describe how much the world has changed to my students is as follows: If I go to the art gallery to buy a poster, the gallery gives me a tube to carry the poster. You can think of the labour market between 1945 and 1976 as an art gallery tube. The employment of the skilled, unskilled, men and women were all developing much the same rate, so you could place these series in this narrow tube and they would all move comfortably along within the narrow space from one year to the next. That also means that the average change of all these series was not a bad representation of the change of any of the groups. Then, all of a sudden, from 1975, the tube is no longer effective. All the series begin to diverge along different directions. The series cannot be confined in such a narrow space. What you find is that **inequality** within groups, inequality within men, within women, as well as within all the economic or social categories, has widened dramatically. This has happened in the US, in Australia and all around the world.

Another major change that has occurred, as you suggested, is that women have done much better in the labour market than men. In some countries the economic situation for women has improved very quickly, like in Australia in the mid-1970s. In some countries, the improvement has been much slower, in the United States, for example. But there's no doubt that women are doing better in the labour market than men. So their average income levels and employment has increased over the past 40 years.

And then lastly, within the men and within the women it has been the least skilled that have done worse. Now the deterioration of the least-skilled labour market bottom has stabilised, at least in the US and Australia, and it is the labour market for those who earn the top incomes that is changing the most. The well-paid have had very large wage and income increases. You hear these stories in most countries. In the US for example, half or more of the increases of wage income over the last decade have gone to the highest paid 1 or 2 per cent of individuals. That is truly remarkable.

JL: Are such increases in income inequality justified by the human capital story?

BG: No, I don't think so. Human capital was a reasonable predictor of an individual's earnings during the 1950s and 1960s. But the predictive ability of human capital, as measured by years of education, has weakened. The reason why is pretty obvious. When I was a student it was primarily the top 4 per cent, IQ wise, that studied for a degree. Then the relationship between a degree and earnings was pretty close because IQ, privilege, family and labour market connections and all things that matter for earnings were highly correlated. Today about 40 per cent of young cohorts have degrees and, as a result, the correlations among variables that matter for earnings is weaker. So knowing that a person has a degree is not a good enough predictor anymore of their wages. The education prediction is still there, if you want to earn more money on average it's better to get more education. But the ability of education to predict employment and income outcomes is weakening because the correlation between education, IQ, social status and family connections are all weaker.

Take male–female earnings for example. It is true, relative to men, that women have acquired an increasing share of the income growth over this period, quite substantially actually. And it's true that women have more education than they used to, but that's not the source of their gain. The main source of the relative income gain for women was the result of something else, namely the Australian equal pay decisions. A degree may get you into the interview, but when the employer interviews you, he is trying to figure out how smart you are, how good your social skills are, whether you are likely to be loyal and so on.

These non-formal requirements matter more and more. Economists are now trying to measure the contribution of these factors to labour income and – surprise, surprise – they are becoming increasingly important. And in fact, looking back, it's amazing how education was so well-correlated with those things, and that it was such a good predictor of earnings, whereas now it's nowhere near as good a predictor as it was.

JL: Let us consider some of the important factors in the labour market. You mentioned **minimum wage** legislation, is that a good thing? The theory we teach our first-year students is that if the minimum wage is set at a level that's above the equilibrium it's going to lead to some involuntary unemployment. So what do the data say?

BG: Well as soon as you say 'a good thing', that means you're talking about value judgements. We know a couple of things about the minimum wage. One thing we know is that if the minimum wage is increased, a group of workers get more money – they are paid more per hour. If the individual has a job at the minimum wage, they get a pay rise when the minimum pay increases. So for all those people, an increase in the minimum wage has to be good. Another thing we know is that some people will not get a job because the minimum wage is higher. And for them, presumably, the wage increase is not good.

Then the important question for me is: how many people fall into each set? I've always been of the view, and this puts me in the minority I think, that what is gained from an increase in the minimum wage in the Australian context outweighs considerably what is lost. So I have never thought of minimum wages as the key to either the general unemployment problem or the unskilled employment problem that we have been discussing. But as I said, not everybody holds that view.

JL: Well, I think you'd only be in the minority among economists, but you'd be in the majority when you consider the whole population.

BG: Exactly. But we do not want the analysis to be decided by ignorance or by vote. Policy can be decided this way but not the analysis. Once we get the analysis right, values then matter. The other lesson I have learnt when looking at the world and how it works is that you need to have stereotypes in your head to make progress. If I told you minimum wage workers were married men with two children and an invalid wife, are you in favour of increasing the minimum wage? You would probably say 'yes'. But if I told you minimum wage workers are kids from rich families mucking around at McDonalds when they're 16, on their way to a law degree to become highly paid barristers, are you in favour of a minimum wage rise that increases the price of fast food for the poor? You would probably say 'no'.

So that goes to the data again; when one group loses and another group gains, it is important to know who the groups are and how large is each group. And then we need to know how much people move between the groups. So suppose, for example, the unemployed minimum wage worker today was to be employed at the minimum wage tomorrow, then what he might say is: 'When I'm employed I will get 20 per cent more. I might also be unemployed 10 per cent more. Then I gain on balance so I am in favour of a minimum wage increase.'

So you have to know all the facts. I'm quite keen on the view that it is not good to come to these policy issues from economic theory alone, because economic theory is not rich enough, and can never be, to provide correct answers. Economic theory can never tell you who the people are, how many fall into each group and so on. Furthermore, as I pointed out earlier, economic policy designed by the application of good theory may well not be the policy that you end up with.

JL: Andrew Leigh, currently a Member of Parliament and previously your colleague at ANU [see Chapter 3], examined exactly the kind of data you mention in his 2007 paper. He looked at who the average recipient of the minimum wage is and found it's someone more likely to be from a medium-income household than a low-income household. He ran various simulations and found that minimum wages sometimes actually increase inequality rather than decrease it.

BG: That's partly right. That knowledge goes back a long way. Sue Richardson from Adelaide was one of the first to put a lot of emphasis on this point in Australia. She identified minimum wage workers and their families. Those from very rich families tend not to work at the minimum wage. But, by and large, minimum wage workers are 'middle class' kids, or middle class wives, who want to drop into the labour market for a while. In fact yesterday I was at a dinner party for a student and his wife; she has just completed a Master's degree, comes from a high-income foreign family and is working at the supermarket as a check-out person. For her, the minimum wage was not her career wage. At this stage of her life it simply suited her. So there's a lot of variation as to who is paid the minimum wages. But should this example lead us to conclude not to increase the minimum wage?

Let me make another point: Suppose the minimum wage is increased by 10 per cent, what happens to the person who's above the minimum wage? Well, if the salary is a little bit above the minimum wage, that person will probably receive a 10 per cent increase too. So, increasing the minimum wage leads to (declining) wage increases up the wage distribution. Suppose the minimum wage is $15 an hour and you get $20 an hour. The minimum wage is increased to $16, I would say that the $20 worker would also receive an increase. So that immediately suggests that we shouldn't think of a minimum wage change as only affecting minimum wage workers. We should be looking at the spillover up the wage distribution. And that introduces a range of new ideas as well.

It could well be that while the rich are involved in the $15 an hour jobs because they're in the retail area, the rich may not be involved in $18 or $20 an hour jobs. These workers may be the traditional type of person I mentioned earlier – the person you want to help. So the instrument to affect the traditional poor that you're interested in might well be to change a wage that does not directly affect them. Perhaps the point of changing the minimum wage is not to help those on the minimum wage but to help those many more workers who are paid slightly above the minimum. You can see that once there is data access and data-based analysis, the simple question of whether the minimum wage should be increased becomes quite a rich question that is far more important and has far-reaching effects. Then it becomes a lot of fun to try and figure all these things out.

JL: In your answers you mentioned education a number of times. And you were in fact part of the committee that made the decision to introduce student income-contingent loans in Australia, the so-called 'HECS', subsequently imitated by many countries. Can you tell us how it works and how the decision-making process went?

BG: Oh, the decision-making process was a lot of fun. The Labor Party introduced HECS but the Labor Party was also firmly against university fees, full stop. So the Minister said to us: 'An education system of no fees is unsustainable. If we don't give universities more money, we just can't have the growth in universities that we want.' So they started to look around for ways of getting more money into universities. One way was to accept foreign students as full fee payers. But this was not going to be sufficient.

So the government set up a committee of which I was a member – the Wran committee – to explore options to raise more money. Wran was the political heavyweight to help introduce the recommendation; he had been the Premier of New South Wales. He didn't come to many meetings but he turned out to be very effective. I was on the committee with Meredith Edwards, who was an important person in this story. In the committee research support group was ANU economist Bruce Chapman. The instructions to the committee – delivered by winks and nods – were: 'We want you to introduce fees for a university degree, but we can't introduce fees. So come back to us and solve this problem.'

So we played around with fees and loans and then Bruce and Meredith came up with the HECS idea. The essence of the idea was there will be university fees – that's good, that's what the winks and nods were about, but it is also bad because the Labor government did not want fees. How can you have fees and not have fees? This is where HECS became important. We thought if fees could be coupled with a generous loan system it might work for the government. The obvious source of loans was private banks or a new institution. But it became clear fairly quickly that this was not a good idea. In the US and every country that have student fees, private bank loans do not seem to work.

Meredith had been working in the Prime Minister's department, and had introduced a new, truly innovative policy. The tax department would collect income support for deserted parents and children. The tax department would do this as part of the tax return process. That innovation was the key to HECS. Bruce and Meredith thought: 'Why don't we get the tax department involved in education loans?' This had never been done anywhere in the world and Bruce ran with this, he thought it was a terrific idea. I thought: 'Why don't we just get the banks to collect the money even though it is not ideal? Why do we want the tax department involved? Can they do it?'

JL: Was the tax department keen on getting involved?

BG: No, but Bruce and Meredith kept developing this idea and they sold me, the committee and Wran fairly quickly once the feasibility had been demonstrated by the deserted mothers' scheme. Wran brilliantly sold the scheme to the Labor Party. I agree with Bruce, it is a terrific scheme. By the way, the Department of Finance was opposed, just like the Treasury had been opposed to floating the exchange rate earlier. The department wanted university fees and private loans.

JL: I think the key reason we want the government involved – and this is Bruce's way of looking at it – is that the government can be more sensitive to people's income circumstances. By making the education loan repayment dependent on the graduate's income, the government effectively takes on an insurer's role.

BG: I didn't mention that in my earlier answer but that is correct. HECS divides into two interlocking ideas: one is the collection mechanism and the other is the insurance element.

JL: And it also affects the decision to study since the loan only has to be paid back if income is above a certain threshold. So if a prospective student is not sure whether all this tertiary education's going to be worth it, but knows that the government is taking care of it if he or she is unlucky and has a low income, then he or she might be more willing to study.

BG: That's right, but there are complications. If the individual had to borrow money for the education and came from a poor background, then no one would lend the money. And in any event, the individual may not want to borrow money because of the point you made – they are just not sure what's going to happen. So HECS should take all these considerations out of the decision process and that's why it's such a good scheme. After the event, we found a couple of outcomes that were expected. First of all, the introduction of fees with a government loan scheme didn't really make that much difference to the social class distribution of who goes to a university. Fees and HECS did not seem to scare off any particular group of people.

JL: Which is a good thing …

BG: Yes and no. We did not want to scare anyone off, that is right, but we also wanted to alter the distribution of students by dragging more people from poor families into universities. But HECS did not seem to do this. All social groups increased their university attendance more-or-less pro rata to their earlier attendance. And the other thing I learnt, which was quite weird, was our main opposition to HECS came from women. I would say to the women when I was trying to sell the scheme: 'Look, this is a pro-woman policy because if you ask the question who is most likely to have low income it's the women. Who is likely to earn less with a degree and therefore afford less to have a degree? It is women. Women look after children, women drop out of the labour force, women get discriminated against in the labour market a bit and receive lower salaries. So the fact that the individual does not have to pay HECS until they are paid a relatively high income is in favour of women.'

JL: Yes, I suppose they wanted to retain the status quo, where they didn't pay any fees at all.

BG: That's right. And I kept saying that the status quo is not on. And then they just got terribly upset about all this. This story goes to the point that in policy debates it is important to know the counterfactual. In my mind it was quite clear; it was either fees or HECS. I guess in their mind it was HECS or no fees, and they were unwilling to buy the argument that no

HECS or no fees meant lower opportunities for women at universities because universities would not expand.

Let me also tell a Wran story. Wran was a barrister, a QC, State Premier, a big figure in the Labor Party. He didn't come to the meetings, so we got to him the day before the plan is to be sold to the Labor Party to brief him. And then Meredith rings me before the meeting and says: 'We've got to go to the press announcement to protect Wran. And we have to do it in a way which doesn't undercut him.' We go to the meeting, Wran stands up and I couldn't believe it, he was so good! He sounded as though a) he invented the scheme and b) he knew everything about it. And he just sold it. I looked at Meredith and said: 'What are we doing here?' And that was when I learnt that a class lawyer is very good at selling policies which perhaps they really don't understand. He was terrific and he got it through.

JL: They might be good at selling things; they might not be so good at the substance of economic policy.

BG: Right, but at least you need to get the mix right to introduce radical change. That is, you couldn't get an academic up to try to sell this policy. The academic would just get killed. As I have stressed throughout this interview, introducing good policy is a combination of good economics and good politics. Good policy still requires good salesmen, good politicians, good back-room people; good policy requires a good team.

JL: Let's move from the labour market to short-term macroeconomic stabilisation policies. There is **monetary policy**, there is **fiscal policy**. You have vast experience with monetary policy, having served on the Reserve Bank of Australia (RBA) Board. Can you summarise for us whether the two policies should be used in trying to minimise economic fluctuations? And if so, which one is more effective in your view?

BG: When I started in economics, the prevailing view coming straight out of John Maynard Keynes was that fiscal policy mattered most. Fiscal policy was, based on the experience of the 1930s' Great Depression, mainly about varying government expenditure rather than varying taxes. Monetary policy had to be loose, but it was relatively ineffective in terms of stimulating demand. I felt very comfortable with this view. It seemed like common sense to me. But from around the mid-1960s this view of macroeconomic policy began gradually shifting. This story is complex and I hope the following can be understood and captures the main shifts.

Initially, attitudes as to the role of monetary policy began to change. The most important influence was Milton Friedman. He suggested that monetary policy should be steady and rarely change, because inflation is the enemy, not unemployment or lack of aggregate demand. And the way to fight inflation is to control the money supply so that it grows at a low rate. Furthermore, the lags between a monetary policy change and its effect is very long and variable. Hence, policy monetary changes can be destabilising. The aim then becomes to target inflation and keep the growth of the money supply constant. If governments want to pursue macro stabilisation adjustment, this should be done with fiscal policy. So, where did these ideas come from? My view is that they did not arise either from detailed empirical work (although there was a lot of research) or from new theories. I think they arose because inflation was increasing and had become the central problem. In economics through the ages, inflation and money supply have always been linked together.

When I joined the RBA Board, which is 30 years after the Friedman contributions, the attitudes had changed again. The general view when I arrived was that fiscal policy in Australia should be fixed and steady. What governments should do is to get the balance right between how much they spend and how much tax they collect and in doing this governments should save more. Monetary policy should be the swinging instrument directed towards macroeconomic stabilisation. It's the one that should vary to stabilise real output. But the old view was that money didn't really have much effect on real output.

So you get well-trained economists who in one direction say monetary policy should be directed towards inflation control and yet, in practice, governments are using monetary policy to influence real output. So this becomes very, very murky. I felt very strongly that there was no coherent policy/theory underpinning monetary policy and I believed that there couldn't be except in the very broadest of terms.

There was another idea that I found weird. It had been argued by many economists that because all agents understand what is happening in the economy and know the effects of policy, monetary policy only works if a policy change is a shock to expectations. The only way for monetary policy to have a real output effect is to surprise everybody. Today, nobody says this anymore. Central banks now try to avoid surprises and try to make clear how the policy will evolve and what the future path of interest rates is likely to be.

JL: The New Keynesian consensus coming out of Friedman seems to be that in the long run monetary policy can only affect the level of inflation, not the natural level of unemployment and output. But in the short run it can affect these real variables too. This is why central banks seem to primarily focus on inflation but, subject to that, also on stabilising the short-term swings in unemployment and output.

BG: Well, the balance between policy instruments is changing all the time and there is insufficient awareness of this in textbooks. Seven years ago at the beginning of the Global Financial Crisis, fiscal policy was at centre stage to target output growth. Then as government debt grew the unconventional monetary policy took centre stage. The lesson to be drawn from this is if there are two policy instruments, monetary and fiscal policy, and they impact differently on the economy in terms of what they affect, with different lags, then the policy instrument mix should vary as circumstances vary.

This is one of the themes I've been trying to push through this conversation, that good policy should not be derived from classroom or textbook economics alone. The classroom and the textbook alone cannot capture sufficiently the complications of the real world. We need the classroom teaching to give structure to the analysis but then we should respond to the real-world situation. Policy has to be flexible.

JL: I agree, but sometimes flexibility goes against the desired predictability of policy you mentioned – for example, the effect on inflation expectations. In an interview with Professor Adrian Pagan [Chapter 9], who was also on the RBA Board, we discussed the future outlook on this front. He is not so much worried about higher US inflation down the track, despite the fact the balance sheet of the Federal Reserve (the US' central bank) more than tripled over the last few years. Prof. Pagan was confident that they should be able to wind this **liquidity** back without it being inflationary.

BG: Good for him! That's what everybody hopes, but throughout history, big monetary expansions have always been followed by big inflation. I would agree with Adrian that a monetary expansion is the right thing to do now and that the inflation is not immediately around the corner. We are looking a long way down the track before inflation emerges as a problem – in fact, deflation seems to be the problem now.

JL: So if you were to assess monetary and fiscal policies in responding to the crisis, do you think they have been appropriate, and effective?

BG: That's debatable, people argue over that. Quite apart from whether they were effective or not, I believe a strong response was appropriate, because there was nothing else to do. The crisis was so severe that Keynesian fiscal expansion seemed to me to be the only possible answer. And so was increasing the money supply as part of expansionary monetary policy. And I think in the short run both policies were indeed effective, but these things wear off. I supported Australian government policy on the fiscal front; I thought Australia reacted pretty well. Australia was in a position where it could react; our government balance sheet is really quite extraordinary. Commentators often do not give enough credit to what good shape we are in fiscally. That's why this crusade today for a quick return to a budget surplus is a bit weird.

JL: I think that's a really good example of the fact that, if you want to be able to use fiscal policy for stabilising such big shocks, it is important that a country is in a sound long-term fiscal situation with low debt. European countries and the US are now finding that they can't really engage in more expansionary fiscal policy.

BG: Yes, I agree. The Greeks can't spend more because of their balance sheet. The Greeks just have to go ahead with fiscal consolidation which will make domestic output worse in the short run. So Australia needs to move towards a budget surplus but I do not see the need to achieve this in a year or two.

JL: Let us think a little broader in relation to the role of government. There seem to be two camps of people, with very little overlap. One thinks that generally we have a market failure that needs to be rectified by the government. The other group is concerned that we are more likely to see a government failure, arguing that public policies and regulations make the outcomes even worse. This division was highlighted by people's assessment of the causes of the Global Financial Crisis and implications for regulation reforms. Is this a reasonable division?

BG: I never think in terms of market failures, I don't teach in those terms either. It seems a bit pedantic to me or at least for my course. But when you hear what I say, it can be turned into that language. For example, I do believe that we need more bank regulation, so I guess that's code for responding to market failure. But in general, I prefer governments not to be involved in making things or making commercial decisions. So I guess that puts me more in the government failure camp in some sense, right?

But I never use the externality failure language per se and I just tend to react on an issue-by-issue basis. I never begin a policy discussion by looking for the market failure although I endorse this approach as a good one in the classroom. When discussing policy I tend to ask: 'What will happen if we do this and will it be sensible?' In my early career, which was devoted to international trade and commercial policy, I was very clear that I did not like governments giving high tariffs for industries and I did not believe in government subsidies to industries. So, on industry policy I'm very right-wing and against government intervention in general. On social issues, however, I'm sort of left-wing. And I don't find any real problem with my lack of left-wing right-wing consistency because, as I keep saying: 'When things are different, you should and will behave differently.'

JL: You must find it very painful now, because many countries do exactly the opposite. For example, the US is more left-wing on industry policy than it used to be and more right-wing on social issues (although President Obama has been attempting to change this through the *Affordable Health Care for America Act* and other policies).

BG: Yes. I am not so upset about the car industry policy responses in the US because the car industry is sort of special in the sense that it is a big employer and it's geographically located. We know that geographic areas do get depressed and can stay that way for a long time – the Detroit problem. So, often governments do not have much choice. I didn't worry too much, however, about removal of car subsidies in Australia over the last few years. Protection has more-or-less gone now.

I wanted the government, however, to go much further on banking regulation and they have been a bit slow on that. They've been nowhere near as radical or changed things in the way I would like. I understand how financial institutions can get around regulations, and that too much regulation is bad, but I still want a little more than we have presently. The GFC has been so horrendous that we should be doing something to stop this happening again. It can't be a good system that allows a Global Financial Crisis because banks and other financial institutions lend money to people who can't really pay for the loans. Now the government wasn't completely clean in all this, because government also got involved in various ways of making these people look as though they were financially okay. Anyway, I'm in favour of more banking controls.

JL: This leads nicely into a question I ask all my guests. Can you briefly mention some other policies that research implies would improve overall wellbeing, but politicians have shied away from?

BG: I have no big ideas here but I have some comments in the context of the Australian budget deficit – which I mentioned earlier has to be addressed over time. First, Australia should wind back some superannuation concessions. I don't see why those on large superannuation incomes, like me, should not pay some tax. I also doubt whether superannuation concessions increase savings. They primarily encourage people to reallocate their savings to reduce their tax obligations.

Second, I don't know why cutting company taxes or high income taxes in the current environment is so important. I am not arguing for large increases in marginal tax rates. But it is absurd for the government to focus only on expenditure and argue that it is better to cut school expenditure, hospital expenditure, government pensions and so on rather than increase taxes on the well-to-do.

Third, we need to scale back negative gearing. Negative gearing just forces house prices up as house investors begin to replace home owners and force them out of the market. A very simple knowledge of general equilibrium tells you that if policies encourage the population to invest in rental property, someone has to give up house ownership to rent that property. This process is achieved by those who are seeking negative gearing forcing house prices up.

JL: I would like to ask one last general question. If you were to sell economics to prospective students, how would you advertise it? What would you highlight about a career in economics?

BG: Oh, I wouldn't sell it as a career. Career sounds like some way to make money. If a student wants to think about careers, look to be a surgeon, banker, or top-rate lawyer. Now this is a very personal comment directed towards those thinking about academia. I always wanted to try and understand more about the world, essentially by reading rather than doing. So being an academic or an intellectual paid to try and understand more about the world is sheer heaven for me. I would argue: 'Go into those areas where you want to learn things.' So the question, for those of an academic bent, is: 'What part of the world am I interested in? What matters?'

I don't think learning more about the law, for example, is an important part of learning more about the world but I think learning economics is. Economics really matters for the world. The Global Financial Crisis is a clear case in point. More damage has been done in the last five years because of the GFC than has been gained, and this is going to sound preposterous, in medical research over the last 20 years. You could argue that the fact that we had a GFC is indication that maybe it is not possible to learn about the world and avoid these crises. Maybe so, but I want to try.

For those who are going to become university professors and so on, the answer to your question seems clear, at least in the first instance. Just do what you're good at and what you like. Look at the top mathematicians – surprise, surprise – they're good at maths and they like it. And the top economists are good at economics and they like it.

JL: It sounds like the concept of **comparative advantage** ...

BG: No, choose what you like rather than what you are good at relative to other people. But what you like and what you are good at usually go together. I've always found economics fun. What is cause and effect I don't know. Maybe I like it because I am good at it or maybe I am good at it because I like it. So as an individual, pick what you like rather than what someone tells you to do. I think liking what you do is a necessary condition for success.

One advantage of economics is that it is not a unified field with fixed borders. I can bring into this room 20 economists and, after hearing them talk, you might think that they are researching completely different disciplines. The mathematical economists often sound as though they know nothing about society and real-life economics. The economists of a more sociological bent may sound as though they know little about economic theory. Everybody is different. In economics, you can choose to specialise in what you feel comfortable with. You can do policy, theory, empirics and so on … I think it's terrific that there is so much choice. You can go into economics without necessarily having to be very narrow.

But increasingly to be a good academic you need to know maths. Maths is becoming more and more necessary – it may not be desirable across-the-board, but you just have to get good at maths, that is the way it is. Finally, it doesn't help for economists to fight each other and say economics should be this or should be that. There are so many examples of famous economists laying down the law as to the right way to proceed. There is no right way to proceed. Economics is a very broad church. That's the great thing about it. That is what we should encourage.

JL: Thank you, Bob, for very interesting views. The economics profession is very grateful for the many contributions to academic research and public policymaking you have made over the years!

2.3 Key economic insights and policy lessons

Economic insights	Implied policy lessons (for public officials and voters)
Individuals and businesses generally prefer stability and predictability to fluctuations and uncertainty.	Policymakers should promote stability of the economic environment.
All economies experience business cycles, and these are of varying duration and magnitude.	Policymakers should strive to use macroeconomic policies in a way that has a counter-cyclical effect (reduces economic cycles) rather than a pro-cyclical effect.
There usually exists a large degree of uncertainty regarding the state of the economy and its future prospects.	Policymakers should be cautious in evaluating new information and responding in never-tried-before ways.
Large economic swings (such as the GFC) are often driven by underlying long-term imbalances in the economy.	Policymakers should neither create nor overlook long-term economic imbalances.
'All that glitters is not gold' tends to be true in economics. Countries rich in natural resources may be subject to the Dutch Disease – underdevelopment of other industries and associated long-term problems.	Policymakers should implement resource taxes and use the proceeds to ensure proper development of non-mining sectors. Furthermore, budget surpluses should save some of the benefits of a mineral boom for the future.
Most public policies and regulations have redistributive effects; both at a given point in time and across time.	Policymakers should carefully consider the redistributive effects of their planned policies.

Economic insights	Implied policy lessons (for public officials and voters)
There is no universal prescription for whether a country should run a trade surplus or deficit.	Policymakers should identify the reasons why a trade surplus or deficit occurs before trying to rectify the situation.
Short-term foreign currency speculation is like buying a lottery ticket or gambling in a casino.	Policymakers should explain to the public that following 'proven' expert advice regarding frequent currency buying and selling leads to expected losses.
Using foreign currencies to hedge against exchange rate risk may be a good idea.	Policymakers should diversify a country's holdings of foreign reserves rather than only hold US dollars.
Flexible (floating) exchange rates allow the economy to adjust to foreign developments rather than forcing the price level to do so, which is the case under fixed exchange rates.	Policymakers should generally advocate flexible exchange rate regimes, unless a fixed regime is a step towards forming a common currency in an optimum currency area.
Economists have identified several main causes of unemployment, but they are uncertain about their relative importance.	Policymakers should support randomised policy experiments (such as are done in medical research and starting to appear in economic development research) to find the most cost-effective policy solutions. Identifying ways of reducing long-term unemployment is one such area.
Unskilled men face a greater probability of being unemployed and of not getting married, which has a negative effect on them as well as on women.	Policymakers should pay attention to the unskilled men problem, e.g. by ensuring flexible labour markets and by promoting access of lower socioeconomic groups to quality education.
Aggregating labour market data for various groups (such as males and females or full- and part-time workers) often leads to incorrect conclusions.	Policymakers should beware the aggregation problem in interpreting economic data.
Most countries have experienced increases in income inequality over the past several decades, the reasons for which are not fully understood. But taking the world as a whole, its inequality has actually decreased substantially over the past few decades.	Policymakers should carefully examine the trends in inequality in order to establish whether/how to respond to them.
Social skills and other non-IQ factors are becoming increasingly important in the labour market.	Policymakers should support education that encourages independent thinking and development of relevant soft-skills rather than rote learning and memorising facts.
Minimum wage legislation affects individuals and firms through a number of channels, on both the supply and demand side, and its overall welfare effect on the economy is not certain.	Policymakers should carefully analyse the effects of minimum wage legislation, and adjust their policies accordingly.
The welfare effect of a policy depends on the counterfactual, i.e. the choice of an alternative policy that is used as a benchmark for comparison.	Policymakers should clearly specify the counterfactual, i.e. which policies are being compared, how and why.
Monetary and fiscal policies impact the economy with different lags and in different ways.	Policymakers should always consider the right mix of monetary and fiscal policy as it may vary over time, noting that under normal circumstances monetary policy has a comparative advantage in macroeconomic stabilisation.
Throughout history, big monetary expansions have been followed by high inflation.	Policymakers should make sure that unconventional quantitative easing-type policies used during the GFC do not lead to excessive inflation.

Economic insights	Implied policy lessons (for public officials and voters)
If public debt is large, fiscal policy cannot effectively stimulate the economy in response to an adverse shock.	Policymakers should ensure that public finances are in good shape over the long term to have ammunition to respond to large adverse shocks.
Superannuation savings get very favourable tax treatment in Australia.	Policymakers should make superannuation taxes more in line with the principles of progressivity and intergenerational equity.
Negative gearing legislation creates perverse incentives for people to buy houses for investment purposes. This inflates their value and pushes home owners out of the market.	Policymakers should explore ways of doing away with negative gearing legislation.

2.4 Discussion questions

1   Using your own words, summarise the debate of Section 2.2 in three to five sentences.
2   Write down one idea discussed in the interview that you found new or interesting, or that you disagree with, and briefly explain why.
3   Write down one question on any topic covered in the interview that you would ask the speaker if you had a chance.
4   Consider the cartoon in Section 2.1, and explain the point to someone who has not read the section and does not have any knowledge of economics.
5   Examine Figure 2.1 from the perspective of a policymaker. Describe its key message to the public and explain what kind of policy improvement is implied by the data. Do the same for Figure 2.2.
6   Suppose you take part in a debating contest, in which the topic is the opening quote of the chapter by William H. Beveridge:

> Unemployment is like a headache or a high temperature –
> unpleasant and exhausting but not carrying in itself any
> explanation of its cause.

   Prepare a speech you would give for the affirmative side. Then (you or your classmate) prepare a speech for the negative side. If possible, organise an audience and perform the debate.
7   Explain in your own words what the 'Dutch Disease' is and how Prof. Gregory discovered this economic linkage.
8   What is a 'tariff'? In your view is it beneficial or detrimental to a country's economic performance? Why?
9   What does Prof. Gregory suggest the Australian government do during a resource boom? Try to come up with some additional policy ideas.

10 Explain Prof. Gregory's view on whether countries should run trade deficits or surpluses. Do some research on the internet to write a list of arguments for and against trade deficits and surpluses.

11 Is it a good idea to engage in short-term speculation on the foreign exchange market? Use some economic theory and data to support your answer.

12 What is the relationship between the exchange rate and the trade balance, i.e. exports and imports? Should countries have a fixed or a floating exchange rate? Why?

13 What are the major factors that contribute to unemployment? Suggest the main ways in which unemployment is harmful to individuals and society. Outline Prof. Gregory's discussion of how unemployment has changed over time in Australia, also mentioning the observed skill mismatch.

14 Find data on the rate of unemployment for the United States and Australia, separately for males and females, possibly also a more detailed demographic division according to race or age. Plot these in a graph and attempt to provide explanations for the various trends you see.

15 The effect of education on unemployment is discussed in this chapter. What other personal characteristics do you think are important in gaining a good job? Think about your resume in this light and identify its strong points as well as areas you could improve upon.

16 What is Prof. Gregory's view on the desirability of the minimum wage legislation? Have you or someone you know ever been affected by this legislation? How?

17 What is the HECS scheme? Do you think it may affect a prospective student's decision to pursue higher education? If so, how?

18 What is Prof. Gregory's take on the use and effectiveness of monetary and fiscal policies – both in general and in relation to the Global Financial Crisis?

19 Prof. Gregory discusses his view on the role of the government in the economy, and the distinction between market and government failure. Summarise his view and contrast it to your own.

20 Propose a set of policies that you think best achieves a low and stable unemployment rate and ultimately promotes people's wellbeing.

2.5 Where to find out more

Boesler, M. (2015), 'What the Unemployment and Labour Force Participation Rates Would be if all of the Discouraged Workers Came Back', *Business Insider*, 20 January, available at **www.businessinsider.com.au/ unemployment-rate-if-discouraged- workers-came-back-2014-1**

Corden, W. M. and J. P. Neary (1982), 'Booming Sector and De-industrialisation in a Small Open Economy', *The Economic Journal*, 92, pp. 825–848.

Forbes (2013), 'Why Family Wealth Is a Curse', 3 January, available at **www.forbes.com/ sites/deborahljacobs/2013/03/01/why- family-wealth-is-a-curse**

Gregory, R. G. (1976), 'Some Implications of the Growth of the Mineral Sector', *Australian Journal of Agricultural and Resource Economics*, Australian Agricultural and Resource Economics Society, 20(2), pp. 71–91.

Gregory, R. G. (2012), 'Living standards, terms of trade and foreign ownership: reflections on the Australian mining boom', *Australian*

Journal of Agricultural and Resource Economics, Australian Agricultural and Resource Economics Society, 56(2), pp. 171–200.

Gregory, R. G. (2012), 'Dark Corners in a Bright Economy: the Lack of Jobs for Unskilled Men', *Australian Bulletin of Labour*, National Institute of Labour Studies, 38(1), pp. 2–25.

Leigh, A. (2007), 'Does Raising the Minimum Wage Help the Poor?', *The Economic Record*, The Economic Society of Australia, 83(263), pp. 432–445.

Mitchell, B. (2013), 'Australian Labour Market Data – Urgent Need for Fiscal Stimulus', Billy Blog, available at **http://bilbo.economic outlook.net/blog/?p=25654**

RBA (2015), 'The Australian Economy and Financial Markets, Chart Pack', available at **www.rba.gov.au/chart-pack/pdf/chart-pack.pdf**

Richardson, S. (1998), 'Who Gets Minimum Wages?', *Journal of Industrial Relations*, 40, pp. 554–579.

3 Designing effective microeconomic policies

The first lesson of economics is scarcity: there is never enough of anything to fully satisfy all those who want it. The first lesson of politics is to disregard the first lesson of economics.

Thomas Sowell, writer and economist, *Is Reality Optional? and Other Essays*, Hoover Institution Press, 1993.

Economic concepts discussed

Easy-to-understand explanations of all the concepts listed below appear in the glossary at the end of this book.

- Ageing population
- Aptitude distribution
- Baby bonus
- Confidence intervals
- Consumption smoothing
- Convex preferences

- Earned-income tax credits
- Econometrics
- Fallacy of sunk cost
- Gender pay discrimination
- HECS
- Minimum wage

- Payroll taxes
- Percentile
- Prediction markets
- Reverse mortgages
- School productivity
- Statistical significance

3.1 Motivation and overview

Economists sometimes lament that politicians do not listen to them carefully, and criticise various economic policies as ill-designed or badly implemented. Only a small fraction of economists, however, have the courage (and elbows) to take the matter into their own hands and enter politics.

One such exception is Dr Andrew Leigh, MP. Prior to entering politics, he was an economics Professor at the Australian National University, and recipient of the 2011 'Best Australian Economist under the Age of 40' award. Currently he is a Member of the Australian House of Representatives (for the Labor Party) and Shadow Minister for Competition. In an interview with me recorded on 5 September 2012,[1] Dr Leigh uses his expertise in both economics and politics to demonstrate that economic research can be valuable in designing and implementing effective public policies, and hence greatly improve the lives of individuals.

---

[1] The full video-interview is available at **http://youtu.be/ULm0bpmyy5U**. For more details regarding Dr Leigh's research and policy involvement, see **www.andrewleigh.com**.

What determines the quality of school teachers? How is it linked to students' performance and economic growth? Should the government pay parents a '**baby bonus**'? What is the effect of **minimum wage** legislation? What is the best way to predict election outcomes? Are divorce rates influenced by the gender of the couple's children? In the next section Dr Leigh answers these and many other questions, and considers their implications for the desirability of various microeconomic policies.

The first discussion topic is the downward trend in the quality of Australian school teachers that Dr Leigh documented in his research (Leigh and Ryan, 2006). Figure 3.1 shows this trend, comparing the ability of new female teachers in 1983 and 2003, which the authors summarise as follows:

> *Over this 20-year period, the fraction of women in the top achievement quintile becoming teachers fell from 11 per cent to 6 per cent, while the fraction of women in the second-top achievement quintile fell from 12 per cent to 6 per cent.*

Figure 3.1: Ability distribution of new female teachers as proportion of ability group in each quintile (20%) of the whole population in 1983 and 2003

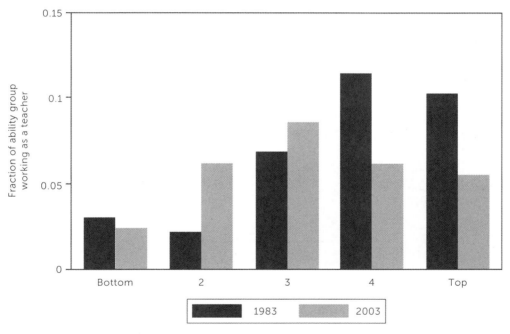

Source: Leigh and Ryan (2006), based on data from Longitudinal Surveys of Australian Youth. Used by permission.

Dr Leigh outlines possible explanations for this trend, which also occurred in the United States (see Hoxby and Leigh, 2004). The primary factor identified is a decline in teachers' pay relative to other occupations. He discusses the policy made during this period, which consisted of cutting class sizes without increasing the overall salary budget commensurately:

> *Roughly you saw a 10 per cent cut in teacher pay, relative to other occupations, and a 10 per cent cut in class size. So it's*

*almost like the new teachers were being paid out of the
wallets of the existing teachers.*

It is important to note that these trends in teachers' quality have been associated
with a decrease in numeracy and literacy scores of Australian school children, as
documented in Leigh and Ryan (2011). Dr Leigh discusses the possible causal link
between these undesirable developments, and outlines public policies that could reverse
them. The debate also covers tertiary education. Dr Leigh explains that the returns to it
are large; based on his estimates there is on average a 15 per cent increase in pay for
every year of tertiary education. He therefore addresses the natural question of the right
level of government subsidy towards university tuition.

The discussion then moves onto other areas, namely well-intentioned public policies
that turn out to have undesirable effects on people's incentives and behaviour. One such
policy was the introduction of the 'baby bonus' in Australia on 1 July 2004. In Gans and
Leigh (2006) it was shown that the introduction of the policy was ill-designed and created
incentives for birth shifting. This is because a child born just before midnight on June 30
would not be eligible for the $3000 bonus, whereas a child born moments later would.
The paper estimated that the policy led to more than a thousand (caesarean section and
induction) births shifted from late June to early July in 2004 in order for the parents to
receive the payment. Dr Leigh explains that 'a non-trivial share – maybe a few hundred –
were shifted by a couple of weeks'.

Figure 3.2: The number of children born in Australia around the introduction of the baby
bonus on 1 July 2004 (top); the deviations in the number of births from normal
(bottom)

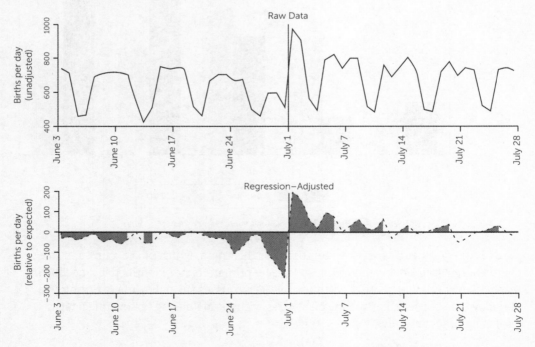

This is apparent in Figure 3.2, which shows the number of children born in Australia around that time, with the baby bonus introduction indicated by the vertical line. The first day of the baby bonus recorded the greatest number of births in Australian history!

While the health effects of such birth shifting are difficult to establish, even the pure consequence of overcrowding maternity wards in the first week of July 2004 speaks volumes of the poor implementation of the scheme and the perverse incentives it created, depicted in the cartoon below. As Dr Leigh explains, it could have easily been phased out over time to avoid such birth shifting.

Concept by Jan Libich © 2015, drawing by Veronika Mojžišovà. Used by permission.

The discussion then turns to the demographic trend of **ageing populations** and its effect on the budget, the elderly and the young. Minimum wage legislation is then scrutinised, both from the perspective of the workers and employers. This is in the light of Dr Leigh's study, in which he showed that a typical Australian worker on a minimum wage is from a middle-income rather than a low-income household, and thus the legislation may not always reduce inequality as much as desired (see Leigh, 2007).

The next part of the interview discusses Dr Leigh's research findings regarding election predictions (see Leigh and Wolfers, 2006; and Wolfers and Leigh, 2002). Perhaps surprisingly, predictions based on betting markets tend to be much more accurate than predictions based on polls. An implication of this is that the ability of betting markets to aggregate information and forecast the future should be used more broadly, not only in politics but other areas (some firms and government bodies already take advantage of them).

The last topic relates to the effect of economic research on personal life. It centres on the findings of Leigh (2009) showing that parents tend to prefer having children of both genders. The study reports some consequences of that: 'Compared to parents with a boy and a girl, parents with two children of the same sex are 1.7 percentage points less likely to marry if they are unmarried' (and possibly also more likely to get divorced). As proof that even political elites' powers are limited when it comes to natural forces, we find out in the interview that Dr Leigh's third child, due to be born in one week's time, is again a boy – like his two elder siblings.

3.2 The debate

Dr Jan Libich (JL): In our consideration of how economics can contribute to public policy design we cannot but start with education. This is because research shows that human capital accumulation through quality education is the key determinant of economic growth and prosperity. In your 2008 paper with Chris Ryan, you examined the quality of school teachers in Australia. You found a downward trend – a slight decline in the quality of Australian teachers. Then you look at possible explanations and come up with teachers' pay as one of the key variables. Can you tell us what happened to teachers' pay over time, and how it may link to teachers' quality?

© Andrew Leigh. Used by permission.

< Dr Andrew Leigh (AL): The story of the academic aptitude of new teachers is that in 1983 the typical teacher was at the 70th **percentile** of the **aptitude distribution** – in the top 30 per cent of her class. By 2003, she was at the 62nd percentile – the top 38 per cent of her class. Chris Ryan and I talk about a number of possible explanations. One is this trade-off that policymakers made from the late 1980s to the early 2000s between cutting class sizes but not increasing the overall salary budget commensurately. Roughly you saw a 10 per cent cut in teacher pay, relative to other occupations, and a 10 per cent cut in class size. So it's almost like the new teachers were being paid out of the wallets of the existing teachers.

Then, you had some other factors going on. You had the fact that **gender pay discrimination** in the professions was rampant in the 1950s and 1960s. It was almost like we were corralling Australia's most talented women into teaching and nursing, and as those gender pay gaps fell we then saw a drop-off in the share of suitably talented women entering teaching. Thirdly, I think there's also an increase in earnings inequality in the rest of the labour market, which posed a particular challenge for teaching. Teachers traditionally operated off uniform salary schedules.

JL: Let's think through the consequences. You have a 2009 paper where you examine student outcomes. You look at the numeracy and literacy scores for Australian schoolchildren and you find a worrying trend, a decline in test scores. Given the increases in expenditure per student, at face value it would imply a fall in 'school productivity'. Can you tell us a little bit about that and how it actually links to your previous study about lowering teachers' pay?

AL: School productivity is one of these ugly phrases that economists love and educational policymakers hate. But essentially, what you described is the trend we found. We went back through the dusty archives to try and find instances in which precisely the same Maths or English question had been asked of successive cohorts. So, same wording, certain share of kids get it right in one test, another share of kids get it right in another test. We find flat or perhaps even declining test scores across a couple of different tests. One possibility is that the trade-off between dropping teacher pay relative to other professionals, and cutting class sizes, was actually the wrong trade-off to be making in that period.

Then there are other possibilities, such as changes in curriculum affecting learning outcomes. There's also a set of social changes, but to the extent that Chris (Ryan) and I can hold them constant in our data analysis, it doesn't look as though things like more TV watching or a rise in single-parent households or a rise in kids from non-English-speaking backgrounds explain much of the downward trend in students' test scores. You've actually got trends that go in the opposite direction. Not just the increase in inflation-adjusted spending per student, but also the fact that more kids than ever before have a parent with a tertiary education. So, it's a bit of a black box. We can tell that Australia's school kids in Year 8 or 9 aren't scoring better than they did a generation ago, and I think that poses a pretty big challenge for policymakers like me.

JL: If you combine the two findings, it seems like a no-brainer. We have lowered teachers' pay, consequently we got lower-quality teachers and therefore worse student outcomes. Or are you suggesting that this might be too simplistic, that this may not explain the whole story?

AL: I certainly think that teacher quality is important. One of the things that always surprises me is that parents worry a huge amount about which school their child attends. Yet, they worry very little about which teacher their child is taught by within a school. Yet, we know that the within-school variance in quality is higher than the between-school variance. So I think that does suggest that we ought to be focusing on teacher quality. I think programs such as 'Teach For Australia' and 'Teach Next' are important in attracting alternative career entry. I think it's also really important to think about retention of great teachers in the profession. That's a key issue for policymakers. It's not the only one. Test score accountability and the right level of principal autonomy matter as well, but teacher quality is pretty much my number one educational issue.

JL: I agree. What would be some of the policies that can reverse this unfavourable trend in students' performance? You mentioned class size, does that matter as much as it is often argued?

AL: We know that cutting class sizes down from 40 to 30 has a big impact on student outcomes. Cutting class sizes once they fall below 30 probably has smaller impacts. The research is varied. You have 'Tennessee Project STAR' suggesting still positive effects going from 22 down to 18. But I think now you're probably down to a point where you want to think about teacher quality and teacher pay as being the top priority.

JL: One of the worldwide critiques of the policy approach to education is that it's more of a top-down approach. Politicians seem to have an idea what the education system should look like and try to impose it on schools, but there is evidence that school autonomy in shaping the curriculum and other things is beneficial. What do you think about this trade-off?

AL: I think determining the right level of school autonomy is extremely important. That partly depends on what principals feel they're able to do. If you've got a principal who is comfortable managing the lawn-mowing contracts and wants the flexibility to save money on lawn-mowing so they can spend it on textbooks, then that's fine. But if you've got a principal who mainly wants to be an educational leader and actually doesn't want to spend a lot of their time working out how the budget's going to look, then you don't want to thrust upon that principal more autonomy than they're ready to handle. So I think this is one of these areas where the people who become principals are important to thinking about the autonomy we should give them.

JL: Let's move to tertiary education because similar themes apply there. You have a 2008 study looking at the returns to education. You find that there's a high personal gain from tertiary education, on average around 15 per cent increase in salary for every year. In relation to that, there's a recent Grattan Institute report with similar findings (Norton, 2012a). Its author argues that we can actually start reducing tertiary education subsidies because students are getting most of the private benefits. What's your view on this?

AL: Clearly the private benefits of tertiary education are very large, as you said, 15 per cent a year. So a three-year Bachelor's degree is earning a student something in the order of a 50 per cent increase in earnings. Then the question is: how much are the private returns also matched by social returns? And, sadly, the social returns are easier to list than they are to measure. You can list returns such as better productivity, so if you have more education and we're sitting next to each other in adjoining cubicles, I might learn a lot from you and become more productive. A higher education might also mean that you have less of an impact on the healthcare system. It's probably unlikely to have much of an impact on crime. Increased secondary schooling I think could well have social payoffs in crime, but I'm less sure about universities. And there might be political participation payoffs to tertiary education of which I think we're fairly uncertain. So all of that adds up to, I think, big **confidence intervals** around what the social payoff to tertiary education is.

The Grattan Institute report seems to take a strongly rational view on debt. It seems to say we can ramp up student contributions without affecting equity outcomes. But what I worry about is there might be some degree of debt-aversion which, even if it isn't backed up by a rational model, could still lead kids from disadvantaged backgrounds to baulk at a high sticker price. And to refuse to take on a university education despite it being good for them and having big social payoffs.

JL: The report seems to present some evidence that people from lower socioeconomic backgrounds would not be disadvantaged and higher deferred fees wouldn't impact too much on them entering university. What is your view on that?

AL: The authors are testing out of sample, Jan. The two best experiments we have are the ones that Bruce Chapman and Chris Ryan look at: the introduction of the Higher Education Contribution Scheme (**HECS**) and then the introduction of differential HECS in the late 1990s, which saw higher HECS bills again. But those increases were of a much smaller magnitude than is proposed in the Grattan Institute report. So students now may be asked at the end of their university education to pay back a debt equivalent to a small car. I don't think that then tells us that we could increase their debt to equal the value of a small plane, and they wouldn't baulk at it.

JL: Let's move to other microeconomic policies. You were quite instrumental in your research highlighting the fact that some government policies, if badly implemented, can have severe distortionary effects on people's behaviour. The study that pops into mind is your 2006 paper with Joshua Gans where you look at the introduction of the baby bonus and the timing of births. Can you tell us what it was about?

AL: The 'baby bonus' study centres around a policy change put in place by the Liberal Party government under Prime Minister John Howard. They said any baby born on or after the 1st of July 2004 will receive $3000. They were asked: what about a baby born on the evening of the 30th of June? And the Minister was very clear that such a family would not receive the baby bonus. There were rumours around this time that the policy had caused shifting of births and overcrowding in maternity wards. Joshua (Gans) was very close to the issue because his wife had one of their children in the July just after the baby bonus came into effect.

JL: Was his child one of those that was moved?

AL: Well, they had some difficulty getting an obstetrician at the time and that's indeed what we find from the data. This is one of those studies where you actually don't need much fancy **econometrics**. There is one day on which more babies were born than any other day in Australian history, and that's the first day the baby bonus was introduced. You just see the graph spike up and then what's troubling is that you see the birth rate higher even in the second week of July than it should have been. It suggests that of the thousand births that were shifted from June into July, a non-trivial share – maybe a few hundred – were shifted by a couple of weeks. Generally, when we're thinking about the health of babies, we're worried about premature births, but there's also some evidence that babies that are in the womb well past term might suffer health consequences as well. So, while we didn't find anything that was conclusive, we were concerned that the sharp introduction of the baby bonus had actually had adverse health consequences.

JL: The sad thing is that you warned the government about this, but the policy was not changed and there was another jump increase in the level of the baby bonus. Unsurprisingly, birth shifting occurred again.

AL: That's right, yes. So the Howard government then went and increased the baby bonus. Having introduced it in July 2004, they increased it in July 2006, and just in case you'd thought the first result was a fluke, we saw the same effect in July 2006 again. We had released our study just prior to that in order to try and persuade the government to just step in the change, make the payment increase gradual. They didn't and you again saw births shifting.

JL: I am starting to understand why you felt the need to enter politics … We are now moving onto the important question of how we can improve the design of policies to avoid these kinds of distortionary outcomes.

AL: We want to think about 'introduction effects' – it's what Joshua (Gans) and I call it. Normally when we think about policy distortions, we think about the longer-term, steady-state effect of a policy. I think we ought to also make sure that when a policy is being put into place, it doesn't generate perverse incentives. Those introduction effects are not as critical as the enduring effects, but they matter and there are simple ways to get around them. So for example, the Health Minister wrote to obstetricians prior to Labor's increase of the baby bonus to make them aware of the fact that there had been births shifting previously and to encourage them to make sure that birth timing was only done with the health of the baby and the mother in mind. I hope that had some effect in reducing the degree of births shifting.

JL: It's peculiar because the government could easily change the implementation of the policy. Instead, they write to all obstetricians asking them to do something rather than actually fixing the policy and the perverse incentives it creates. Anyway, so far we've assumed that the baby bonus was actually a good policy, but is it really the case? Do you think it's desirable?

AL: Well, the best argument you can make for the baby bonus is that if families are credit-constrained at the time of the birth, then this provides extra liquidity for families at the time the baby is born. And that any drop in expenditure at the time of the birth could have substantial adverse· consequences. Think about a family that has difficulty keeping the heat on, providing enough food, making sure that the parents are in good harmony. If you can stop there being shouting in the household in the first few months of a baby's life, you might well improve the child's life overall.

JL: Currently it is no longer a once-off bonus, but it's phased out over time – it's paid fortnightly. Is it perhaps less helpful to a credit-constrained family?

AL: Why so? It just means that the family then has payments that they receive through the ensuing six months or so, either through a baby bonus or paid parental leave. I would've thought potentially that's even better for liquidity constraints, if you're worried that a lump of cash might not be spent entirely on baby-related things.

JL: In some countries one of the aims of the baby bonus, together with the **consumption smoothing** you described, is to address the undesirable demographic trends of dropping fertility and populations ageing. Is trying to provide extra incentives for people to have kids an intention of the baby bonus in Australia?

AL: I think it was always principally income support, trying to top up payments at around the time of the birth. To the extent that it was a birth incentive, I think that was given life by then-Treasurer Peter Costello's statement on budget night: that mums and dads should have one for her, one for him and one for the country. That, I think, is probably a pretty weak argument for the baby bonus. Joshua and I didn't look at this issue, but there's a Melbourne Institute study by Mark Wooden and co-authors (Drago et al., 2009) that estimates that for every extra baby born thanks to the baby bonus the cost to the budget is over $100 000.

JL: Are there any other policies that could deal with the adverse demographic trends? When baby boomers retire there will be a big negative impact on the budget ...

AL: The aged-care reforms that are going on at the moment are aimed at a lot of that. One of the things that we just announced yesterday, which I think is quite clever, is thinking about the training of aged-care workers. At the moment we train aged-care workers and doctors very differently. Doctors are trained in teaching hospitals, which have regimented curriculum programs and experienced doctors to mentor them. Aged-care workers tend to just find themselves in whatever aged-care home they work in. So we're actually setting up teaching aged-care centres to try to improve the quality of care. And we also try to think about the way in which aged-care is financed, which is important.

JL: Yes, but this is going to impose more expenditure on the budget, it's not actually going to help solve the problematic fiscal outlook.

AL: Well, it imposes more expenditure on Australians as a whole. And I think one of the ways in which you've seen the debate shift in the last 15 years is away from the notion that government ought to pay for everything, to the notion that if an elderly couple finds themselves in a situation where they have substantial assets and they want a better quality of aged-care, it might be appropriate to ask them to pay for it. Because, really, who's ending up paying for it is the children who are receiving slightly smaller inheritances while their parent receives a better quality of aged-care.

I think that conversation's gotten better in Australia than it was in the 1990s. And structuring appropriate bonds, protections around **reverse mortgages** – to make sure reverse mortgages can work. These are natural policies to economists to make sure the tax system doesn't generate perverse incentives not to make a contribution to better quality aged-care for those that can afford it.

JL: True, but I think the extent of the demographic problem is much bigger than most people realise. The projections over the next two to three decades suggest that the proportion of people over 65 in Australia relative to working-age population is going to increase by almost 50 per cent; from about 0.2 to around 0.35. So it will have a major fiscal impact. And it's not only through the pension scheme, it's also through healthcare. A large part of the health expenditures occur in the last year of life, so having a lot more elderly people is going to have a severe impact on the healthcare budget.

AL: But I think one of the good things that economists have brought to this debate, Jan, is the notion that we ought to not just think of a 64-year-old as a 64-year-old. In some sense, you know, as Paul McCartney from the Beatles actually said when he turned 64, it's quite different from what he thought it would be when he wrote his famous song 'When I'm Sixty-Four'. And you see this. David Cutler has some nice work where he looks at the functional physical mobility of someone who is 64 now and someone who was 64 a generation ago. And you're finding increases in the order of about 10 years, today's 64-year-old is as mobile as a 54-year-old a generation ago. That means people enjoy longer life spans. And another aspect I think the demographers miss is that they often ignore price effects. As prices change, you also see demands change as well. So I worry that a little bit too much of this modelling is driven by simple age structure and not enough by the way in which we would think about it as economists with the prices included.

JL: The increased mobility will naturally have labour market consequences, which brings us to a different microeconomic policy, the minimum wage legislation. You have a 2007 study where you're trying to assess to whom the minimum wage actually goes, who the recipient is. And surprisingly, you find that it's actually not low-income families but more often it's medium-income families. And when you run simulations, in the scenario that I found most realistic, minimum wage actually leads to an increase in income inequality rather than a decrease. So, we think of minimum wages as a way of reducing poverty and inequality, but your research seems to imply that they may actually have the opposite effect. As a politician now, where do you see the minimum wage legislation?

AL: I find the minimum wage debate enormously frustrating. There's one side of the debate that doesn't acknowledge that raising the minimum wage has benefits in terms of higher earnings.

JL: Income effects?

AL: Yes. You raise the minimum wage, a bunch of people get wage rises and while they're not all poor, they are disproportionately poor. And then there's another side of the debate, people who don't accept that there could be any dis-employment effects; that some workers lose their job as a consequence of the minimum wage legislation.

Both of those extreme cases don't make much sense. I think there are dis-employment effects, but they're probably fairly small. I think there are also positive wage effects, although it actually turns out we have no studies in Australia looking at what the wage effect is, and understanding better how much a minimum wage increase flows through into wage packets is really important. You can write theoretical models in which the answer is 'none', or in which the answer is 'all'. Therefore, theory tells us nothing and we'd like to have some more empirics. So I think minimum wage legislation is part of an anti-poverty toolkit but I think it will never be the only effective part of alleviating poverty. Things like **earned-income tax credits**, focusing on the impact of **payroll taxes** and income taxes, and of course education are all going to be at least as important in fighting poverty as the minimum wage.

JL: You have a very interesting study with Justin Wolfers about forecasting election outcomes. It compares the accuracy of election predictions by three methods: economic models, the polls and prediction (betting) markets. The interesting finding is that betting markets usually give a better answer than the polls. Being a politician now, is your party paying more attention to **prediction markets**?

AL: You always learn good things from co-authors. With the baby bonus study I was sure when we began that we wouldn't find any effects, and with the election forecasting paper, I said: 'Justin, why do you want to include this prediction market stuff, isn't it more interesting just to look at the economic models and the polls?' And then he persuaded me that prediction markets were truly fascinating to look at. I certainly look at them, but there's a large degree of path dependence in politics. That's true in the commentariat, that's also true within political parties themselves.

So I think the temptation to continuing surveying is going to be with us for quite a time to come. Despite the fact that polls are so extraordinarily volatile. You and I know if you're measuring something that has a margin of error of a couple of percentage points either way and you want to look at the change in that thing, then if two things measured with a two percentage point margin of error differ by two percentage points, then chances are you're just looking at inaccurately measured data: what economists call 'noise'. But that's not the impression you'd get if you looked at the front of a major broadsheet on the day they brought out their in-house poll.

JL: Let me ask one last policy-related question. Can you briefly mention some public policies that economics implies would improve overall wellbeing, but politicians have shied away from?

AL: One of the unusual things about economists is that we think in terms of prices. So it's intuitive to us that the optimal price for emitting a tonne of carbon isn't zero – an insight that hasn't always been apparent to my friends in the Liberal and National parties. Economists often point to the considerable costs involved in traffic congestion, which is becoming a particular problem in Australia's largest cities. Electronic tolls have become commonplace in Australia but, so far as I'm aware, the only one which charges a different price at peak times is the Sydney Harbour Bridge. In all other cases, the charge is the same at 5 am and 5 pm.

JL: So far we've discussed the influence of academic research on policy, but let's get a bit more personal. You authored an interesting study published in 2009 where you look at how divorce rates, and generally people's happiness, are affected by the composition of their children. You find that if people have a boy and a girl they are more likely to get married and less likely to get divorced. Given that your first child was a boy, I hope I can disclose that you were wishing for a girl as your second child ...

AL: This is what economists call **convex preferences** over child gender. You can write down models in which people ought to enjoy having two children of the same kind; for example, because they can pass down the blue clothes or the pink clothes to the next child. But in general, you see convex preferences – people prefer one of each gender. This is partly exhibited in the fact that parents with two kids of the same gender are more likely to go for a third than parents of two kids of different genders. My research showed they were also less likely to get married and more likely to split up. Not by a great deal, by 1.7 percentage points, which accounts for maybe a tenth of the total variation in marriage rates among those families.

But I don't know whether this is because we've talked ourselves into it or whether having 'one of each' was always our preference. My wife and I are delighted by the fact that we're expecting a third boy. I feel like I know how to raise boys, I feel as though I know what sort of holidays we'll have. They're going to be active holidays in which we try and all exhaust one another. And I feel as though I know what kinds of empirical lessons I'll be sitting down to teach my sons; making sure by the time they turn 10, they understand the **fallacy of the sunk cost** and they can think at the margin.

JL: Congratulations! I would like to wish you best of luck for the birth and thank you very much for your ongoing contribution to economic research and public policy. Please keep in mind that if things don't work out for you in politics, we'd be very happy to have you back in economics.

AL: Thank you very much. It's likely an 'absorbing state', but I very much enjoy dabbling in economics. I think the popularisation of economics is enormously important to the future of our discipline.

3.3 Key economic insights and policy lessons

Economic insights	Implied policy lessons (for public officials and voters)
Incentives are a powerful force in determining a person's behaviour. Ever-present in economics, they can be compared to the role of gravity in physics.	Policymakers should think through the impact of proposed policies on people's incentives, including the indirect second-round effects.
Policies can create undesirable market distortions not only in terms of their longer-term ('steady-state') effects, but also via their short-term ('introduction') effects.	Policymakers should design the implementation of policies carefully so as not to create perverse incentives and behaviour (such as birth shifting around the introduction of the baby bonus).
The baby bonus policy does not seem to be very effective in encouraging families to have children.	Policymakers should treat the baby bonus primarily as an income support tool rather than a fertility-boosting measure, and design it accordingly.
The public benefits of quality primary and secondary education are very large, partly because education positively affects many other social and economic outcomes.	Policymakers should put increasing the quality of education at the top of their priorities.
If a reduction in the class size is not accompanied by a corresponding increase in the school budget, teachers' pay generally falls.	Policymakers should not ignore the various trade-offs they are making in education and other areas.
Empirical research shows that the benefits of a good teacher, as measured, e.g., by increases in the students' future wages, are enormous. If teachers' pay falls relative to other comparable occupations, then (other things equal) teachers' quality declines – as has been the case in Australia since the early 1980s.	Policymakers should put incentives in place to attract great teachers and retain them in the profession.

Economic insights	Implied policy lessons (for public officials and voters)
The optimal degree of school autonomy differs across schools and their principals.	Policymakers should set up a flexible system in which the degree of a school's autonomy is tailored to the needs of the particular school.
The social benefits (positive externality) of all levels of education are known, but their individual contribution is difficult to measure.	Policymakers should support research and experiments to discover the most cost-effective ways of improving the quality of education.
Research shows that increases in life-expectancy and improvements in health make today's average 64-year-old as mobile as a 54-year-old a generation ago.	Policymakers should appropriately account for improvements in life expectancy and health in designing changes to their pension, healthcare and welfare policies.
Minimum wage legislation has desirable income effects as well as undesirable dis-employment effects.	Policymakers should acknowledge both types of effects of minimum wage legislation and, if deemed desirable, design it based on careful data analysis regarding the existing pros and cons.
Markets are very good at aggregating information, which is why betting (prediction) markets tend to offer more accurate forecasts of economic and social events than polls.	Policymakers should carefully design prediction markets and use them to collect information on the current and future trends in the economy.
If a variable is measured with a wide margin of error (such as political party preferences in polls), then minor changes in the measured value are likely to be random rather than reflecting an actual change in the variable.	Policymakers should more carefully communicate uncertainty (and statistical significance) around empirical findings, and take it into account when designing policies.
Traffic congestion is very costly from a social point of view.	Policymakers should use existing electronic congestion pricing methods for road use and parking whereby the charge varies with traffic (rises in peak times).

3.4 Discussion questions

1   Using your own words, summarise the debate of Section 3.2 in three to five sentences.
2   Write down one idea discussed in the interview that you found new or interesting, or that you disagree with, and briefly explain why.
3   Write down one question on any topic covered in the interview that you would ask the speaker if you had a chance.
4   Consider the cartoon in Section 3.1, and explain the point to someone who has not read the section and does not have any knowledge of economics.
5   Examine Figure 3.1 from the perspective of a policymaker. Describe its key message to the public and explain what kind of policy improvement is implied by the data. Do the same for Figure 3.2.

6   Suppose you take part in a debating contest, in which the topic is the opening quote of the chapter by Thomas Sowell:

> The first lesson of economics is scarcity: there is never enough of anything to fully satisfy all those who want it. The first lesson of politics is to disregard the first lesson of economics.

Prepare a speech you would give for the affirmative side. Then (you or your classmate) prepare a speech for the negative side. If possible, organise an audience and perform the debate.

7   Summarise Dr Leigh's discussion on 'school productivity' and explain what the main challenge is for educational policymakers. What were the key findings of his research on teacher quality in Australia? Based on the interview and research you can find on the internet, list the arrangements that seem to affect educational outcomes and those that don't.

8   What are your thoughts on education as a possible determinant of economic growth? Use other studies and available data to bolster your argument.

9   Compare the research findings on the economic benefits of tertiary education reported by Chapman and Ryan (2005), Leigh (2008) and Norton (2012a) – the links are provided below. Highlight the similarities and differences, including those regarding policy implications.

10 Critically evaluate the following statement: 'The baby bonus was a well-intentioned and appropriately designed public policy. It is not the government's role to act as a gatekeeper for the negative consequences of people's decisions.' Suggests ways in which the implementation of the baby bonus could have been improved.

11 The composition of society as well as people's lives have changed considerably since The Beatles released their popular single 'When I'm Sixty-four' in 1967. What has changed for this demographic in Australia? Use your imagination and outline what you think your life will look like when you turn 64 (or if you already have, in 10 years' time).

12 Outline Dr Leigh's research on the relationship between children's gender and marriage/divorce rates. Find out whether results for other countries suggest similar or different patterns. What are the possible explanations for this relationship?

13 Dr Leigh finds the debate on the minimum wage 'enormously frustrating'. Explain why, and suggest additional factors that should be taken into account in assessing the pros and cons of the minimum wage legislation. What is your personal view on this?

14 In a study with Prof. Justin Wolfers, Dr Leigh compares the predictions of election outcomes obtained from surveys and betting markets. The latter channel seems to provide more accurate forecasts; why do you think that is? Can you think of some ways in which prediction markets can be used more effectively in various areas of policymaking? Find some real-world examples.

15 Like other economists, Dr Leigh has undertaken research on a wide range of social and economic issues. What do you think are the advantages of having economists working within the government? Can you see some disadvantages as well?

16 Dr Leigh expresses the view that 'the popularisation of economics is extremely important to the future of the discipline'. Do you agree with him? On what grounds? (For some ideas, see Dr Leigh's interesting book *The Economics of Just About Everything*.) Suggest how academic economists could better bridge the gap between academic research and real-world policymaking.

17 Propose a set of policies that you think best promote a sufficiently high fertility rate that stops the population from shrinking.

3.5 Where to find out more

Chapman, B. and C. Ryan (2005), 'The Access Implications of Income-contingent Charges for Higher Education: Lessons from Australia', *Economics of Education Review*, Elsevier, 24(5), pp. 491–512, available at https://ideas.repec.org/p/auu/dpaper/463.html

Cutler, D., E. Meara and S. Richards-Shubik (2011), 'Health Shocks and Disability Transitions among Near-Elderly Workers', 13th Annual Joint Conference of the Retirement Research Consortium, 'Innovations in Retirement Security', Washington DC, available at: http://crr.bc.edu/wp-content/uploads/2011/08/Health-Shocks.pdf

Drago R., K. Sawyer, K. M. Shreffler, D. Warren and M. Wooden (2009), 'Did Australia's Baby Bonus Increase the Fertility Rate?', Melbourne Institute of Applied Economic and Social Research, Working Paper Series wp2009n01.

Gans, J. and A. Leigh (2006), 'Born on the First of July: An (Un)natural Experiment in Birth Timing', published in 2009 in the *Journal of Public Economics*, 93(1–2), pp. 246–263.

Hoxby, C. M. and A. Leigh (2004), 'Pulled Away or Pushed Out? Explaining the Decline of Teacher Aptitude in the United States', *American Economic Review*, 94(2), pp. 236–240.

Leigh, A. (2007), 'Does Raising the Minimum Wage Help the Poor?', *The Economic Record*, The Economic Society of Australia, 83(263), pp. 432–445.

Leigh, A. (2008), 'Returns to Education in Australia', *Economic Papers*, The Economic Society of Australia, 27(3), pp. 233–249.

Leigh, A. (2009), 'Does Child Gender Affect Marital Status? Evidence from Australia', *Journal of Population Economics*, 22(2), pp. 351–366.

Leigh, A. (2014), *The Economics of Just About Everything*, Allen & Unwin.

Leigh, A. and C. Ryan (2006), 'How and Why Has Teacher Quality Changed in Australia?', Discussion Paper Number 534, Centre for Economic Policy Research, The Australian National University.

Leigh, A. and C. Ryan (2011), 'Long-Run Trends in School Productivity: Evidence from Australia', *Education Finance and Policy*, MIT Press, 6(1), pp. 105–135.

Leigh, A. and J. Wolfers (2006), 'Competing Approaches to Forecasting Elections: Economic Models, Opinion Polling and Prediction Markets', *The Economic Record*, The Economic Society of Australia, 82(258), pp. 325–340.

Norton, A. (2012a), 'Graduate Winners: Assessing the Public and Private Benefits of Higher Education', The Grattan Institute Report, August, available at http://grattan.edu.au/wp-content/uploads/2014/04/162_graduate_winners_report.pdf

Norton, A. (2012b), 'Mapping Australian Higher Education', Grattan Institute, Melbourne, available at http://grattan.edu.au/report/mapping-australian-higher-education-2012/

Norton, A. and I. Cherastidtham (2014), 'Mapping Australian Higher Education, 2014–15', Grattan Institute, Melbourne, available at http://grattan.edu.au/report/mapping-australian-higher-education-2014-15

Siegfried, J. J. (2010), *Better Living through Economics*, Harvard University Press.

Wolfers, J. and A. Leigh (2002), 'Three Tools for Forecasting Federal Elections: Lessons from 2001', *Australian Journal of Political Science*, 37(2), pp. 223–240.

4 Public policy and microeconomic regulation

*Government's view of the economy could be summed up
in a few short phrases: If it moves, tax it. If it keeps
moving, regulate it. And if it stops moving, subsidise it.*

Ronald Reagan, the 40th President of the United States, 15 August 1986, Remarks to State Chairpersons of the
National White House Conference on Small Business, Ronald Reagan Presidential Library and Museum.

Economic concepts discussed

Easy-to-understand explanations of all the concepts listed below appear in the glossary
at the end of this book.

- Australia Post disease
- Comparative advantage
- Congestion pricing
- HECS
- Intellectual property rights
- Market concentration
- Market failure
- Medicare

- Medicare levy
- National Broadband Network (NBN)
- Natural monopoly
- Patent
- Postage stamp pricing
- Price discrimination
- Privatisation
- Progressive taxation

- Regulation
- Regulatory capture
- Reserve Bank of Australia (RBA)
- Subsidy
- Superannuation
- Unconscionable conduct
- Use it or lose it rules

4.1 Motivation and overview

Is Ronald Reagan's above description of how governments view the economy accurate?
Are governments always the evil institutions that interfere with the markets through
excessive taxation and bureaucratic **regulation**, or can government policies actually
improve economic outcomes and people's wellbeing?

Professor Stephen King discussed his views on the optimal design of microeconomic
policies and regulation in an interview with me conducted on 21 May 2014. He is well
equipped to provide insights into public policy due to his unique blend of experience: as
author of influential academic research, as Dean of Business and Economics at Monash
University, and as Commissioner of the Australian Competition and Consumer
Commission (ACCC). He has also served as an expert witness in numerous inquiries by

public agencies (such as the Senate, Australian Federal Court and Australian Competition Tribunal), and has advised many private businesses on competition matters.[1]

Questions of interest include: 'How does the Australian healthcare system compare to other countries?', 'How can healthcare financing and services be improved?', 'Should the government build roads and own utilities or should the private sector do so?', 'What has been "one of the worst policy disasters" of Australian public policy in the last decade?', 'Is lifting the government cap on tertiary education fees charged to students a good idea?'. These questions and many others will be answered by Prof. King in the next section.

The discussion starts with the Australian healthcare system and why, despite being relatively good compared to other countries, it still suffers from '**Australia Post disease**'. Prof. King explains how various redistributive transfers are hidden within the system, and how it should be reformed to become more transparent and thus more effective in delivering quality care in a fiscally sustainable manner. This includes, among other things, the right balance between public and private health insurance.

Figure 4.1 suggests that healthcare is one of the key public policy challenges worldwide. It shows that there has been a trend of increasing healthcare spending, both per capita and as a proportion of GDP, driven partly by technological improvements in healthcare. Importantly, the demographic trend towards an ageing population implies that such increases in the healthcare bill will, in an absence of policy reform, continue at an even faster pace. They may thus threaten fiscal solvency.

Figure 4.1: International comparison of total spending on healthcare (public plus private) during 1980–2010; per capita (left, adjusted for purchasing power parity, PPP) and as proportion of GDP (right)

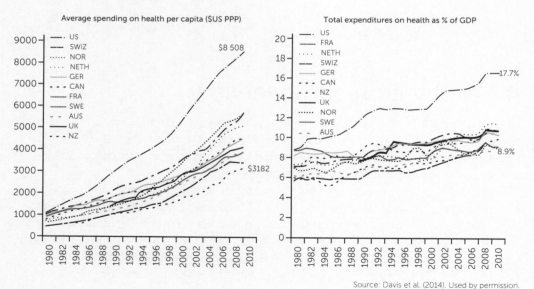

Source: Davis et al. (2014). Used by permission.

---

1 The full video-interview is available at **http://youtu.be/40LAb_VxQ6Q**. For more details regarding Prof. King's research and policy involvement, see **www.australiancompetitionlaw.org/experts/king-stephen.html**

A related issue is one of efficiency of the healthcare system. Data clearly show that higher spending does not necessarily deliver better care. For example, the United States has by far the greatest per capita healthcare spending, US $8508 in 2011, but in terms of the quality of healthcare it ranked last of the 11 countries considered in Figure 4.1 (see Davis et al., 2014). In contrast, the UK topped the healthcare quality ranking despite having the second lowest expenditure of the considered countries. Australia ranked fourth in quality and had the third-lowest per capita spending, at only about 45 per cent that of the United States. Detailed analysis of healthcare systems suggests that a part of the explanation for such puzzling findings may lie in the perverse incentives implied by the relationship between the patients, doctors, health insurance and pharmaceutical companies (as depicted in the cartoon).

Concept by Jan Libich © 2015, drawing by Veronika Mojžišová. Used by permission.

Prof. King is, however, fairly optimistic in terms of the future of the Australian healthcare system, explaining why Australian institutions and public policies tend to improve over time and thus be of high quality compared to most other countries. His view is that: 'the Australian policy debate tends to come up with a very good mix of equity and efficiency'. This is in contrast to both the US, where the focus seems to be too much on the efficiency side, and Western European countries which focus predominantly on the equity side. Nevertheless, Prof. King argues that: '… there are still lots of areas where we need microeconomic reform in Australia', and expresses his belief that: 'A key task for economists in our universities is to push the intellectual case for these reforms.'

The next topic of discussion was the government's involvement in infrastructure building, as well as public ownership and regulation of utilities such as electricity networks. Prof. King explains that state ownership and regulation are linked in the sense that the latter may substitute for the former. He argues that:

> Microeconomics, and this is one of the triumphs of our discipline over the last 30 years, has come up with a whole lot of really interesting ways that you can design better regulatory regimes … there's less need to have the large company under government ownership. We can put it under private ownership … [where] there's more incentive to lower cost.[2]

Nevertheless, many countries (e.g. China, United Arab Emirates and Russia) have not yet gone down that route and the largest companies are predominantly owned by the government; see Figure 4.2.

Figure 4.2: International comparison of the shares of government-owned enterprises (weighting equally shares of sales, assets and market values) among the countries' 10 largest firms

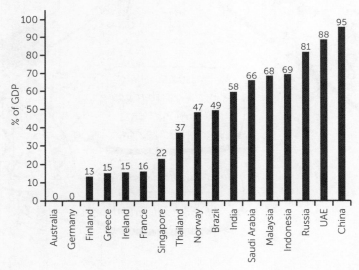

Source: Based on data from Kowalski et al. (2013).

In this respect, Prof. King explains why the building of the **National Broadband Network (NBN)** by the Australian government is, in his view, a very bad idea. He believes that a Rural and Regional Broadband Network would have been a more sensible and cheaper policy solution, because private providers have sufficient incentives to ensure broadband

---

2 The 2014 Nobel Prize in economics was awarded to French economist Jean Tirole for his contribution to the body of research on regulation.

coverage in highly populated urban areas. This topic is related to the issue of **natural monopolies**. Prof. King explains why competition fails in such instances, and offers recommendations regarding regulation to alleviate this **market failure**.

Primary and secondary education is another area discussed in the interview. Prof. King stresses the 'club good' nature of schools and argues that the government's financial per-student contribution to schools, both public and private, should be inversely related to the parents' income. This is to: '… set up an incentive scheme so that students from less well-off backgrounds become the most desirable students for schools', which would be beneficial in strengthening human capital and thus prosperity in Australia.

This is followed by a discussion of tertiary education, with emphasis on the May 2014 Australian budget which proposed to remove the cap on student fees. Prof. King offers some interesting insights explaining why the current ownership and control arrangements at Australian public universities are 'dysfunctional'. He believes that:

> unless you fix the ownership structure, a large number of
> Australian universities will be getting a massive, great big
> windfall, and I think the Australian community may not see a
> lot coming out the other end.

Available data back up Prof. King's concern: for example, the fact that the salaries of vice-chancellors at Australian universities are, appropriately adjusted, three times higher than those in the United States and United Kingdom (see Frijters, 2013). Prof. King's remarks on the proposed removal of the fee cap have been widely discussed in the media, and have helped to shape public opinion away from the government proposal. This is another example of how economics can improve real-world policies.

The debate then moves onto other topics such as regulation of credit card fees, problematic **intellectual property rights**, avoiding international **price discrimination**, and fixing the **patent** system. Prof. King was an expert witness in the recent Samsung versus Apple court case, and his perspective on the issues is quite illuminating. The audience questions then lead the discussion into **market concentration** and possible lack of competition in the Australian supermarket industry, as well as the need for avoiding **regulatory capture** which is apparent in the United States in many areas.

4.2 The debate

© Stephen King. Used by
permission.

Dr Jan Libich (JL): Ten years ago you wrote a book called *Finishing the Job*, co-authored by Professor Joshua Gans. It was full of ideas about how to improve public policies. Today we will look at many of them, starting with healthcare and its financing. Can you tell us what the problems in this area are and how they can be solved?

< Prof. Stephen King (SK): The best division that we can start off with is to separate healthcare financing, as you mentioned, from the provision of healthcare. Those two things are sometimes confused, not just in Australia, but around the world. The big question that we tried to tackle in that book was to look at the current Australian system of health insurance, which is health financing through the public **Medicare** system and through private insurance companies, and consider the incentives and constraints that the governments put on that system. In particular, we were interested in trying to work out whether the incentives are right in terms of helping people get healthcare or actually stand in the way of people getting healthcare.

JL: And what was your conclusion?

SK: Well, the Medicare system run by the Australian government suffers from what I call the 'Australia Post disease'. It is the use of pricing for one product to either subsidise another product, or to subsidise other consumers of that product. The classic example being postal services worldwide, where urban consumers end up subsidising rural consumers, and in fact uniform pricing is called '**postage stamp pricing**' for that very reason. It's done in every country. So there's a **subsidy** built into the price. The same happens with Medicare where it's actually quite explicit. The Medicare scheme is designed so that everybody pays their taxes under the progressive tax scheme that we've got in Australia. Wealthier individuals will pay more towards Medicare than poorer individuals, which is a good thing.

JL: There's also the **Medicare levy**.

SK: There's also the Medicare levy, which is part of your income taxes, and obviously if you earn more, you pay more, because that's a flat 2 per cent. There are also incentives for wealthier individuals to buy private health insurance. If you earn more than a certain amount and don't buy private health insurance, then you get a big whack in your tax from the government. Private health insurance does two things. It covers things that Medicare doesn't cover. It covers the 'extras', so if you want a private bed, a choice of your own doctor, if you want to avoid waiting lists for some elective surgery, private health cover is the product for you. But it also doubles-up with Medicare. So a lot of the payments that are made by private insurance companies when you go into, for example, a public hospital for emergency care would be paid for by the Medicare insurance scheme if you didn't have private health insurance. This doubling-up is quite deliberate to try to make the rich pay more.

JL: And if I recall, your argument was that we want to have more people in the private insurance sector because that frees up some of the resources from the public sector for lower income individuals.

SK: That's the idea behind the argument, it is essentially like **progressive taxation**. I personally would prefer a much more transparent scheme. I would prefer if we simply said: 'We've got a universal health cover system called Medicare. If you want the extras, if you want the private health insurance to get your own doctor, private room, to avoid the waiting lists, that's fine, you go out and pay for that separately. And we have higher tax rates so that there's explicitly a transfer from the wealthiest parts of Australia to pay for the health insurance of the poorest parts of Australia.'

The trouble with the current system is that it makes the richer people pay more by this sort of transfer – you pay for the same insurance twice. But this is not the only group paying more. One question we ask in the book is: 'Who else would want private health insurance?' The answer is: 'Those who are at the highest risk of requiring health cover.' In particular, health cover for things that are not emergencies but are still pretty deleterious. There's two main groups in society that probably want private health cover but aren't necessarily rich. The first group is the elderly. If you want a hip operation and you haven't got private health cover, the waiting list can be a year. That's a lot of pain for a year. So there's an incentive for the elderly, even if they're not rich, to get private health insurance to avoid the year wait. The other group is young families with young children. Young children tend to do things like break bones.

JL: Why on Earth do they do that?!

SK: I don't know why they do that. Why do they play these nasty, rough games like football? You are also at a stage of the child's life where you're learning about the child's health prospects; it's those early first five to six years where a lot of long-term health issues may first be diagnosed, and where that private health cover provides you with a back-up. So, we've got a system that tries to push the wealthy into private health cover by doubling up, by having this: 'If you don't buy it, you get penalised'; but it also is essentially paying twice for the same coverage. That captures the elderly as well and young families, exactly the sort of people that we don't want to pay twice – they're the people we want covered by the public system!

JL: This is I think why you call it anti-insurance.

SK: That's exactly why.

JL: What do you do with that? How do you design a better system?

SK: Well, the correct way to get around the problem is to say that the current system has been designed to be progressive. It's trying to make the rich pay more, which is good. I personally am in favour of a much more progressive tax system in Australia than the one we've currently got. Currently we're quite a low tax country. I think we should be taxed more for things like a universal healthcare system. But, at the moment, we do it through the back door, we try to hide the tax. We say: 'There will be a tax, but only if you don't go out and buy private health insurance.'

A much better system would be to simply say: 'You know what? Medicare is truly universal. It covers everybody for the services they need at a particular level of care. There may still, and almost certainly will, be waiting lists for certain procedures. If you want the extras – private room, private doctor, or to get around the waiting list – you pay and buy explicitly private health insurance.' And we can have a more progressive tax system. You know, let's have families who are earning over $100 000 a year pay higher taxes, and have that money 'dedicated' towards the Medicare health insurance system. Make it clean and transparent.

JL: I guess some people would argue that the better services would only be for the rich, but this is already happening anyway.

SK: Yes, that's already the situation!

JL: But there's a bigger issue here. It seems that most healthcare systems around the world are struggling financially. The per capita expenditure has been growing much faster than productivity in the economy. And the projections are not looking good, especially when you take into account the trend towards ageing populations, because the more elderly people you have, the more the public purse has to pay. And we know that relying predominantly on private healthcare is also not the solution. If you look at the United States, which does so, they spend on healthcare twice as much of their GDP as other high-income countries and their health outcomes are actually not very good. Can you think of a solution? If healthcare shouldn't be all private and shouldn't be all public, where's the balance?

SK: I actually think Australia's pretty close. As part of our project looking at health insurance in Australia, Joshua (Gans) and I looked at a range of different health insurance systems around the world. This included the American system, which is almost completely private ...

JL: 'Obamacare' has recently tried to change this ...

SK: Obamacare is changing that ... On the other side of the spectrum there is the Canadian system, which is very strongly public with very little private involvement. But of course, you know, on one side of the border, on one side of Lake Michigan in Chicago, you end up with individuals unable to pay for cancer treatment. On the other side of Lake Michigan in Toronto, you have individuals who, because of the waiting lists in the public hospitals, can die of a heart attack whilst they're on the waiting list for surgery. Neither of those sound like particularly desirable solutions.

I actually think in Australia we've got a pretty good balance, a good mix of public and private insurance. We should be looking at redesigning our system around the edges, but it doesn't need a major overhaul. I don't think anyone came up with a brainstorm and said: 'Let's come up with this system we've got in Australia.' It's evolved over time since Medibank was originally introduced back in the early 1970s by the Whitlam government. It's evolved to our current system, but it actually works well.

There are two main areas where it could be improved. In addition to the anti-insurance problem we discussed, it is the issue of who provides the services. At the moment we have this division between public and private health insurance and that spills over into public and private provision of health services. If you've only got public health insurance that doesn't mean you have to go into a public hospital. Or it does, in Australia – but it shouldn't mean that. The government should actually be saying: 'We want to now work out how to buy the health products that we want for our citizens in the best possible way, the best mix of public and private hospitals.' So that's the other area where Australia's lagging, but compared to most of the world, on no grounds should we do a massive change in our health insurance system because we are actually one of the best in the world.

JL: You argue that we have slowly converged to a pretty good system, and it seems to be the case in many other areas of public policy in Australia. I recently interviewed Professor Bruce Chapman [Chapter 5] who was the designer of the **HECS** loan system for tertiary education students, and we seem to have one of the best financing systems in the world. Similarly the pension systems; when I asked Professor John Piggott [Chapter 7] about designing the optimal pension system he said the Australian system's pretty close to that ideal. So it brings up the issue of why Australian institutions seem to be of high quality compared to most other countries. Do you have a view on that?

SK: I think that the Australian policy debate tends to come up with a very good mix of equity and efficiency. If you have the same debates in say the US, it tends to be a strong efficiency line and not very much on the equity line, or a lot less than in Australia. If you have the debate in some European countries, then I think the equity arguments tend to dominate the efficiency arguments. In Australia, whether it's due to our background, or whether it's due to our magnificent cultural mix that we have in this society, we've got a great balance between equity and efficiency.

So there are a lot of policies that need fiddling around at the margins to improve. Heath insurance is one. I think the HECS scheme for tertiary education is a brilliant idea, subject to issues in the 2014 federal budget. It's been translated overseas. And on the other one, which is pensions and the **superannuation** scheme, I think we've got pretty close to a well-designed scheme up until the time you retire. I don't think that we can say post-retirement we've got a great scheme. Because at the moment the incentives aren't quite right and I know John Piggott himself has also written on that issue. That being said, I think as our population gets older and more people retire with superannuation balances, I would expect in the next three to six years we'll see changes in superannuation to try and fix up the problems that we have post-retirement.

JL: Let's move on to other areas of public policy starting with infrastructure. There's always this issue of who should provide infrastructure: the public or the private sector? People generally agree that governments should build roads and other essential infrastructure projects. But things like the National Broadband Network (NBN) offering Australia-wide internet coverage, should it be provided by the government or should it be in the realm of the private sector?

SK: Well, I'm not going to necessarily let you get away with the 'governments should build roads' argument. We've got an East–West link tunnel that's on the drawing boards in Victoria. The strategy is for the government to take a risk-owning role, so the government will control the risk associated with traffic flows on that road, but for it to actually be a private road. The plan is for it to be developed privately and the party that runs the road will be paid for their services. You start getting into these grey areas with contracts about who actually owns what.

JL: I suppose this goes back to the 'Australia Post' situation. I agree your qualification about the private sector building roads may apply to some lucrative areas but probably not regional roads. So this is again where the richer areas subsidise the less financially viable areas.

SK: Yes, it depends.

JL: And in relation to the National Broadband Network, in many countries this is actually done privately.

SK: Okay, the NBN in my personal view is one of the worst policy disasters that we've had in the last decade, well and truly. Go back 40 years; it's hard to find one that is as poorly designed as the NBN. The first question when contemplating a public policy or project is to always ask: 'What's the problem? Why do we need government investment in this area? Why isn't the private sector, left to its own devices, going to be successful?' And with the NBN, the answer's obvious. You can't run broadband out to rural and regional Australia. It's simply never going to be profitable. The density of population isn't there.

But how do you then solve that problem? Well, a sensible solution would've been to say: 'Okay, we the government are going to step in and build broadband infrastructure in rural and regional Australia. We're going to make sure there's equity of access to high-speed internet across Australia and we're going to cover those areas where the market isn't going to work.' That would've been a sensible thing. We would have had a

'Rural and Regional Broadband Network'. Why did we end up with a National Broadband Network?

First thing to note, there is no problem in the cities. For example, if you look at the Melbourne CBD and inner city area, we've had competition there for at least 12 to 15 years. One of the things that the ACCC does is it regulates telecommunications systems, but it never regulated central business district telecommunications when I was there. Why? Because there's so much broadband, so much fibre in the centre of Australian cities, that if you want high-speed broadband, there are 10 companies that can provide it to your door. So there's no problem there.

There's really no problem in the outer suburban areas either until you start getting into low population. Why? Well you've already got the ADSL, so you've got the copper; you've got at least two cables going past a lot of the suburbs, and certainly one cable which is the Foxtel cable. The Optus cable is also still out there to provide broadband. And you immediately have, with perhaps some separation of Telstra, a couple of competing broadband suppliers.

JL: It seems like Telstra would have built something similar to the NBN by themselves?

SK: Well, let me get to Telstra because Telstra's a great example of what the problem is. We've got a situation where the government wants to provide a rural and regional broadband network. That's expensive. We can't charge commercial rates, that's just not going to make any money, that's why we have to intervene. That means higher taxes. Higher taxes – that's electorally unpopular. Let's hide the tax! How are we going to hide it? What we're going to do is build a national broadband system and make the people in the cities pay for the country users. So we'll have a postage stamp, or a uniform price across Australia, but that means the price in the cities is massively above a competitive price and of course, it's a subsidised price in the bush, which is what we want there.

So the NBN is national. We've got all this infrastructure being built that quite frankly would have been built privately: the private sector would have taken the risk in the cities. And the pricing is going to have a hidden tax on internet usage. What madness! We're building the NBN because it's the future of the Australian economy, because it's going to help transactions, it's going to help commerce, it's going to help entrepreneurs, we're going to have e-medicine, we're going to have e-learning – and we're going to tax it! We've come up with a system where we're going to put a great big tax just on the thing that we think is going to be the huge productivity-enhancing part of our economy. It's completely insane.

JL: This doesn't seem to be the only area where government policies may be well intentioned but actually turn out to be counterproductive. Why is it? Is it that politicians don't listen to economists enough and don't think through the incentive issues? We can go back to the post-2008 fiscal stimulus and the insulation fiasco. Why is it that government policies may fail so badly?

SK: Well, we're economists and we both know that economists have unique and overarching wisdom. Unfortunately, politicians seem to have this view that they need votes.

JL: They haven't read your book …

SK: They haven't read the book! If only they did, they would be inspired and work out the truth. Politics is a process where the government's got to pretend it's not putting up taxes – so it puts levies on. At the same time, there are more demands for government spending. It's got to try and balance those from a political perspective and that's hard. What we see in Australia is that attempt to balance – meaning that we try to hide a whole bunch of taxes. That's just bad policy.

JL: Let's think about some other areas, namely utilities, things like electricity and rail networks. There's been a lot of **privatisation** in many countries, as well as in Australia, but there are still people who argue that utilities are somehow special industries and they shouldn't be fully privatised. What's your view on government ownership of utilities?

SK: The first thing to realise about utilities is – in areas like electricity transmission or distribution, gas transmission or distribution – they're what we call natural monopolies. So they're situations where competition isn't going to work. And that's not just a theoretical argument – we have about 200 years of history of attempts for competition on natural monopolies, and that competition failing.

It goes back to the canals in Europe, early transport networks – before you even had rail, far less cars, you built great big canals and you had barges moving back and forth along the canals. And it was pretty quickly realised that if you had one canal which was making a lot of money and someone tried building another canal next door to try and get some of that money, all that happened was, once you built the second canal, the marginal cost of an extra barge on the canal was very low. You had prices crash; one of the companies went bankrupt and was taken over by the other company. So they were early natural monopoly infrastructure. And then you go through roads, bridges, electricity systems, gas systems. The electricity system, for example, wasn't originally publicly owned in a number of countries. It ended up being publicly owned or nationalised because competition meant the companies were failing.

JL: So, natural monopoly occurs wherever the fixed cost of building the infrastructure is too high?

SK: Where the fixed cost is very big relative to the marginal cost, at least up until you hit a capacity constraint. And so, in the case of electricity distribution, one set of wires down a suburban street is more than enough to carry all the electricity for that street. Even if the company was charging a monopoly price and making lots of money, if somebody else came in and strung up another set of wires, that would just lead the price to crash. They wouldn't be able to make any money. One of them would have to drop out and the other company would take it over and create the monopoly again.

So there is a definite role in natural monopolies for regulation. You have to have a regulator sitting in there, regulating the prices and making sure that you have reasonable economic prices because competition isn't going to work. That's a different question to the one you asked, which was about government ownership, and that's a much trickier question. That comes back to this issue: you want regulation, what's the best way to regulate? Traditionally, the best way to control one of these large companies – a large electricity company, a large gas company, or a road company – was to actually have it under government ownership and to directly control it through that ownership.

But microeconomics, and this is one of the triumphs of our discipline over the last 30 years, has come up with a whole lot of really interesting ways that you can design better regulatory regimes. You can get over, at least partially, the issues of asymmetric information – that the person running the company always knows much more than the regulator trying to set the prices. So, as that regulation's improved, there's less need to have the large company under government ownership. We can put it under private ownership. That's got some good things; there's more incentive to lower cost. Of course, there's also more incentive to push up prices, but because we've got better regulatory instruments, because we know so much more now about regulation than we did 30 years ago, we can probably control the bad side of private ownership and keep its good side.

JL: So your view would be more towards full privatisation with good regulatory oversight?

SK: Well I think, again, by luck or management, we've actually ended up coming out of the Hilmer report in the early 1990s with a good process put in place to isolate the natural monopoly and work out where the problem is. So you don't have government-owned electricity generators in Victoria anymore. It was realised pretty early on that you could have competing electricity generators, there's no need for government ownership. That's not where the problem is. What about the transmission or the distribution system? There is a natural monopoly; there you have to work out what's the balance. Do you want to keep it under government ownership, where you have some issues relating to the way the system's run? It may not be run at least-cost but is that better, or is it better to have private ownership with an arm's-length regulator?

That debate is still going on in practical terms in Australia but certainly in electricity I think the 'privatise and regulate' model has shown that it works. In fact the bizarre thing about the last two years of debate in electricity is that it has all been about there being high prices in electricity transmission. Where? Where the government still owns the assets. So in Victoria the transmission prices under the private system looked like they're considerably lower than in New South Wales and Queensland where they're still government-owned assets. So I think that's the final nail in the public ownership coffin – at least, electricity assets – and we'll see those moving out into private ownership with arm's-length regulation.

JL: Let's move on to another public policy area, education. We're on academic soil and you as former Dean at Monash University obviously have a lot of insights into this area. We can start with your 2004 paper that looks at the primary and secondary school systems, and identifies some problems as well as solutions. Can you summarise them for us?

SK: I guess we all follow our experience, and my wife and I had kids at primary school at that time. Our starting point, in research for the Victorian government, was to ask: 'How should you think about schools from an economic perspective?' Schools are a classic case of what economists call a 'club good'. It's something that we desire that's produced best by a community or a group of people. You could have private tutoring for everyone, but it is not very efficient. What we'd prefer in general for educating our children is to have a community institution – we call it a school – with parents contributing to that school and their children being educated appropriately at that school. And we have a mixture of publicly and privately owned schools in Australia.

The problem for the publicly owned schools in Australia is that they're then put into very, very tight straightjackets. In particular, even if 90 per cent of the school community said we want some more resources, we want to be able to pay fees to hire a new science teacher or to have a new gym or to have better facilities for our children, they're very limited in their ability to do that, except through fundraising-type drives. So it would have to be a 'charitable donation', it couldn't be treated as a 'fee' for attending that school. And the reason for that is an equity argument. What about the 10 per cent? If there's 10 per cent of poorer families at that school it may not be fair on them.

How do you then get around that trade-off? We want a school community to be able to build and have a real sense of investment and ownership of a publicly owned school. But how do you protect the poor? The way that we were thinking was that rather than the government simply saying every student is identical, the government can say we will have a certain contribution to the school or the education of a particular child. But that contribution can depend on the income of the parents.

So if you come from a low-income family, the government may say that's $10 000 for each student, whichever school they go to, that's $10 000 given to that school to help with the costs of educating that child. What about if you come from a wealthier family? Well maybe the contribution from the government's only $6000, or maybe only $5000. The school can then determine the level of fees up to the maximum. So let's say the maximum's $10 000. So the poorer families, they're covered completely by the government. The school can then work out exactly what resources it wants within that range between $5000 and $10 000 and can then work out where the resources are spent. It can do so through the school council, through the school principal, through the teachers and the broader school community.

JL: But it seems the effect it would have is to push the wealthier families more towards private schools.

SK: But the funding then has to be the same for the private sector as well as for the public sector. So the private sector has a choice. Private schools can say: 'No, we're just going to set our fees and give up our current government funding.' The private school system gets significant federal government funding at the moment. Or it can say: 'We want to be a part of that system, in which case we have to play by the same rules as the publicly owned schools.'

Now, to a degree, one of the things we explored in the paper was if that's too much of a restriction on some of the schools, should schools be able to pay more? So if the maximum amount was $10 000 for a poorer student, should a school be able to set $12 000 or $14 000 as a scholarship? And our suggestion there was you may want to allow that so long as you say, perhaps for every dollar over $10 000 you raise in fees, 20 per cent or 25 per cent has to be used to support poorer students, or students from minority backgrounds, Indigenous students and so on. The whole aim of this is to set up an incentive scheme so that students from less well-off backgrounds become the most desirable students for schools. At the moment you have a bit of a race to the bottom in Australian public education where, as you mentioned, the wealthier families leave. They still get government funding but go off to a private school where there are no constraints on the fees that a private school can charge. What we want to do is create the incentives where schools – whether they're private or public – say: 'You know what, we want more minority students. We want more students from poorer backgrounds, we want a more diverse mix of students.'

JL: When you say 'we want' you presumably mean the interest of the whole society as such, because it may not be in the interest of an individual school.

SK: That's right. My personal view is, and this is where economics starts stepping over the line into social views, it's a good thing for society.

JL: Let's move on to tertiary education. Since the May 2014 Australian budget proposal to remove the cap on student fees, there has been a lot of debate on the topic. Some people worry that student fees might increase two- or even three-fold. What's your view on this whole area of regulating tertiary education fees and lifting the cap?

SK: I think this is a classic situation where the government, and some of its advisors, just haven't thought through the issues. The first issue is that there will still be a HECS–HELP deferred loan scheme – the same as there has been for postgraduate study. We can actually use postgraduate study as a bit of guidance as to what would happen in the undergraduate area with the ability to charge higher fees. What we've seen there is very big price dispersion. All the fees will go up, there's not even any point debating that. England's the most recent example where the government allowed higher fees. They set a cap on the high fees and, surprise, surprise, every university just went up to the cap and it's coordinated on the cap. So we would see fees go up for undergraduates.

JL: In the UK they basically removed all the subsidies within that government loan scheme, whereas in Australia we still have about 55 per cent subsidy, right?

SK: Yes. And the government is trying to get rid of some of the subsidies. The interest rate is proposed to go up from the CPI to the government bond rate, but there would still be a non-trivial subsidy going on there. You'd still be able to defer the payment. It's still the sort of loan you wouldn't be able to walk into a bank to get. So we would expect to see undergraduate fees go up. We could also expect to see a big difference in fees. Who would be the winners? The Group of Eight, the elite universities, would be massive winners on this.

I think you would see some of the Group of Eight universities' fees going up – by three times is not out of order. The way to see that is to ask where their international fees are. So the international undergraduate fees at the Group of Eight universities in, say, a business course, which is the one I'm familiar with, are around $30 000 a year. The undergraduate fee at the moment in Australia for a domestic student is around $10 000 a year.

It doesn't take a genius to work out that when the university is saying: 'Oh, $30 000, $10 000 – $30 000, $10 000?', they will choose $30 000.

JL: In fact there are some economists, for example Professor Rabee Tourky, who believe the fee set for Australian students could actually end up being higher than the fee for international students because of all the additional benefits of HECS domestic students enjoy. It's the low interest and no-repayment threshold which increase the value of that education for Australian students, and hence potentially their willingness to pay for it as seen by university leaders.

SK: Could be. And if universities were competitive, well-run institutions, I would agree that that's a possibility. My view though is politicians haven't really thought through what the fees would be. They haven't thought through the implicit subsidy in HECS. That's all fine. My big problem is they haven't actually thought through the way that universities are governed. The universities in Australia are all public institutions. Their ownership is a bit grey, but they're all set up under either state or federal legislation. They are overseen by their councils. The councils are sort of appointed by a mixture of people, but the vice-chancellors have a fair amount of control over who gets appointed to the councils. And each university is run day-to-day by the vice-chancellor and an administrative team.

But there's very little in the way of a line of responsibility and a line of control. Not just compared to the private sector, but even compared to standard public organisations. When we were at the ACCC, as a receiver of taxpayers' money, as a public organisation, we had to appear before Senate estimates at least two times a year. A senior team of the ACCC were up there being grilled by the senators, and believe me, you got a grilling on your performance. They knew well and truly what you were doing. The vice-chancellors don't go up before senators. They don't get grilled in that way. They just have to answer to a council, which is part-time members drawn from a very broad community, some of them recommended by the vice-chancellors. This is a very bizarre and quite frankly, I think, a dysfunctional ownership and control arrangement.

You're now going to say to these institutions – and it's not clear who actually runs and controls them: 'You have to compete by setting prices as if you were a private firm. You don't have any of the private firm incentives and nobody's getting a dividend from this. Go out there and compete and pretend like you're a private firm, but we're not going to check up on what you do!'

JL: So given this ownership structure, you think lifting the cap on fees is a bad idea?

SK: I think unless you fix the ownership structure, a large number of Australian universities will be getting a massive, great big windfall, and I think the Australian community may not see a lot coming out the other end. What we've really got to ask is, if we're giving more money to our universities, which is what this fee change is proposing to do, who's responsible for making sure it's spent appropriately? Where is that money going to be spent? Is it going to be fed back into undergraduate education? You and I are both academics. I don't know about your views, Jan, but I wouldn't be betting on much of that money going back into improved undergraduate education. It may go off into very expensive toys for science and medical research. That might be a good thing. But we're talking about billions of dollars here, without even the controls that you normally have on public institutions. And I think that's a recipe for disaster.

JL: Let's hope the proposal will not get through. I would like to ask you about some other areas potentially in need of public regulation. One such area is credit card fees. There was an inquiry by the **Reserve Bank of Australia (RBA)** and you have a 2003 paper on this, again with Professor Joshua Gans. Can you tell us what your suggestions and subsequent policy outcomes were?

SK: The RBA did part of what we suggested, but then didn't do the rest of it. Joshua (Gans) and I looked at this interesting issue, what economists call a two-sided market. You've got merchants and you've got consumers. Consumers want to carry a credit card that merchants accept; merchants only want to accept credit cards that consumers carry. So there's a coordination issue going on there. They each have a bank and there are interchange fees, the fees that the banks charge each other. In credit cards, the interchange fee is positive, so the merchant's bank pays the fee to the customer's bank. Interestingly in EFTPOS, which is a traditional debit card in Australia, the interchange fee actually runs the other way. There's no reason why the fee has to run one way or another way; it just depends on how the system's set up.

There was a problem around the world, and Australia was one of the early leaders on reform in this area. The credit card systems had rules that made it impossible for the merchant to say: 'Hang on, this card is costing me a lot more than if you paid with another card or if you paid with cash. I'm sorry, but you're going to have to pay an extra two dollars or an extra 1 per cent if you want to pay with that card.' That option was not available to merchants. There was a 'no surcharge' policy, so if you accepted, say, Visa, you were not allowed to charge a different price to anyone with a Visa card than if they had a MasterCard, Diners Club or cash.

So what were the RBA's reforms? The RBA was worried about the interchange fees. They saw the fees as being too high – and they were correct. The reason they were too high was because of this 'no surcharge'. Merchants have to cover their costs, so if credit cards are costing more than cash, what happens? You set a price that balances out. Those paying cash pay more, those paying with a credit card are subsidised. And who pays cash? Well, the statistics are quite clear, the poorest parts of the community pay cash. So we had this bizarre situation where the credit card company rules were meaning the poorer people were paying for richer people.

JL: And policymakers naturally don't want this regressivity ...

SK: It didn't sound very good. What were our recommendations? Easy, change the rules. Once you allow surcharging, that interchange fee, it's just a price, it's not going to matter very much. If the Reserve Bank really wants to regulate it, it can regulate it, but you can show that the effects of regulation are second order. Fortunately the RBA did the good thing; it did require the credit card systems to change their rules. And we've had some surcharging, we've seen some differentiation. We now have merchants who quite clearly – on the very expensive cards, Diners and Amex – say: 'If you want to pay us with those, it's 5 per cent extra,' because essentially that's what the merchants are charged. The Reserve Bank also tried regulating the interchange fee, but I think there it was wasting its time. Once it fixed the rules and allowed surcharging, it should have stepped back and let the market work.

JL: Another area of regulation relates to the topical issue of intellectual property and piracy. For example, those annoying regional restrictions on DVDs, are they a good idea to stop intellectual property violations? People who download stuff illegally argue that the big studios and other producers charge too much money for their products, who's right here?

SK: Well, I was going to make a joke about 'You buy DVDs?', but I won't just in case there's anyone watching this – I always buy DVDs and don't know what torrent streaming services are, thank you. Normal programming will now resume. This is just the price discrimination we teach our undergraduate students. If you can charge a higher price to the people who have less sensitive demand, less elastic demand to use the economic term, and a lower price to more price-sensitive customers, you want to do that to maximise your profits. So that's what all these inter-regional DVD restrictions are. DVDs are actually a minor part of it now.

The big area is electronic goods that can be downloaded through the internet or the physical goods that you buy over the internet. Don't believe me? Get onto Amazon and try ordering some of the stuff with an Australian credit card. You'll suddenly find out you are not allowed to buy this stuff. There's a price, they've got the goods, I want to buy them, why won't they let me buy them? Well, because the suppliers have got rules in place saying: 'Look, Amazon, it's okay for you to sell to the US at that price, but there's no way you can sell to Australia at that price because we want to charge them a higher price.' This international price discrimination is occurring more and more. The days where it was just DVDs we could ignore it. Now it's becoming a real problem.

How do we solve it? There was a Senate inquiry last year and it came up with 'We're not sure how to solve it.' Hopefully a bit of pressure will get the companies to change their rules. Adobe is a classic example where what you can download here for $4000 you can download for $1000 if you're based in the US and have a US IP address. Same server, same software. The Senate hoped something would fix it up automatically. I think their hope is not well based. The Canadians have got really annoyed about this because they sit there looking below the border and saying: 'Why are we paying so much more than those guys south of the border?' They're actually thinking of bringing in a new rule into their competition laws to say that you're not allowed to sell it cheaper in the US. If you sell it cheaper in the United States, you must sell if for that price in Canada. That's probably going to be a complete nightmare. How do you enforce something like that?

JL: Do you have any suggestions on how the problem can be fixed?

SK: I think what we need to do in Australia is think carefully about the rules these companies are using to be able to price higher to us, and make sure that we're not supporting those rules. So what rules? Well, the obvious one is copyright or intellectual property laws. Why can't I just go to the US, download a copy of the Adobe software, bring it back to Australia, copy it a thousand times and sell it? Well, because I'd be breaching Adobe's copyright over that material. But hang on, this is the same company that wants to charge us $4000 and refuses to sell it to us – the same product, at the same price, from the same server in the US. So we've got to think about, well, we're using our own rules, our own interpretation of copyright to allow them to rip us off! That seems to be bizarre.

We need to think about things like 'use it or lose it' rules. If you don't sell a product in Australia, and you're selling that product overseas, there should be no barrier to anyone legitimately buying it overseas in any quantities they like and bringing it into Australia, and if you try to stop them, that's a violation of competition laws. We need to think about our copyright laws and say: 'Well, actually, if someone buys a legitimate copy of your good anywhere in the world, they can resell it in Australia. And you know what? They can buy it 50 times or 60 times, and resell it 50 or 60 times in Australia.' So at the moment, I think our own laws are our worst enemy in this. Fix up the laws and then the market will work.

JL: A similar area to copyright is the patent system, which seems to be badly broken. You were in court as an expert in one of the recent cases,

Samsung v Apple. Can you tell us a little bit about the case, what's wrong with the patent system and how we can fix it?

SK: I'll be very specific because I'm not an expert on the patent system, but I do know more than I ever thought I would want to know about patents, intellectual property and things like mobile phones. The starting point to realise is that when you pull out a mobile phone, you're pulling out a mass of intellectual property. And the standard, say 4G, which is essentially the main standard for any new phone that you buy in Australia, is set on an international basis. It's set by a standards-setting organisation for phones based in Europe.

The standards-setting organisation is actually a group of market participants who get together and decide what intellectual property, what features they are going to include in this standard, in terms of how signals communicate with each other, how signals go in one way and come back another way, how signals get downloaded to a phone, how signals get uploaded from a phone. All of that involves intellectual property and intellectual goods. They basically come to an agreement about what intellectual property will be embodied into that standard. And all the parties to that standard, all of the parties that have some of that intellectual property, have to put their hand in the air and say: 'Yes, I have patents; I have intellectual property that you will need to make a 4G phone. You can't make a 4G phone unless you've got my intellectual property somewhere there in it. And I guarantee that I'm going to license my intellectual property on a fair, reasonable and non-discriminatory basis.' FRAND it's called.

JL: What does that really mean?

SK: That's a good question. Why are these companies like Apple, Samsung and Google fighting each other all around the world? Well, certainly in the case of the Apple and Samsung matters, the basic case is that Apple looked at Samsung and said: 'Hang on, you're copying our phones, you're taking some of our intellectual property.' Samsung, which had intellectual property as part of the 3G and 4G standards, then came back and said: 'You, Apple, are violating our intellectual property by selling phones that are 3G or 4G phones.' So the Samsung claims related to these standard essential patents. Apple came back and questioned the 'fair, reasonable and non-discriminatory' clause. And they've been fighting ever since about what that actually means.

JL: They have had like 50 court cases around the globe ...

SK: One extreme is the US where they basically said: 'For God's sake just go away and sort it out for yourselves.' On the other hand there are some authorities, I think it's the Dutch or the Germans in Europe, that have said that Samsung's broken the anti-trust law, it's abusing market power by not giving what the court thought was a fair, reasonable and non-discriminatory licence to Apple. So you've got this huge range. It's clearly a system that's broken. It's clearly a system that's shown it can't work.

What's been the defensive mechanism, by the way? Well, Apple has realised it needs a seat at the standards-setting table, so it bought somebody with some intellectual property relating to mobile phone standards, just so that this wouldn't happen to it in the future. Google – same situation. It buys Motorola, takes out the patents, sells on the rest of the business. All it wanted was the intellectual property so that, as a producer of mobile phone operating systems and mobile phones, it could get a seat at the table to set the standards.

JL: In an excellent book on the problems of intellectual property rights by Professors Boldrin and Levine I learnt that Microsoft is actually adding more than a thousand patent applications every month in the US alone. And the cost associated with all this patent bureaucracy for most of the high-tech companies is actually greater than the money they spend on innovation itself. There really is something wrong with that.

SK: Clearly the system is broken and we need to work out a way of fixing it. There's a big debate about how FRAND should be interpreted, there's a lot of economists particularly in the US involved in this debate. I think the underlying issue really has to be: 'Is this the best way of setting standards?' At the moment, you set the standard and then ex-post you start talking about the price. That doesn't seem very sensible! I would've thought you talk about the price before you start buying the thing or making it essential. It needs a whole rethink.

I don't think there are any easy answers, because these are very complex products. And by the way, 4G is built on 3G, which was built on 2G. So even if you came up with a new system for fifth generation phones or sixth generation phones, then you're still going to be sitting there with a whole bunch of parties who say: 'Well, sorry, you're still using our intellectual property, and we're not playing by the new rules. We're still covered by the old rules.' So this isn't a problem that's going to go away, it's going to get worse.

JL: There is one last question before I hand it over to the audience. Can you briefly mention some public policies that economics implies would improve overall wellbeing, but politicians have shied away from?

SK: Where do I begin! Another issue that Joshua Gans and I touch on in *Finishing the Job* is road pricing. With modern technology for electronic toll collection, governments can easily charge motorists appropriate **congestion prices**. The charges will mean better road use and the funds can be used, for example, to boost public transport. But despite these tolls becoming more common (and often publicly popular) overseas, our state governments have shied away from them.

Then there is a range of unfinished business in competition reform. We have restrictive taxi rules that mean that buying a taxi licence can cost hundreds of thousands of dollars. New Zealand got rid of these restrictive rules many years ago and provides an example of a low-cost efficient taxi system. In contrast, Australian governments have put taxi deregulation in the 'too hard' basket. This may all change as Uber, Lyft and other smartphone-based systems become more popular, allowing anyone with a car to act like a taxi driver. But currently, if a private car driver provides services on Uber in Victoria or New South Wales, then they are breaking state laws.

Similarly, we still have highly restrictive rules on where a pharmacist can open a new pharmacy. These rules make no sense other than to protect existing pharmacies from competition. We have 'cabotage' rules that limit foreign companies competing to deliver goods and people around Australia. So it is impossible for, say, Singapore Airlines to fly Singapore–Perth–Sydney and pick up passengers and goods 'on the way'. This benefits Qantas and Virgin, but hurts the public. There are still rules in agriculture that limit farmer and consumer choice. So in Western Australia there is a Potato Marketing Corporation that tells farmers what potatoes they can grow and how many. The end result is less choice for consumers.

We still have significant 'corporate welfare' in Australia. While the federal government has decided that it should not be propping up an inefficient car industry, there are still government subsidies going to a range of businesses. These make the individual company's shareholders better off, but hurt consumers and taxpayers. Further, there has been recent lobbying by the Business Council of Australia (BCA) for a new round of corporate welfare. Of course, it is not called that. Rather, the BCA argues the government should support areas where Australian business has a '**comparative advantage**'. Sounds good, but if the businesses actually have a comparative advantage then they do not need a government handout! So there are still lots of areas where we need microeconomic reform in Australia. And, in my opinion, a key task for economists in our universities is to push the intellectual case for these reforms.

JL: Very interesting thoughts, I hope our politicians will seriously consider these policy suggestions!

Audience member 1: Thanks for your elucidation of the university ownership and responsibility for accounting. That was quite enlightening for many of us. I would like to ask what it is about Australia that makes it more amenable to having monopolies in the supermarket industry.

SK: Supermarkets are really interesting. Is this market more concentrated in Australia than around the world? So that's the first question. Your assumption that we've got higher concentration is broadly correct, but be very careful how you interpret 'more concentration'. Australia's big two, Coles and Woolworths, have about 80 per cent of the dry grocery market. As soon as you broaden it out though, the share comes down. Once you start getting to fresh meat, fish and fruit and vegetables, the market share is a lot lower. Australians, unlike people in some European countries for example, buy a lot of their fruit and vegetables from fruit and vegetable stores, a lot of meat still from butchers, a lot of fish from fishmongers. So once you get down to that level, you're talking more like 40 to 50 per cent for Coles' and Woolworths' share combined. It's still a lot, but you do have to be careful.

The second area where you have to be careful is to look at Australia versus other countries, and remember that our population's low. So if you look at Australia compared to the United States, we look very concentrated. If you look at Australia compared to, say Florida, then our supermarkets don't look that concentrated. All of that's really just to say you've got to be a bit careful. Yes, we are concentrated in my opinion, so not wanting to avoid the premise but just to clarify it.

Why has that occurred? Very easy – logistic chains, and it's happened all around the world by the way. The real difference is population. If you've got a bigger, denser population you can support more supermarkets. But the reason why the mum and dad stores have tended to disappear is just that integrated logistic chains have developed, and the infrastructure, the software to drive those changes became so much more sophisticated that big supermarkets are now much more efficient than smaller supermarkets.

Where do we get to in Australia? Australia is sort of odd. I was involved in the ACCC's grocery inquiry in 2008 and that inquiry was driven by the concern that the supermarkets were pricing too high. We looked at that. Wesfarmers had just taken over Coles. Coles was competing quite badly. Woolworths essentially had the game to itself. We said: 'Look, there are some problems here, but if Coles can actually get its act together ... there are some issues in the industry but they're not detrimental. Let's see what happens next.' We were also influenced by the fact that Metcash, the wholesale supplier to the IGA (Independent Grocers of Australia) stores, was actually growing quite substantially at that stage. Well, what's happened next is Wesfarmers with Coles started a discount price-war. It's usually beneficial to the consumers but is clearly having some problems for suppliers. So the issue in Australia has now flipped on its head, where the concern is now not that consumers are being ripped off, but that the suppliers are being ripped off.

JL: What can we do about it?

SK: There's no point wishing for smaller grocery chains in Australia. You can only do that if you had big inefficiencies in the logistics chain. Metcash supplies all the IGA stores. It finds it hard enough to run an efficient logistics chain for its market share. So that's not a great way of going. That's going to mean higher prices for consumers. I think the current ACCC 'unconscionable conduct' case is really interesting and I think it's a good idea to start making sure that the boundaries of those relationships between suppliers and the supermarkets are very clear. During the grocery inquiry we heard lots of stories about the way that suppliers were treated. Most of them, or a fair number, unsavoury.

At that stage, you didn't have the current law, so 'unconscionable conduct for business-to-business transactions' wasn't available. That was changed a couple of years ago so the ACCC was given a new stick and they're now using that stick. I think it will be really interesting to see what happens. Hopefully the outcome will be fairer transactions between suppliers and the big supermarket chains without destroying what's been very beneficial competition for consumers. If we can get a fairer landscape but still keep the competition then we're all going to be winners.

Audience member 2: Excellent talk. When discussing the solutions in public policy, they often gravitate around regulatory outcome. Do you feel that 'regulatory capture' is not a problem in Australia as it is in the United States? I mean the idea that regulatory agencies generally hire executives in firms, or at least are sympathetic to the firms in the industry.

SK: Yes. We have regulatory capture but it's different to the United States. As you may know, there's currently a Harper review of competition reform. One of the things that they should be looking at is the structure of our regulators, and in fact we've got a Monash business policy forum paper that's been written on exactly that. In Australia at the moment we don't have a lot of individual company-type regulators. We used to have, for example, AUSTEL, which was the telecommunications regulator and it just dealt with telecommunications. It's now part of the ACCC. We used to have individual electricity and gas regulators, a bit like the UK and a bit like the public utility regulatory authorities in the US. They've now been rolled into the Australian Energy Regulator and overall that's a good thing and it's helped prevent that sort of capture.

Where has there been capture? Interestingly, in Australia the capture tends to be from the new entrants and the customers, not from the incumbent. We don't have a long history of people leaving the regulators and working for the incumbent, or people from the incumbent moving into the regulators. That's not been traditionally a path in Australia. Certainly in the old AUSTEL days, who had captured AUSTEL were probably the new entrants.

So AUSTEL went from being, in a sense, an arms-length regulator, the referee, to being a bit of a participant. 'Go Optus, go entrants, go Optus, go entrants!' And that was also a problem. That's not a good result for regulation either. A bit of that, I think, spilt across to the ACCC. We have seen – and when I was at the Commission I was trying to fight this from the inside – a bit of a culture within the telecommunications group to say Telstra is the enemy, not the firm that we're regulating. So there has been some capture but it's a different type of capture in Australia.

We need to rethink how we structure our regulators. I think the utility regulator, like the telecommunications group within the ACCC, the rail and water groups within the ACCC, should actually be separated out from the competition regulator. They have very different roles. The utility regulator is all about interfering in the market. Their job is to come out and set prices and set standards. Their whole raison d'être is to manage the market. On the other hand, competition regulators are more like referees. They've got a set of rules and have to enforce those rules to make sure we have fair and equitable behaviour in the market place.

The last thing you want with the competition regulator is for them to get in there and say: 'Let's start designing the market, maybe we should break up Coles today.' That would be a disaster for the way the economy works. Unfortunately, they have very different cultures, and having those same cultures in one body means that the ACCC has a bit of bipolar disorder. It has got a competition hat and an interference hat. It needs to have those hats separate and I think in separate bodies.

JL: Stephen, let me thank you very much for your views and far-reaching contribution to Australian public policy. I'd like to wish you all the best for the future and we all hope that your contribution will continue in the years to come.

4.3 Key economic insights and policy lessons

Economic insights	Implied policy lessons (for public officials and voters)
Most economic rules and regulations advance either the economy's efficiency at the expense of equity, or the other way round.	Policymakers should strive to find the right balance between efficiency and equity.
Firms and governments sometimes use pricing of one product to either subsidise another product or other consumers of that product.	Policymakers should be mindful when using uniform pricing so that it does not lead to the 'Australia post disease', as is the case with the National Broadband Network.

Economic insights	Implied policy lessons (for public officials and voters)
Australia is a fairly low-taxing country in international comparisons.	Policymakers should explore ways in which a greater degree of progressivity could be implemented without a major adverse effect on labour supply.
Politicians tend to hide various taxes they consider to be electorally unpopular.	Policymakers should enhance financial literacy in the population to be able to better explain to voters the motivation for various desirable policies.
Healthcare provision and financing systems in most countries, including Australia, tend to create perverse incentives and inefficient health outcomes.	Policymakers should impose more transparency in healthcare and avoid the anti-insurance problem.
International healthcare comparisons suggest that too much emphasis on the private system (such as in the US) or on the public system (such as in Europe) is not optimal.	Policymakers should seek the right balance between private and public healthcare schemes.
The existence of natural monopolies means that competition cannot work in some areas – those with a large fixed cost relative to marginal cost.	Policymakers should implement sophisticated yet transparent regulation regarding natural monopolies, based on a large body of economic research.
In most areas of utilities it seems preferable to have ownership by the private rather than the public sector, but with strong regulatory oversight.	Policymakers should consider the 'privatise and regulate' model, and ways of perfecting it.
Schools are an example of a 'club good', best produced by a community of people.	Policymakers should build in mechanisms for parents and educators to best contribute to the club good and help schools thrive.
The cost involved in educating a child tends to depend on his or her socioeconomic characteristics.	Policymakers should consider varying their per-student contribution to schools with the family's income.
The structure of ownership and accountability of Australian universities seems dysfunctional.	Policymakers should first fix these aspects before possibly considering the introduction of more competition in the sector, e.g. before lifting a cap on the fees universities can charge to students.
The HECS system provides sizeable public subsidies to students through several channels.	Policymakers should take the nature of the HECS subsidies into account in regulating tuition fees to make sure the benefits are not effectively diverted away from the students.
No-surcharge credit card rules mean that poorer people (who tend to use cash) subsidise richer people (who use credit cards).	Policymakers should allow merchants to put a surcharge onto high interchange fee credit cards.
Companies attempt to engage in international price discrimination, e.g. through regional DVD restrictions or different prices of goods purchased online for different countries.	Policymakers should make sure their rules and regulations (e.g. copyright legislation) do not actually support this welfare-reducing price discrimination.
The intellectual property protection system seems badly broken, especially in the technological area, which hinders innovation and economic growth.	Policymakers should consider ways of reforming intellectual property and patent legislation to be in line with social objectives.
Technological companies tend to spend more money on patent-related administration than innovation itself. This problem is likely to get worse over time.	Policymakers should, as part of intellectual property reform, make the patent process much cheaper and more transparent.

Economic insights	Implied policy lessons (for public officials and voters)
Restrictive regulation of the taxi, pharmacy, agriculture, or airline industries tends to lead to inferior outcomes to those under competition.	Policymakers should consider ways of liberalising these industries.
There still exists significant 'corporate welfare' in Australia provided by the government, which tends to hurt customers and taxpayers.	Policymakers should look into winding back various subsidies to private businesses.
The Australian supermarket industry is more concentrated than in other countries, but it is largely driven by a high degree of urbanisation.	Policymakers should look beyond simple market concentration measures before concluding that a market is insufficiently competitive and requires intervention.
'Regulatory capture' in Australia is not as big a problem as it is in the United States, and its nature differs.	Policymakers should make sure that the regulators favour neither the incumbent firms nor the new entrants.
The utility regulator and the competition regulator have very different roles. The former intervenes in the market whereas the latter tries not to, only enforcing existing rules.	Policymakers should consider separating (to a greater extent) the utility and competition regulators within the ACCC.

4.4 Discussion questions

1   Using your own words, summarise the debate of Section 4.2 in three to five sentences.
2   Write down one idea discussed in the interview that you found new or interesting, or that you disagree with, and briefly explain why.
3   Write down one question on any topic covered in the interview that you would ask the speaker if you had a chance.
4   Consider the cartoon in Section 4.1 and explain the point to someone who has not read the section and does not have any knowledge of economics.
5   Examine Figure 4.1 from the perspective of a policymaker. Describe its key message to the public and explain what kind of policy improvement is implied by the data. Do the same for Figure 4.2.
6   Suppose you take part in a debating contest, in which the topic is the opening quote of the chapter by Ronald Reagan:

> Government's view of the economy could be summed up in a few short phrases: If it moves, tax it. If it keeps moving, regulate it. And if it stops moving, subsidise it.

Prepare a speech you would give for the affirmative side. Then (you or your classmate) prepare a speech for the negative side. If possible, organise an audience and perform the debate.
7   What is 'Australia Post disease'? What are its major ailments that are relevant to the current issues in the Australian healthcare system? Outline Prof. King's argument for

a more transparent system providing fiscally sustainable quality healthcare. Can you add to his argument with opinions of your own?

8   How does Australia's healthcare system stack up compared to other countries? Like Prof. King, do you believe that Australia has a good healthcare system that only needs 'fiddling around the edges'?

9   What is Prof. King's assessment of the pre-retirement part of Australia's pension system? What is your view on this? Prof. King further states: 'I don't think that we can say post-retirement we've got a great scheme.' Using data from the internet, outline the basis for Prof. King's view. What reforms do you think he would advocate, and why?

10 Prof. King believes that the Australian National Broadband Network (NBN) is a bad policy; what are his main criticisms? What are his ideas for a potential solution? What is your view on the NBN, and why?

11 Explain the term 'hidden taxes' and give some Australian examples.

12 Why does a 'natural monopoly' occur? What are the possible approaches of the government towards ownership and regulation of utilities such as electricity, gas and road networks? What is Prof. King's view on which approach is the most efficient? Use data or examples from the internet to support your answer.

13 Paraphrase Prof. King's arguments for equity in schools and outline the incentive issues he mentions. Is it realistic to think that even with improved incentives schools would be keen on 'diversifying' their socio-demographic composition?

14 Prof. King argues that the current ownership and control arrangements at Australian public universities are 'dysfunctional'. What is the essence of his argument? Do you think that in order to provide quality education, universities should be able to set their own fees? Based on your personal experience discuss specific policies that could improve the quality of higher education in Australia.

15 Is Prof. King an advocate of the 'no surcharge' policy on credit cards? Outline his argument.

16 Can you think of other goods aside from computer software to which international price discrimination applies? Is there an economic need for price discrimination? What is Prof. King's suggestion for eliminating such practices? Do you have other ideas about how more socially desirable pricing could be achieved?

17 Outline what the main problems are in relation to intellectual property, for example, regarding the *Samsung v Apple* court battles. Can you think of any ways to alleviate the problems?

18 Over the course of the interview Prof. King often comes back to the importance of public policy and regulation reforms for the social and economic equality of Australian citizens. Why do you think equity is important? Do you share his view that Australian institutions are generally of high quality because they strike the balance between efficiency and equity?

19 Propose a set of policies that you think would best reform the Australian healthcare system and ultimately improve people's wellbeing.

4.5 Where to find out more

Australian Competition and Consumer
Commission website: www.accc.gov.au

Boldrin, M. and D. K. Levine (2008), *Against
Intellectual Monopoly*; the book is freely
available at http://levine.sscnet.ucla.edu/
general/intellectual/againstfinal.htm

Davis, K., K. Stremikis, C. Schoen and D. Squires
(2014), 'Mirror, Mirror on the Wall, 2014
Update: How the U.S. Health Care System
Compares Internationally', The
Commonwealth Fund, available at
www.commonwealthfund.org/~/media/
files/publications/fund-report/2014/jun/
1755_davis_mirror_mirror_2014.pdf

Frijters, P. (2013), 'Timothy Devinney on Overpaid
Vice-Chancellors', Core Economics blog,
available at www.economics.com.au/?p=9716

Gans, J. and S. King (2003), 'A Theoretical
Analysis of Credit Card Reform in Australia',
The Economic Record, The Economic Society of
Australia, 79(247), pp. 462–472.

Gans, J. and S. King (2004), *Finishing the Job:
Real-World Policy Solutions in Health, Housing,
Education and Transport*, Melbourne
University Publishing.

Harper, I. (2014), 'Review of Australian
Competition Policy', available at
www.australiancompetitionlaw.org/
reports/2014harper.html

Hilmer F. (1993), 'Report on National
Competition Policy', available at

www.australiancompetitionlaw.org/
reports/1993hilmer.html

Jose, C., S. King and G. Samuel (2013), 'Agenda
for National Competition Policy Inquiry',
Monash Business Policy Forum, Monash
University, available at www.buseco.
monash.edu.au/mbpf/agenda.pdf

King, S. (2014), 'The NBN Makes Australia
Post's Privatisation Inevitable and
Desirable', *The Conversation*, available at:
www.theconversation.com/the-nbn-
makes-australia-posts-privatisation-
inevitable-and-desirable-22439

Kowalski, P., M. Büge, M. Sztajerowska and
M. Egeland (2013), 'State-Owned Enterprises:
Trade Effects and Policy Implications', OECD
Trade Policy Papers, No. 147, OECD
Publishing, available at www.oecd-
ilibrary.org/trade/state-owned-enterprises_
5k4869ckqk7l-en

Royal Swedish Academy of Sciences (2014),
'Jean Tirole: Market Power and Regulation',
compiled by the Economic Sciences Prize
Committee, available at www.nobelprize.
org/nobel_prizes/economic-sciences/
laureates/2014/advanced-economic
sciences2014.pdf

Tourky, R. (2014), 'An Example of a HECS
Distortion with Uncapped Fees', Core
Economics blog, available at
www.economics.com.au/?p=9972

5 Education financing: government as risk manager?

He who opens a school door, closes a prison.

Attributed to Victor Hugo, French writer and statesman, date and source unknown.

Economic concepts discussed

Easy-to-understand explanations of all the concepts listed below appear in the glossary at the end of this book.

- Adverse selection
- Consumption hardship
- Default
- Econometrics
- Economies of scale
- HECS

- Income-contingent loan
- Insurance
- Legal aid
- Moral hazard
- Nominal/real interest rate
- Opportunity cost

- Paid parental leave
- Positive externality
- Regressive system
- Retention rate
- Risk aversion
- Risk pooling

5.1 Motivation and overview

Imagine you can choose between two options. The first one is 'safe': you simply receive $10 000. The second one is 'risky'; if you get 'heads' in a coin toss you receive $21 000, but if you get 'tails' you receive nothing. Which option would you go for? If you settle for the first option, you are, together with a large majority of the population, '**risk-averse**'. Most people like certainty, stability and predictability better than uncertainty and turbulent times. Because of that, they are generally willing to pay in order to reduce some of the risks they are facing.* In the jargon of economics and finance it is called **insurance**. Most people associate this term with a person in a suit working for a commercial insurance company, and an insurance contract with lots of vague words written in small print.

Professor Bruce Chapman from the Australian National University will show you in this chapter that this is not the whole insurance story. He argues convincingly that the government, too, can act as a risk manager, and in fact be more effective in many areas than private insurance providers in reducing people's risks. The main focus of the interview, recorded on 21 March 2014, is on the area of tertiary education. It explores the following question: 'How should the university sector be run to ensure sufficient funding and quality, but not subject graduates to the risk of **default** on their student loan or

---

*In our example, by choosing the first option you sacrifice $500 in expected value to avoid the danger of getting nothing.

consumption hardship?' As the architect of the Australian Higher Education Contributions Scheme (**HECS**), Prof. Chapman is a world-class authority on this issue.[1] In his pioneering scheme, the loan repayments are socially sensitive as they are income contingent, i.e. dependent on the graduate's wage, not a mortgage-type fixed amount. This idea became very popular and many countries have followed in Australia's footsteps by implementing the scheme.

The discussion touches on many aspects of the government's risk-managing role in higher education as well as in other areas: 'What are the benefits of education?', 'Why is it not a good idea for tertiary education to be "free"?', 'What is the problem with private banks offering student loans?', 'Does an HECS loan make it harder for a graduate to buy a house?', 'Should elite, highly paid athletes pay back the financial support they received while training at the Australian Institute of Sport as teenagers?', 'Can the government use income-contingent loans for artists, exporters, farmers' drought relief and failing banks instead of the existing non-repayable grants, subsidies and bailouts?'. The interview implies answers to these and many other topical policy questions.

It starts with the political and economic background of the birth of HECS. Reading the story, one gets to appreciate the complicated adoption process of many economic policies, and the non-economic factors that are often at play. Prof. Chapman then explains how introducing student fees in combination with government loans can, paradoxically, increase the enrolment of students from low socioeconomic backgrounds compared to 'free' education. This is by bringing in more financial resources, which can make the system accommodate more students, even from disadvantaged backgrounds. It can therefore avoid a decline in quality that tends to occur in the 'free' education systems (as highlighted in the cartoon below).

The next point of discussion is comparing the government-run system with loans provided by private banks. Based on the experience in many countries, Prof. Chapman highlights the market failure associated with the latter scheme. It is simply too risky for private banks to offer such loans, because there is no collateral:

> If you go to the bank to buy a house, the bank owns the house.
> But if you go to the bank for a student loan, the bank can't own
> your brain, basically. There is not an efficient market for brains.

For this reason, in many countries governments provide guarantees for student loans in the event of default. But Prof. Chapman explains that this is associated with **moral hazard** on the part of banks: 'If you as a student borrower don't pay back, then the bank doesn't care. In fact it stops banks chasing the loans … they'll go to the government and say: "Give us the money please".' Furthermore, the banks are not authorised by legislation to know a person's income; the only such institution is the government tax or social security office which is, as Prof. Chapman makes clear, another reason the government is well-suited to run student loans. However, he stresses that this is only feasible in fairly developed countries with quality governance and sound institutions, which are prerequisites for the system to function effectively.

---

1 The full video-interview is available at **http://youtu.be/ctI1R6gkVV8**. For more details regarding Prof. Chapman and his research, see **https://crawford.anu.edu.au/people/academic/bruce-chapman**

Concept by Jan Libich © 2015, drawing by Veronika Mojžišová. Used by permission.

The interview then discusses two other advantages of the HECS scheme. One is the low cost compared to private banks' loans. Prof. Chapman states that annually the HECS debt administration by the Australian Tax Office 'costs about $40 million per year … but HECS actually brings in about $1.8 billion, so it's extremely efficient.' The key advantage of HECS, however, is that the repayments of the debt are more sensitive to people's financial circumstances.

This is achieved by two features of HECS: (i) there is an income threshold below which one does not have to repay the loan at all; and (ii) for earners above the threshold the repayment is 4–8 per cent of annual income, not a fixed amount. These features mean that a student loan cannot bring a person to bankruptcy or cause consumption hardship. This is apparent in Figure 5.1, which shows an example of an income profile of a representative male and female before and after HECS repayment for full-time working graduates. The student loan deduction is hardly noticeable, and is much less than the forgone income (the so-called '**opportunity cost**') during the course of the studies. As Prof. Chapman explains, an income-contingent loan is: 'an instrument that governments

Figure 5.1: Income profile in 2014 dollars of an Australian male (left) and female (right) with a Bachelor's degree and a typical student debt of $20 000 (the solid line shows gross income, the dashed line gross income after HECS deduction)

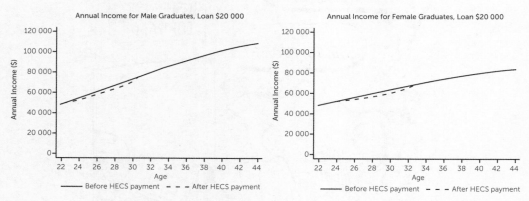

Source: Libich and Macháček (2014), based on Bruce Chapman's calculations. Used by permission.

have that allows people to tax themselves in the future and give themselves the money now when they need it.'

The discussion then looks more broadly at the benefits of education. Time after time, economic studies have found the quality of education to be a key determinant of people's prosperity and wellbeing. As Prof. Chapman argues:

> If you want to get a high return for an investment, just to use the terminology of economics, it's in education as an individual. Those returns would be higher than the average returns from the stock market or from government bonds ...

But in addition to such private benefits, Prof. Chapman also highlights the social benefits of education. In particular, the quality of education is closely linked to a country's economic growth (recall Figure 1.1 in Chapter 1), because it has spillover effects (positive externalities): essentially, people learning from their smart peers. The latest research attempts to measure this indirectly by estimating the returns to a good teacher, and the numbers are nothing short of staggering.

An example is presented in Figure 5.2, which compares the effect of good and bad teachers in the United States, as derived from the data by Professor Eric Hanushek from Stanford University (interestingly, he was Prof. Chapman's PhD supervisor at Yale University in the late 1970s). Compared to an average teacher, a 75th percentile teacher (that is, the 25th best out of 100) increases the lifetime wage of each of her students by about $14 000 on average. So if the teacher is in charge of a class of 30 students, in a given year she generates a wage premium of more than $430 000 dollars for her students. A 90th percentile teacher (that is, the 10th best out of 100) generates more than $820 000 annually in combined extra wages, again compared to an average teacher. Importantly, a bad teacher has negative effects on wages of the same magnitude, as Figure 5.2 shows.

Figure 5.2: Impact of teacher's quality on student lifetime incomes (compared to an average teacher) as a function of the class size

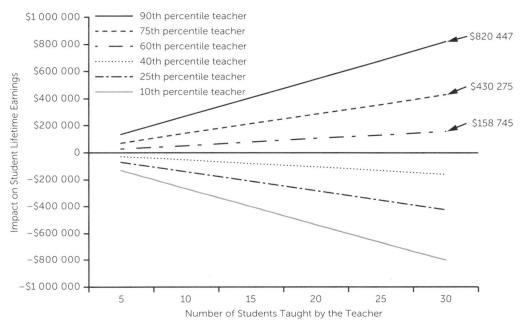

Source: Hanushek (2011).

The final part of the interview is devoted more generally to the role of the government as a risk manager. While public policies such as healthcare, unemployment benefits, or deposit insurance already attempt to reduce the risks people face, Prof. Chapman advocates the use of **income-contingent loans** in several other innovative areas. For example, extending **paid parental leave** via HECS-type loans may help parents deal with a temporary increase in their expenses and revenue losses associated with the rearing of small children. Athletes may also repay some of the cost of their training if they 'make it big'. Artists may pay back their government grants if their projects are successful and generate a lot of revenue. Similarly, farmers, exporters or struggling financial institutions may be offered financial assistance that is repaid once their situation improves. The idea can even be used in the collection of criminal fines, as Prof. Chapman's research suggests.

His message is that government assistance in the form of a loan repayable based on income is preferred to a non-repayable government grant or subsidy. It is also consistent with Australia's principle of a 'fair go', because successful recipients contribute back to society by repaying the loan. Furthermore, this means that the government can offer such assistance to a much greater number of people. And the icing on the cake is that it is done in a fiscally prudent way, which does not threaten the sustainability of public finances and does not burden future generations.

5.2 The debate

Dr Jan Libich (JL): Let's start with your most influential idea. You were the main designer of the system of tertiary education loans run by the Australian government, the so-called Higher Education Contributions Scheme (HECS). Its key feature is that the loan's repayment is contingent on the graduate's income, not a fixed amount. The scheme was so successful that it was subsequently adopted by a number of other countries. Can you briefly outline what the scheme is about and why it has been so popular around the globe?

© Bruce Chapman. Used by permission.

< Prof. Bruce Chapman (BC): Perhaps I'll start with some background about the policy debate. It was a long time ago – in fact 25 years ago. There was a Labor government that had several influential members of Cabinet who wanted to reintroduce university fees into Australia. University fees had been abolished in 1974 by another Labor government led by Prime Minister Gough Whitlam, because it was seen to be socially progressive not to charge university students for tuition. But the 1980s Labor government led by Bob Hawke had a different view – at least several of the ministers did.

It was a view held by John Dawkins and Peter Walsh, who were the Ministers for Education and Finance, and who believed that the so-called 'free' university system is actually a **regressive system**. What economists mean by the word 'regressive' is that it tends to redistribute financial resources from poorer people to the people who are relatively well-off. And the argument used then and still today was that the people that go to university tend to come from fairly privileged backgrounds. Not all, but on average. I'll give you some of the data that was used then. If you came from a professional or managerial household, the chances of going to university were approximately four times greater than if you came from an unskilled or less-skilled background. So that was the first point. The people at university were not representative of the population, they were the advantaged in general.

JL: Some people may now wonder: 'How can fees change that? If university is free, it should not disadvantage people from low socioeconomic backgrounds and prevent them from going to university?'

BC: That's the critical part of the story, but let me just finish the bit about the regressive nature as argued by the Labor Cabinet at the time. People who go to university and graduate, on average, do very well financially. They earn about a million and a half dollars more (over their lifetime) than non-graduates. Hugely different earnings!

JL: There's a study by your former colleague, Andrew Leigh [Chapter 3], who estimated that in Australia every year of a Bachelor degree increases a person's income by about 15 per cent. So that's a sizeable private benefit of tertiary education.

BC: Yes, if you want to get a high return for an investment, just to use the terminology of economics, it's in education as an individual. Those returns would be higher than the average returns from the stock market or from government bonds or whatever. The other problem facing Labor at that time was that the school **retention rates**, that is, the proportion of young people who finish high school, was going through the roof. That number was about 40 per cent at the beginning of the 1980s and by the time it came around to the HECS debate in the late 1980s that number was close to 70 per cent. So there were increasingly long queues of people who couldn't get into the university system and the government was not prepared to use taxpayers' money to make the system bigger.

When I first met the Education Minister John Dawkins, I must say I cringed at what he said to me, because the idea of being involved in introducing university fees was not what I would call a welcoming and warm concept to me. I was an economist at the Australian National University and I'd been a consultant with him for about a day when he said to me: 'Your job is to help me reintroduce university fees'. And I thought: 'My job should not be here, this will be really unpopular and hostile and not very pleasant.' But he said: 'Go away' – not in a nasty way – 'I want an options paper.' And the terms of reference were very clear; there were going to be fees. No matter what happened there would be fees. And then it was a matter of trying to get the fairest system.

JL: Could you draw on the experience of other countries?

BC: I'd looked at other countries' systems and most countries have banks involved in loans, with the repayment guaranteed by governments. But in my view that's not a very good idea, particularly for students. The banks can't be involved without assistance from government and the reason is that if you as a student go to a bank and say: 'Hey, I'm really motivated and I want to go to university, will you please give me some money to pay tuition or for income support?', the bank won't do it. The reason is that you're too risky. Something like 25 per cent of people who attend Australian universities don't graduate. And most importantly, there's no collateral. If you go to the bank to buy a house, the bank owns the house. But if you go to the bank for a student loan, the bank can't own your brain, basically. There is not an efficient market for brains.

JL: Well, the bank can be entitled to your future income ...

BC: It's very hard to know how to enforce that. Banks are not allowed the legal jurisdiction to know what your income is. Only one institution has the legal jurisdiction, which is the government. So one model would be that we could have adopted the Canadian or the US system where the banks give the student the money and then, in the event of default, which could be as much as 15 to 20 per cent (e.g. in Canada), the government guarantees the money to the bank. Now that's a really lovely loan for a bank because it's riskless. If you as a student borrower don't pay back, then the bank doesn't care. In fact it stops banks chasing the loans. You've got a kind of behavioural problem that if a student is late, they can say: 'Well that's the end of that', and they'll go to the government and say: 'Give us the money please.'

JL: So there are some moral hazard and **adverse selection** issues associated with the private bank loan scheme ...

BC: There's a moral hazard which basically means that people change their behaviour as a consequence of the policy. In this instance the bank would stop chasing the repayments and the taxpayers would pick up the cost. But there's a bigger problem in my view. If you're a student with a debt and you have to pay it back over a fixed 10-year period (that's what it is in Canada and the US), or a 20-year period for a mortgage, the bank will be insensitive in its collection engagement to your circumstances. For example, if you are unemployed, don't finish university, have a bad accident, need to look after elderly parents or for whatever other reason you earn a low income, the bank is still knocking on your door saying: 'You owe this money.'

And you might say: 'Well, does it really, really matter?', because you can go bankrupt and that's the end of the story and the taxpayer picks up the bill. Are we all fine? And the answer is: 'Absolutely not!' Because if you default on your student loan that problem stays with you forever. It strongly and adversely affects a person's credit reputation to have defaulted on the repayment of a student loan, and this means that the next time they approach a bank for a loan – for example, for the purchase of a house – they will have great trouble securing the money.

JL: So your ingenious idea was that the government can be more sensitive to people's circumstances, also because the tax office has information about people's income. In particular, the government can make the loan repayment contingent on the person's wage, and thus take into account these kinds of adverse circumstances in people's lives.

BC: Yes, and the critical point is the one you've implied; an 'income-contingent loan' (ICL) scheme is just technical jargon for 'pay when you can'. It is capacity to pay that drives the repayments, not time. What that means with HECS is that if you don't earn $52 000 (the 2014 approximate first income threshold of repayment) that year you repay nothing. This threshold basically protects people against poor circumstances and that's the critical difference between a mortgage-type bank loan, which is what happens in many other countries for students, and an income-contingent loan in Australia.

The way the system often gets characterised in the media is, I think, not very useful. But the way to think about it is that it's an insurance system designed around taking risk away from the debtor (the student). If you've got a financial problem, the government will look after you in that period by requiring no repayments. If you don't have a problem and you're doing very well, then we want a lot at that time. It's a bit like the progressive tax system. You don't pay anything if you're below the threshold, and then it's progressive above that.

So the HECS system is designed as an insurance mechanism but the critical focus in the media is it's about tuition. It's a bit disappointing in one sense. Every January is what I call 'the no news happening January story'. There's a headline in the newspaper, this has been going on for 25 years: 'HECS debt out of control,' it says. And that's because there's nothing else going on in January.

JL: What about the Australian Open, the tennis Grand Slam tournament?

BC: Okay then, there are two things going on, the HECS debt and the Australian Open! But HECS debt only gets one headline. And the focus is on the fact that it's a debt and the implication is that the stock of the debt is important, when it is actually a trivial issue. The really important characteristic of this loan is its sensitivity to people's capacity to repay.

JL: You mentioned this aspect of the government acting as a risk manager, and the government already acts in this capacity in many areas, such as with respect to unemployment benefits, bank deposit insurance, natural disaster relief and public healthcare. You have a forthcoming book with the Nobel Laureate Joseph Stiglitz, in which you outline many interesting, innovative areas where the government can act as a risk manager using income-contingent loans. But before we get to them, let us explore the HECS system a little bit more. You mentioned that if your income is below a certain threshold you don't have to repay the loan at all. How does one set a threshold like that?

BC (shrugging)**:** This shrugging means 'How can you accurately know the right level for the first income threshold of repayment?' You can't do it with reference to economic theory or with reference to some kind of optimal model so the concept of fairness is really important here. The Australian threshold is a relatively high one. The other countries that have income-contingent loans – New Zealand and the United Kingdom for example – have lower thresholds. But what drove the original setting of the threshold was the politics and that's often the case with economic policy. Because the original threshold was not $52 000, in today's terms (current dollars) it would be about $70 000. And the reason? It was the average income of all people working for pay in Australia.

JL: Average? Why not median?

BC: It was average, but it included people working part-time. So it was not just full-time workers, it was the average income. That allowed the minister at the time, and other people who were promoting HECS, to say: 'Do you think it is fair that graduates will be paying – at the time – $8 a week and repaying 25 per cent of the total cost of going to university? Is it reasonable that when graduates are earning above the average income they should pay back this proportion?' And once you use the average, the political debate is quite different.

The other 75 per cent was direct government subsidy picked up by taxpayers. It's not 75 per cent anymore; it's about 55 per cent now with political plans for further reductions. In New Zealand, that threshold is about $15 000 or $16 000 per year, but it's a marginal-based system, so the repayment is only 10 cents in the extra dollar of income above that. In Australia, once you earn above the threshold the amount to be repaid is a proportion of your total income, including income below the threshold.

JL: But again, even $16 000 is still higher than the zero that you effectively have in countries where banks run the system. They still require the payment even if you have no income.

BC: It's a really important point and this debate needs to be framed in those insurance terms. I'm not saying the banks are insensitive, but it's not their job to look after you socially. It's their job to run financial markets. If I miss my mortgage, the bank's not going to phone me up and say: 'Are things okay, Bruce? Did you lose your job? If you did, don't worry about this, we'll pick it up next year!' No, you've got a basic problem. And the problem is not just default, although default is a very serious problem for the graduate because it affects their credit reputation forever. The problem is what economists call 'consumption hardship'. There are some countries in the world in which the student loan obligations are so large that many people can't afford to repay their student loans ...

JL: Can you give us an example – using your wealth of experience in designing such systems around the world?

BC: The government of Colombia in South America invited me to have a look at their new loan system, about eight years ago. And the first thing that they said was: 'We want an outside person so you could not be involved in the politics of Colombia', which was highly attractive to me, not to be involved in the politics of anywhere really! Colombia had a reputation where you didn't feel necessarily all that comfortable, although I just found things fantastic in Colombia in general. They told me about their loan scheme: 'The first point is that it doesn't cost any money, there's no government subsidy.' And I thought: 'Whoa, that's pretty weird'. I've never heard of any public student loan scheme that doesn't have a subsidy, mostly in the form of relatively low interest rates. Moreover, in Colombia it had a very short time period of repayment – eight years. And it was to cover tuition plus living costs.

And I said: 'How do you afford this? How can the subsidy be zero?' And I was told it was because the interest rate was 18 per cent per annum in nominal terms. Given inflation was around 5 per cent this was a pretty high interest rate, 13 per cent in real terms. And the politicians said to me: 'Will this scheme work?' And I said: 'I don't know, but let me go and talk to the education officials.' So I went over and sat in their Department of Education. I didn't speak any Spanish. They didn't speak any English but we got on just fine because we had one language in common, which was **econometrics**, data analysis. And it was really amazing. I had more to talk to them about in communication, not in actual words, than I do with my next-door neighbour. And we all had the techniques and we all had similar training.

And we asked a very simple question. Take the poorest of graduates, that is, in the bottom 25 per cent of the distribution of graduate income. Not people that just went to college or university – graduates – so they're the people that actually finished higher education successfully. And the poorest group were young women in the bottom 25 per cent of the distribution. Let's look at their income and ask the question: 'If they had this loan, what proportion of their income would they have to use to pay off the loan?' And the answer was 85 per cent for the bottom 25 per cent of female graduates. For the bottom 10 per cent of the income earners, it was like 150 per cent. So for them it was impossible to repay, they would have to borrow from their parents or friends – since banks wouldn't help them. They probably wouldn't have their friends for too long because they wouldn't be able to pay it back. The other alternative was default. Can this loan system work? No, it can't work, the default rates would just be too high.

JL: You mentioned that a government-run system can be more sensitive, and it's not only through the no-repayment threshold. It's also because the repayment itself is a proportion of the person's income, not a fixed amount. In Australia, if you just reach the threshold, you pay a mere 4 per cent of your annual income. And this proportion increases with your income up to a maximum of 8 per cent.

BC: That's right.

JL: These are very different numbers from what you found in Colombia.

BC: Yes, and we've done this kind of work for many countries now. In relatively poor countries, these kinds of loan systems basically can't work. And when I say 'relatively poor countries', Colombia is kind of a medium-income country. We've designed hypothetical loans schemes for growing, but low-income, countries such as Vietnam, Indonesia, China and Thailand. In all cases, 'normal' types of loan schemes (not ICL) can be shown to have major issues of collection.

JL: And you're actually involved in the proposals in the US to move in the direction of ICLs ...

BC: Well, the US is another example. Many people say: 'The student private bank loan scheme in the US is fine because on average the graduates only pay 4 per cent of their income.' But the really important methodological point, the data point, is that almost none of the action is at the average. What really matters is the relatively poor debtors, the poor graduates and those who dropped out.

Now that you've brought up the US, I'll give you an interesting example. If you study law in the United States, and I hear people in Australia complaining about $6000 to $8000 HECS charges per year, but it is about US $25 000 in the United States if you go to a high-cost law place. Their debts end up often being $130 000 to $150 000, usually with a 10-year repayment period. If you've got a student debt of that level it is likely to affect your job choice. You cannot afford to work for the government or in **legal aid** because incomes are too low to allow you to repay your student loan with ease. You can't afford to work with the police or as a prosecutor or as a public defendant.

The above problem actually motivated US President Bill Clinton to try to change the system in 1993 into an income-contingent one. He wasn't successful and most people in the US have still never heard of it. So the critical point is that the bank loans system can not only cause people to default and affect their credit reputations and their lives. It can also cause a lot of hardship in repayment and negatively affect, as it does in the United States, occupational choice. You can't get really terrific, young lawyers going into work in the government because they can't afford to, because their debts are so high.

JL: In addition to this sensitivity to people's circumstances, what are some other advantages of the government running an income-contingent loan scheme. Is it because it can do it in bulk and thus keep the cost low?

BC: There are two advantages, and one is closely related to the relatively low cost of government **risk pooling**. It comes down to a legal jurisdictional issue. Only one institution has the legal power to know your income as an individual – and that's the government through the income tax office. So, that's the first point. Now you could possibly collect these loans through the private sector if you gave the private sector the capacity to know an individual income, but you actually wouldn't want to do it.

And the reason for using the tax office is what we call 'economies of scale'; if it is done on a larger scale it is cheaper. The income tax system in OECD countries, or relatively rich countries like Australia, is pretty comprehensive and it's very efficient. To collect a HECS debt is just like collecting income tax. So if you're working as an employee, and not as a self-employed person (that's a different situation, but not that much), the employer takes money out for income tax every week or every two weeks and sends it to the tax office. If you're a graduate, they take a little bit more out, the 4 to 8 per cent you mentioned, and send it off to the tax office. That actually costs, on top of the income tax system, less than 3 per cent of the total revenue. So it costs about $40 million just for that part of HECS collection but HECS actually brings in about $1.8 billion, so it's extremely efficient.

And you indicated that I'm working on a book with Joseph Stiglitz, who's a terrific economist and invented a whole new area in our discipline, the economics of information. He's written a paper on the aspect you've just raised, Jan, on the efficiency of the use of the tax system. And being Joseph Stiglitz, he can encapsulate it in just a couple of words and you know what's going on. And he calls it 'transactional efficiency'. That is, it is really very cheap for the government to use the income tax system, or in other countries it's called the 'internal revenue service', to collect debt. And I've given you the data for Australia, the data for the UK are pretty much the same.

JL: For comparison, the cost of private insurance varies across the type of insurance and across countries from about 20 to 50 per cent of the total revenue. So the cost is about 10 times greater than for the government-run insurance, at least in countries with quality public institutions.

BC: It's a funny thing that when this system was being designed this issue didn't occur to anyone, including me. People would say: 'How much does it cost to run this system?' 'Don't worry, it doesn't cost that much, you know, it's 3 or so per cent of annual revenue.' Well actually, Joseph Stiglitz and another economist in Australia by the name of Richard Denniss, who runs The Australia Institute, have both been strong proponents of the efficiency of this system. And it's now become a major talking point in discussions about income-contingent loans, whereas people like me would traditionally focus on other benefits of ICL: consumption smoothing and default insurance.

JL: So far, we have been comparing the HECS system with a system of private bank loans, but the other alternative is 'free' tertiary education with no student fees. In such a system the government cops the whole bill and funds higher education through general tax revenue, as is the case in Scandinavia, Germany and other countries. In my home country, the Czech Republic, even foreign students can study for free as long as they study in the Czech language. You mentioned some problems of this system at the beginning, the fact that many students may not be able to get in due to the limited number of places, and the declining quality of education due to lack of finances. Are there any other issues?

BC: Let me comment on this question of equity because it was a really big deal in Australia and a lot of people – including me – changed our minds about the benefits of so-called 'free' education. The word 'free' is a very potent word. But there is no 'free'. Everything has a cost. So the word 'free' as applied to higher education means 'free upfront, free to the student'. And in a way, I think that the Whitlam government's abolition of university fees in 1974 was a bit similar to HECS in the sense that both ideas were designed to take away all the costs at the point of entry so that relatively poor students could actually come to university without having money. The difference was paying back in the future but only when they're doing okay.

And the equity point, the one that you just raised, is a really important deal. At the time that fees were abolished in Australia, only about 10–15 per cent of people went to university. And I assure you that, on average, they were very privileged. About 70 per cent or more of young people had left school before Year 12 or equivalent. They were in the labour market aged 14 or 15, and they were the poor ones. And they were the ones whose taxes were being used to pay for so-called 'free' university education. It is such an important point. And I must say that HECS hasn't changed this. HECS has not made it relatively easy for poor people to come into the system, but what's happened is that, particularly in the early years up to about 1994–95, the extra money was used to make the system much bigger. And that meant a lot more poor young people went to university, but a lot more rich young people did too, and a lot more in the middle as well. The system doubled in size.

JL: What's the proportion of high school graduates now in Australia that go to university?

BC: About 40 per cent.

JL: It's among the highest in the world, right?

BC: Yes. There are a number of countries that are around 40 per cent, but there wouldn't be too many above that, perhaps the US is, by a bit. But it's still the case that the Australian system has large subsidies to undergraduates of about 55 per cent.

JL: This is the average and it is worth noting that the subsidy varies substantially across the disciplines. In science, the government contribution is actually more than 80 per cent, so the HECS debt is less than 20 per cent of the actual cost. In contrast, in economics and law the government contribution is below 20 per cent, in humanities it is about 50 per cent, in medicine about 70 per cent. So the important point is that once you have fees combined with government loans, you do not actually have to charge the student the full cost of going through the degree, there may still be a sizeable public subsidy.

BC: True, and there are many arguments for not charging the full cost. We believe that there are positive spillovers from higher education. It's extremely hard to quantify them but one thing we do know is that education generates skills and wealth, and it therefore generates additional income and thus tax revenue. So that's a contribution to the broader society. But I think the major contributions come through the adaptation to technical change, the capacity to facilitate the adoption of new technologies, which we're pretty confident is associated with higher levels of education.

Your basic point about the cross-subsidies is a very important one. Medicine is hugely expensive, so is veterinary science, so is dentistry, and the charges are nowhere near the cost. Law is very inexpensive, like economics, sociology and history. What's interesting, in England, when the conservatives won government in 2010, they abolished all subsidies in their HECS-type system. It was really kind of startling. The average price went from £3000 per full-time year to £9000 per year. What was kind of interesting is that the behavioural response, that is, what this did to people's interest in going to university, was close to nothing. So a radical change in the price didn't change the behaviour and I think that comes down to the notion that students basically know what it is all about. They may not use the language of economists but they understand that HECS is an insurance system ...

JL: ... and that the private benefit of tertiary education is high ...

BC: Yes, and you've kind of got nowhere else to go. If you want to be in the skilled labour market you've got to go to a university or equivalent and that means taking on the debt. I am quite confident that if that money was an upfront charge, you'd get huge responses because this capital market does not work very well. As we said before, without guarantees the banks won't help.

JL: Let's think a little bit more broadly. We mentioned the forthcoming book with Joe Stiglitz and it's actually looking at many other areas where we can use this idea of government being the risk manager offering income-contingent loans to individuals and companies. This would replace the status quo whereby the government acts as a donor, and gives grants and subsidies that do not have to be repaid. Can you mention some of the possible applications of income-contingent loans?

BC: There's a remarkable 2002 book by David Moss, an economic historian from Harvard University. Please have a look at this book, it's called *When All Else Fails* and it's about the history of public policy in the United States. Many of us use a very simple model about the nature of the engagement of government. It's left-wing, high tax, high-spending, high regulation, or right-wing, low tax, low-spending, low regulation. And that kind of model I think is useful, but it is not the only important way of thinking about the role of the public sector generally.

David Moss promotes the idea of thinking about government not in left- and right-wing terms only, but also as a manager of risk. And there are great examples, such as limited liability when people form companies. If you didn't pay debts from a bankrupt company a couple of hundred years ago, then you'd go to prison. So this was kind of the end of you and the end of your family really, and limited liability stopped that. Other examples include occupational health and safety regulation, speed rules on roads, and the best example in Australia – Medicare.

Medicare is an insurance system. It's universal. The government says: 'If you're unlucky enough to get really, really sick, we are going to cover you.' And an income-contingent loan like HECS is just a subset of risk management instruments that governments use in all sorts of ways. The progressive income tax system, even something as basic as that, is a risk management instrument. If you earn nothing, you pay nothing; if you earn more, you pay a greater proportion of income in taxes.

So I read the book by Moss about six or seven years ago and it kind of blew my mind. I thought I was too old to have my mind blown, you know what I mean! But I thought: 'Wow, that is so useful a way to think of it!' And it mentioned income-contingent loans, but in the United States there has not been an income-contingent loan for the financing of college, so it didn't get much attention. But income-contingent loans have of course been in Australia for 25 years and in New Zealand for 20 years. We kind of 'get it' more than they do in the United States. This whole concept of the government being able to help people balance their lifecycle is the essence of an income-contingent loan.

JL: Can you give some specific examples of possible areas in which these can be used? I recall you have talked about elite athletes ...

BC: Elite athletes. That's a good one, although you get a lot of hostility. I got a critical letter from Lleyton Hewitt's manager. I've got absolutely no problem with Lleyton Hewitt as a person – but let me give you some facts. Lleyton Hewitt got a tennis scholarship when he was 16 or 17 years old to play tennis at the Australian Institute of Sport. In current dollars, that was worth about $100 000. Well, I was sitting in the dentist one day. I don't know what you do at the dentist, but I read those crappy magazines and there was an article: Lleyton's $400 000 diamond ring for his fiancée. And I thought: 'Great, Lleyton, why don't you pay back your $100 000 first?' Not a lot, 2 per cent of income, that should do it. Lleyton Hewitt has earned $35 million in his life, but the scholarship was a gift to Lleyton Hewitt. Do we think that's a reasonable way to use taxpayers' resources? Well, it's certainly not very progressive.

There are other examples. Jelena Dokic – about a quarter of a million dollars' worth of financial assistance from the Australian Institute of Sport. And I'm not particularly picking on the Australian Institute of Sport, but you can see examples that are quite profoundly obviously unfair uses of taxpayers' money. That's a lot of money that could be used for all kinds of things, like hospital beds or making schools better or medical assistance that would be fairer.

JL: Having them actually repay the loan if they become successful seems consistent with the Australian idea of a 'fair go'. A person is offered a hand, but when in the position to give something back, they should do so.

BC: Well, it's an interesting term that you've used because you've mentioned Andrew Leigh before. He made a speech in parliament about all this and said that contingent loans are very Australian because of the 'fair go'.

JL: I think that's where I got it from …

BC: A 'fair go' is just Australian language for progressivity. It means that if you're going to do something as a government, do your best to redistribute resources from not-poor people to poor people. That's essentially what it means. And the other point to make in the context of contingent loans is you've got to think of the lifecycle as well, because people who are poor today may not be poor in 10 years' time. That is generally true of graduates; they're poor as students but they're not poor as graduates. And it can also be true that people who are well-off today may not be well-off tomorrow. If you have a nasty accident and you lose your job, or you lose your leg, or you can't work for some reason, you want systems in place to look after people. And that means paying account and giving weight to models and instruments that actually take the lifecycle into account, like an income-contingent loan.

JL: This reminds me of a similar proposal regarding paid parental leave. In most countries, parents receive payments when they have small kids. Often it is actually a subsidy from poor singles to rich families, or families that might need the money now when raising kids but later on they will be well-off. So there doesn't seem to be much reason for not having the scheme as an income-contingent loan.

BC: That particular example is one we've done a lot of work on. There is a PhD thesis by my ANU colleague, Tim Higgins. Let's put it into a little bit of a contemporary context. At the moment – although this is likely to change because of Tony Abbott's alternative suggestion of paid parental leave – you can get 18 to 20 weeks as a grant. Now 18 to 20 weeks' leave to look after a newborn is not that long. And if you want to take a year off, what would you do? Well, if you haven't got the money, you can't do it. So the idea was, let's imagine the 18 to 20 weeks model stays as it is, but you want more money to live on to look after a small child for another six months. And you need, say, $10 000. So Tim and I designed exactly what you're talking about – an income-contingent loan for extensions of paid parental leave. And then we added the debt onto a HECS debt to see how much it would cost the government, because there are always interest rate subsidies if you don't adjust for that. And it turned out to be pretty cheap.

There was only one group where the subsidy was very high. And they would be single mothers, in the bottom 25 per cent of the single mothers' income distribution. But everyone else would have the capacity to pay back in part and the vast majority of people would be able to pay back in full. And what were we doing here? This was an instrument that governments have that allows people to tax themselves in the future and give themselves the money now when they need it. And that's what HECS does basically. It says you need the money to go to university. You haven't got it. Just imagine when you're 40 years old, in 15 to 20 years' time and you've got it, wouldn't you like to say: 'I was really struggling then as a student, I'm going to transfer this money hypothetically through time to myself when I'm 20 or 25 and I really need it.' A government's got the capacity to do that whereas the commercial sector does not. And that's the essence of it; it allows lifetime income smoothing when banks can't help you.

JL: It's not only fair in the sense that the government can actually offer financial assistance to many more people – because some of them will repay back. But it's also more sustainable from the fiscal point of view. Many countries are now running into problems of financing their spending and their debt projections look really grim, Australia is one of the few exceptions. So there's a strong fiscal sustainability argument for using income-contingent loans. But let me just mention some of the other novel applications; for example, artists. Currently, they get a grant to shoot a movie and they don't have to repay it even if it becomes a blockbuster. Why not? Similarly, support to farmers and exporters, climate change adaptation; you have also explored using income-contingent loans to deal with brain drain …

BC: Yes, we had a lot of these, maybe 15 or so in total. I think I've been really fortunate professionally because I've been able to work with lots of different people in lots of different areas. Take farmers who used to get billions of dollars for drought relief. And some of their properties were pretty valuable, and we knew that the farmers could pay back over time when the drought had gone. So I worked with Linda Botterill, who's a drought expert, and we designed a revenue-contingent loan for farmers in drought. And all that means is they get the same money now, but when their profits recover, the government gets it back. And that's fairer to taxpayers without damaging the people on the properties.

JL: In relation to that, I once read that the highest proportion of ownership of the luxury Porsche car was among the farmers in Greece. This just tells you something about the government farming subsidies in Europe, although in Australia they are much lower.

BC: When Linda and I used to put out a paper and it got a bit of media coverage, we'd end up doing interviews; for example, for ABC Radio in country Australia. And a lot of the people listening were farmers. Then they'd have talkback and Linda and I would roll our eyes and think we were going to get beaten to pulp. But it never really happened. Most people would call in and say: 'I don't qualify for one of those government drought grants, but my neighbour does because they've got a line on the map. And if I was on the other side of the highway I'd be getting this. And you know what? You know where they are?' And we'd say: 'No, where are they?' 'Well, they're in Switzerland on a skiing holiday.' That's what they'd say, or 'They just bought a Porsche'. Well, it mightn't have been the Porsche but it might've been a new beaut tractor or whatever. And that's always a critical issue for all government engagement: 'Is it fair? Is it progressive?' And in that particular area it's very easy to argue that it's not.

I'll give you another example which seems such a long, long way away from economics, but I think makes the point similarly in terms of the capacity of governments to change people's lives through a contingent loan scheme. It's the payment of criminal fines. This idea came from a friend of mine, John Quiggin. If you read blogs, you'll know John Quiggin, who is a very smart and creative economic theorist. And he said to me one day: 'There's something that might be as good as HECS', and explained to me what happens with the criminal justice system.

When people commit low-level criminal offences such as theft, assault or drunken driving, they get a fine. It is mostly young men with very low levels of education. And 50 per cent of those who are fined don't pay the fine. The police go and round them up, they plonk them back in the court. The judge says: 'Well, you're a bad person, we're going to double the fine.' Fifty per cent don't pay that. Then they get put into community service. Thirty per cent of them don't turn up. They'll take away their driver's licence. Many of these people get caught driving illegally. They might have an accident with drunken driving. They can go to prison. If they go to prison that is an appalling result for them because they've got criminal offences against their name. Their life in the future labour market is much poorer than it otherwise would be. And it's also a really bad result for taxpayers. It costs about $80 000–90 000 to keep someone in prison for a year.

So, John's idea was to turn the fine into a contingent fine. Have the first threshold of repayment quite low compared to HECS, but the repayments would be low too. So if you earn $25 000, 2 per cent goes to the fine and that means that you can pay this off with default insurance. You don't have to go to prison, and you can get your money back into the system. I went down to the courts as an observer to see what the magistrates were doing, and they're kind of already doing it. So here's a classic case. Eighteen-year-old young man, drunken driving, driving without a licence. Judge says: 'You're a very bad person. The fine is $1000 and you've got one month to pay.' And if the person looks deeply uncomfortable, which they do, the judge will say: 'What's your current employment situation?' And they will say: 'I'm unemployed.' 'Alright, you've got six months', says the magistrate.

JL: This sounds like the judge is using an income-contingent scheme …

BC: Yes, it's not operated the way we think of HECS but it is a contingent fine when they are allowed time for their income to recover. And we've talked about this at legal conferences and several magistrates have come up to me and said: 'Do you know, I never fine those people what I should be fining them. I put a fine of $800 but it should be $3000. And the reason I don't make it $3000 is that they would default. And if they default, they could end up in prison, which is a terrible outcome.' So what you could do – and this is John Quiggin's thought as well – the system can make the fine a lot higher but without any possibility of jail, without any possibility of default. You get the money back without ruining their lives and costing taxpayers a lot. I think it's extraordinary how flexible this instrument might be. And there have been many other examples; you've talked about a few of them.

JL: Before turning to the audience, I ask my guests a final question about public policies that economics implies would improve overall wellbeing, but that politicians have shied away from. Let me make it more specific in your case: are Australian policymakers actually considering some of these innovative proposals for income-contingent loans?

BC: The answer is: 'kind of', and also 'I don't really know a lot'. There was the adoption of the Austudy (Loans) Supplement in 1994 which allowed people to trade in some part of youth income support for a higher level of contingent loan. But I don't know where it's at except that HECS has now spread throughout the tertiary education sector – into postgraduate, private universities and into the vocational education sector. I have done projects with governments over the years that are about adopting ICLs. And there is ongoing work that I think most people look at and say: 'That sounds fair.'

Let me give you an example which I've recently done some modelling on; it's legal aid. Legal aid is in trouble, it basically doesn't have enough money from governments. And if you've got a property dispute or a child custody dispute, there is no legal aid for you. So imagine that you've just had a marital separation, or a break-up with a de facto, and there's a child involved and there's a property to be divided. And one of the partners has got a lot of money and the other one does not. And they disagree, which is kind of common. The rich partner can take the poor partner to court until his or her money has gone. So it will end up being in the jurisdiction of the more powerful person because there's no legal aid.

I believe you can actually have a legal aid system which takes into account the capacity to pay, and gives assistance to people who are pretty disadvantaged. I can't say that the government's contemplating that, but I have had discussions with people in government and that kind of thing is not off the table. And what's interesting (and a bit depressing), through all my experience in public policy I've never seen a more fiscally tight environment than it is today. I've seen it before but not as parsimonious as now. And I think the Commission of Audit and the next budget [May 2014] are likely to be dominated by fiscal parsimony and probably crisis points with government outlays. So if there's going to be a chance to save government money, this might be the occasion.

Audience member 1: I'm going to ask a controversial question. Given the UK experience and the current government's motivation for fiscal parsimony as you described it, do you think there's scope for Australia to have higher HECS fees? Especially because in the UK the participation rate in higher education did not drop when fees were trebled. It should be said that as part of the changes in the UK, they increased the income threshold for paying back, but it was still lower than it is in Australia now. Do you have an opinion on that?

BC: One of the things that seems very clear is that the level of fees doesn't matter too much in terms of student behaviour, but it may matter to student happiness and unhappiness. I'll give you a few examples. When HECS was introduced, the price was previously zero. And it went in current dollars to $3500 per year basically overnight. The system expanded for two reasons. Number one: the government used the money to make the system a lot bigger to solve the problem with queues.

Number two: the students weren't that much affected by the introduction of HECS, because these decisions about going to university don't happen at age 18. They're a lifecycle thing. And I've seen enough data to know that this is pretty clear. There are several relevant longitudinal surveys in Australia. The one that I've looked at with Chris Ryan asks 12-year-olds: 'Do you plan on going to university?' And then the survey process follows them, annually, and we see where they are in their early 20s. More than 90 per cent of the 12-year-olds who said: 'Yes, I'm going to university', even if they don't quite know what that means, are in university in their early 20s. And something like 3–5 per cent of the 12-year-olds who said: 'No, I'm not' end up in university.

In other words, you can start to predict these lifetime choices at very young ages and I think it's because this whole question of educational choice starts even before you're born. You know, they say that the most important decision you make is who your parents should be. That's absolutely important with respect to education. And you can see it going on when people are very young. You can see it in the nature of their choice of school subjects and peer groups and what they're doing at home. Parents who are really interested in education will be investing in educational capacity when their children are very young. So that's one reason why you don't get that much effect when university fees are changed.

JL: I should say we're very happy that you chose the parents you did because they apparently supported you through university studies and enabled you to contribute to Australian public policy in such a major way.

BC: Sometimes when I was deeply horrible as a teenager I didn't think they were all that happy, but they were always hugely encouraging about me going to university. But let me add that another reason why contingent loans don't really affect behaviour very much is the insurance aspect. That was the idea in theory and it's worked, I think, in practice. Because even when the charge increased radically in 1989 by HECS being introduced and then importantly in 1997 when the incoming government essentially doubled it, there was no effect, like in the UK.

But that doesn't mean you want to keep doing it. There are some people that say: 'Oh, let's charge whatever we like because they're going to come anyway.' There has got to be a sense in all government policy about equity and justice. And on the basis of empirical evidence you cannot say what the right charge is. That's got to be made politically. The political judgement at the time when HECS was introduced was that at about 25 per cent of the recurrent costs, the level of the charge seemed about fair. At the moment it's about 45 per cent. I can comment on that as an individual but I haven't got any expertise in this at all. I'd leave it on average about where it is. It looks about fair.

And even though you could raise a lot more money by increasing the charge, I think it's the sense of the justice of it all. And the UK government, by making the subsidies zero, is effectively saying to students that there's no social value in higher education (only on paper, in reality there are still interest rate subsidies). So a sense of fairness is kind of what ultimately drives the parameters that are chosen. But if you ask me as an individual, I'd leave it roughly where it is in Australia.

JL: It's not just the fairness argument but it's also the positive spillovers you mentioned from human capital to everybody else in the society, and economic growth. If people don't internalise this **positive externality** they tend to underinvest in their education, so through the subsidies the government encourages them to invest more. On the other hand, there's a 2012 Grattan Institute report by Andrew Norton (and subsequent work) arguing that the subsidies in Australia should be phased out over time and reduced by about 50 per cent. There's a debate.

BC: I've seen the report and I've spoken a lot to Andrew Norton who wrote the report, and we've done other work which looks at the extent of the spillover benefits. It's so hard to pin down. You need so much structure on the models and so many limiting assumptions to get any numbers at all. One of the reasons is that we don't know how to model it. We don't know if going to university causes people to be healthier or whether or not it's just associated with people who are interested in a healthy lifestyle and investing in education. We don't know if it's the act of going to university that reduces the probability that people will commit crime or whether or not we're just selecting groups.

And with those uncertainties, it's very hard to pin it down. In the end it comes down to political judgements and that's what politicians have to make all the time. But don't let anybody fool you and say: 'The right number is this, the right subsidy is zero, or the right subsidy is 100 per cent.' They don't know. And I know enough about this to know we don't know.

Audience member 2: The recent Kemp–Norton review talked about using real as opposed to **nominal interest rates** for HECS. Do you have a view on that?

BC: The **real interest rate** issue is very important and it's really hard to get hold of. Let me try and explain why I think it's very complicated. A real interest rate does not make it harder to repay at any point in time (compared to a nominal one of the same value), it just means you pay back longer. And that's an important point. So long as you've still got a maximum payment between 4 and 8 per cent of your income, the real interest rates won't actually affect behaviour, they'll just redistribute income away from graduates. The real interest rate question though has a lot to do with the optics of it all. In New Zealand they introduced a real interest rate in their system and the nominal debt went through the roof. People went: 'Oh my god, this is really unfair,' they looked at the stock of the debt and that got politically very unpopular. The Australian system is subsidised, that's true. And it has a real interest rate of zero since the loan is only adjusted for inflation.

JL: People really need to study more economics: if only to be able to tell the difference between nominal and real variables …

BC: The hardest thing in my experience with HECS is making it clear what the interest rate issues are. And they're actually extremely important. In New Zealand now they've reduced the interest rates in nominal terms to nothing. You know what that means in subsidy terms? 70 per cent. In Australia, our subsidy for our interest rate ratio is about 15 per cent. I wouldn't touch it, I think the system is basically okay as it is. And as the policymaker you don't actually get that much. For all the pain that you inflict with the optics and the poor politics of big interest rates, it's not worth it in the money terms, if I was a minister. But by the way, I'm not the minister.

JL: Minister or not, let me thank you Bruce on behalf of the millions of students around the globe for improving their lives with your ideas. I'd like to wish you all the best for the future, and look forward to many other influential insights of yours.

5.3 Key economic insights and policy lessons

Economic insights	Implied policy lessons (for public officials and voters)
If individuals do not fully understand the difference between nominal and real variables (such as interest rates), they tend to make erroneous decisions.	Policymakers should encourage the media to always report both nominal and real variables where relevant, and lead by example in this respect.
There is no such thing as 'free' tertiary education.	Policymakers should clearly explain to the public how 'free' education and other government-provided programs are financed to highlight the policy trade-offs.
'Free' tertiary education tends to be regressive, i.e. redistribute money from poorer people (without degrees) to richer people (graduates).	Policymakers should avoid regressivity in tertiary education as well as in other policies.
'Free' tertiary education systems tend to experience lack of financial resources, leading to restricted access and declining quality.	Policymakers should ensure sufficient financial resources in the tertiary education sector, from public or private sources.

Economic insights	Implied policy lessons (for public officials and voters)
Tertiary education systems with tuition fees and student loans from private banks do not generally function well due to informational asymmetries. Further, they may lead to consumption hardship, personal bankruptcy and distortions in occupational choice.	Policymakers should not automatically 'solve' the information asymmetry problem in higher education by offering banks guarantees as this simply moves the financial risks from the student to the taxpayer.
The private benefits of tertiary education in Australia are substantial, on average a 15 per cent salary increase for each completed year.	Policymakers should carefully weigh the quantifiable private benefits and non-quantifiable (but large) social benefits of tertiary education in setting the right level of subsidies.
The Australian HECS system, in which the government runs student loans directly making repayment contingent on income, seems a good compromise between fully private and fully public tertiary education financing.	Policymakers worldwide should consider emulating the Australian HECS system.
HECS enables the government to be sensitive to the graduate's circumstances as well as to save the graduate some money by using the tax office for collection (compared to private bank schemes).	Policymakers should shift from the paradigm of the government as a donor and broaden its role as a risk manager.
Moving from nominal to real interest rates on HECS debt does not make it harder to repay at any point in time, it just takes longer, and some people may be put off by a high nominal debt.	Policymakers should carefully consider the right level of interest rate subsidy inherent in HECS, and how it is explained to the public.
Government can, through income-contingent loans, help people manage risks in many other areas; in a way that is both fairer (more people receive government support) and fiscally sound (much of the support is repaid to the public purse).	Policymakers should replace existing subsidies, grants and bailouts to exporters, farmers, sportspeople, artists and collapsing banks by income-contingent loans repayable when the recipient's situation improves sufficiently.
The collection of low-level criminal fines is a big problem worldwide, both for the government and the affected individual.	Policymakers should pursue proposals for using income-contingent loan principles for collection of criminal fines, and thus avoid personal bankruptcies and imprisonment while increasing the proportion of fines that get paid.
Lack of legal aid may have major negative consequences on low-income individuals that are inconsistent with the right to fair and equitable legal treatment.	Policymakers should investigate ways of using income-contingent schemes in legal aid to help the disadvantaged.
In countries with political instability and an absence of sound institutions, income-contingent loans are unlikely to work effectively.	Policymakers should attempt to create a quality institutional and legal framework that supports their role of helping people to insure various life risks.
Using the average of a variable (e.g. wage) can be very misleading. It may differ substantially from the median and/or conceal what happens at the low end of the distribution.	Policymakers should always consider the whole (wage) distribution, not just the averages, and explain to the public why this is desirable.
Decisions about studying at university do not happen at the end of high school but many years earlier.	Policymakers should not judge the true effect of tuition fee changes solely in terms of the changes in that year's enrolment.

5.4 Discussion questions

1   Using your own words, summarise the debate of Section 5.2 in three to five sentences.
2   Write down one idea discussed in the interview that you found new or interesting, or that you disagree with, and briefly explain why.
3   Write down one question on any topic covered in the interview that you would ask the speaker if you had a chance.
4   Consider the cartoon in Section 5.1 and explain the point to someone who has not read the section and does not have any knowledge of economics.
5   Examine Figure 5.1 from the perspective of a policymaker. Describe its key message to the public and explain what kind of policy improvement is implied by the data. Do the same for Figure 5.2.
6   Suppose you take part in a debating contest, in which the topic is the opening quote of the chapter by (most likely) Victor Hugo:

> *He who opens a school door, closes a prison.*

    Prepare a speech you would give for the affirmative side. Then (you or your classmate) prepare a speech for the negative side. If possible, organise an audience and perform the debate.

7   Outline the background to the HECS scheme; why and how did it come into being?
8   What are the main features of an income-contingent loan and its rationale?
9   Provide some examples of countries using a full-subsidy system featuring no tertiary education fees. Compare it to the HECS scheme and discuss the advantages and disadvantages (attempt to support your answers with data). Is the former type of education really 'free', as is usually stated?
10 Based on your research, provide some examples of countries in which student loans are provided by private banks (possibly with a government guarantee). Compare it to the HECS scheme and discuss the advantages and disadvantages.
11 Compare the New Zealand and United Kingdom income-contingent loans schemes with the Australian system. Using some internet sources, make a case for whether one of the systems works better than the others, and why.
12 Based on the comparison in the previous question, suggest how the Australian HECS system could be improved.
13 Why does Prof. Chapman believe that income-contingent loan systems are unlikely to work in relatively poor countries? Using research by Prof. Chapman available on the internet, summarise what he recommends as the best solution for those countries.
14 Based on the US case, explain how the type of higher education financing may affect occupational choice. Can you think of some other examples?
15 Do you think that it's the government's job to act as an 'insurer' and help individuals reduce various risks they face? In your answer, discuss the desirability of the examples given by Prof. Chapman such as paid parental leave and fines for low-level criminal offences.

16 Striking the right balance between equity and efficiency is an important goal of policymakers. How would you best design natural disaster (e.g. flood or drought) relief programs? Make sure you think through the incentives of the program, including the possible moral hazard problem.

17 Suggest a novel area in which you think income-contingent loans may be beneficial, and explain why. Do not be afraid to 'think outside the box'.

18 Propose a set of policies that you think best promotes the quality of the tertiary education system and ultimately people's wellbeing.

5.5 Where to find out more

Barr, N. (2001), *The Welfare State as Piggy Bank: Information, Risk, Uncertainty and the Role of the State*, Oxford University Press.

Botterill, L. C. and B. Chapman (2009), 'A Revenue Contingent Loan Instrument for Agricultural Credit with Particular Reference to Drought Relief', *Australian Journal of Labour Economics*, 12(2), pp. 181–196.

Chapman, B. and C. Ryan (2005), 'The Access Implications of Income-contingent Charges for Higher Education: Lessons from Australia', *Economics of Education Review*, Elsevier, 24(5), pp. 491–512.

Chapman, B. J. and T. Higgins (2009), 'An Income Contingent Loan for Extending Parental Leave', *Australian Journal of Labour Economics*, 12(2), pp. 197–216.

Chapman, B., T. Higgins, and J. E. Stiglitz (2014), *Income Contingent Loans: Theory, Practice and Prospects*, Palgrave Macmillan.

Denniss, R. (2003), 'Funding Sport Fairly: An Income-Contingent Loans Scheme for Elite Sports Training', The Australia Institute.

Hanushek, E. (2011), 'The Economic Value of Higher Teaching Quality', *Economics of Education Review*, 30(3), pp. 466–479.

Hanushek, E. (2014), 'What's A Good Teacher Worth? A Public Lecture by Eric Hanushek', 22 September, available at https://blog.cerge-ei.cz/?p=2586

John Quiggin's blog, available at www.johnquiggin.com

Kemp, D. and A. Norton (2014), 'Report of the Review of the Demand Driven Funding System', 13 April, available at http://education.gov.au/report-review-demand-driven-funding-system

Leigh, A. (2008), 'Returns to Education in Australia', *Economic Papers*, The Economic Society of Australia, 27(3), pp. 233–249.

Libich, J. and M. Macháček (2014), 'Do People Need Insurance by their Government or Against their Government?', under review.

Moss, D. (2002), *When All Else Fails: Government as the Ultimate Risk Manager*, Harvard University Press.

Norton, A. (2012), 'Graduate Winners: Assessing the Public and Private Benefits of Higher Education', Grattan Institute Report, August, available at http://grattan.edu.au/report/graduate-winners-assessing-the-public-and-private-benefits-of-higher-education

6 On fiscal policy rules and avoiding public debt crises

*If I owe you a pound, I have a problem; but if I owe you
a million, the problem is yours.*

Attributed to John Maynard Keynes, British economist, date and source unknown.

Economic concepts discussed

Easy-to-understand explanations of all the concepts listed below appear in the glossary
at the end of this book.

- Age dependency ratio
- Anchoring fiscal
  expectations
- Annuitisation
- Balanced budget rule
- Budget deficit/surplus
- Charter of Budget Honesty
- Credit rating

- Fiscal Commission
- Fiscal crisis
- Fiscal gap
- Fiscal policy
- Fiscal sustainability
- Government bonds
- Growth and Stability
  Pact

- Inflation targeting
- Maastricht Criteria
- Myopic agents
- Open market operations
- Ponzi scheme
- Public debt (gross/net)
- Ricardian equivalence
- Sovereign default

6.1 Motivation and overview

Since 2008, politicians across the globe have devoted most of their time to responding to
acute economic problems. This has unfortunately left most of them with little
'willpower' to address the root causes, and the big-picture problems in the pipeline. The
aftermath of the Global Financial Crisis (GFC) can therefore be compared to a fire brigade
extinguishing a fire and choosing to ignore the explosives in the house next door, which
could potentially bring about even more destructive blazes. Here is how it goes: 'Lots of
bad bank assets? Let's pour money into the banking system!', 'The European monetary
union not working? Let's bail out affected countries!', 'The **budget deficit** growing? Let's
cut expenditure on education and infrastructure to balance the books!'. Such a short-
sighted firefighting agenda, however, tends to be unsuccessful as it does not deal with
the underlying driving forces of the problems.

In this chapter, based on an interview recorded on 26 September 2012, Dr Stephen
Kirchner, from the Australian Financial Markets Association, discusses the main long-
run drivers, namely populist governance in combination with the demographic trend of
an ageing population. Apparent in most high-income countries (with Australia being one

of the few partial exceptions), this deadly combination of populism and ageing has led to an unsustainable **fiscal policy** stance and growing debt projections for decades to come. This results in a high degree of uncertainty and underperformance of the economy with a negative impact on people's wellbeing.

Dr Kirchner has knowledge of this topical economic policy area from several different perspectives. He has worked as an adviser to members of the Australian House of Representatives and Senate, as a Senior Lecturer at the University of Technology Sydney, as Research Fellow at the policy-oriented think tank Centre for Independent Studies, and Director of Economic Research with the financial company Standard & Poor's. His blog, Institutional Economics, has been ranked highly both on scholarly impact and policy influence.[1]

The discussion starts with an overview of the fiscal problem, i.e. the 'explosives' placed at the heart of most countries' public finances. And the time bomb of an ageing population that threatens to trigger the debt blaze. One of the implications is that in many countries **government bonds** are a risky asset, and the threat of **sovereign default** within one or two generations may not be negligible. The 2011 **credit rating** downgrade of the US government indicates this also (for more information, see *Washington Post*, 2011). Such reality is depicted in the cartoon below, taking inspiration from the classic Australian movie *The Castle*.

Concept by Jan Libich © 2015, drawing by Veronika Mojžišová. Used by permission.

---

1 See e.g. Mixon and Upadhyaya (2010). The full video-interview is available at **http://youtu.be/4XW4J3oTCig**. For more details regarding Dr Kirchner and his research, see **www.institutional-economics.com** and @insteconomics on Twitter. The views expressed in this interview are those of the interviewee and are not to be attributed to current or future employers.

The consensus on the gravity of the problem can be documented by the 2014 Global Risks report featuring assessments by more than 500 experts and policymakers at the World Economic Forum. The report sees 'fiscal crises' as the number 1 risk in terms of the perceived financial losses, ahead of all other geopolitical, societal, technological and environmental risks – see Figure 6.1. Furthermore, fiscal crises are perceived as likely to occur in the next 10 years.

The subsequent discussion focuses on ways of improving the discipline of politicians in conducting fiscal policy and thus ensuring the long-term sustainability of public finances. Dr Kirchner outlines his 2009 reform proposal (with Robert Carling, former

Figure 6.1: The 2014 Global Risks by the World Economic Forum, showing the likelihood and impact of various events. The possible answers of experts ranged from 1 ('very unlikely' and 'low impact') to 7 ('almost certain' and 'high impact')

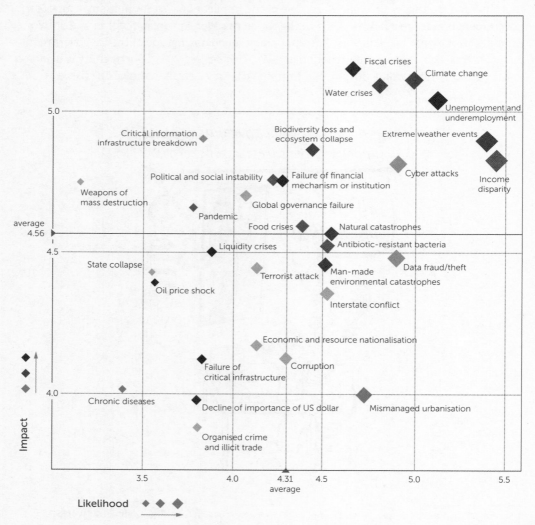

Source: WEF (2014).

Executive Director at the New South Wales Treasury), which aims to achieve these objectives. The proposal's underlying agenda is to increase the transparency of the budgetary process and thereby ensure greater accountability of politicians for the accumulation of debt. It attempts to align their incentives with the long-term public interest rather than follow their short-term populist 'instincts'.

The proposal consists of three main quantitative rules. The first one can be thought of as a loosely defined '**balanced budget rule**' limiting the size of budget deficits and surpluses to 2 per cent of GDP. The second rule stipulates the maximum value of net **public debt** to be 10 per cent of GDP. As Dr Kirchner explains:

> the rules are designed to interact and reinforce each other.
> You could actually run budget deficits just below 2 per cent of
> GDP for many years and still be consistent with our budget
> rule. So the idea of the net debt rule is to limit how long you
> can do that, while still giving governments the flexibility to
> run deficits for extended periods if necessary.

The third rule is a ceiling on the GDP shares of tax revenues and government expenditures, which is set at 25 per cent of GDP. It is motivated by the trend of recent decades in high-income countries, where the redistributive role of the government in the economy and in the lives of individuals has grown steadily. Figure 6.2 (see page 136) shows that this trend also has been apparent in Australia since the early 1990s (the drop in tax revenue from 2008 is largely due to the GFC). Despite this trend, Treasury (2013) reports that 'The Australian Government's total taxation revenue as a percentage of GDP averaged 22.5 per cent over the period from 1980–81 to 2010–11', suggesting that Dr Kirchner's rule is well within the bounds of Australia's past experience.

In summary, the proposed rules attempt to institutionalise sound budgetary processes, to provide 'a less discretionary approach to fiscal policy' as Dr Kirchner puts it. The discussion then considers the similarities and differences with the fiscal rules in the European Union, which seem to have failed in preventing fiscal excesses prior to 2008. The issue of accountability and automatic enforcement is key here, and one of Dr Kirchner's suggestions is the creation of an independent **Fiscal Commission**. He explains that it would 'conduct research into fiscal policy and monitor compliance with the rules. It would also enforce the rules in terms of imposing pecuniary penalties on politicians for breaching the rules, essentially a fine on all Members of Parliament.'

The latter feature is rather innovative, and Dr Kirchner mentions the experience of British Columbia in Canada where 'provincial politicians can have their salaries reduced significantly if they breach the fiscal rules'. In fact, since the proposal was published some countries have moved in this direction; for example, in Slovakia Members of Parliament's pay gets cut by 5, 10 or 15 per cent if the budget deficit is above 3, 5, or 7 per cent, respectively.

Figure 6.2: Australia's tax-to-GDP ratio over time by level of government, compared to the OECD average (the thin line at the top)

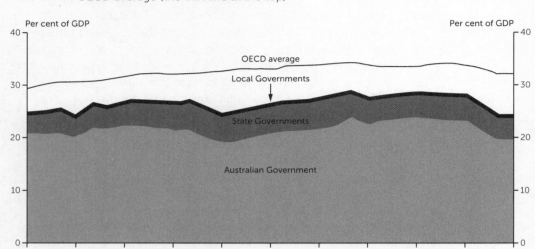

Source: Treasury (2013).

Many other topics are touched on in the interview. For instance, the importance of using a comprehensive measure of public indebtedness, the '**fiscal gap**', is debated. Reforms towards transparency and accountability that have occurred in monetary policy since the late 1980s are mentioned, and their lessons for fiscal policy highlighted. Their benefits include better guidance for the public, the so-called expectations 'anchoring'. The healthcare and pension systems in Australia are also discussed (for more, see Chapters 3 and 7, respectively), because the need to put them on a sustainable path is paramount. The GFC is covered too, including the effectiveness of fiscal stimuli.

6.2 The debate

Dr Jan Libich (JL): Let us start by summarising the key problem of public finances. What's wrong with the long-term setting of fiscal policy across the globe?

© Stephen Kirchner. Used by permission.

< Dr Stephen Kirchner (SK): I think that one of the problems with fiscal policy is that it's not focusing on what it's good at. In principle, tax and expenditure policy should be driven by microeconomic considerations. We want them to create good incentives for working, saving and investing; we want them to stack up on a cost/benefit basis. Unfortunately politicians tend to use fiscal policy for macroeconomic purposes, they use it to stimulate or restrain economic activity. That's something that fiscal policy is not very good at and it diverts politicians away from those microeconomic considerations.

JL: You are right that most economists consider fiscal policy to be unsuitable for short-term macroeconomic management – unless there is a major adverse shock such as the GFC. But even the minority of economists advocating discretionary short-term stabilisation fiscal policy agree that it has to be balanced over the long term, that it has to be sustainable. This does not seem to be the case in most countries.

SK: Yes, there's an issue around **fiscal sustainability** in that we know politicians have an incentive to spend more than the tax revenue they are bringing in at any particular time. And in a sense, Keynesian economics provides an intellectual justification for doing something that politicians have a temptation to do anyway, and that is to spend beyond their means.

JL: What exactly is driving this temptation?

SK: Well, it's an electoral incentive. Politicians feel that if they are spending on things that are popular this will help them get re-elected, and they can send the bill to future generations in terms of rising debt.

JL: But ultimately it must mean that voters are either not fully informed to be buying those excessive election promises, or short-sighted in that they do not care sufficiently about the negative consequences of such actions on their children. But in any case voters seem to encourage such inappropriate actions of politicians.

SK: Yes, there's a big question about how forward thinking voters really are. There's the idea of **Ricardian equivalence** which says that current voters understand this game. They recognise that debt must be paid for sooner or later, and when the government announces an unfunded fiscal stimulus they understand that the government is implicitly also announcing a future tax increase. And such Ricardian-type voters do not respond to the fiscal stimulus by increasing their spending, but by increasing their saving to pay for the future tax hike. This of course makes the fiscal stimulus ineffective. So empirically it's an interesting question as to how big that Ricardian effect is.

JL: Yes, there is only partial support for Ricardian equivalence in the data. The deviations from this theory could be due to, for example, existence of borrowing constraints or **myopic agents**. For example, one issue that many people seem to ignore is the trend towards an ageing population. What is that about?

SK: We have the baby boom generation hitting retirement age, starting around now. And this leads to an increase in the **age dependency ratio,**

which is the number of old people relative to the number of people still in the workforce.

JL: The changes seem very large quantitatively, going from six workers per pensioner a few decades ago to two or less in some countries by 2040 …

SK: It is a large change but there is a precedent for this, which was the post-war period. Countries experienced a big increase in the total dependency ratio when the baby boomers were children. And that didn't lead to a significant fiscal problem because the welfare state was much better contained in the early post-war period and government spending was more under control than it is now. So a big increase in the dependency ratio in itself is not necessarily a problem. The problem is unsustainable public expenditure that we have attached to this ageing population. So my view would be that you need to tackle this unsustainable expenditure profile.

JL: It is instructive to document the extent of the problem with some statistics. In the United States the budget deficit to GDP ratio is currently between 8 and 9 per cent, which may not seem like a big number. But it's a bit misleading because the government doesn't actually own the GDP. A more informative way to think about it is that out of every $3 the US government is spending, only $2 are financed through tax revenues and $1 (i.e. a third) must be borrowed.

SK: But if you look at the US, it was running **budget surpluses** up until the late 1990s.

JL: Under President Clinton …

SK: Yes. Then you had the recession in 2001 which sent the US federal budget into deficit, and the position really didn't recover. Then we went into the GFC and a very severe economic downturn, which I think is worse than the fiscal position. If you look around the world, the countries that have the worst fiscal policy outcomes are the countries that have had the worst recessions, so there is a big cyclical component to the US budget deficit. And it's actually hard to separate out the cyclical and the structural component.

JL: Well, there is a 2009 paper by the International Monetary Fund that calculates the fiscal cost of the GFC as a proportion of GDP and compares it to the impact of ageing populations. It finds that on average in G20 countries the impact of ageing populations on the fiscal position was over 400 per cent of GDP, which was 10 times higher than their estimate of the average fiscal cost of the GFC. So it seems to me that as far as fiscal crises go, the worst is yet to come. What are the possible solutions? You have a proposal with Robert Carling about reforming the fiscal legislation, what are your suggestions?

SK: Our proposal is in the Australian context. If you look around the world there are a number of countries that introduced fiscal responsibility legislation in the 1990s; for example, Australia, New Zealand, Canada and many of the Scandinavian countries. That was bringing in a more rules-based approach to fiscal policy, similar to what was being done with monetary policy at approximately the same time. In Australia we have the **Charter of Budget Honesty** which came into legislative force in 1998. What that did was to lay out some principles for fiscal policy; it didn't lay down any hard rules to what fiscal policy should consist of. The Charter said that the government should have a fiscal strategy, but it didn't actually say what that strategy should be.

JL: What is the strategy you suggest? What are your rules to strengthen fiscal discipline?

SK: What we have proposed is a more prescriptive approach to fiscal policy rules including some hard-and-fast enforceable rules. In the Australian context we firstly recommended a balanced budget rule, which says that budget deficits and surpluses need to be kept below 2 per cent of GDP.

JL: On a cyclically adjusted basis?

SK: No, we see this as being an annual constraint, and if you look historically at the budget outcomes for Australia going back to say 1970, you'd be able to accommodate most of the budget balances that we have seen historically within those parameters. As another measure we propose a net debt rule. It says that the net debt to GDP ratio should not exceed 10 per cent, which is again very close to the historical average for Australia since about 1970.

Finally, we propose a rule regarding the size of government. It says that the revenue and expenditure shares of GDP should be capped at 25 per cent. And this is in fact consistent with an existing policy which the current government says it's going to keep. So basically we just suggest a legislative rule that would formalise the government's existing policy commitment.

JL: In other words, you are trying to 'institutionalise' good fiscal policy rather than simply hope that all subsequent governments voluntarily deliver sound budgetary outcomes.

SK: Yes, it's a less discretionary approach to fiscal policy. And part of the reason for that is that we want to refocus fiscal policy back on what it's good at. Its focus should be on the role of tax and expenditure policy in conditioning microeconomic incentives, leaving macroeconomic stabilisation to monetary policy, which has a comparative advantage in that regard.

JL: Considering the three specific rules you propose, there seems to be an overlap between them. If a country is running balanced budgets it will automatically keep its debt in check …

SK: Well, the rules are designed to interact and reinforce each other. You could actually run budget deficits just below 2 per cent of GDP for many years and still be consistent with our budget rule. So the idea of the net debt rule is to limit how long you can do that, while still giving governments the flexibility to run deficits for extended periods if necessary.

JL: There have also been fiscal rules in the Euro area as part of the **Growth and Stability Pact**, among the so-called **Maastricht Criteria**, and they have not been effective. Can you outline the similarities and differences between the European rules and your rules?

SK: The Maastricht rules were designed to do two things. They were supposed to lay out convergence criteria that countries had to satisfy in order to gain Euro accession. But then they also attempted to hold the Eurozone together to avoid a situation where fiscal policy would blow up monetary policy. And in a sense fiscal policy rules in Australia would be designed to do the same thing. You want a fiscal policy regime that is going to support the monetary policy regime. Because if a government is running irresponsible fiscal policy, then it can effectively force the monetary authority to accommodate fiscal expansions. And as the European example shows, it's not just enough to have the fiscal rules. You need an enforcement mechanism that actually gets used.

JL: Do you propose such a mechanism to go with your rules?

SK: We do. The Eurozone had an enforcement mechanism as well, it just wasn't used properly. In 2003 and 2004 both Germany and France violated the rules and they were not held accountable under the Maastricht framework for those violations. This set a bad precedent which was followed by other countries and led to many of the existing problems. What this shows is that it's not enough to have the rules written down, you actually need a culture that says these rules must be enforced.

JL: How do you develop a culture like that in an institution that is fairly new, such as some European Union institutions?

SK: Well, I think the process of designing and implementing enforceable rules is one of the ways you can develop the culture. It's a reinforcing process. But rules by themselves are not going to be enough. If politicians are determined to violate the rules, and electorates don't hold politicians accountable for those violations, then no fiscal policy regime is going to be able to withstand that. Having said that, I still think the rules are important because they are part of creating the culture and the accountability mechanisms that you hope will restrain politicians.

JL: What kind of enforceability mechanisms do you suggest?

SK: In Australia we have proposed an independent Fiscal Commission which would conduct research into fiscal policy and monitor compliance with the rules. It would also enforce the rules in terms of imposing pecuniary penalties on politicians for breaching the rules, essentially a fine on all Members of Parliament. And it's not because we think politicians are necessarily going to be particularly responsive to that sort of pecuniary incentive. We see it as more of a non-pecuniary incentive. If you have an independent body imposing penalties on politicians, this involves a loss of reputation, and politicians guard their reputations quite jealously.

JL: So how would it work in practice? Suppose you have an independent Fiscal Commission similar to an independent central bank, what would happen if it comes up with an intergenerational report showing fiscal policy is unsustainable?

SK: Well, we do have intergenerational reports in Australia at the moment. Part of the problem with those reports is that they are prepared by the Treasury, and they are not seen to be independent of the government. This reduces the authority of those reports so we would expect that the Fiscal Commissioners would be compiling these reports. If you go back to the 2007 *Intergenerational Report* in Australia, it said very explicitly that over a 40-year horizon there was a large fiscal imbalance ('fiscal gap'), and that this would lead to unsustainable debt dynamics. The subsequent 2010 report never used the word 'unsustainable'; they fudged it a little bit.

JL: Despite the fact that the fiscal outlook overall seems, due to the GFC, worse in 2010 than in 2007 ...

SK: Well, actually, on the official Australian numbers the situation improved a little bit between 2007 and 2010, but it is still an unsustainable situation. So part of the role of an independent Fiscal Commissioner would be to comment on the sustainability of fiscal policy but also to then enforce the fiscal policy rules, to say to governments: 'You are in breach of the rules. Here is a penalty and here is what you need to do to get back on track. This is the magnitude of the required fiscal adjustment.'

JL: And that would be non-negotiable, the politicians would have to comply?

SK: Yes. The idea is to make these provisions enforceable. If you look at the existing Charter of Budget Honesty in Australia, the very first provision of that legislation says that nothing in the Charter of Budget Honesty will be subject to administrative or judicial review. So effectively the existing legislation says that there is no enforcement mechanism. Now you can't take politicians to court to make them adhere to the rules ...

JL: Do you think that was a deliberate feature of the Charter?

SK: Of course. Politicians are effectively saying: 'We'll have these fiscal principles but we're not going to lay down fiscal rules, and we're not even going to be accountable for the fiscal principles.'

JL: There are some countries that have gone further than Australia in their fiscal reforms, can you talk a little about them?

SK: New Zealand is a good example. It's still the case that the New Zealand legislation doesn't prescribe so much what the fiscal strategy should be, but it has very good transparency and accountability mechanisms built into it. The Netherlands is another example, with a very good independent fiscal authority that evaluates legislation in terms of its fiscal impact.

Generally speaking, the model we propose defines the parameters within which fiscal policy needs to be made. I don't think you can have a situation where an independent body is telling politicians what expenditure and taxation decisions to make, because governments are not going to surrender their responsibility for those. But what you can do is put parameters around the budget aggregates and the debt position and so on. In addition to ensuring fiscal sustainability, there is the benefit of tying down the public's expectations in relation to fiscal policy.

JL: The so-called 'anchoring' of fiscal expectations?

SK: Yes. Central banks have long recognised that such anchoring of (inflation) expectations is important for monetary policy, but governments haven't recognised it's equally important for fiscal policy. What makes large budget deficits and unstable debt positions harmful is not so much the actual numbers, not so much the existing fiscal policy. It's the public's expectation that future policy along the same lines is going to lead to serious problems and that is very destructive to economic confidence.

JL: Europe provides support for your argument. If you look at Spain and Ireland, their debt to GDP was fairly low up until recently, lower than the values for France and Germany. But they still got under debt pressures, largely due to the markets' assessment of their future. You mentioned monetary policy reforms of the past two decades, where we have observed a trend towards independence, transparency and accountability. You have done a lot of research in this area, can you briefly outline what happened and what monetary reforms can teach us about fiscal policy?

SK: The Reserve Bank of New Zealand (RBNZ) was really a pioneer in this respect in 1989, and since then there has been a move to make central banks more independent from the government. This was in recognition of the empirical literature which suggested that more independent central banks achieved better inflation outcomes. So countries wanted to take monetary policy out of the political arena and separate it from fiscal policy. And at the same time there was a move to a more rules-based approach to monetary policy. Rather than just making it up as you go along and responding to a wide range of macroeconomic variables in ways that were sometimes inconsistent, there was a much stronger focus on defining what monetary policy was trying to do. That new regime ended up being called **inflation targeting**.

The idea is that you want to target a low rate of inflation and this has the advantage of focusing monetary policy on something that it's good at. One thing we know is that monetary policy in the medium to long run can successfully tie down the price level, and thus also inflation expectations. And this actually makes the job of setting monetary policy much easier, because consumers and firms factor that into their price and wage setting.

JL: And they will therefore be less responsive to shocks, which will in turn enable the policymaker to stabilise them with smaller changes in interest rates. I formally modelled this effect in a 2011 paper. But whether it is really the case links back to the issue of accountability we discussed. In some countries the central bank governor is personally accountable for achieving the inflation target over the medium term. Can you think of a similar arrangement in the fiscal arena, can politicians be fired for breaching fiscal rules?

SK: I think the accountability mechanisms basically have to be reputational in nature with fines added to them. In British Columbia in Canada there is a regime where provincial politicians can have their salaries reduced significantly if they breach the fiscal rules. I think they take a 30 per cent pay cut while the state's finances are in breach of the given rules, not a bad incentive. That is the kind of model we have in mind, but I think the more important accountability mechanism is just a reputational one where you have a well-respected independent body criticising politicians. Because then politicians have to go to the electorate and justify their record, they want to be able to say: 'We've done a good job'.

JL: Let me ask about the implementation of your proposed rules in the presence of an ageing population. The pay-as-you-go pension and healthcare systems in most countries can be, in an ageing population, compared to a fraudulent multilevel marketing pyramid, the so-called 'Ponzi scheme'. In this scheme, existing members can only get paid through an inflow of (a growing number of) new members, otherwise they lose out. If politicians do not implement any systemic long-term reform, an ageing population implies that they are going to be faced with a budgetary shortfall that is increasing every year. This is because as the population ages, tax revenues shrink, while pension and healthcare expenditures go through the roof. In order to achieve a balanced budget they will have to do some short-sighted expenditure cuts – the sort of short-term austerity measures we are seeing in Europe. These usually turn out to be counter-productive by undermining economic growth. So would you agree that to achieve the fiscal rules countries actually need conceptual reforms of pensions and healthcare, which are usually unpopular politically?

SK: I think having rules and an independent enforcement mechanism gives politicians a commitment device. They can say to the voters: 'We are being forced to make these unpopular decisions because this is what the law requires us to do.' So it strengthens the hand of politicians who want to pursue responsible policies.

JL: Australia implemented a major reform of its pension (superannuation) system about two decades ago. Can you outline what this reform was about and whether it is working?

SK: Australia's pension system has two advantages. One is that we don't have a universal pension, we have a means-tested pension so not everybody is eligible. That puts Australia in a very strong fiscal position relative to countries where the pension is a universal entitlement. The other advantage is pre-funding, whereby the government mandates that a certain percentage of people's incomes goes into their personal superannuation account.

But I think there are still a lot of problems with our pension system. For example, there's an incentive for people to take their superannuation benefits as a lump sum, spend it on a new home or something like that and then become eligible for the old age pension. There is nothing at this stage to prevent people from doing that. So we need to look at not only what happens with the accumulation stage but also at the decumulation stage. There have been a number of very good proposals put forward by economists like Geoff Kingston, Hazel Bateman and John Piggott [for more, see Chapter 7] arguing for mandatory **annuitisation** of retirement benefits. I think the retirement system we have in Australia is good by international standards, but the international standards are very low, so we still have work to do in improving our system.

JL: I agree. One of the benefits of individual pension accounts is that people know how much they have saved up for retirement and they can therefore make better decisions. This is not the case in the pay-as-you-go system used in most high-income countries, which is not pre-funded. The current younger generations are contributing to the system, but due to the ageing population trend the system's deficit is growing so they are unsure how much they are going to get back.

SK: If you look at the US, people pay social security taxes, and the government takes that money and spends it. The social security liabilities that the United States is accruing are largely unfunded and this is part of the fiscal sustainability problem.

JL: Boston Professor Larry Kotlikoff and co-authors estimated the size of the US 'fiscal gap', which is a comprehensive debt measure including these sorts of implicit government liabilities, to be about 20 times more than the official public debt. And it is not just the United States, the story is similar for other countries – the fiscal problem is immense.

SK: Yes, I think it's enormously destabilising. Younger taxpayers know that their tax burden is going to increase, but they don't know how. This makes them reluctant to save and invest because they might be setting themselves up for a higher tax burden in the future. But on the other hand, these numbers are so bad that something is going to give; either politicians find the courage to address the problem or a **fiscal crisis** forces them to do so.

JL: Yes, but this can be very costly as the example of Greece shows, partly because such fiscal consolidation is designed in a hurry, and implemented at the worst possible time …

SK: Yes, on top of that Greece is in a monetary union and we know that if you have a fiscal contraction in a fixed exchange rate regime, that is going to be contractionary for economic activity. I think the problem for Greece is more being part of the Euro than the fiscal policy situation.

But I'm not convinced that a crisis is necessarily a bad time to implement fiscal reforms towards sustainability. Sometimes you can get better policy coming out of a crisis just because the situation demands it. We saw that in a number of countries. New Zealand, for example, basically had the International Monetary Fund knocking at its door in the early 1980s, which led to a series of dramatic reforms. The same occurred in Sweden in the early 1990s. Sweden had a very severe financial crisis but that led the country to implement a number of reforms which have meant that it's outperforming most of Europe today.

JL: The pension system is one big area, but unsustainable healthcare seems to be an even larger problem due to ageing populations, and there are really no good examples of how to reform it …

SK: It's certainly true that if you look at the intergenerational reports for Australia, a large part of the fiscal gap is attributable to future healthcare costs. This is one thing that we have not been very successful in containing so far, partly because while we means test the pension, we do not means test access to publicly funded healthcare.

JL: So even a multi-millionaire can rock up at a public hospital and get free healthcare …

SK: Yes, they don't qualify for the public pension but they do qualify for government-funded healthcare.

JL: How can we tame the runaway healthcare costs?

SK: Putting a means test to access to Medicare is one suggestion. There are, however, problems because by putting means tests on government benefits you can create very high marginal tax rates. So policymakers need to be careful not to create disincentives for labour force participation, and that's just a trade-off that has to be made.

JL: Let me ask one last question related to economic policy more broadly. Can you mention some policies that research suggests would improve overall wellbeing, but politicians have shied away from?

SK: In the area of fiscal and monetary policy, these can be further reformed in complementary ways. Chicago University Professor Scott Sumner's proposal for 'nominal GDP futures targeting' [Sumner, 2012a & b] is worth pursuing. Essentially, a futures market is established in the level of nominal GDP. The central bank then conducts **open market operations** so that the market's forecast for nominal GDP is consistent with the desired path. Effectively, the market determines the stance of monetary policy. It is a regime in which the market determines whether a given policy stance is effective or not. It is like a halfway house between free and central banking. It also makes clear that monetary policy is responsible for stabilising aggregate demand, allowing fiscal policy to focus on microeconomic incentives and long-run fiscal sustainability.

JL: Thank you very much Stephen for your insights and hopefully we will see countries following your advice regarding stronger fiscal rules and moving towards sustainable public finances.

6.3 Key economic insights and policy lessons

Economic insights	Implied policy lessons (for public officials and voters)
The short-term nature of the political cycle results in the politicians' temptation to spend beyond their means and accumulate debt.	Policymakers should try to tie the hands of future politicians by 'institutionalising' good policy practices.
The demographic trend of population ageing is a major threat to fiscal solvency, especially in countries with generous public pension, healthcare and welfare systems.	Policymakers should carefully consider the long-term budgetary implications of demographic trends in designing their policies in many areas.

Economic insights	Implied policy lessons (for public officials and voters)
Pay-as-you-go public financing in the presence of an ageing population acts as a Ponzi scheme, a fraudulent multi-level marketing pyramid.	Policymakers should move, where possible, away from pay-as-you-go schemes to pre-funded systems.
The size of the budget deficit is reported in proportion to GDP, which may be misleading since the government's revenues are only a relatively small part of GDP (below 25 per cent in Australia).	Policymakers should communicate economic statistics to the public in an intuitive and truthful way.
The most commonly used measure of public debt is flawed as it does not include all public liabilities. The 'fiscal gap' is more comprehensive as it is the expected present value of all future expenditures net of revenues.	Policymakers should use the fiscal gap and generational accounting in the setting of fiscal policy and its institutional framework.
The Charter of Budget Honesty in Australia prescribes that the government should have a fiscal strategy, but does not specify what the strategy should be.	Policymakers should explore ways to make their commitment to fiscal sustainability in the Charter of Budget Honesty more explicit and transparent.
If fiscal expectations are well-anchored, agents tend to adopt a longer-term perspective, which makes their behaviour more conducive to balanced economic growth.	Policymakers should strive to reduce uncertainty regarding future fiscal actions, and thus anchor fiscal expectations.
Explicit quantitative fiscal rules seem to work better than implicit ones in delivering fiscal discipline. Greater accountability can be enhanced through pecuniary penalties and enforcement by an independent fiscal watchdog.	Policymakers should legislate fiscal rules with automatic enforcement by an independent Fiscal Commission, and thereby provide themselves with a commitment device to help them resist short-term populist temptation.
If politicians and voters do not find the courage to address underlying fiscal imbalances, a debt crisis will force them to do so sooner or later, as we have seen in the case of Greece in the post-2008 period.	Policymakers should not postpone solutions to long-term problems until it is too late; they need to deal with them in a conceptual way and explain to the public why they are necessary.
Tax and expenditure policies are much better suited to creating good incentives for working, saving and investing than to reducing economic cycles.	Policymakers should design tax and expenditure policies primarily on the basis of microeconomic considerations; unless a major shock dictates their use for macroeconomic stabilisation.
Evidence in favour of Ricardian equivalence is mixed, most likely because some economic subjects are credit constrained and/or myopic.	Policymakers should support research into Ricardian equivalence to better design and predict the effect of fiscal policies on the behaviour of individuals and the economy.
While the public pension in Australia is means tested, access to public healthcare is not.	Policymakers should explore ways in which means testing could be implemented into the public healthcare system in an attempt to reduce its runaway costs.
In the aftermath of the GFC a hotly debated question has been: should governments save (to deal with long-term fiscal imbalances) or should they spend (to deal with the short-term economic weakness)? This question is inaccurate and misleading as it does not distinguish the policy horizon.	Policymakers should, in the post-2008 downturn, save and spend at the same time. They should first implement credible conceptual reforms of the pension and healthcare systems (i.e. long-term saving), and this will enable them to carry out short-term stimulatory spending. This is precisely the opposite of what many countries (e.g. in Europe) did during 2010–15.

6.4 Discussion questions

1   Using your own words, summarise the debate of Section 6.2 in three to five sentences.

2   Write down one idea discussed in the interview that you found new or interesting, or that you disagree with, and briefly explain why.

3   Write down one question on any topic covered in the interview that you would ask the speaker if you had a chance.

4   Consider the cartoon in Section 6.1 and explain the point to someone who has not read the section and does not have any knowledge of economics.

5   Examine Figure 6.1 from the perspective of a policymaker. Describe its key message to the public and explain what kind of policy improvement is implied by the data. Do the same for Figure 6.2.

6   Suppose you take part in a debating contest, in which the topic is the opening quote of the chapter attributed to John Maynard Keynes:

> *If I owe you a pound, I have a problem; but if I owe you a*
> *million, the problem is yours.*

Prepare a speech you would give for the affirmative side. Then (you or your classmate) prepare a speech for the negative side. If possible, organise an audience and perform the debate.

7   What does Dr Kirchner criticise about the way politicians use fiscal policy? He then argues that:

> *in a sense Keynesian economics provides an intellectual*
> *justification for doing something that politicians have a*
> *temptation to do anyway, and that is to spend beyond their*
> *means.*

What are your views on this?

8   Explain what 'Ricardian equivalence' means. Based on your research, to what extent is this theory supported by data? Write the main possible explanations for deviations from Ricardian equivalence and explain the mechanism behind them.

9   Using United Nations data available online, describe the trends in old-age dependency ratios in Australia and two other countries of your choice. Explain the driving forces behind these trends.

10 What does the observed demographic trend towards an ageing population imply about long-term fiscal outcomes and sustainability of public finances?

11 What is the connection Dr Kirchner makes between recent economic recessions and fiscal policy outcomes? Using the internet, list data for at least three countries to document his argument.

12 Plot on a graph budgetary outcomes for Australia and the US since 1970. Describe the observed trends and offer their explanations.

13 Dr Kirchner, together with Robert Carling, put forward a proposal about reforming Australian fiscal responsibility legislation (see the references). Outline the three rules

in the proposal and discuss their intended effect. Also highlight the suggested enforcement mechanism including pecuniary penalties for politicians.

14 Contrast the proposed fiscal rules with those in the European Union's Growth and Stability Pact. What are the similarities and differences? What could Australia learn from the European experience?

15 What would be the role of an independent Fiscal Commission suggested by Dr Kirchner? How do you think its independence from politicians can be ensured?

16 What does 'anchoring' fiscal expectations mean and why is it important?

17 Dr Kirchner is 'not convinced that a crisis is necessarily a bad time to implement fiscal reforms towards sustainability'. What is your view on that, and why?

18 Propose a set of policies that you think best promote long-term fiscal sustainability and ultimately people's wellbeing.

6.5 Where to find out more

Bateman, H., G. Kingston and J. Piggott (1993), 'Taxes, Retirement Transfers, and Annuities', *The Economic Record*, The Economic Society of Australia, 69(206), pp. 274–284.

Carling, R. and S. Kirchner (2009), 'Fiscal Rules for Limited Government: Reforming Australia's Fiscal Responsibility Legislation', Policy Monographs, available at **http://grattan.edu.au/report/mapping-australian-higher-education-2012/**

IMF (2009), 'Fiscal Implications of the Global Economic and Financial Crisis', International Monetary Fund, IMF Staff Position Notes, No 2009/13.

Kotlikoff, L. J. (2006), 'Is the United States Bankrupt?', *Review*, Federal Reserve Bank of St. Louis, July, pp. 235–250.

Libich, J. (2011), 'Inflation Nutters? Modelling the Flexibility of Inflation Targeting', *The B.E. Journal of Macroeconomics*, 11(1), Article 17.

Mixon, F. and K. Upadhyaya (2010), 'Blogmetrics', *Eastern Economic Journal*, 36 (Winter).

Sumner, S. (2012a), *The Case for Nominal GDP Targeting*, Mercatus Center, George Mason University, **http://mercatus.org/sites/default/files/NGDP_Sumner_v-10-copy.pdf**

Sumner, S. (2012b), 'Using Futures Instrument Prices to Target Nominal Income', *Bulletin of Economic Research*, 41, pp. 157–62.

The Inform Act, 'The Intergenerational Financial Obligations Reform Act', available at **www.theinformact.org**

Treasury, The (Australian Government) (2013), 'Australia's Tax System Compared with the OECD', *Pocket Guide to the Australian Tax System*, part 1, chart 2, available at **www.treasury.gov.au/Policy-Topics/Taxation/Pocket-Guide-to-the-Australian-Tax-System**

Washington Post (2011), 'S&P Downgrades U.S. Credit Rating for First Time', 6 August, available at **www.washingtonpost.com/business/economy/sandp-considering-first-downgrade-of-us-credit-rating/2011/08/05/gIQAqKeIxI_story.html**

World Economic Forum (2014), 'Global Risks 2014', available at **www3.weforum.org/docs/WEF_GlobalRisks_Report_2014.pdf**

7 Population ageing, pension systems and retirement financing

It's nice to get out of the rat race, but you have to learn to get along with less cheese.

Gene Perret, writer and producer, date and source unknown.

Economic concepts discussed

Easy-to-understand explanations of all the concepts listed below appear in the glossary at the end of this book.

- Active/passive asset management
- Annuity payment
- Asset meltdown hypothesis
- Cognitive decline
- De-accumulation of pension saving
- Defined-benefit system

- Defined-contribution system
- Discount rate
- Dividend imputation
- Fertility
- Housing affordability
- Income tax
- Indexation
- Life expectancy

- Notional Defined Contribution (NDC) system
- Pension pillars
- Pension system
- Population ageing
- Superannuation
- Tax break
- Tax churning

7.1 Motivation and overview

Imagine you live in one of the many countries using a 'pay-as-you-go' **pension system**. A given proportion is deducted from every fortnightly pay cheque, but the money does not go into your personal **superannuation** account to be used in the future (like it does in Australia). It goes to a common public pot of money from which the current retirees get their public pension that very same fortnight. The government has promised that when you retire at the age of 60 you will be eligible for a given (appropriately indexed) amount for the rest of your life. What happens to the government's promise when your country experiences lower birth rates and longer lifespans?

Professor John Piggott from the University of New South Wales, Australia's leading scholar in the area of **population ageing** and pension economics, offers an answer to this question in an interview recorded on 22 April 2014. Director of the ARC Centre of Excellence in Population Ageing Research, Prof. Piggott has extensive experience in advising governments on these matters – not only in Australia but also in Japan, Russia and Indonesia. His advice centres on designing pension systems that mitigate the adverse impact of demographic trends on the public purse and people's wellbeing.[1]

Prof. Piggott explains that, in an absence of a pension (superannuation) reform, the prospects of most countries are not looking good. Fewer children per family and higher **life expectancy** lead to an ageing population, whereby the number of workers contributing to the pension pot of money decreases and the number of pension recipients increases substantially. It does not take a mathematical genius to see that the system becomes unsustainable. A natural consequence, which we have observed recently in countries such as Greece, is that the government breaks its promises (as highlighted in the cartoon below). Policymakers must increase the pension age, tighten eligibility criteria and reduce pension benefits dramatically. Such actions do not only have a detrimental effect on the prosperity of retirees.

Concept by Jan Libich © 2015, drawing by Veronika Mojžišová. Used by permission.

---

1 The full video-interview is available at **http://youtu.be/omwYztSNIiE**. For more details regarding Prof. Piggott and his research, see **www.asb.unsw.edu.au/schools/pages/johnpiggott.aspx**

A mere expectation that this may happen down the track increases uncertainty in the economy and thus negatively affects the decisions of individuals and economic growth.

The discussion starts with an overview of the demographic trend observed in virtually all high-income countries and many low-income countries too. Prof. Piggott describes the two main pieces of this population ageing trend, namely decreases in **fertility** and increases in longevity. For example, he reports that:

> *Between 1980 and 2010 ... life expectancy at age 50 has*
> *exploded. In Australia's case, life expectancy at age 50 went*
> *up by seven years over this period.*

The number of children per family has decreased globally over the past half-century. As mentioned in the interview, 'the average world fertility decreased from five kids per family in 1950 to below 2.5 currently, and it is still dropping'.

These trends imply that the average age in the population increases, and so does the ratio of retirees to workers – see Figure 7.1. In the 1960s, high-income

Figure 7.1: The old-age dependency ratio, defined as population aged 65+ divided by population aged 15–64, for G7 countries, Australia and less developed regions based on the United Nations definition

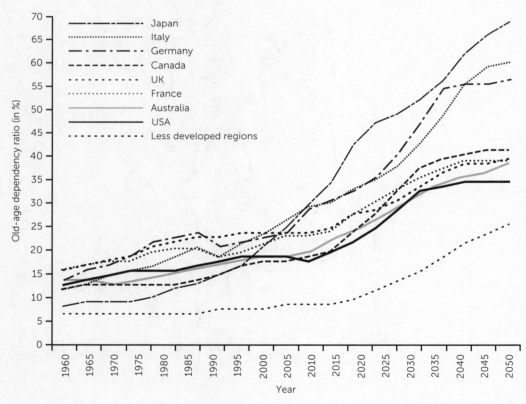

Source: United Nations, 1960–2010 actual, 2011–2050 forecast.

countries generally had more than six workers per retiree, whereas currently it is around three to four (slightly higher in Australia), and projections imply another halving within four decades. Prof. Piggott highlights the estimate for Japan, the fastest-ageing country, which is predicted to have an extraordinary 1.2 workers for every retiree by 2050.

Prof. Piggott then outlines the resulting problem for the pay-as-you-go public pension system, in which governments have made 'very generous pension promises'. He goes on to highlight how governments tend to break these promises by altering the parameters of the system, often in a hidden way. The interview then focuses on existing pension systems and whether or not they are pre-funded, which makes them largely immune to the ageing population trend. Prof. Piggott also describes how globalisation leads to 'weakening of family commitment' in terms of children's support for parents, which has major retirement implications:

> There are 150 million regional migrants in China – people
> who have moved out of rural areas into urban areas.
> They send money back home for some time, but it would
> be a big ask for many of them to return home and look
> after frail parents.

Prof. Piggott then goes on to explain why 'markets work very badly unstructured' in the pension area, and why countries need strong governance, a solid financial system and well-designed government regulation. Importantly, he brings to the fore some of the pension system challenges facing Australia in the decades to come. This is despite the fact that the Australian superannuation system is among the best in the world. Prof. Piggott discusses some areas for improvement when outlining his 'ideal' pension system.

The discussion also covers other implications of an ageing population, in areas as diverse as healthcare, psychology, the construction sector and finance. The specific issues discussed are, for example, the relevance of the **'asset meltdown hypothesis'**, the ineffectiveness of **'tax churning'**, the puzzling 'equity home bias' (French and Poterba, 1991), the development of Australian real estate prices, the way forward for long-term care, the effect of **cognitive decline**, and the demographic (as well as technological) drivers of rapidly rising healthcare costs. The message is that tackling these issues without delay is important for social welfare, and for ensuring long-term fiscal sustainability. Figure 7.2 shows that there is no time to waste as the size of the fiscal imbalance is very large in most countries. Specifically, it demonstrates that primary budgets balances need to move permanently into large surpluses in order to stabilise debt.

Figure 7.2: Fiscal gaps (unfunded liabilities) in selected countries: permanent change in the underlying primary balance to GDP needed to reduce gross financial liabilities to 50% of GDP in 2050 (a positive number indicates a required surplus). The dark columns show the gaps in an absence of pension and healthcare reforms, the light columns assume health and pension spending to remain constant as a share of GDP.

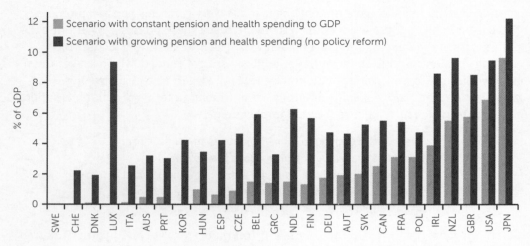

Source: Merola and Sutherland (2013). Used by permission.

7.2 The debate

Dr Jan Libich (JL): Let's start with the basics: what's all this fuss about population ageing, and what does it have to do with the pension system?

© John Piggott. Used by permission.

< Prof. John Piggott (JP): Population ageing has two important pieces to it: increasing lifespan – people are now living a lot longer – and people having fewer children. Both of those changes in the way human lives are being played out have a dramatic effect on the institutions we have around pensions and retirement.

JL: So what's the problem financially?

JP: Well, many countries have very generous pension promises that governments have made and they finance those pension promises from workers. The workers pay a contribution and when it comes to retirement they receive a retirement income. But the retirement income that they receive is actually being financed by the newer generation; the younger generation of workers who are making their contribution. We call this system 'pay-as-you-go' (PAYG).

JL: So the contribution doesn't actually go to an individual account of that person, it just goes to a common pot of money?

JP: It goes to a common pot of money. In some (not many) countries reserves are built up because you'll go through a period where there are a lot of workers and relatively few retirees and then that might switch and you might have fewer workers and lots of retirees. So there may be a build-up of reserves through that first period but that's very different than pre-funding. It's very different from a situation where an individual might save assets to accumulate for his own retirement.

JL: So if we have fewer workers and a lot more retirees due to population ageing, could it be that someone has contributed all their working life towards their pension but the money dries out and there's really no pension that the government can pay that person?

JP: Well, that's very extreme but I think it's certainly true that there is a problem. We must make a number of distinctions. Let's think about developed economies; for example, in Western Europe, or in North America, the US or Canada. What's been happening there is that some of the promises are broken. It's not that you don't get any pension anymore; I think that's a very unlikely scenario. But, for example, pensions are indexed in a less favourable way. A lot of pensions were initially indexed to wage growth, so as wages increased in the community at large, pensions would go up. Then countries switched that saying: 'No, we can't afford that. We'll only index to prices.'

JL: That effectively amounts to cutting the pension …

JP: Yes, that's a form of a pension cut. Or they'll say: 'Well, we promised this at age 60 but we can't really afford that anymore, so we're going to move that to 65.' Or they'll say: 'We have this survivor benefit (once you die) for your spouse. That used to be three-quarters, we'll make that two-thirds.'

JL: So these are all hidden ways in which governments break their pension promises …

JP: These are all hidden ways of reducing the pension liability that these countries are confronting. The underlying reason is that a financing problem already occurs in some countries like Japan, Germany, Italy, and is anticipated to occur in many other countries. The only way to solve that financing problem, other than by breaking promises, is to increase contribution rates. The increase in contribution rates would be a big negative around labour supply. So countries are now finding themselves between a rock and a hard place with demographic transition.

JL: You mentioned population ageing that's underlying a lot of this, and you're Director of the Australian Research Council Centre for Population Ageing Research (CEPAR). Can you outline what the Centre does?

JP: I got involved with pension economics in the early 1990s and once I'd been in that area for five years, it was clear to me that this was a multidisciplinary issue. For example, the link between retirement and health; immediately you bring in healthcare. The link between trying to manage your own financial assets in retirement and cognitive decline; immediately you're looking at economics, you're looking at psychology. The whole question of where increases in life expectancy come from is a demographic question, it's an actuarial question, it's an epidemiological question – not an economic question. That's very interesting.

Let me take that last example. If you take the period between 1950 and 1980, in many countries life expectancy at birth increased, but life expectancy at age 50 didn't do very much. Between 1980 and 2010, life expectancy at birth has sort of continued to trend up a little, but life expectancy at age 50 has exploded. In Australia's case, life expectancy at age 50 went up by seven years over this period. That's huge! And all of that is pension years, all of that is liability for pensions because most of that increase in life expectancy occurs after people expect to retire.

JL: Let us consider the way forward for the pension system, what can be done?

JP: Well, one possible approach is to think about countries' stages. So, if you go back a few centuries in Europe, or if you go back half a century in much of Asia, you have economies and social systems where people didn't move very much. People pretty much worked until they couldn't work anymore. And as the most important source of 'old-age support', they relied on their family which was close by. That's changed completely, families now scatter. We have a globalised economy and with that distance comes a weakening of family commitment. Asia is very keen on promoting the idea of filial piety – and support for parents – but that's beginning to break down.

There are 150 million regional migrants in China – people who have moved out of rural areas into urban areas. They send money back home for some time, but it would be a big ask for many of them to return home and look after frail parents. And as soon as you stop relying on the family, what else is there to rely on? Well, there's markets, but markets work very badly unstructured in this area. You can make markets work in certain circumstances, but you need strong governance, you need a strong financial system and you need good government regulation to make that work. And again, that's one of the challenges at the moment for Australia. If you don't have that, the only other way is to have direct government payments, and that's where most countries have gone over the last century.

JL: We should mention that the government getting involved in the pension system is the idea of the government acting as a risk manager. There's a financial 'risk' that everyone's facing – that they'll live for a long time and the assets that they have accumulated are not going to be enough. Through the public pension system the government's effectively insuring people and saying: 'If you live longer, we're going to look after you and pay you more than you have contributed using the money of those less fortunate who die younger.' But again, the demographic trend is making this system unsustainable because most people live longer.

JP: Well, it depends how you do it, but yes. The sorts of pension promises that were made in Germany and elsewhere were very generous – the 'pension access age' started quite early and people were living very long with these very generous pensions, which were not flat rate. They were geared to your final salary or maybe the average of the best 10 years of your career – and that's become unsustainable. Germany at the moment spends 10 per cent of GDP on pensions.

JL: Australia's figure is a third of that ...

JP: Yes, Australia's figure is about 3 per cent, so you can see how different that is. Some of the difference is that Australia is a younger country population-wise. Some of it is also the nature of the pension promise that is made.

JL: It is worth highlighting the magnitude of the effect. If we look back 40 years ago, there were six to seven workers per one retiree in high-income countries. The ratio is now half of that, between three and four. What's the projection for 40 years into the future?

JP: A number that strikes me is the Japanese number. It's now around 2.5 workers for every retiree, and it is predicted to be 1.2 by 2050. How can you manage that? That seems extraordinary.

JL: Yes, it is a major concern. We talked about the pay-as-you-go public system, which is the first '**pension pillar**' based on the World Bank classification. In contrast, Australia has most of the emphasis on the private second pillar. Can you briefly describe what it's about?

JP: I like to think about the pillars as follows. The first pillar is around poverty alleviation and that's almost always government-run. Now if you do that in a way that is linked with everyone's wages, then high-wage people get a lot of money and that's costly to whatever source it is – the current workers' contributions in most cases. What we did in Australia was to have a flat rate pension set at a level which takes most people out of poverty. The second pillar is then around income replacement, and the third pillar is around encouraging further saving through **tax breaks**. The third pillar is voluntary whereas the second pillar is usually compulsory, in most countries also pay-as-you-go (although not in Australia).

Many countries now combine the first two pillars. They have a social security system which is paid out of current tax dollars and is linked to income, and it's got a minimum associated with it as the poverty alleviation piece. But you've got to contribute to belong. So that means if you don't contribute, you fall outside that net. And you still have an old-age poverty problem – lots of people fall outside the net.

So what we did in Australia – and I'm a strong advocate of this – is to take that poverty alleviation piece and make it a flat rate at a level that's just enough to take people out of poverty. But we'll means test it, so if you're very rich you won't get it. It's not like many means tests around the world, which is sort of targeting a payment at someone who is destitute. What it does is it excludes the affluent; I think of it as 'affluence tested'. And that saves maybe a third of the bill relative to something which is available to everyone.

JL: And we do want progressivity built into the system ...

JP: Yes, there's some progressivity in that. Basically, it's taking a lot of people out of old-age poverty. Half the elderly population get a full pension, a quarter get nothing and a quarter get something in-between – they're the rough numbers. And that seems to work pretty well for us. As you said earlier, at the moment that's costing us 3 per cent of GDP, and in 2050, even after our population ages, it will cost us 5 per cent of GDP or thereabouts. Belgium, by contrast, will be paying 17 per cent of GDP on pensions in 2050. So when people say 'What we have is unsustainable as a pension system in Australia', I'm never persuaded.

JL: The reason the pension bill is fairly small is that we have an emphasis on the private second pillar.

JP: Yes, although we had the first pillar for a long time and no second pillar, we had that aged pension for a long time before we made income-related pensions compulsory in the 1980s and 1990s. In fact, we've had the aged pension since 1909, which is early on; not too many countries had anything prior to that. It's worth noting that nine years after Federation we had an aged pension system – it's quite an achievement in a way.

JL: And we didn't have a population ageing problem back then.

JP: Back then we did not have a population ageing problem!

JL: So, in terms of the second pillar, how does that work? It's private, it's funded ...

JP: Yes, we have something which I think of as 'pre-funded', only a few countries have this. It's requiring individuals to save for their own retirement through the workplace, which has to put a portion of wages into a separate account administered by a registered insurance company or wealth management firm. The contributions accumulate and when you reach the point you need it, which is pretty much after the age of 60 except in exceptional circumstances, you have a lump sum you can use towards your retirement. That's how it works.

JL: So it is a **defined-contribution system**, not a **defined-benefit system**?

JP: Yes. When we talk about the superannuation guarantee in Australia, the only thing that's guaranteed is the contribution, not the benefit.

JL: Some countries tend to define both the contribution and the benefit, but ageing creates a discrepancy between the two.

JP: That's right. If you pre-ordain the benefit relative to salary and then social or economic circumstances change, like you're going to live for longer, or interest rates are lower, then the only way you can make that system continue to balance is to vary the contribution. If you've preset both, you're going to have a system which is potentially unsustainable.

JL: There are a number of ways that individual pension accounts can be set up. We have in Australia what's called the Financial Defined Contribution (FDC) system, which is pre-funded. Some countries have gone the route of not having it managed by the private sector, but having a government-run scheme with 'non-financial' individual accounts. How does that work?

JP: The non-financial, sometimes more commonly called the **Notional Defined Contribution (NDC) system**, is usually a place countries go as a way of systematically modifying the unsustainable promises they previously made. So you begin with a defined benefit pay-as-you-go system. You've made this promise and now you realise that demographic change is going to make that promise unsustainable.

So you say: 'We're going to reform the pension system and pretend that you have accumulated an amount of money through the contributions you have made in working life. We're going to come up with a notional asset value at the end of your working life. And then we're going to pretend that you buy an annuity priced in terms of your life expectancy, prevailing interest rates and so forth, and whatever the value is, that's what we'll give you.' So, no longer are we making a defined benefit promise, we're making a promise based upon a notional accumulation. That's why it's called a notional defined contribution.

JL: The money may still not be there …

JP: The money is not there.

JL: But at least people know how much they've contributed to the system.

JP: Yes, what they don't know is how much they're going to get. But it is still a more systematic way of doing the reforms than other countries have done in the way that I was describing earlier – by raising the retirement age, by changing the **indexation** or the survivor benefit. Instead of doing that, you're saying: 'Now it's all up for grabs, we're going to pretend this is in the market and offer you what the market might have offered.'

JL: And the advantage of doing it more systematically is that you can have some kind of in-built sustainability processes. Some countries have a reserve fund, some countries have a 'balancing mechanism', can you describe that?

JP: What happens there is those countries say: 'Well, we're not going to leave this completely up to the market. If interest rates go down, we're not going to reduce your **annuity payment** automatically; however, if things get too bad we'll introduce this balancing mechanism where everything suddenly gets changed.' Japan has done that, Sweden has done that.

JL: How does it work? When you add up all the liabilities and assets of the system and the liabilities exceed the assets …

JP: Yes, by some margin then there's some sort of cut-off.

JL: Across the board?

JP: That's right.

JL: Some people argue that the system where the government gets involved might in some ways be superior. I interviewed Professor Bruce Chapman [Chapter 5] who was the architect of the Australian system of government-run student loans contingent on income. One of the advantages of the system is that the government can do it in bulk and use the existing tax system for collection, which turns out to be much cheaper than if student loans are financed through private banks.

JP: Indeed, and I think the private pension system that we have is expensive in terms of the administrative burden.

JL: What are the average costs of pension funds in Australia?

JP: Oh, they vary a lot, but the average is between 1 and 2 per cent of assets. One reason there's a large range is we're pushing individuals to take more control. This is something that is happening worldwide – highlighting individuals' responsibility for their own retirement. That means they've got to know stuff they never used to have to know, and there is an advice market. So an important reason why some of these are expensive and others cheap is that the expensive ones usually come with advice. The advice may or may not be good, but that's an important component of the underlying cost which is missing in the cheaper funds.

JL: It seems that another part of the cost is **active asset management** on the part of the fund.

JP: Yes, that doesn't always happen, but that's true.

JL: Critics of the system say that there should be a lot more emphasis on **passive investment**, e.g. through index funds.

JP: I think there's good sense to that, because administrative costs can make quite a big difference. They don't sound like a lot because they're expressed as a proportion of assets, but that means actually they're a deduction from the rate of return. So if you have a system which is offering you, let's say 5 per cent and then you add on an extra 1 per cent of costs, so now it's 4 per cent, that can make a big difference.

JL: I presume you're talking in nominal terms, so in real terms (adjusted for inflation) that might make an even bigger difference …

JP: Yes, in real terms you might be going from 2 to 1 per cent. You get to retirement the fees can make a difference of 30 per cent or more in how much you've accumulated. So it's more significant than people think, and it is a legitimate reservation about the arrangement that we've come to in Australia.

JL: There may be some other potential disadvantages we will touch on later, but let's think about the advantages of the system compared to unfunded pay-as-you-go systems. You pointed to the transparency – people can see how much they've saved. Are there any other advantages?

JP: For me, the important advantage is its sustainability. As I said earlier, when people tell me the Australian pension system is not sustainable I can't really believe it when you look at these comparative numbers. I think what we have is a system which is sustainable for half a century, maybe longer, maybe a century, over which time fertility behaviour could alter dramatically. There are assumptions made about what fertility will be like in 2050 or 2080 but you're talking about the fertility behaviour of women who are yet to be born. I think that's a very risky thing to do.

JL: So we might go back to having four or five kids? People sometimes criticise these predictions for ageing as based on shaky numbers, but it seems to be one of the most robust facts in economics that when people get more prosperous, fertility rates go down. There's been an immense change in this respect; the average world fertility decreased from five kids per family in 1950 to below 2.5 currently, and it is still dropping. Many high-income countries have fertility rates around 1.3–1.4 (1.9 in Australia), well below the replacement rate of 2.1 needed to stop the population from shrinking in the absence of immigration.

JP: Yes, there's never really been a comprehensive study to explain why fertility rates decline in different countries at different times. Everybody knows that Japan has the oldest population in the world. The reason is its fertility plummeted in 1952 or 1953. Why did it plummet then, and not 10 years later like in Australia? Well, that's not clear. It would be very interesting to put together a study which looked at the timing of fertility declines around the world, because that would tell us a lot about what the underlying causes of fertility are. But you're right that population ageing is a global phenomenon, that median age is going up in almost every country in the world, and that the two reasons for that are people living longer and having fewer kids. That's certainly the case.

JL: It seems that another advantage of the Australian superannuation system is its flexibility. You can choose the fund that you're going to accumulate your savings through; you can choose the investment strategy, so more risk-averse people can be more conservative in their investment; you can retire earlier if you have accumulated enough assets and so on.

JP: It is more flexible and its flexibility is, other things equal, good. There's a lot of evidence though that people aren't all that wonderful at committing to things that are a long way off. We all know that.

JL: And it's getting worse, actually. There is some evidence that a generation ago people were a little bit more patient – they had a lower **discount rate**, using the economics term.

JP: Yes. I gave a talk at Hong Kong University of Science and Technology last week, and I said: 'If I asked you before this session begins whether you're going to have an apple or a chocolate brownie at morning tea, you'll tell me an apple. When you go out at morning tea time, you'll have the chocolate brownie.' The idea of committing in advance is at odds with flexibility. So I think that's one reason why we have these kinds of mandatory pension schemes. If we really believed people made optimal decisions throughout their whole lives then social security would not exist.

JL: This is one of the things that critics point out: 'Why do we need the government to get involved in the first place? Why do we have to mandate people's pension savings?' So in your answer you would point to the psychology, to our impatience?

JP: I think that's the reason. We'd be prepared to pay something to organise a commitment to the future. And that's what we're doing with social security and what we're doing with the Australian superannuation system. Some say it's costly. Yes it is, but it does ensure there's something there when you're 65 or even 80. That's a whole new issue around cognitive decline, an open area of policy debate.

JL: One of the things that gets debated about the Australian system is fairness and equity. Is it fair that when someone passes away prematurely the family can inherit the savings? Is it a good thing or a bad thing?

JP: I am an advocate of greater equality and if you came to me with a credible proposal to increase aged pension benefits, for example, or to say that instead of the top quarter not getting it, maybe the top third should not get it, I think you'd be able to persuade me if the case was a reasonable one. I think there are two pieces that people miss in this whole question of inequality. The first is that if you take taxes and transfers and compare how the dollars go from rich to poor between Australia and other OECD countries, we are by far the best. We are the most efficient at getting rich tax dollars into the hands of the poor, and an important reason for that is that we do not have conventional social security which pays benefits to rich people. It is not the only reason, but it is an important reason.

JL: I think it says something about how bad other countries' systems are, because there's a lot of middle-class welfare in Australia. There's a lot of tax churning, an inefficient phenomenon whereby the same person pays taxes and receives government benefits. Last year's study by the Centre for Independent Studies (Baker, 2013) estimated that half of all government expenditure in Australia can be attributed to tax–welfare churning.

JP: That's true. I'm not saying we're perfect by any means. There's huge room for improvement and we could do more to rein in middle-class welfare – I agree with that entirely. But I find much of the debate around inequality and retirement incomes in Australia rests on the notion of tax expenditures associated with superannuation payments. Superannuation is tax-preferred and the tax expenditure estimates that are generated presume that the best system, or the benchmark system, is a comprehensive **income tax**. Well, it just isn't! We don't want a comprehensive income tax; it's never existed anywhere and countries which have tried to approximate it have done badly. It's extremely bad for growth, it's extremely bad for asset allocation.

JL: Because of labour market distortions?

JP: Yes, because it messes up the ways in which different assets are taxed. The owner-occupied housing, for example, is always omitted. That's a major lifecycle asset. If you tax the only other major lifecycle asset – your pension accumulation – very differently, then people will move into housing. And that happens. So the housing market goes out of control then. You need a system which recognises that there are some kinds of saving and investment for your retirement, it's not for a trip next year or something. And that needs to be treated so that the tax system does not distort the prices of that future consumption from the price of your present consumption.

To do that, you need not a tax on income, but a tax on expenditure. Once you do that, these enormous numbers that people quote as to the cost or the lack of sustainability of the superannuation system go away. Not completely, and we could improve it, we could make it more like an expenditure tax than it is, but the vast bulk of it, the big quantitative wave of that argument goes away. So I think there are two things that get missed. First of all, we do well, comparatively speaking, in getting rich tax dollars to the poor in terms of transfers. And secondly, we should not be using comprehensive income as a benchmark to measure the tax cost of superannuation or owner-occupied housing.

JL: It's true that the general sales tax or some kind of indirect taxes, which are less distortionary, are much higher in most European countries than they are in Australia.

JP: That's true. And we could use more of that; we're going to have to use more of that, because we're going to need more taxes with an ageing population. Whether it's healthcare or pensions or whatever, we're going to need more, and we're going to have to increase consumption taxes such as the GST.

JL: As part of the flexibility of the Australian system, it was mentioned earlier that people can actually choose their investment strategy. One thing that has puzzled economists is that people tend to invest too much into domestic assets as opposed to foreign assets, the so-called 'equity home bias'. Why does this occur and is it a problem?

JP: Yes. It's less of a case in Australia than it is in many other countries, but it can be a problem. I think it happens in Australia for two reasons. First of all, we have a corporate tax which pays **dividend imputation** to Australians – not to people overseas. So there's a kind of tax advantage to buying an Australian equity relative to a foreign equity.

The second thing is the exchange rate risk that a superannuation fund faces if it decides to invest heavily overseas. You can cover exchange rate risk, you can hedge it in short periods such as a year or three years. But often the assets and liability matching are around 25–30 years. A 40-year-old is going to need this when they're 65, right? So you don't want to take too much risk on the exchange rate when that's the pattern of liabilities you're going to have to meet. Now, it's probably the case that it would be better if we invested more broadly than we do, but they're the two reasons why I think there is this home bias in investing that you observe in Australia.

JL: Let me ask a broader question about country-specific risks. The recent banking and sovereign crises in countries such as Cyprus, Iceland and Greece highlighted the fact that many countries have some kind of economic weakness. It seems to me that an appropriately designed pension system with pre-funding is well suited to reduce the country-specific risks by foreign diversification of the accumulated pension savings. If the country gets in trouble, people might lose their job and income for some time, but at least they do not lose their pension invested in foreign assets. But the public pay-as-you-go financed first pillar does not allow that; in fact, it exacerbates the domestic risks because people can lose much of their pension as well if their country gets into fiscal stress. This in turn deepens the economic downturn and makes job loss more likely. It seems to me that this foreign diversification advantage of the capital accumulation pension system is not discussed sufficiently.

JP: That's true, that's a fair point. I think there's something to be said for what I call 'system diversity'. If you're relying on the government for the first poverty alleviation pillar, then maybe it's worth relying upon the market for the second pillar. And then the government could let you down or the market could let you down, but maybe they both won't let you down. It gives you a bit of risk diversification like that.

JL: This touches on the issue of what the 'optimal' system should look like. If you could design a pension system from scratch for some country, what kind of attributes would it have – in addition to being a combination of the public and the private sector?

JP: I think that's the first thing. I think our tax system is very messy in Australia and I think the way we deal with distribution of the saved assets, the **de-accumulation**, is just not present. We need to do a lot more work in policy there. But if you fixed those two things up, the broad design of the Australian system is very close to what I would advocate if I was starting *de novo*.

I'd have a flat rate pension which is non-contributory, like the Australian aged pension. So you don't have to be a member or pay anything. It's there if you are resident for some period of years to prevent people coming for six months and picking it up. I think the figure in Australia is 10 years. Resident for 10 years, you're entitled to this, subject to the other means that you might have. That makes good sense to me.

I think then you need pretty tight tapers. So you need to set this at a minimal level which takes people out of poverty and when you get to it, you need a tight taper that is probably tighter than what we have now. It's probably 60 to 70 per cent. I know people say that's a very high effective marginal tax rate, but it's affecting fewer and fewer people. The tighter you have it, the fewer people are around that income area. Probably not 100 per cent, but it could be tightened. So that would be the first piece that I would have. I would also index the payment to wages. But the age should be indexed to life expectancy at age 60 or 65.

JL: Not life expectancy at birth?

JP: Not at birth. I think you need to take account of sudden increases in life expectancy. In such cases retirement age gradually goes up as life expectancy goes up. Not the amount that's paid, but the access age. I think that needs to be indexed, that's where I would begin. And then I would have a system not that dissimilar from ours, but I would have the specification of the payment as the amount going into the account. So we have a superannuation contribution of 9 per cent of wages at the moment, going to 12 per cent. But from the payment that the employer makes to the insurance company or fund, fees are taken out before it ends up in the account. I think it's better, instead of 12 per cent, to specify 10 per cent, let's say, but the 10 per cent is net. The 10 per cent ends up in the account.

The tax treatment would also differ in my preferred scheme. There would be no fees on the superannuation contribution or the fund investment earnings. So the fund goes away and earns and invests your money and only when you retire, you pay tax. You pay an income tax on whatever you draw out. So it's just treated under the normal income tax. That way you get progressivity, you get a taxation of the benefit. And you get, in the situation where you have a demographic change, the government picking up revenue from those benefits at the same time that it's facing liabilities for things like healthcare. We currently have a different kind of tax system. We don't do anything about the income stream in retirement, which is another piece that I think we should have. We need better income streams than we currently have, exactly how I don't know, but there should be more than we have. So I think those things I would have as part of my ideal system, but I think we've got the building blocks in Australia now.

JL: How can a country that already has the first pay-as-you-go pillar move successfully on to this system? Australia implemented its private second pillar more than 20 years ago …

JP: Well, Australia didn't have a social security system. It had this flat-rate aged pension so it never had to replace a social security system with something pre-funded, and that was a huge advantage for us. Now, two or three other countries have done something similar and they've done it from scratch, pretty much. The Netherlands and Switzerland both have pre-funding and they both pretty much did it from the beginning.

Chile is a country which has started with a social security system and changed it around. And it's getting there. It's better than it was, but it's been very hard. I think some of the reasons it's been hard in Chile relate to its stage of development. Although Chile is a middle-income country and coming along well, it's got quite a large informal sector. And people noted that when they converted, they gave what they called 'recognition bonds' to people who'd made payments into the old social security system. So you began with an asset in the new defined-contribution system, and then that accumulated further with your contributions.

And people looked at these contributions and said: 'Oh, membership is very high.' But they didn't look at what's called the density of contributions.

So people would work for a few months in the formal sector and then they would go work in the cash economy for a few years and then they'd come back and work formally for a few months. So when it came to maturity time, which was 20 years, and people started looking at payouts, the payouts were virtually nothing. Because people had not contributed continuously for the 20 years as everyone had assumed they would, they had contributed for three or four.

JL: You've just identified one of the important prerequisites for the system to work, and that's the country having stable and transparent institutions including quality legal and administration systems.

JP: I think that's actually true in both a pay-as-you-go system and in a pre-funded system. Pay-as-you-go systems can be completely messed up by governments – and they have been – particularly in the developing world, but we've talked about how promises have been compromised in the developed world as well. So that can happen without strong governance and unless you have strong governance around the financial sector and considerable financial sophistication, these very long-term contracts on investment and saving that you're talking about with retirement income are very difficult to guarantee.

JL: That's precisely why many countries that are trying to move in the direction of pension system sustainability and have implemented some Australian-type second pillars seem to be back-tracking now. The Hungarian government nationalised a large chunk of private pension funds, Poland's reversing its policy to some extent, and the Czech Republic implemented a private second pillar and scrapped it soon after. So it seems there's a lot of political opposition, also partly because some people worry that if it's run by the private sector there's always a danger of pension fund bankruptcies, fund managers running away with the money.

JP: Particularly in Central and Eastern Europe, the countries you mentioned, this has happened several times. I think there's a combination of reasons for that. The first is that they probably did not have sufficiently strong governance or financial sophistication to manage the system, or maybe even political maturity. So there have been cases where governments have expropriated the accumulated assets and simply moved them back into consolidated revenue. The other thing is that many of these countries started this system in the first half of the 2000s and they just got going when the Global Financial Crisis (GFC) hit. So it was very inopportune timing. Maybe if it had happened at the beginning of the 1990s then things would have developed differently.

JL: I should mention that you've actually advised a number of governments on pension matters. You worked with the government of Japan for more than 10 years, also with the Russian and Indonesian governments.

JP: A lot of that's just information provision, but in the case of Russia, for example, they wanted a system of benefits which took out the systematic risk and so it was quite a complicated thing to design. I don't think it was ever implemented because the pension system moved on, but that was the assignment that I was given, and it was very interesting to do. I learned a lot about Russia, I learned a lot about the Russian pension system, and I learned a lot about pension economics. That problem had never really been analysed properly previously.

JL: Let's look at the consequences of population ageing in the financial markets, housing markets and healthcare. What implications does ageing have in these three areas?

JP: Well, there are two stories about asset pricing. One is that the old own the assets and if you take the case of housing, they've expropriated those assets to themselves. House prices have gone up and that generation has benefited at the cost of younger generations because now it's impossible to buy into mature housing markets in large cities.

JL: Is that narrative accurate?

JP: I don't know how much it's a plot; it's just something that has happened. In the Australian case, a lot of it lies on the supply side. We need to radically rethink things like zoning, density and the associated infrastructure, and then I think housing would become more affordable. We're in an unusual situation in having an economy which is very agglomerised and almost everyone wants to live in the four big cities, so the site rents around housing are extremely high.

JL: This is partly the reason why, unlike in many countries where property prices fell quite dramatically after 2008, it didn't happen in Australia.

JP: That really didn't happen here. Australia survived the GFC better than most other countries, that's true. The housing market itself had not gone through such a boom, so if you looked at the United States, the housing prices actually went up quite rapidly prior to 2008. If you look at the Sydney market for example, it hadn't gone up much at all in the five years prior to the crisis (although it did before that). So maybe the increase in prices we've seen in the last year would've occurred two or three years earlier without the crisis. But there was room for an upward adjustment and I think that helped cushion potential falls.

JL: My recollection is that Australian house prices increased quite a lot prior to the crises, over 100 per cent in real terms between 1996 and 2006. But it is true that relative to income the rise was less dramatic than in the United States, so **housing affordability** did not decline that much.

JP: Incomes were rising very fast in Australia during that period. In terms of your second area, financial assets, I'm not sure what the effect of population ageing is. It seems to me that there are many opportunities for investment with high returns. I think the broader, long-term story on population ageing – the verdict isn't in. So what happens when global population starts shrinking and fertility is as people project? Is there going to be the same demand for new capital that there is now? For the moment, I don't subscribe to the 'asset meltdown' scenario.

JL: Can you briefly outline what that is?

JP: Well, the idea is that the baby boomers have accumulated assets for their retirement. Now they're going to spend them down. The only way they can spend them down is to sell them. So the market for these assets will become a buyer's market because everyone will be seeking to sell and the prices will plummet. That will mean that what senior people thought they had, which was enough wealth to go through their retirement years, will not be there any longer.

JL: This hypothesis, I was told by some of my German colleagues, was influential when a pension reform was being discussed in Germany. It was one of the arguments against a reform: 'Okay, we're going to have all these private pension funds and pre-funding, but because the price of assets is going to decrease dramatically, the system is going to face the same kind of problems as the public pay-as-you-go system.'

JP: It's a very globalised economy we're operating in, and although population ageing is occurring everywhere, it's occurring at very different rates and at very different stages. So I think there are opportunities for investment in Asia. There's decades of investment in Asia before the marginal return on capital declines to a point where you would have an asset meltdown. It might be true in Germany if it was just a national market, but I think in a global market it's very unlikely.

JL: I agree. There are studies, for example by Sebastian Schich, that show that the asset meltdown hypothesis might be correct in theory, but quantitatively it's likely to only lead to a small reduction in the return on assets. What about the third major area, healthcare? Are there any lessons from the pension reforms for healthcare, which seems to be a big long-term problem for public finances in virtually all countries?

JP: Healthcare is important and it's a major part of government expenditure. The basic story is that in order to continue to provide healthcare which is commensurate with where technology is – the growth in healthcare expenditure is partially technologically-driven – tax increases are inevitable. I really don't see a way around it; it's very difficult to pre-fund healthcare. Once again, I'm not opposed to the arrangement in Australia where a private insurance option is available that people can take up and relieve a bit of the pressure on the public system. But eventually you have a healthcare system which delivers to the populace and the primary funder of that is going to be the taxpayer. The taxpayer, of course, is the primary beneficiary as well which needs to be taken into account.

Something else along that same theme is that new policy imperatives will grow with population ageing, and an important one would be aged-care. Long-term care is something which this country has not paid much attention to until recently. And then a year or two ago we had an aged-care policy and that's, I guess, proceeding and gradually being developed over the next 10 years. Not a moment too soon, but actually in time. There are going to be these areas where there will be new demands on the public purse as a result of the ageing demographic.

JL: Can you give another example?

JP: Take cognitive decline. I'm not really talking about dementia, although that's a piece of it – just people not being able to figure things out so well when they're 80 as when they're 60, or when they're 40. That's going to mean that perhaps there's room for a policy of pre-commitment at late age. Germany has this pre-funded pension that you alluded to, the Reister pension. You have considerable freedom over your benefits, but there's a piece that has to be preserved to age 85, and then it's a pension. And that's to cope with cognitive decline. So that's another element of population ageing where you get this interaction between health, psychology, economics, finance and policy.

JL: It seems like ageing has many different facets and it's going to influence our society in many diverse ways.

JP: Very much. I'd say climate change and population ageing are going to be the two twenty-first-century stories really, from a social point of view.

JL: I think your view is well grounded. The 2014 Global Risks report by the World Economic Forum ranks, in terms of expected adverse financial impact, fiscal crises as number one and global warming as number two problem.

JP: There you go!

JL: There is one last question I ask my guests regarding public policies that economics shows would improve overall wellbeing, but politicians have shied away from. Today we have discussed several such examples, but would you like to briefly mention anything else?

JP: Let me take a broader 'population ageing' perspective. What I would like to see is political leadership discussing the necessity for increased taxes driven by changes in the demographic structure. We will need more taxes per person to stay where we are, which is a good place, in delivering support to people who are older, who have no capacity to work anymore, and who have limited financial resources. If our leaders embrace the idea that government should be there for those in need who have exhausted their capacity to earn, those additional taxes would enable this goal to be delivered in a fiscally sustainable way. And we'd be on more secure ground in retaining and enhancing the community solidarity which I think Australia currently possesses – to a greater degree than many countries. It is an asset worth investing in.

JL: John, I would like to thank you very much for your time and for your ongoing contribution; not only to research on population ageing and pensions, but also in the policymaking arena. Let's hope countries will be able to successfully address the demographic changes and ensure sustainable retirement systems and public finances in general.

7.3 Key economic insights and policy lessons

Economic insights	Implied policy lessons (for public officials and voters)
High-income countries and the world as a whole have been going through two major demographic shifts: declines in birth rates and increases in lifespans.	Policymakers should carefully study how fertility and longevity trends affect population ageing and what their fiscal implications are.
Population ageing has a major impact in a number of areas such as pensions, healthcare, aged-care, financial markets, housing, psychology and epidemiology.	Policymakers should take into account the multidisciplinary nature of population ageing in designing policy solutions.
The number of workers per retiree in high-income countries has decreased from a value of 6–7 half a century ago to about 3–4 currently. Demographic estimates imply values below 2 within three decades.	Policymakers should be incorporating the predicted dramatic rise in the old-age dependency ratio into their budgetary processes as it leads to a major increase in mandatory expenditures and decrease in tax revenues.
In light of the ageing population trend, the pension promises most governments have made to their future retirees are unachievable (with Australia being one of the few partial exceptions).	Policymakers in many countries should, sooner rather than later, come clean about the dire long-term outlook of the public pay-as-you-go pension system.
A pension system cannot generally be sustainable when both the contribution and the benefit are defined, because demographic changes lead to misalignment between the total sum of money collected and the sum to be paid out.	Policymakers should, if insisting on pay-as-you-go financing, favour defined contributions systems in which the pension benefit is calculated ex-post based on the system's long-term balance.
Governments have started reneging on their pension promises, often in hidden (ad hoc) ways that increase uncertainty in the economy and disadvantage some individuals and generations relative to others.	Policymakers should design a conceptual pension reform that takes ageing into account and respects the principle of intergenerational equity.
In a globalised economy featuring active migration, there is a weakening of the family commitment to look after aged parents ('filial piety').	Policymakers should design retirement financing systems that help offset the weakening of within-family support.

Economic insights	Implied policy lessons (for public officials and voters)
Most high-income countries have eligibility in their first public pension 'pillar' linked to previous contributions, but not means tested. Australia's system is the opposite.	Policymakers should carefully consider the eligibility and means testing features of their pension systems. The advantage of the Australian system is that it alleviates old-age poverty without burdening the public purse excessively.
Only a handful of countries have a pre-funded Australian-type superannuation scheme (second pillar) that is largely immune to population ageing.	Policymakers should consider following the Australian scheme in which a person's and employer's contributions accumulate in the person's superannuation account rather than in a common pot of money.
The Australian superannuation system with capital accumulation through private pension funds is relatively expensive in terms of administrative charges.	Policymakers should seek inspiration from the Swedish model in which a publicly run low-fee fund is among the available investment options.
Passive investing using a 'buy and hold' strategy, e.g. with the use of index funds, has been shown to consistently outperform active asset management due to much lower fees.	Policymakers should highlight to the public the advantages of a passive investment strategy, and make it a default option where relevant.
Research shows that people are not very good at committing to actions such as retirement saving, the consequences of which are far into the future.	Policymakers should attempt to educate people about the importance of retirement saving, but unless/until they succeed they are well advised to make such saving mandatory.
The tax system in most countries including Australia is excessively complex and opaque.	Policymakers should strive to streamline the tax system to reduce its implicit costs on taxpayers.
Australia is more efficient than other countries in redistributing money from high- to low-income people, but it still has substantial tax–welfare churning.	Policymakers should explore ways of reining in middle-class welfare, i.e. minimising the inefficient situation in which an individual pays taxes and receives government handouts at the same time.
If superannuation income has higher tax than housing, people will move to the latter, which has a number of negative consequences.	Policymakers should unify the tax treatment of major lifecycle assets to eliminate perverse incentives regarding acquisition of housing for investment.
Data show an 'equity home bias' – investors' strong preference for domestic stocks relative to foreign, also due to favourable tax treatment of dividend and exchange rate risk minimisation.	Policymakers should think through the consequences of tax laws on people's behaviour in many seemingly unrelated areas.
Pay-as-you go pension systems do not, unlike pre-funded systems, allow reduction of country-specific risks through diversification into foreign assets.	Policymakers should evaluate the benefits of foreign diversification of domestic risks (such as a country's excessive reliance on its banking or mineral sectors), and reflect them in their pension system design.
Diverse systems tend to be safer and more resilient than homogeneous ones.	Policymakers should promote system diversity in many areas by spreading the load between private and public schemes.
The de-accumulation (post-retirement) part of the Australian superannuation system is poorly designed.	Policymakers should improve the de-accumulation superannuation options of retirees, and discontinue features that create perverse incentives and social welfare losses.
The means tests on eligibility for Australian public pensions are fairly generous, and the pre-specified minimum age is inconsistent with the trend of growing lifespans.	Policymakers should contemplate tightening the means tests on public pensions and indexing the age to life expectancy (at age 65 rather than birth).

Economic insights	Implied policy lessons (for public officials and voters)
Countries with a large informal sector, sub-par institutions and/or an underdeveloped financial sector find it hard to reform their pension systems.	Policymakers should strengthen the quality of the country's institutional framework to maximise the chances of a successful transition to a sustainable pension system.
Inopportune timing of pension reforms implemented during the GFC is partly responsible for their failures.	Policymakers should recognise the importance of timing long-term reforms in the expansionary part of the business cycle.
Various regulations by different levels of Australian governments such as zoning are partly responsible for the restricted supply of housing and the resulting house price increases.	Policymakers should rethink the constraints they put on the supply of housing in Australia.
While the 'asset meltdown' hypothesis has theoretic foundations, the quantitative reduction of asset returns due to an ageing population is estimated to be fairly small.	Policymakers should carefully investigate the effect of population ageing on the financial markets and asset returns.
Pre-funding of the healthcare system seems even more challenging than pre-funding of the pension system due to greater uncertainty about technological progress and more complex risk-pooling.	Policymakers should explore ways of ensuring sustainability of the healthcare system. Educating and incentivising people to assume greater responsibility for their health seem important elements of the solution.

7.4 Discussion questions

1   Using your own words, summarise the debate of Section 7.2 in three to five sentences.
2   Write down one idea discussed in the interview that you found new or interesting, or that you disagree with, and briefly explain why.
3   Write down one question on any topic covered in the interview that you would ask the speaker if you had a chance.
4   Consider the cartoon in Section 7.1, and explain the point to someone who has not read the section and does not have any knowledge of economics.
5   Examine Figure 7.1 from the perspective of a policymaker. Describe its key message to the public and explain what kind of policy improvement is implied by the data. Do the same for Figure 7.2.
6   Suppose you take part in a debating contest, in which the topic is the opening quote of the chapter by Gene Perret:

> It's nice to get out of the rat race, but you have to learn to get along with less cheese.

Prepare a speech you would give for the affirmative side. Then (you or your classmate) prepare a speech for the negative side. If possible, organise an audience and perform the debate.

7   Prof. Piggott explains the two main demographic changes behind the ageing population trend. Summarise this debate and support your answer with data showing both changes.

8   Discuss the World Bank pension pillars in terms of whether they are (i) run by the private or public sector, (ii) mandatory or voluntary, (iii) defined contribution or defined benefit, and (iv) funded or unfunded.

9   Carefully describe the 'pay-as-you-go' pension scheme used in most countries, and discuss the implications of an ageing population for this type of system.

10 What are the explicit and hidden ways in which governments can (and do) renege on their pension promises? What are the negative consequences of this reneging?

11 Describe the Australian pension (superannuation) system. Compare it to other countries in terms of its sustainability, and explain how Prof. Piggott would reform it.

12 What is the Notional Defined Contribution (NDC) system? Use an example of at least one country to describe how it works.

13 What is 'tax-churning'? Is it desirable? Prof. Piggott argues that, compared to other countries, Australia is good at 'getting rich tax dollars to the poor'. Assess this argument using available data.

14 Critically evaluate the statement: 'The government should not get involved in the pension system, because people can best make their saving and retirement decisions.'

15 What are the consequences of population ageing for investment, financial markets and housing markets? What is the 'asset-meltdown hypothesis'? Find some research assessing the relevance of the hypothesis and summarise it.

16 What are the consequences of population ageing for healthcare and long-term care?

17 Propose a set of policies that you think best reform the Australian pension system and ultimately improve people's wellbeing.

7.5 Where to find out more

Baker, A. (2013), 'Tax Welfare Churn and the Australian Welfare State', 27 March, available at www.cis.org.au/publications/target30/tax-welfare-churn-and-the-australian-welfare-state

Bateman, H., G. Kingston and J. Piggott (1993), 'Taxes, Retirement Transfers, and Annuities', The Economic Record, The Economic Society of Australia, 69(206), pp. 274–284.

Chomik, R. and J. Piggott (2012), 'Pensions, Ageing and Retirement in Australia: Long-Term Projections and Policies', Australian Economic Review, The University of Melbourne, 45(3), pp. 350–361.

French, K. R. and J. Poterba (1991), 'Investor Diversification and International Equity Markets', American Economic Review, 81(2), pp. 222–226.

Hernaes, E., S. Markussen, J. Piggott and O. Vestad (2013), 'Does Retirement Age Impact Mortality?' Journal of Health Economics, Elsevier, 32(3), pp. 586–598.

Libich, J. and M. Macháček (2014), 'Insurance by Government or Against Government? Overview of Public Risk Management Policies', under review.

McGrattan E. R. and E. C. Prescott (2013), 'On Financing Retirement with an Ageing Population', NBER Working Papers 18760, National Bureau of Economic Research, Inc.

Merola, R. and D. Sutherland (2013), 'Fiscal Consolidation and Implications of Social Spending for Long-term Fiscal Sustainability', 31 March, available at www.voxeu.org/article/fiscal-consolidation-and-implications-social-spending-long-term-fiscal-sustainability

Rocha, R., D. Vittas and H. P. Rudolph (2010), 'The payout phase of pension systems: a comparison of five countries', Policy Research Working Paper Series, No 5288, The World Bank, available at http://elibrary.worldbank.org/doi/book/10.1596/1813-9450-5288

Schich, S. (2009), 'Revisiting the Asset-Meltdown Hypothesis', *OECD Journal: Financial Market Trends*, 2008/2.

Sinn, H. and S. Uebelmesser (2003), 'Pensions and the Path to Gerontocracy in Germany', *European Journal of Political Economy*, 19(1), pp. 153–158.

Tapia, W. and J. Yermo (2008), 'Fees in Individual Account Pension Systems: A Cross-Country Comparison', OECD Working Papers on Insurance and Private Pensions, No. 27, OECD publishing, doi:10.1787/236114516708.

United Nations (2012), *Department of Economic and Social Affairs, Population Division, World Population Prospects: The 2012 Revision*, The United Nations, available at http://esa.un.org/unpd/wpp/

Whitehouse, E. (2006), 'Pensions Panorama: Retirement-Income Systems in 53 Countries', The World Bank, available at http://documents.worldbank.org/curated/en/2006/01/7190679/pensions-panorama-retirement-income-systems-53-countries

World Economic Forum (2014), 'Global Risks 2014', available at www3.weforum.org/docs/WEF_GlobalRisks_Report_2014.pdf

8 Economics and policy of climate change

The climate change problem is at its heart an ethical problem ... [about] intergenerational income distribution ...

Ross Garnaut, Climate Change and Social Justice Conference, University of Melbourne, 2008.

Economic concepts discussed

Easy-to-understand explanations of all the concepts listed below appear in the glossary at the end of this book.

- Adaptation policies
- Atmospheric concentrations
- Carbon tax
- Climate change
- Confidence interval
- Emissions trading scheme

- Garnaut Review
- Global warming
- Greenhouse gases
- Intergovernmental Panel on Climate Change (IPCC)
- Kyoto Protocol
- Mitigation

- Natural monopoly
- Negative externality
- Oligopolistic market
- Parts per million
- Prisoner's dilemma
- Stern Review
- Uncertainty

8.1 Motivation and overview

What's all this fuss about **global warming**? Don't most people prefer summer to winter and warm showers to cold ones? In this chapter, based on an interview conducted on 8 May 2014, Associate Professor Frank Jotzo from the Australian National University sheds light on this apparent 'paradox'.[1]

Informed by his longstanding research and his role as lead author of the 2014 **Intergovernmental Panel on Climate Change (IPCC)** report, A/Prof. Jotzo's summary is highly informative. It provides answers to many policy-relevant questions such as: 'Is there strong scientific evidence that human activities cause **climate change**?', 'What is the mechanism behind global warming?', 'What are the environmental and economic costs of letting the planet warm?', 'How do these compare to the cost of mitigating climate change?', 'What are the options policymakers have in dealing with climatic

---

1 The full video-interview is available at http://youtu.be/oLsMav4FbwQ. For more details regarding Prof. Jotzo and his research, see https://crawford.anu.edu.au/people/academic/frank-jotzo

changes?', 'What can we do as individuals to help the environment in this respect?'. The key message of Prof. Jotzo is clear: human-induced global warming is a major threat to both nature and to our economic systems, whereas the cost of mitigating climate change is likely to be fairly small in comparison. We should therefore take action (rather than use flawed arguments such as depicted in the cartoon below).

Concept by Jan Libich © 2015, drawing by Veronika Mojžišová. Used by permission.

The discussion starts with an overview of the science behind climate change. Prof. Jotzo explains the role of **greenhouse gases** such as CO_2 and methane in trapping the heat in the Earth's atmosphere. He stresses that in terms of their concentrations: '… we are, through our energy systems, pushing the Earth's atmosphere right out of the boundary of historical precedent'. Compared to the current climatic changes, the warming that occurred after the last ice age looks miniscule, both in terms of its magnitude and its speed.

Prof. Jotzo then outlines the projections for global air temperatures until 2100, and they are indeed alarming. In the absence of climate change action the average air temperature on Earth is likely to increase from 14 degrees Celsius to somewhere around 17–18 degrees Celsius, possibly much more. To document this, Figure 8.1 reports the predicted temperature changes from a scenario featuring a relatively low mitigation effort.

Figure 8.1: Estimated changes in average surface temperature in 2081–2100 relative to 1986–2005 for a medium-to-low mitigation scenario from the 2013 multi-model simulations of the Intergovernmental Panel on Climate Change

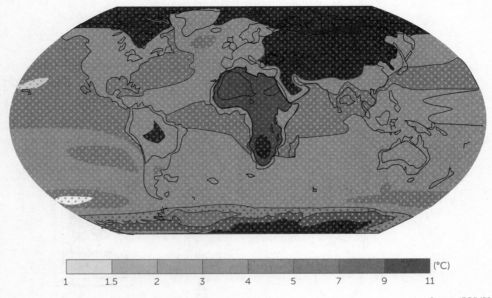

Source: IPCC (2013).

As Prof. Jotzo argues:

> … *even when the risk is small, perhaps less than 10 per cent, but the outcome from that risk is catastrophic such as the end of our economic system and social system as we know it, then as a global community we would be very well advised to take precautionary steps to reduce the risk of truly harmful outcomes.*

The interview then discusses the possible impacts of climate change. They are large because: '… all of our human infrastructure, our economic infrastructure, the way we live our lives, in fact humanity itself, is built on the current climate'.

Prof. Jotzo also stresses that the costs are very location-specific. An obvious example is the amount of rainfall. There will be some areas with more rainfall, implying more frequent flooding, but also areas likely to have less rainfall and thus experience droughts and water shortages. Southeastern Australia, for example, is predicted to be in the latter category. The infrastructure solutions to these climatic changes, such as better flood and drought management or even moving towns further away from rivers, may be extremely costly for countries and individuals. In addition, research suggests that yields for rice, wheat and other major crops may be impacted negatively in many areas, with enormous adverse consequences for the affected people.

In contrast to that, the estimated costs of climate change mitigation are quantified to be surprisingly low. Prof. Jotzo reports that:

> *IPCC estimates from several hundred models and modelling*
> *runs tell us that the economic cost in terms of forgone*
> *increase in GDP is something below 0.1 per cent per year.*
> *So rather than the world economy growing by 3 per cent per*
> *year, if that's the number you want to assume for the next*
> *50 years or so, it would increase by 2.9 per cent a year.*

However, Prof. Jotzo stresses the large degree of **uncertainty** around these estimates (wide **confidence intervals**, to use the language of statistics). This is because the models are 'trying to extrapolate out what our economic systems might look like in 50, 80, 150 years down the track'.

The debate then moves onto the arguments of climate change sceptics, and shows that they do not square with the overwhelming scientific evidence on the issue. They are, however, unlikely to disappear from the public discourse, despite having been refuted numerous times. As Prof. Jotzo explains, this is because they tend to be driven by vested interests, i.e. economic subjects that would disproportionately bear the cost of climate change mitigation efforts. This implies an important role for policymakers in helping these companies and individuals during the transition while still providing incentives for businesses to adopt cleaner technologies.

Prof. Jotzo discusses how this can be achieved in practice, starting with **emissions trading schemes** and highlighting the main issues of the Australian and European systems. **Carbon taxes** are debated next, and how both types of policies, if well designed, have been found effective. This is by providing the price signals needed for individuals and companies to change their production and consumption patterns in the direction of reducing carbon emissions. An alternative policy of 'direct action', whereby the government deals with environmental issues and projects on a case-by-case basis, is inferior and insufficient, argues Prof. Jotzo.

That pricing signals are needed to change production and consumption choices can be illustrated by the striking fact that the greenhouse gas called sulphur hexafluoride is still widely used as an electrical insulator and tennis ball filler. This is despite the fact that it is 23 000 times more potent than carbon dioxide in trapping the heat, and 1 kg of this gas amounts, in terms of global warming, to driving five cars for a whole year.

Prof. Jotzo then discusses the prospects for international cooperation in implementing climate change policies. The problem, identified by economists a long time ago, is the '**prisoner's dilemma**' nature of international agreements. Prof. Jotzo explains that:

> *each individual country is too small a decision-making unit*
> *and so their own contribution to solving the global problem*
> *is a relatively small one. Too much of the overall benefit*
> *of the action gets diluted to everyone else. And that's*
> *why we need cooperation, but cooperation's hard to*

> *achieve, because everyone just wants to free ride on*
> *everyone else's effort.*

This is why many economists are sceptical in this respect (for example, Prof. Frijters in Chapter 1) and turn their hope to technological progress and various geo-engineering solutions to climate change.

Many other issues are touched on in the interview: for example, the accuracy of climate forecasts, pitfalls when quantifying potential adverse effects of global warming, the failure of policymakers and economists to better communicate climate change issues to the public, the role of China in international negotiations, and the potential problems of some 'clean energy' options such as shale gas. Various ways in which individuals can reduce energy consumption and thus help reduce global warming are also suggested. In relation to that, Prof. Jotzo discusses the relevance of the 'message' in the media that appeared after the release of the 2008 **Garnaut Review**: 'Garnaut says we should eat kangaroo rather than beef.' Figure 8.2 shows a comparison of greenhouse emissions intensities in this regard and indicates that our dietary choices can indeed have a major impact on the climate.

Figure 8.2: Greenhouse emissions intensities of selected major agriculture and forestry areas over the 1960–2010 period

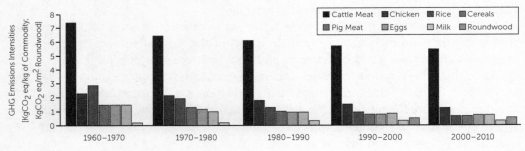

Source: IPCC (2014b).

8.2 The debate

Dr Jan Libich (JL): Can you start by briefly summarising the issue of climate change for us?

© Frank Jotzo. Used by permission.

< A/Prof. Frank Jotzo (FJ): Okay, let me talk about the science of climate change in just one minute. We're really talking about the enhanced greenhouse effect. The Earth's atmosphere lets energy from the Sun in and keeps the heat – traps it – inside. Without this greenhouse effect the Earth would be too cold to support life, so we need this for the Earth to be habitable. But the greenhouse gases we have been emitting into the atmosphere, principally carbon dioxide as well as methane and a few other heat-trapping gases, make the wall of the greenhouse thicker. The gases accumulate in the atmosphere and make the blanket we have around the Earth thicker, so it gets warmer.

JL: Is it like putting a lid on a saucepan and the heat can't come out as much as it otherwise would?

FJ: That's exactly right, it's like making the walls of the saucepan thicker or the lid sealed more tightly.

JL: So what's the problem associated with that? Most people like warm weather, so is the warming actually a bad thing?

FJ: Yes, it is. One argument you often hear is: 'Why is the status quo, the current climate that we have, the best climate?' The answer is that all of our human infrastructure, our economic infrastructure, the way we live our lives, in fact humanity itself, is built on the current climate. Imagine a drastically different climate, as has existed on planet Earth in geological time, and the basic preconditions for our civilisation and possibly our species to survive are no longer there. So we're fit-for-purpose in terms of the climate that we have. Any major deviation from that poses a grave problem for many species – humans included. In terms of greenhouse gases, there is a geological timescale variability in CO_2 in the atmosphere. And we are, through our energy systems, pushing the Earth's atmosphere right out of the boundary of historical precedent of a time period for which we can sample atmosphere concentrations.

JL: There are some people who say that after the last ice age we did see a warming too. But that was of a much smaller magnitude, around 0.6 degrees Celsius, and over a much longer span – 2000 years or so. What are the temperature predictions in terms of the next hundred years?

FJ: Very good point, Jan. Rate of change and potential magnitude of change are really the issues here. Over the time span of just a hundred years or so, we have pushed **atmospheric concentrations** of CO_2 to 400 **parts per million** from an equilibrium level of perhaps 280, right out of the measured envelope of variability over hundreds and thousands of years. If we keep going like that, if we don't do anything about mitigating or reducing greenhouse gas emissions, then the projections are that we might double that concentration yet again over the course of this century.

JL: What would that mean in terms of air temperatures?

FJ: That's where we're beginning to get some uncertainty. We know from elementary physics that there is a positive relationship between atmospheric concentration of greenhouse gases and temperature, but the 'multiplier' is a matter of empirical contention and therefore the projections for temperature rises differ. It could be something like

4 degrees Celsius above pre-industrial averages. It could be as high as 6 to 8 degrees, or possibly even higher.

JL: To put things in perspective, the current average global air temperature is about 14 degrees Celsius, so this would amount to a massive increase. The 2006 **Stern Review** considered an increase in global temperature of 5 to 6 degrees Celsius 'a real possibility'. But even the median projections for global temperature increases, generally between 3 and 4 degrees by the end of the twenty-first century, are still very large.

FJ: It depends on what you assume for your emission SCRoF (Selective Catalytic Reduction on Filter) scenario. Many people latch onto the notion of a potential 4 degree increase. But the point really is not in the expected mean, in what we might consider the most likely scenario; the point is in the 'possibility' (you used that word just then) of a high-end, high-impact scenario. Of course, there's a probability distribution. It might end up not being quite as bad as we think, and then we'll be lucky. But equally, there's a risk that things turn out worse, potentially much worse than our expectations. So this is really climate change policy as 'worst mitigation policy'. Even when the risk is small, perhaps less than 10 per cent, but the outcome from that risk is catastrophic such as the end of our economic system and social system as we know it, then as a global community we would be very well advised to take precautionary steps to reduce the risk of truly harmful outcomes.

JL: There seem to be two types of sceptics when it comes to climate change. The first group basically denies global warming is happening. What would you say to these people? How would you convince them with scientific evidence?

FJ: Look at the basic atmospheric physics of the issue; it has been clear and undisputed for the last 200 years. You put CO_2 and other heat-trapping gases into the atmosphere, and it'll get warmer. That is not usually the point of attack, really. The point of attack on the science is more often along the lines of what is the contribution that humans are making right now to temperature increases. And then, all you need to know is that the overwhelming majority of reputable scientists in this area, and we're talking about well over 99 per cent, and all of the notable academies of science in the world are unanimous in stating that human-induced climate change is real and very, very likely to pose a problem – unless we do something about it.

JL: There's a meta-study by Professor Lawrence Powell who examined all the academic papers regarding climate change published since about 1991. And he found that out of roughly 14 000 such studies, only 24 of them actually argued that there's no climate change or they wouldn't attribute it to human actions. This is a mere 0.1 per cent. So as you say, climate action proponents form an overwhelming majority in the scientific community.

This is probably why the second type of sceptic usually admits that human-induced climate change is happening, but because there's so much uncertainty around it, they argue we shouldn't do anything. What would you say to that?

FJ: Well, it's a fine example of how, in an area that is scientifically complex, and also very complex in terms of how we react to it as individuals and as society, it's quite easy for people to throw sticks in the spokes. It is easy to throw confusing arguments into the debate, for whatever reason, but there's usually specific vested interest at play here.

All you really need to do is step back and take it to principles. Okay, let's grant that there's no certainty around global warming. It may be 99 per cent, but there's a 1 per cent possibility that everything will turn out fine. What is the adequate response for societies? Is it to wait and see whether we get lucky with a one in a hundred chance? And if the draw is one out of 99 then bad luck? Or is the sensible approach to assume that, in all likelihood, this is a problem and we had better get on top of it before it gets on top of us? The answer is of course crystal clear.

The reason why we're seeing these sceptical arguments, I would say, is fundamentally because doing something about the problem of greenhouse gas emissions will cause substantial changes in some well-defined paths of our economies, which will in turn have substantial ramifications for the economic value of existing infrastructure and existing structures of ownership and profitability.

JL: And the parties involved may not always see that as a positive to them.

FJ: Yes, people are obviously putting up a fight whenever there is a major structural change in the economy. We see that with everything. We've seen this with agricultural liberalisation, we see that whenever there's a suggestion that the government might withdraw subsidies from a particular part of the economy. In most of these cases, it's quite readily possible to come to some kind of arrangement where these interests are being bought off in a way. But this is something that's not just some very small part of the economy, like chlorofluorocarbons (CFCs) in terms of ozone-depleting substances, which was only about fridges and firefighting equipment. Climate change is bigger and more pervasive, so it's more difficult.

JL: Let's talk about the negative consequences of climate change. Scientists warn about the melting of the glaciers, the sea level rising, the Australian Great Barrier Reef disappearing, many species becoming extinct, or major changes in industry. Can you talk a little about some of these issues, which of them is the most important in your view?

FJ: What the most important climate change impacts are depends on the specific geographical, natural and economic factors; it's very location-specific. In broad terms, what we're talking about is a warmer climate, and that will have ramifications for regional and local climatic patterns as well.

For example, consider the amount of rainfall that you're likely to see in different parts of the world. There will be some areas with more rainfall and others with less. More rainfall means more runoff and more frequent flooding. What do you do about that? Well, there are usually infrastructure solutions: better drainage, flood management systems. Perhaps you will need to move your city from down the river delta to further up the hill. Enormously costly in terms of the existing economic infrastructure that you've got to write off and build new, or in terms of additional infrastructure that you've got to put in as a defensive measure.

In other parts of the world, it might get drier. And this is a distinct possibility – not a certainty – but a distinct possibility for the south-east of Australia. We are already dealing with droughts and attendant water shortages in a cyclical fashion, causing problems for city water supply and for agriculture. If you had a scenario where that intensifies, you can quite readily see the ramifications for agriculture, for where we live and how we deal with these things.

JL: One of the interesting findings in the 2014 report of the Intergovernmental Panel on Climate Change (IPCC), which you were a part of as one of the lead authors, is that the yield of some of the main crops, like rice and wheat, is likely to be impacted negatively rather than positively. While some areas may experience a positive change, overall it's more likely that there'll be a negative impact on crop yields. Again, there's high uncertainty around that prediction, but as a risk-mitigating measure it should probably be addressed.

FJ: Yes. Food security is usually seen as one of the big 'meta-factors' that could face a strong risk from climate change. If we do see crop yields drop substantially as a result of climatic change, then it has ramifications throughout our economic and social systems. That could cut straight to the heart of how the world actually works, where people live, where there are wars between different groups of people, migration pressures. We have to see this in a systemic context. Professor Garnaut, for example, in his 2008 Climate Change Review for Australia ...

JL: ... which you were a part of ...

FJ: Yes, I was really lucky to be in a position to help advise on that Review. Professor Garnaut always made sure to place impacts on Australia in the regional and global context. So we trade a lot with the rest of the world, right, we rely on investment from other parts of the world, we are an immigration country. And all of these things could be affected – potentially in a very substantive way – as climate change impacts the countries that we are connected with, who trade and invest here.

JL: Suppose you were talking to an economic rationalist who only cares about the hard economic numbers and ignores all the environmental (non-economic) costs of climate change such as the extinction of many species. What are the estimates of the purely economic costs of global warming, assuming that we take no action on climate change?

FJ: So here we are right in one of the big controversies this year around the release of the IPCC Working Group II report on impacts and adaptation. Economic estimates of damages are a really complex issue and when you see these numbers that say economic damage from climate change in the year 2100 will be X per cent of GDP, take them with as big a grain of salt as you can possibly find. Because we're trying to extrapolate out what our economic systems might look like in 50, 80, 150 years down the track. And if you back-ask that, if you were in the year 1910 and you tried to imagine the economy of 2014, you would have come up with some wildly distorted picture that has very little to do with where we are at now.

JL: You're saying we wouldn't have predicted the iPad …

FJ: Yes, I am saying that indeed! And then you go and say: 'We take that future hypothetical economy that we don't know what it will look like, impose climate change on top of it, and we measure the difference.' That's essentially what goes on in these economic models. We really can't say much.

JL: But if you had to come up with some range of estimates? I recall the Stern Review quantified the expected economic loss to be around 5 per cent of GDP each year, and including various other risks it reached a number as high as 20 per cent of GDP annually. So we're talking large losses, although these numbers have been disputed and the IPCC ones are lower.

FJ: I will not come up with a number because I'm a sceptic of our capability of modelling these things in terms of the economic effects and economic costs and benefits. Talking about these cost estimates, the point really is the range. So the Stern Review's headline numbers were 5 per cent of GDP annually for climate change impacts, and up to 20 per cent once you include equity adjustments, stronger weighting on more extreme impacts and some valuation of the non-market impacts. That's a ratio of four to one; the more inclusive estimate compared to the bare bones kind of market values estimate.

Let me take those three included things one by one. Valuation of non-market impacts, that's the value of your ecosystems. For example, the value that we might place in Australia on the existence of the Great

Barrier Reef, that perhaps people in other parts of the world might place on the existence of Australian animal species that might go extinct. We don't trade these things in markets; nevertheless, it's probably indisputable that as societies we place some value on them.

Secondly, equity. Straight down the line in an economic model, a dollar is a dollar. Someone loses their house with a view of the river in Brisbane, $2 million loss if it's a nice big house. Someone loses their house in a river delta in Vietnam or Bangladesh, $20 000 loss. Is one 100 times worse than the other? Well, probably not. So we need to adjust these estimates by placing a greater value on the loss imposed on someone on a low income. Finally, it is the value of insurance, or the disamenity from the risk of really severe climate change impacts. This goes back to the issue of a low risk of a very severe impact, and that needs to be reflected in our overall estimates.

JL: In this context, you mentioned natural disasters like floods and cyclones. Can we attribute a specific event of this sort to climate change? What does climate change actually predict about natural disasters? Will they be more frequent, will they be greater in magnitude?

FJ: In general terms, under scenarios of global warming, you would expect an intensification and greater frequency of many types of extreme weather events. I'm choosing my words very carefully here and I would like to reiterate that my field is economics and policy and not the natural science of climate change. But research shows we should expect greater intensity and greater frequency of some types of extreme weather events, and hence, typically a greater damage bill. One of the more straightforward examples, in the Australian context, is bushfires. Hotter summers will mean more frequent and more extreme conditions for bushfires, large-scale burning of natural forest land, with the attendant cost for infrastructure in terms of housing, lives, health and emergency services.

JL: Very costly indeed. Let us move from the cost of global warming onto the cost of actually doing something, mitigating climate change. I am asking because the sceptics argue: 'We would have to go back to the trees, it would just be too costly for us to change our lifestyles.' Is that really the case?

FJ: No, it's not. In the mitigation case we're reducing emissions but economic output keeps going up. It's just marginally less in terms of the rate of increase over time. IPCC estimates from several hundred models and modelling runs tell us that the economic cost in terms of forgone increase in GDP is something below 0.1 per cent per year. So rather than the world economy growing by 3 per cent per year, if that's the number you want to assume, it would increase by 2.9 per cent a year. In other words, the world would double economic output and consumption in 24 rather than 23 years. Those are the kind of economic cost estimates. Of course, around central estimates like that, there's a lot of uncertainty yet again. Some models say it will be more than that. Other models say it will be even substantially less than that.

JL: How do these estimates compare to the Stern Review?

FJ: There are two distinct ways of reporting the cost. The GDP costs are normally reported in terms of the difference in levels between two alternative scenarios at a particular point in time. So the IPCC numbers, the envelope given there, is between 2 and 6 per cent of GDP at 2050; the Stern Review in 2006 had about 1 per cent. Now, if you take the IPCC estimates back to annual growth rates, then you arrive at less than 0.1 per cent per year as I mentioned. Actually, there are some studies, including by a colleague at CSIRO, Dr Hatfield-Dodds, about how people perceive these numbers that are being reported. And it's often with confusion in terms of the 0.1 percentage points annual growth rate, as opposed to the 2–6 per cent accumulated over time.

JL: The bottom line is that these numbers are certainly lower than what most people think. We're talking about big changes in the way energy is used, but scientific research suggests that they would have a very low cost. Can you explain the intuition behind this?

FJ: The cost is low relative to the size of the global economy or any particular economy. The cost is large if you go down to the micro scale and look at what needs to happen in any country's energy supply system, in any country's heavy industry sector, in any country's building sector, in any country's transport sector. Once you 'get down and boogie' at the sector level, the costs suddenly don't look so small, because you're talking about hundreds and hundreds of billions of dollars of investment per year that need to go into modernisation of these systems.

Think about the electricity supply sector of a country where fossil fuels play a big role, such as Australia, China and the United States. If you take an optimistic 2 degrees warming scenario requiring strong global mitigation then, all other things equal, we will probably have to turn a very carbon-intensive power sector into an almost zero carbon electricity supply. From high carbon to no carbon in the space of 30 or 40 years.

JL: At a glance that would seem pretty costly …

FJ: Exactly. What that means is that we would need to stop investing in fossil fuel generation assets – pretty much now or very soon. And go for zero carbon options instead, perhaps combined with lower carbon options such as gas, and very high efficiency coal for a limited period of time.

JL: Many people put their hope in the fact that technology progresses quickly and will drive the cost down.

FJ: That's right. At the end of the day, changes in consumption patterns and habits have some role to play, but really it's about the technology as to how we provide the services. People will want to live comfortably in houses and flats, people will want to get around. The world will be richer and people will increase their demand for travel. Unless of course we have some further enormous improvements in telecommunications technology that may reduce travel needs to some extent. So, all of that will go on. To the extent that all of this uses energy, how do we get to a point where we provide most of that energy in a carbon-neutral way?

The technological opportunities are already there. I mean, we would not need further technology development than what we already have right now in order to make that transition for the world. It would just be, on current evidence, much more expensive than the governments of the world are actually prepared to commit their economies to do. On the bright side of course, the costs of these new clean technologies are coming down all the time. Solar panels these days cost a small fraction of what they cost two decades ago.

JL: Let's talk about the possible mitigation strategies. Some countries have emissions trading schemes to encourage innovation and movement towards cleaner energy. Some countries have environmental taxes, some use direct action with the government micro-managing environmental-related activities, there are also geo-engineering solutions. Can you briefly talk about all these and what you think is the way forward?

FJ: There's a great diversity of policy instruments that countries use and can use potentially. The choice of these policy instruments is tightly linked to policy objectives. The actual policymaking is not always just about reducing greenhouse gas emissions, it's about co-benefits such as reducing air pollution. It's a very big motivating factor in China right now where successful attempts at limiting the growth of coal consumption have been made. And it's also of course a function of tradition, a function of existing institutional frameworks, and at the end of the day, politics as well, as we see in Australia.

All these factors explain the diverse policy approaches. From an analytical point of view, in a market economy we will always come back to the conclusion that putting a price signal on greenhouse gas emissions will be the backbone and the core of a cost-effective strategy to reduce emissions. One way to implement a price signal is through an emissions trading scheme. The government issues permits and market participants – companies – can trade these permits with each other, because they have a scarcity value.

JL: Which is the current system in Europe and New Zealand.

FJ: That's right, and a system that has been used for other pollutants as well. Many other countries and states are considering or already implementing this system. California is one and there are Chinese pilot schemes for emissions trading; there's a significant amount of uptake of this policy instrument. Conversely, you can – and many countries have – put a carbon tax, a tax on emissions.

JL: Economic theory shows that under reasonable circumstances it has a very similar effect to an emissions trading scheme, right?

FJ: Well, at the end of the day, the effect tends to be the same. The emitter – the factory, the power station that puts greenhouse gases into the atmosphere – faces a price signal. There's an opportunity cost of doing this. By cutting back, by putting in a more efficient piece of technical gear, by switching from a high-carbon fuel to a low-carbon fuel, they can save themselves money because they have to pay less carbon tax. Or they have to buy fewer of the emissions trading permits. And in both cases, to the extent that they still emit greenhouse gas emissions, they will pass that carbon cost onto their consumers.

So a carbon-intensive product will go up in price, and a low-carbon intensive product will go down in price, and consumers will then have an incentive to actually modify their choices in that regard. It goes right through the economy and requires relatively little administrative effort. You will therefore be very hard pressed to find an economist who says that this approach is not the right one, and some more direct regulatory or subsidy approach is superior.

JL: It seems that the devil really is in the detail, because many would argue that the European emissions trading scheme is not really performing well.

FJ: What's going on with the European emissions trading scheme is that you have a severe economic downturn there and a fixed emissions target. So much less needs to be done to actually achieve that short-term emissions target to 2020. And there's a host of non-pricing policies in existence as well, regulation for energy efficiency, massive subsidies for the deployment of renewable energy, and that leaves very little for the emissions trading system to do. So the prices are low and the instrument 'isn't working', but if you infuse that instrument with ambition, then it will work again.

JL: Let me just add that Australia is the opposite case. Its carbon tax seems to be working, but the Coalition government elected last year is actually trying to scrap that scheme.[2] They prefer 'Direct Action', which is essentially the government picking and choosing projects on a case-by-case basis.

FJ: Well, it has some effect right here, right now.

JL: You've been very critical of this kind of approach; for example, in your submission to the Senate inquiry on Direct Action … But that's for another debate, let's instead consider the prospect of dealing with climate change on a global scale – given it requires coordinated action across all governments. Can you talk a little bit about the past – for example the **Kyoto Protocol** – as well as the future in terms of the global targets and whether we're moving in the right direction?

FJ: The world community has gone through this amazing journey of elevating climate change to a position of central importance for the cooperation of nations. We were really there in 1992 at the Rio de Janeiro Earth Summit. Out of that the Kyoto Protocol was born with legally binding quantitative targets for greenhouse gas emissions.

JL: And everyone ignored it …

FJ: Well, it was only for the developed countries, and without ratification by the US Congress, so it was really a bit of a house of cards. Since then, the journey has gone further than that, and in a sense, back to the national level as well. There has been a realisation that quantitative targets negotiated in the middle of the night at some UN conference don't necessarily mean that much once they're taken back to the Cabinet rooms in national governments, and exposed to all manner of economic and political change that comes afterwards.

Now, the thinking is that countries, governments, leaderships need to come to their own domestically determined positions on what they can do. And then take that to the international table, show it to everyone else and say: 'Look, this is what we intend to do, what do you intend to do? And you, slacker over there, you should be doing something as well.' It's actually a much more traditional approach to international negotiations and diplomacy than the kind of approach that was tried, and to a large extent, failed.

JL: But it still doesn't seem to be dealing with the main problem, which is the 'prisoner's dilemma' nature of the international situation. Each country wants everyone else to mitigate, but because of the cost, it would prefer to free ride and not mitigate. Is this preventing cooperation across countries?

FJ: Yes, certainly. The basic theory of why all this isn't working is that each individual country is too small a decision-making unit and so their own contribution to solving the global problem is a relatively small one.

2 Two months after recording the interview, the Australian Senate repealed the carbon tax, and the planned emissions trading scheme was never implemented.

Too much of the overall benefit of the action gets diluted to everyone else. And that's why we need cooperation, but cooperation's hard to achieve, because everyone just wants to free ride on everyone else's effort. That's a simple game-theoretic caricature description of what is likely to happen.

JL: This is what Stern called the greatest **negative externality** …

FJ: 'The greatest externality the world has ever faced.' Certainly that's true. However, if you really get an understanding of what goes on in international relations, the picture isn't quite so simplistic. There are relationships that states have, there is reputation at stake, this is not a one-shot game. This is a repeated interaction and it is a game of mutual assurance.

JL: China seems to be deviating from this 'prisoner's dilemma' scenario by moving in the direction of climate change mitigation – more strongly than one would expect.

FJ: China is in a sense reluctantly moving itself into a leadership position globally on climate change. Reluctantly, because for so long China has seen itself as a developing country that will, like other developing countries, do something once the developed country group have really done something useful about climate change. Instead, the situation we have is the developed country group as a whole, with great differences between countries, have done something but really not an awful lot on climate change mitigation. And we're now in a situation where the global problem really cannot be solved unless China and other industrialised and developing countries do what needs to be done. Practically all of the incremental growth in global greenhouse gas emissions from year to year now comes from developing countries.

JL: China is, I believe, the biggest emitter of greenhouse gases in the world. But their argument has been that they want the rich countries to do something first. It seems justified in the sense that China's per capita emissions are at 25 per cent relative to the United States. I think India has about 8 per cent, so they're in a way still entitled to have their share of emissions.

FJ: Well, China is now above the global per capita average, so when you think of a scenario where per capita emissions peak at some point, and then decline, as they will have to for any kind of meaningful global climate mitigation, Chinese emissions will have to come down faster and more strongly than global averages. But more to the point, in China there's an increasing realisation that this presents an opportunity.

Chinese leadership these days is strong on the quality of growth. They don't want to be the heavy-duty workshop of the world anymore. They want to lead in services, in high-value-added manufacturing, and clean energy is a tremendous opportunity for China. China is already the market leader in wind turbines and solar panels. If China can go ahead and infuse stronger climate change action globally, that will increase the global demand for wind turbines and solar cells, which is good for Chinese manufacturers. The same is true for nuclear power stations and other zero-carbon technologies that are coming or may come in the future.

JL: We talked about what countries can do, what policymakers can do, but I think there's a lot we can do at the individual level to actually help reduce global warming. Recycling, using public transport, purchasing energy-efficient appliances and so on … At the beginning you said that these are not so important compared to the changes in industry, but a lot of the emissions come from, for example, the meat industry which is related to our meat consumption. In fact, this is probably the greatest emitter – even bigger than transportation. So should we change our diet and eat less meat? Or should we ride bicycles more? What are the things we could do to help slow down the warming process?

FJ: You know, Jan, this always creates the most vigorous debate, precisely because it takes it down to the individual level. I remember back in 2008 with the release of the Garnaut Climate Change Review, one of the really big headlines in the media was: 'Garnaut says we should eat kangaroo rather than beef.' Yes, of course. Here's one red meat, and another red meat. One causes tremendous amounts of methane emissions, the other doesn't, and it's a logical conclusion. But it was not a prescription that individuals should do this, that or the other. The point is that if you had a rational system and a cost-effective way of dealing with greenhouse gas emissions in terms of a pricing system, then beef would rise in price, and other substitute meats from 'non-human-farmed' animals would fall in price. And people would make their consumption choices along those lines.

JL: Just scrapping some of the farming and water subsidies would lead to the price of meat being much higher than it is now.

FJ: You should perhaps talk to the European Union about that. But seriously, in terms of individual consumption choices, it is at the end of the day constrained by the system we live in. However, there are big opportunities at the individual level, in particular for energy efficiencies, the purchasing decisions that we make for appliances. The slightly more expensive fridge or television that uses less power, smaller cars versus large cars, hybrids versus non-hybrid. Also housing, especially free-standing houses, and especially insulation. Those are the things where individuals can make really big differences in terms of the energy use footprint and thereby also the carbon footprint that we have.

JL: In terms of our job as academics, I was really surprised to find out that a laptop computer generally consumes only about 10 per cent of a desktop computer. Similarly, one of the reports I read about the UK was looking at energy consumption associated with the kettle to boil water. It found that about a third of all the energy is wasted by overfilling the kettle, and strikingly, that wasted energy would be enough to cover half of all the street lighting in the UK. So there are a lot of things individuals can do as our personal climate change action with little or no 'sacrifice'.

But let me pose a final question I ask my guests before turning to the audience. It regards public policies that economics shows would improve overall wellbeing, but politicians have shied away from. Today we have touched on many such examples in relation to climate change, but would you like to briefly mention anything else in this respect?

FJ: Climate change really is a perfect example of the political system shying away from steps that are in the strong longer-term interest of society. It illustrates the power of vested interests over policymaking. It also illustrates the difficulties in getting complex solutions in areas that are difficult to communicate and where one side of politics is intent on using the issue for political gain. Australia's carbon price is the archetypal example. It is also the emblematic case of the difficulty of establishing deep and lasting international collaboration, and of short-term bias inherent to governments in democracies getting in the way of action for long-term societal benefit.

Other big themes in Australia today, where politics is taking a direction that seems at odds with the longer-term national interest as I would see it, are foreign aid and education. Education is the key to lasting prosperity. A well-educated, capable and creative workforce is needed to attract the high-value-added, knowledge-based industries of the future. This matters particularly as the resources boom is coming to an end. And it would matter greatly for Australia in a world that acts strongly on climate change and switches away from fossil fuels. A strong push in education is needed to keep Australia's economic prospects bright for the coming decades. Moves to cut public funding for education, especially tertiary education, are taking the country in the wrong direction.

Finally, aid cuts are currently seen as an easy target to help consolidate the federal budget. But this has more than just a moral downside. It undermines Australia's standing in the world – we now contribute among the lowest percentage of aid as a share of GDP among all developed countries, despite being one of the richest countries on Earth. It also reduces the opportunities for Australia to help achieve better development outcomes in countries in our region and the influence Australia has on developments in those countries. Cuts to foreign aid, beyond improvements in aid effectiveness, reflect a combination of short-termism and a narrow definition of the national interest.

Audience member 1: My question is in regards to implementing a price system. If people aren't willing to pay and sacrifice beef consumption in favour of lamb consumption because lamb's too expensive, what makes us think that they're going to vote to arbitrarily change that price? How do you convince the voting public to actually implement the environmentally optimal price? They're obviously not willing to do it of their own accord.

FJ: The point is that we need to think in terms of changes in relative prices. Where one price in the economy increases, another decreases. Where the government raises revenue from a tax, the government has money to lower another tax, or to provide extra public services. This is the point that any economist working in this policy space, and in fact in many other walks of policy life, needs to work harder to get across in public communication. Because the experience in Australia with the carbon tax debate was that a substantial proportion of the population only got the message that the price of some goods and services, principally electricity and gas, will go up. Full stop. End of story.

In reality, it's not end of story. Because relatively speaking, the price of other goods and services will decline and the money from the increased price of electricity and gas goes somewhere. The majority of it ends up with the government and it can cut taxes, in this case income tax, and increase welfare payments. So I have to say that as a community of economists, I think we have, to a significant extent, failed in public communication of this point.

Audience member 1: Sorry, I don't think you quite answered my question.

FJ: I think I failed again!

Audience member 1: My question is, if people are not already willing to change their consumption patterns, what makes us think that they're going to vote for the government to force them to do it?

FJ: So voting for change comes back to the free-rider problem that we discussed earlier. And I think in any society you will find people who take a strong moral or ethical value-based position to these issues and say: 'Well, I want to be part of a nation that does what is right.' And what is right will then again differ but there will be a broad range of features that most people would agree on. The right thing is, for example, to contribute more strongly to the global good than a relatively poor country such as India.

And there will be other people who put the emphasis more on the near term and more on their own individual situation, and who say: 'Well, I don't really care so much about the greater global public good and our nation's role in it. What I care about is my financial position at the end of the year.' They will tend to be less enthusiastic or even actively opposed to such public good provision. But this is not the first time that a nation comes to a decision point like that; these public policy decisions, with their international ramifications, are being made all the time. Think of any nation's – or Australia's – decision to make a contribution to international security efforts or, in fact, to ongoing wars. We send soldiers there, we make enormous contributions financially in terms of equipment, to the effort that, rightly or wrongly, is going on in different parts of the world. These are complex issues that are being worked through the public policy, the public debate and ultimately the electoral policies as well.

Audience member 2: What is your view on the fact that the alternative, so-called 'greener' forms of extracting minerals may in fact be quite harmful to the environment? In particular, coal seam gas is pitched as being better for the environment, but high levels of toxins are injected into the Earth. And you've got cases where there's a high incidence of earthquakes throughout the United States, mudslides, sink pits and things like that. We've just recently allowed fracking on the Great Barrier Reef and there has already been environmental damage and ramifications in those regions. So what is actually green and what is not?

FJ: Your question touches on where our energy supply comes from. Where does our gas come from? Is it traditional natural gas or is it unconventional gas; the so-called shale gas, coal seam gas? I live in Canberra and it gets pretty cold in winter, so I turn up the heating, and in my house it's gas. I don't really have much choice as to how that gas is produced or where it comes from (although this is changing now). The main choice that I do have is to invest in better insulation of my house and persuade my kids to wear a jumper rather than turning up the heater even more.

In terms of where the gas comes from, this unconventional gas is a wonderful example of the trade-offs between different types of environmental and societal objectives. We've really seen the gas boom within the United States and it's done tremendous things in terms of bringing the US greenhouse gas emissions trajectory on a significant downward trend. In about 2007 it was peak CO_2 for the US and it's practically certain that this will be the case probably forever. And gas has had a lot to do with it, because it's just simply uneconomical at the moment to build new coal-fired infrastructure in the United States; gas is cheap because of fracking.

But as you pointed out, there are all sorts of local and environmental problems that you have as a result of it. How big a value should you place on CO_2 as a global long-term environmental problem versus pollution, loss in local amenity because of everything that goes on with shale gas exploration? It's an open question and I think that it's ultimately for each society, each jurisdiction to determine. I don't think there's any objective answer to that question.

JL: Well, the same thing is true for all the geo-engineering solutions that have been contemplated: pumping sulphur in the air, using mirrors and so on. We don't know exactly what the possible negative consequences might be and we are unlikely to find out unless we try them.

Audience member 3: I've been studying the electricity supply chain and I'm finding that there's a lot of policy intervention downstream, because it's an **oligopolistic market**, fossil fuels, et cetera. But at the distribution stage, which is a **natural monopoly**, I find that there's actually not a lot of government intervention there. So I'm curious to understand the mix of mitigation and **adaptation policies**. How do you explain that? Because it's the same electricity that's flowing but there's a lot more happening at different stages of the supply chain. So when you mentioned 'sector' I think that's a bit misleading. I don't think that it's sectoral; I think it's almost at the different stages of the value chain.

FJ: I'll take your question as an excuse to delve into the electricity supply system and markets for a little bit. What we have is generators of electricity, both high in carbon and low in carbon, and a national or quasi-national market in electricity, in which distributors and retailers buy the electricity and then sell it onwards to you. Most of the cost you're paying in your electricity bill is not actually for the generation of the electricity; it's for the poles and wires and the distribution network; the overwhelming majority of it.

Now, as the electricity system changes its structure, its composition, with a greater share of renewables such as solar and wind in the system, the cost composition in the system changes as well. These are practically zero running-cost options, so all the cost of renewables is in the initial capital investment. Once the thing is there, when the Sun shines it will produce electricity and won't cost a cent extra. However, to run a gas, or to a lesser extent, a coal-fired power plant, it costs you because you've got to put fuel in, and there's also maintenance costs related to the running of the equipment. So you've got a market structure you alluded to, where the pricing for electricity is determined on the variable cost. It's a wholesale market, competitive, and the highest marginal cost producer determines the price.

This is becoming an issue in countries where the share of renewables is a very high one. Germany, for example, with very high subsidies for renewables, seems to be coming to a point where the returns for the electricity generator become very low. And they may in future become so low that it's actually not viable to invest in further renewable generation capacity, because the payments just won't be there. People at all ends of the spectrum in electricity markets are coming to the realisation that the current market model is not suitable for a system that has much more renewables in it. It is also not suitable for a system where electricity demand is falling, as it currently is in Australia. We might therefore see different models of how electricity markets are organised.

JL: Let's hope economists will continue to play an important role in designing alternative policy arrangements in regards to climate change. Frank, I would like to thank you very much for your ongoing efforts, both in research and policymaking, to help deal with global warming. Let me wish you – as well as the rest of us – that your efforts are successful and ensure a bright future for our kids.

FJ: Thank you very much Jan, it's a tremendous thing this interview series you're running. Thanks to everyone in the audience too.

8.3 Key economic insights and policy lessons

Economic insights	Implied policy lessons (for public officials and voters)
All existing social, economic and environmental activity is predicated on the current climate. A significant deviation poses major problems for all species including humans.	Policymakers should carefully predict climatic trends, and examine their likely consequences.
Over the past 250 years, atmospheric concentrations of greenhouse gases increased dramatically, e.g. CO_2 and methane by over 40% and 140% respectively. Most of the increase occurred in the last 50 years.	Policymakers should consider the direct and indirect effects of all proposed policies on concentrations of greenhouse gases in the atmosphere and on energy consumption in general.
Around 99.9% of scientific studies conclude that the growth in greenhouse gas concentrations has been caused by human activity, and that it poses a problem due to its warming effect on global climate.	Policymakers should accept the overwhelming scientific consensus on climate change and beware of the attempts of global warming sceptics to obscure this fact.
Unless we actively seek to reduce greenhouse emissions, CO_2 concentrations may double over the rest of the twenty-first century. This could increase the average global temperature from around 14 to 18 degrees Celsius or even significantly more.	Policymakers should devote their efforts and public resources into finding (cost-effective) ways of actively mitigating greenhouse gas emissions and preventing large temperature increases.
Such increases in temperatures are unprecedented. The warming observed after the last ice age was around 0.6 degrees Celsius over 2000 years.	Policymakers should actively support a society-wide debate making the public more aware of the gravity of the environmental problem.
The likely adverse consequences of significant global warming include widespread extinction of animal species, demise of many natural wonders (e.g. the Australian Great Barrier Reef), more frequent natural disasters (floods, cyclones, droughts, bushfires) and major disruptions to most industries.	Policymakers should, in addition to mitigation efforts, also engage in available adaptation policies designed to reduce the negative impact of climate change.
Expected climate change consequences are very location-specific, e.g. some areas will experience much more rainfall and some much less.	Policymakers should recognise and factor in the regional specificity of climate change impact.

Economic insights	Implied policy lessons (for public officials and voters)
The estimates of costs of letting the planet warm tend to substantially exceed the costs of reducing greenhouse emissions and mitigating climate change.	Policymakers should base their proposals of possible solutions to climate change on careful cost-benefit analysis.
Reported consensus estimates related to climate change are obtained from a large number of different models and varying assumptions, but they are still far from certain. Uncertainty about the social and economic costs is higher than uncertainty about the cost of climate change mitigation.	Policymakers should take uncertainty regarding climate change estimates into account. In line with risk-management practices, in their mitigation efforts they should not only focus on the average estimates but also on the worst-case scenarios.
Despite the low overall cost of climate change mitigation, the process requires major changes in agriculture and some industries (heavy on fossil fuels), which affects the economic value of existing infrastructure and profitability.	Policymakers should acknowledge that the burden of climate change mitigation falls disproportionately on some businesses, and design transparent redistribution channels to assist those in the transition process.
The cost of environmentally friendly technologies, such as solar and wind has been decreasing substantially over time.	Policymakers should pursue a flexible approach to the support of environmentally friendly technologies, reflecting their declining cost. This, however, needs to be done in a transparent and predictable way so as not to create unnecessary uncertainty by ad hoc policy adjustments (e.g. arbitrarily reducing the promised subsidies).
Generating greenhouse gases is associated with a negative externality; if the polluter does not pay the environmental cost, they tend to overproduce the pollutants.	Policymakers should carefully address the negative externality leading to global warming.
Putting a price on greenhouse gas emissions, either through carbon taxes or emissions trading schemes, seems the most cost-effective strategy to alleviate the negative externality. This is unlike the Direct Action approach in which the government deals with climate regulation on a case-by-case basis.	Policymakers should implement carbon taxes or emissions trading schemes to affect the choices of firms and consumers towards cleaner (and overall lower) energy use. They should stay clear of ad hoc micromanagement through Direct Action.
Securing a global agreement on climate change action is challenging. Its negative externality nature leads to a prisoner's dilemma situation, in which countries have a temptation to free ride on the mitigation efforts of others.	Policymakers should attempt to devise commitment mechanisms to overcome the free-riding problem and intensify global cooperation regarding climate change.
High-income countries seem to have a moral obligation to lead climate change mitigation efforts, also because their per-capita greenhouse emissions are still substantially higher than in low-income countries (e.g. in Australia roughly 30 times higher than in India).	Policymakers (in high-income countries) should openly acknowledge the moral obligation in leading global climate change efforts.
Many geo-engineering solutions to climate change have been contemplated. They, as well as usage of less conventional fuels such as shale gas, are associated with a number of environmental and social trade-offs.	Policymakers should support research into geo-engineering options and their careful experimental assessment, and be explicit about the various associated trade-offs.
There are a number of things individuals may do to help alleviate global warming such as recycling, purchasing energy-efficient appliances, using public transport and eating less (of certain types of) meat.	Policymakers should promote environmentally friendly practices of households and businesses (which also includes reconsidering existing agriculture subsidies), and use the public sector to lead by example.

8.4 Discussion questions

1   Using your own words, summarise the debate of Section 8.2 in three to five sentences.

2   Write down one idea discussed in the interview that you found new or interesting, or that you disagree with, and briefly explain why.

3   Write down one question on any topic covered in the interview that you would ask the speaker if you had a chance.

4   Consider the cartoon in Section 8.1 and explain the point to someone who has not read the section and does not have any knowledge of economics.

5   Examine Figure 8.1 from the perspective of a policymaker. Describe its key message to the public and explain what kind of policy improvement is implied by the data. Do the same for Figure 8.2.

6   Suppose you take part in a debating contest, in which the topic is the opening quote of the chapter by Ross Garnaut:

> The climate change problem is at its heart an ethical
> problem ... [about] intergenerational income distribution ...

Prepare a speech you would give for the affirmative side. Then (you or your classmate) prepare a speech for the negative side. If possible, organise an audience and perform the debate.

7   Explain what the terms 'climate change' and 'global warming' mean, briefly outlining the basic physics behind them.

8   Evaluate whether there exists agreement among scientists about global warming. What is Prof. Jotzo's view on climate change sceptics?

9   What are the expected effects of global warming on the environment and the economy? Which one do you think is harder to predict, and why?

10 What does Prof. Jotzo say about the link between global warming, food security and natural disasters? Find some scientific predictions in this respect; for example, from the 2014 Intergovernmental Panel on Climate Change.

11 Using online sources, report the likely effects of climate change specific to Australia.

12 What is the difference between climate change mitigation and adaptation? Give examples of both, and assess whether one is more important than the other.

13 Compare the estimates of climate change mitigation costs with the costs of no action. What do you think this implies for policy?

14 Various technological 'geo-engineering' solutions to climate change have been discussed. Find some information on these, and assess whether they seem promising.

15 Provide arguments for and against the emissions trading scheme and carbon taxes. Compare these to the Direct Action approach advanced by the Coalition government since its election in 2013.

16 Describe the 'prisoner's dilemma' in relation to climate change, and how this links to the failure of past global negotiations. Can you think of a way in which this problem can be remedied?

17 What are the changes at the individual level that we can make to help deal with global warming? In your view, how does their importance compare to the necessary changes at the industry level? State one specific action through which you would like to personally endeavour to make a positive contribution to the effort on climate change.

18 Propose a set of policies that you think best deal with climate change and thus improve people's wellbeing.

8.5 Where to find out more

Garnaut, R. (2008a), *The Garnaut Climate Change Review*, Cambridge University Press.

Garnaut, R. (2008b), Keynote Address; Climate Change and Social Justice conference, 3 April.

Hatfield Dodds, S. (2007), 'The Economic Impacts of Deep Cuts to Australia's Greenhouse Emissions', *ECOS*, CSIRO, Issue 134, pp. 12–15.

Intergovernmental Panel on Climate Change (2013), 'Summary for Policymakers', in *Climate Change 2013: The Physical Science Basis*, available at www.ipcc.ch/pdf/assessment-report/ar5/wg1/WG1AR5_SPM_FINAL.pdf

Intergovernmental Panel on Climate Change (2014a), 'Technical Summary', in *Climate Change 2014: Mitigation of Climate Change*, available at www.ipcc.ch/pdf/assessment-report/ar5/wg3/ipcc_wg3_ar5_technical-summary.pdf

Intergovernmental Panel on Climate Change (2014b), *Climate Change 2014: Impacts, Adaptation, and Vulnerability*, available at www.ipcc.ch/report/ar5/wg2/

Jotzo, F. (2013), 'Keep Australia's Carbon Pricing', *Nature*, 502, p. 38.

Jotzo, F. (2014), 'Direct Action's 9 Weak Links', *Business Spectator*, 4 February, available at www.businessspectator.com.au/article/2014/2/4/policy-politics/direct-actions-9-weak-links

Murphy, T. (2011a), 'Galactic-Scale Energy', blog post 12 July, available at http://physics.ucsd.edu/do-the-math/2011/07/galactic-scale-energy

Murphy, T. (2011b), 'Can Economic Growth Last?', blog post 14 July, available at http://physics.ucsd.edu/do-the-math/2011/07/can-economic-growth-last

Pezzey, J. and F. Jotzo (2012), 'Tax-versus-Trading and Efficient Revenue Recycling as Issues for Greenhouse Gas Abatement', *Journal of Environmental Economics and Management*, 64, pp. 230–236.

Powell, J. L. (2012), *The Inquisition of Climate Science*, Columbia University Press.

Stern, N. (2007), *The Stern Review on the Economic Effects of Climate Change*, Cambridge University Press.

Tol, R. S. J. (2014), *Climate Economics: Economic Analysis of Climate Change and Climate Policy*, Edward Elgar, Cheltenham UK.

9 Past and future of monetary policy

Inflation is the one form of taxation that can be imposed without legislation.

Milton Friedman, economist and 1976 Nobel laureate, *The Guardian*, 21 September 1974.

Economic concepts discussed

Easy-to-understand explanations of all the concepts listed below appear in the glossary at the end of this book.

- Asset bubble
- Banking regulation
- Basis points
- Central bank
- Consumer price index
- Credibility
- Credit crunch
- Enterprise bargaining
- Fan chart

- Forecast
- Forward looking
- Friedman's k-per cent rule
- Inflation forecast targeting
- Inflation target
- Lender of last resort
- Look through a shock
- Macroprudential policies
- Monetary aggregate

- Monetary transmission mechanism
- Negative gearing
- Policy lags
- Quantitative easing
- Supply/demand shocks
- Time-inconsistency problem
- Wage–price spiral

9.1 Motivation and overview

Is money the root of all evil, as some people believe? Are central banks (still) the mystical institutions that secretly run the economy using occult techniques that a mortal human being cannot possibly comprehend? (See Greider, 1989). Professor Adrian Pagan, former Reserve Bank of Australia Board member, will demonstrate in this chapter that nothing could be further from the truth.

His insightful overview of monetary policy comes from a 24 October 2012 interview, and it has a very real-world focus. It details how monetary policy, generally the most potent tool of macroeconomic management, is performed by major **central banks**. Despite being one of the world's most esteemed academic econometricians, after whom a widely-used econometric procedure is named, Prof. Pagan's explanations and insights are offered in a very clear and accessible way.[1]

---

[1] The full video-interview is available at **https://youtu.be/esS85Z6-Y1o**. For more details regarding Prof. Pagan and his research, see **http://sydney.edu.au/arts/economics/staff/honorary/adrian_pagan.shtml**

In the aftermath of the Global Financial Crisis (GFC), the term 'central bank' has become one of the most widely used economic terms. The public and politicians see the Federal Reserve, the European Central Bank, the Reserve Bank of Australia (RBA) and other central banks as possible saviours that can re-capitalise failing commercial banks, incentivise firms to create jobs, turn household pessimism into optimism, and find a magic-bullet solution to the sovereign debt problems. In addition, many people hope that central banks can recognise and deflate a possible **asset bubble** without negative consequences.

One of the implications of the debate is that such expectations are unrealistic – monetary policy is fairly limited in what it can achieve. Despite this, central bank policies can have a dramatic impact on the wellbeing of individuals through a number of different channels. In particular, the chapter will offer answers to questions such as: 'What are the specific goals of the RBA, and why?', 'What level and what type of inflation should central banks target?', 'What is the **monetary transmission mechanism** between the policy instrument and macroeconomic outcomes?', 'How should central banks respond to rapid increases in real estate prices?', 'Why should central banks be independent from the government, but accountable to it?', 'Should central banks publish their forecasts or even voting records?', 'What should monetary policy do in a major crisis such as the GFC?'.

The discussion starts with the goals of monetary policy in Australia, and this may pose a surprise for some readers. The RBA's goals, legislated in its Act of 1959, are (i) to preserve the stability of the currency, (ii) to maintain full employment, and (iii) to contribute to the prosperity and welfare of the Australian people. These goals may seem too diverse and possibly incoherent, which is why the Treasurer and the Governor of the RBA periodically release a joint Statement on the Conduct of Monetary Policy (see RBA, 2013). The statement explains that:

> These objectives allow the Reserve Bank Board to focus on price (currency) stability, which is a crucial precondition for long-term economic growth and employment, while taking account of the implications of monetary policy for activity and levels of employment in the short term … In pursuing the goal of medium-term price stability, both the Reserve Bank and the Government agree on the objective of keeping consumer price inflation between 2 and 3 per cent, on average, over the cycle. This formulation allows for the natural short-run variation in inflation over the cycle while preserving a clearly identifiable performance benchmark over time.

One might wonder why there is so much emphasis on stability in both nominal variables (prices) and real variables (production and unemployment). The reason is people's preferences: individuals and businesses prefer stability and predictability to chaos and frequent unexpected changes. And a stable macroeconomic environment allows them to better plan for the future and avoid mistakes, increasing their overall wellbeing (as the RBA Governor Glenn Stevens 'proves' mathematically in the cartoon below).

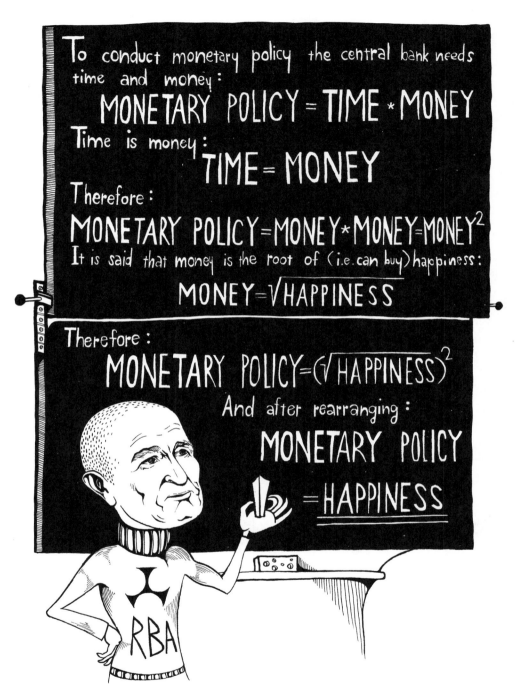

Concept by Jan Libich © 2015, drawing by Veronika Mojžišová. Used by permission.

Prof. Pagan then describes the job of a monetary policymaker using an intuitive analogy of driving a car:

> When you drive a car, there's no point just looking at what's happening to the guy in front of you. You always have to be thinking about what's going on into the distance ... By the same token, central bankers cannot just focus on what the inflation rate is now, but what they think the inflation rate is going to be in the future. And the reason why you have to do that with a car is that it takes a long time once you put the foot on the brakes; it doesn't stop immediately. The same is true for the effect of interest rate changes on the economy, there is a lag.

To demonstrate, Figure 9.1 shows the usual **policy lag**, i.e. the delay in the effect of a policy interest rate change on inflation and GDP, based on the simulations of the Bank of England (1999). Real GDP responds quicker than inflation, and the maximum effect is realised after about one year. In contrast, inflation tends not to respond for a year and reaches the maximum effect after nine to 12 quarters. Such delay implies the need for **'forward-looking'** monetary actions. Policymakers cannot wait for inflation to deviate from the target; they need to respond pre-emptively once their **forecast** of inflation deviates from the target. Such an approach is called '**inflation forecast targeting**'.

Figure 9.1: The effect of an unexpected 1 percentage point increase in the official policy interest rate (maintained for one year) on real gross domestic product (left) and inflation (right)

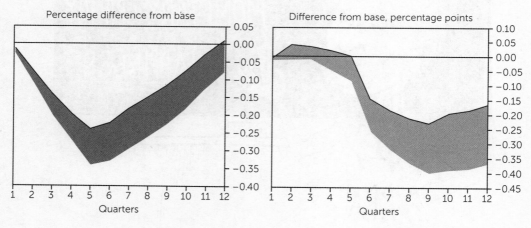

Source: Bank of England (1999).

In presenting the mechanics of monetary policy, let me take Prof. Pagan's analogy one step further. Assume the car has some optimal speed, say 100 km/hr, which balances the risk of an accident with the need for getting to the destination quickly. This is in the same way that an economy has some 'natural' rate of economic growth, for example, 3 per cent, which balances the risk of inflationary pressures against the desire to grow wealth.

When the economy slows down below its natural rate due to external shocks, central bankers behind the wheel step on the accelerator in order to bring the speed back up to 100 km/hr. They do so by lowering the interest rate and increasing the money supply in the economy, which tends to stimulate consumption and investment. In contrast, if the economy is overheating, central bankers behind the wheel step on the brake by increasing their interest rate instrument, which dampens consumption and investment. This reduces the danger of a car accident, i.e. the likelihood of various imbalances such as bubbles in asset markets that have damaging consequences further down the road.

The interview then goes into more detail about the transmission mechanism of monetary policy. It affects not just inflation, consumption and investment, but also people's confidence about the future and thus stock market indices, real estate prices, exchange rates and foreign trade. Prof. Pagan also discusses whether monetary policy should respond to **supply shocks** such as natural disasters, swings in petrol prices and changes in the GST.

The discussion then moves onto the institutional design of monetary policy. It explains why modern central banks tend to be independent from the government, which was not the case prior to the 1990s. Prof. Pagan also discusses the drivers of the worldwide adoption of the inflation targeting regime, characterised by legislating a numerical **inflation target** and a high degree of transparency and accountability. Central banks now actively communicate with the public and explain all their actions, including possible errors. They publish their models, forecasts in the form of **fan charts** (see Figure 9.2), minutes of the policy meetings, and some central banks even publish their voting records. Prof. Pagan discusses the pros and cons of these actions on uncertainty in the economy, monitoring costs of the private agents and anchoring of their inflation expectations.

Prof. Pagan then shares his experience from the large-scale review of the modelling framework of the Bank of England he was asked to perform (his findings and policy recommendations are available in Pagan, 2003). The discussion then moves onto the GFC, and covers many aspects of the recent crisis. Attention is paid to the 'unconventional' monetary policies such as '**quantitative easing**' that many central banks have used once they lowered their policy interest rates all the way to zero (some even slightly below zero). Prof. Pagan discusses their logic and effectiveness, as well as the concerns that such 'money printing' will have inflationary consequences. His fairly optimistic views are in contrast to those of Prof. Gregory in Chapter 2 and Prof. McKibbin in Chapter 11, and it is interesting to consider their different perspectives.

Many other topics are touched on in the interview. For example, Prof. Pagan highlights the role of fiscal policy in the aftermath of the GFC, including proposals for innovative measures such as varying the rate of the GST for the purposes of stabilising the economy. He also outlines the central bank's role in conducting **macroprudential policies** that ensure financial stability, and assesses possible improvements to the inflation targeting framework. His narrative focuses firmly on making sure that central banks are able to steer the economy over a bumpy road in the short term and maintain the optimal speed over the longer term.

Figure 9.2: Fan chart for consumer price inflation from an official November 2014 Czech National Bank forecast. The coloured bands express the uncertainty around the median estimate (solid line), namely the darkest band reports 30 per cent probability and the widening lighter-coloured bands the 50, 70 and 90 per cent probabilities, respectively

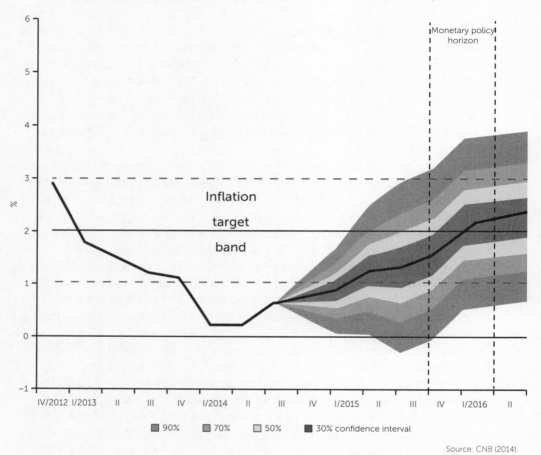

Source: CNB (2014).

9.2 The debate

Dr Jan Libich (JL): Welcome Adrian, thank you for coming to La Trobe University.

© Adrian Pagan. Used by permission.

< Prof. Adrian Pagan (AP): Thank you very much Jan. And as Robert Frost once said: 'Hell is a half-filled auditorium.' Well, we have a complete auditorium here today so I'm very pleased that you could manage to arrange that!

JL: Thank you. Let's start with the big picture and policy goals. What is it that central bankers are trying to achieve in terms of monetary policy?

AP: Well, that's not an easy question to answer. If you look at the foyer in the Reserve Bank of Australia (RBA), you'll see a statement from the 1959 *Reserve Bank Act* with three main monetary policy objectives. They are to preserve the stability of the currency, to maintain full employment and to contribute to the prosperity and welfare of the Australian people. With those sorts of objectives, it's pretty clear that anyone could satisfy them with any sort of definition. So you need something more than that. In practice, it often comes down to something involving a rate of inflation, something involving a rate of economic growth and some other constraints that at various points in time might be relevant.

When I joined the Board, for example, there was a lot of discussion about what the potential rate of growth of the Australian economy was. At that point in time it was regarded as 3 per cent, and in fact today [in 2012] it's regarded as 3 per cent too – as you can see from various statements by the Treasurer recently. During the 1990s though, when I was on the Board, we had rapid productivity growth so the sustainable rate of GDP growth at that time was probably higher than 3 per cent. And a lot of discussion and modelling was about 'Is it 3, or is it 3 and a half?', because that affects what you think the central bank can do.

JL: In the last two decades many countries have implemented the monetary regime of inflation targeting. They have legislated a numerical inflation target and I think one of the reasons is precisely what you have highlighted. It is the fact that the natural rates of economic growth and unemployment are changing over time based on economic fundamentals, so the central bank can't really have a long-term numerical target for these real variables. It can only have such a target for a nominal variable it can control, which is inflation. Is that correct?

AP: Well, I think that the point of the numerical inflation target is its clarity. If you go back and look at the minutes of the monetary policymakers before inflation targeting, you'll discover that everyone probably had a different opinion on what the inflation target was. And you sit around and someone's got a target of 6 per cent, and someone else has got it at 1 per cent. In that situation, it's very hard to get a consensus on what monetary policy should be.

One of the things I think has been fantastic about inflation targeting is that it focuses the mind wonderfully. You don't debate what in fact the inflation target is; you debate how to get there. And I think that actually has had an enormous impact upon – for one thing – how long these meetings actually lasted. The RBA meetings used to go for a whole day before I was there. They eventually went for about three and a half hours and I think today they go for two hours. A lot of that was to do with the more precise targets.

JL: So how does the central bank actually achieve the inflation target in practice? What's the transition mechanism, as seen through the lens of a central banker, between a policy decision and its short-term effect on economic variables such as unemployment, GDP and the price level?

AP: I think every central banker probably has a different view of this. There are obviously direct effects. You raise interest rates; they have a direct impact upon expenditures of households and firms' investment. If you raise them enough, they have enormous effects on expenditures, as we saw at the end of the 1980s, and as we saw in 1974.

But there are also an awful lot of indirect effects. Some people emphasise confidence. They talk about how interest rates are important for the confidence of economic agents. Other people talk about the effects on asset prices. Other people talk about the impact on liquidity. I think they're all part of the transmission mechanism but some people give bigger weights to one than to the other. The Europeans, for example, have always been very focused on monetary issues. As another example, in an open economy you'd be very interested in the effects on the exchange rate, because it has a tremendous impact upon economic activity. So, all of these things have to be brought in and I don't think there's just one transmission mechanism. There are lots of them, and people just put different weights on them.

JL: You mentioned Europe, and there was always a view, advanced by the German central bank (Bundesbank) in its 'two-pillar' policy. It consisted of both an inflation target and a monetary target to make sure that the amount of money in the economy grows at an appropriate rate. Prior to the GFC, many people were critical of this policy arrangement, pointing out that the inflation and monetary pillars may be mutually inconsistent. But it seems that the crisis lent support to the Bundesbank's view. It showed the problem of ignoring the growth in credit and money, which was the case in many countries. The role of the **monetary aggregate** also seems to be more important than what is captured in pre-2008 New Keynesian-type models.

AP: Well, I think that's true of a New Keynesian model but I don't think that central banks have ever ignored things like liquidity, or even things like credit growth. When I was on the RBA Board, one of the things we looked at a great deal was how fast credit was growing and whether that would actually ultimately have an impact on aggregate demand, and therefore upon what the inflation rate would be. I think that the simple model has always ignored money, but the types of models that central bankers use have never really ignored it; perhaps just downplayed it.

If you take the Australian experience as an example, in 1974 we had a **credit crunch** and all the models were adjusted to have many equations capturing the behaviour of banks because of that effect. And 10 years later they dropped all those equations because there'd never been another credit crunch. And it's always like that. Money and credit have always been there but sometimes policymakers downplay their role and sometimes they don't.

JL: One of the periods the role of money was certainly downplayed was the early to mid-2000s. Credit growth was 10 or more per cent annually in many countries, which was essentially double what the '**Friedman's k-per cent rule**' prescribed at the time. But central banks were focused on consumer price inflation and didn't respond to excessive credit growth sufficiently, which economists agree was a mistake. But let us frame the discussion in terms of interest rates rather than money growth as it seems more natural to people.

The simplest prescription for monetary policy is: 'If inflation deviates above the target, raise interest rates to stop inflationary pressures and prevent the economy from overheating. If it goes below the target, lower interest rates to stimulate the economy and stay clear of deflation.' The implementation is however tricky, because there are long lags from the policy decision to its effect on output (roughly one year) and inflation (roughly another year). Central banks therefore pursue 'inflation forecast targeting' – they react pre-emptively based on their forecasts rather than wait for inflation to deviate from the target. Can you outline how this works?

AP: Well, it's very much like driving a car. When you drive a car, there's no point just looking at what's happening to the guy in front of you. You always have to be thinking about what's going on into the distance: 'Is someone coming in from a side road that you have to worry about?' By the same token, central bankers cannot just focus on what the inflation rate is now, but what they think the inflation rate is going to be in the future. And the reason why you have to do that with a car is that it takes a long time once you put the foot on the brakes; it doesn't stop immediately. The same is true for the effect of interest rate changes on the economy, there is a lag.

What you can't respond to is the car suddenly coming in from the right and going through the red light. You just have no idea this is going to happen, and the same applies to monetary policy. That would be called a 'shock', because it would definitely shock the car and you. But that's the sort of thing macroeconomics is about – shocks and the responses to shocks. And in many ways I think there's an art to monetary policy, essentially an art in learning: 'What are the likely shocks, and am I seeing them happening now?' This is necessary in order to work out what types of adjustments you actually want to do. And some people are very good at this. In fact, some of the people I've sat with on the RBA Board were extremely good at it.

JL: My third-year students sitting in the audience have improved their skills in this respect through a monetary policy simulation game developed by a Swiss economist, Yvan Lengwiler. The user acts as a central bank governor, who has various economic data at its disposal and must change the interest rate in response to shocks to keep inflation on target. One of the lessons they have drawn is that some shocks are harder to stabilise than others, namely supply shocks compared to **demand shocks**. How do central banks generally respond to supply shocks that move inflation and economic output in opposite directions?

AP: Well, there's a great variation in this around the world. Some people actually write into the central banking legislation a clause which enables the central bank to discount certain types of shocks, particularly oil price shocks for a country that's very sensitive to oil prices. Others require the central bank to actually make a written statement to the political authorities about why they ignored a certain development.

JL: For example, the UK ...

AP: That's the UK case. In other countries it just becomes a matter of the central bank trying to explain why it can't do anything about those shocks. And we've had a number of those in Australia in the last 20 years. The biggest was the GST introduction. There we had a 6 per cent inflation rate for one quarter and the bank kept on making speeches long before this occurred, and making forecasts that we'd get 6 per cent price level rise. And they argued, quite rightly, that this should not actually cause any rise in wages. The reason is what you'd call the second-round effects. What you don't want to see is a 6 per cent rise in prices due to the GST becoming a 6 per cent rise in wages, because this could in turn become another 6 per cent rise in prices, and so on. Economists call this the 'wage–price spiral'.

So that was quite successful and it was against a great deal of opposition. One of the unions, I think it was the CFMEU, said that they would have vicious strikes in order to make sure that workers got compensation for that 6 per cent. But most of the people doing the enterprise bargains at the time in the unions actually took the lesson that this was something that was a one-off and so shouldn't be built into **enterprise bargaining** contracts. I think we have similar sorts of things with the carbon tax today. The carbon tax would cause some extra inflation, the RBA's already made some statements about that. Similarly, inflation goes up due to floods and cyclones. And in all of these instances the bank has to say: 'Well, there's not much we can do about these things, they're outside of our control.' I think that's the most common way in which central bankers deal with supply shocks around the world.

JL: Central bankers sometimes use this terminology of 'looking through' supply shocks, which means ignoring them and letting them fade away.

AP: Yes, they do. But you have to be careful with what exactly a supply shock is. It's pretty clear with a flood and a cyclone that you have a supply shock. But, for example, take an oil price rise for a big economy such as the US. There it may not be right to consider that as a supply-side shock. This is because one of the reasons why oil prices may have risen is due to fast US growth, and so it's something you can affect if you're a big enough economy. Australia can't affect the price of oil; if oil prices went up here we wouldn't bother doing anything about it. So you have to be careful about whether you can do something about the shock or you can't.

JL: What you're saying is that some developments are not genuine shocks, they might be driven by economic fundamentals and/or the policy setting?

AP: Yes. I don't think cyclones or floods are things that the central bank has much control over. On the other hand, GST was a policy decision by the federal government and therefore we had some control over it. Once it's made, policymakers have to commit to it and convince people that this is a one-off thing, but that's very tricky.

JL: Now that we have a rough idea of what conventional monetary policy is about – and we'll talk about unconventional monetary policies like quantitative easing a little bit later – let's look at the institutional design of monetary policy. We've seen some dramatic changes over the last 25 years on this front. We've already mentioned inflation targeting, but another key change was the move towards independent central banks. What's the point of the central bank being independent from the government, and how did that affect your decisions on the RBA Board?

AP: It's not easy to work out why central banks got independence. The Reserve Bank of New Zealand (RBNZ) was the first one to get formal independence in 1989, although the German Bundesbank had been de-facto independent for quite a long time before that. I think the RBNZ probably got independence because New Zealand's economy was in such a mess. People felt that it couldn't be any worse if in fact the RBNZ was made independent.

But in lots of other cases it's not so clear why central banks got independence. I think there is a fear that if you leave the politicians to tackle what are difficult decisions, then they'll try to avoid them. We can think of a recent one, the second Sydney airport, which has been discussed for 40 years. And it still hasn't come about because it's not the sort of thing any politician wants to bring in. In terms of monetary issues, we had a great deal of regulation of interest rates in the 1970s and the federal government was very reluctant to raise interest rates, even though inflation was starting to take off. And that was something that an independent body might have actually done. I think that such de-politicisation was probably the reason that a few of the early central banks got independence – and that looked successful so other countries decided to do it.

JL: I agree that the motivation seems to have come from the high inflation in the 1970s. The subsequent theoretic literature called this the 'time-inconsistency problem'; essentially, politicians tempted to lower the unemployment rate by excessively low interest rates, which has inflationary consequences. So granting independence was suggested as a way of eliminating this temptation and making monetary policy more credible. But this trend went hand-in-hand with increases in transparency and accountability of the central bank, partly to ensure the system is democratic. Central banks are now open about virtually all aspects of their undertakings, whereas in the 1980s you had books about monetary policy mystique and how the Federal Reserve (Fed) secretly runs the economy [Greider, 1989]. What drove the trend towards transparency and openness in monetary policy and what were the effects?

AP: The movement towards central bank transparency and openness is really just an extension of what was happening with all government. Thirty years ago we didn't have Freedom of Information (FOI) requests. Thirty years ago we only started to introduce Ombudsmen for all sorts of things. So the public service and government in general has become more and more open. In many ways, you might argue that the central banks were one of the last ones rather than one of the first ones. And so it's not surprising that they eventually felt under pressure to release more information than what they had been previously.

It's said that when 'Nugget' Coombs was Governor of the RBA, he spent three years and never once talked to a journalist. I don't mean literally, personally. I mean he never went out and talked anywhere involving news people. In those days you could get away with that but today you couldn't. I think that is probably how it happened. What effect did it have? Well, I'm not sure it had a great effect actually ...

JL: What about anchoring expectations?

AP: Well, I think the inflation target itself is meant to anchor expectations, I don't think transparency does that by itself. One of the things that was a little ridiculous is that decisions were made about interest rates in the 1980s and they were never announced. So the private sector had to guess what the interest rate decision was, and that seems rather silly in retrospect.

JL: There were large teams of people in commercial banks trying to work out what the RBA was doing, it was very costly.

AP: That's exactly right. Mardi Dungey, economics Professor at the University of Tasmania, wrote a note where she tried to interpolate what the actual interest rate decisions by the RBA were [Dungey and Hayward, 2010]. I think gradually it didn't make much sense for the central bank not to reveal what the interest rate decision was. So transparency had an impact on reducing that level of uncertainty, which was worth getting rid of.

JL: There are still some aspects of transparency where central banks differ. Some now publish their forecasts for key variables, but some don't. Do you think it is desirable for central banks to publish their forecasts?

AP: Well, I'd have to ask you what you mean by forecasts?

JL: Say the consensus forecast for inflation and output a few years down the track.

AP: Let me be more precise in my question. Do you mean the forecasts that went to the central bank Board?

JL: No, I mean the consensus forecast that the Board wants to communicate to the public.

AP: Well, is that the forecast that contains the current interest rate decision? Or does it contain an interest rate path the Board intends to implement in the future?

JL: Well, the RBA, for example, used to publish forecasts with an assumption of a fixed interest rate and now they're using the projected interest rate path. I think the latter is the most sensible thing to communicate to the public because it shows that the central bank has some control over the economy and intends to stabilise it using its interest rate instrument.

AP: Yes, but if the central bank shows the path, then it should be that by the end of the period, two or three years out, all you should be getting in the forecast is the target. So in a sense, is that an informative forecast? I think it's probably more informative to see what the forecast was that went to the Board. And that's the actual one the RBA published historically, rather than what is based upon the interest rate decisions. I raise this because there are, as you mentioned, many types of forecasts that people provide and they all revolve around: 'Do you take the policy changes into account, or don't you?' And you get enormous variations.

If you look at the Bank of England, for example, their inflation fan charts are really not so much a forecast of inflation but about the sensitivity of what the inflation forecast would be to risks. And in particular, they identify three major risks and attach probabilities to them, so they give a spread of what the outcomes might be. But it's not actually what will happen; it may be quite a long way away from what will happen, because none of those risks might actually eventuate.

JL: I agree that the forecast going to the Board may be more informative for a policy expert like you, but I am not sure that's the case for the general public. A future inflation path showing a return to the inflation target within three years may also be good for anchoring expectations and building the central bank's **credibility** – if it can deliver the projected values successfully. You mentioned the Bank of England, and it should be pointed out that you were hired to do a review of its modelling framework. Can you tell us about the process and what your findings were?

AP: They wanted me to come in and look at the existing models and forecasting methods. In particular, at that time they were building a new model and they wanted me to comment upon whether it was 'state-of-the-art'. And state-of-the-art doesn't mean highest academic standards because no central bank model really tries to be at the research frontier. It uses things that have been tried and true. So my job was to answer the question from that policy perspective. The monetary policy department at the Bank of England had 134 people in it at the time, so as you might expect it was pretty close to state-of-the-art. I don't think there was any doubt about that. I made various suggestions, both in my final report [Pagan, 2003] and as the report went along, about what they should do. Some of them they agreed to and put into the model, and some of them they didn't and they left them out.

JL: The Bank actually released a formal report addressing your findings, so again the process was very transparent and open. Is there anything that central banks should not publish? One of the questions is whether the minutes of the Board meeting should be published, or even the voting records, and whether these should be attributed to individual Board members or non-attributed. What's your view on that?

AP: I don't think I'd like to see the voting records published. That just produces more froth and bubble in the commentary on monetary policy, and the newspapers are already full of froth and bubble trying to guess who will vote which way in the next round. I think it's really not a good use of our time, and the public shouldn't be constantly bombarded with it.

JL: It may also put pressure on the individuals to vote in a certain way, and thus compromise their independence.

AP: Well, I think it can. Mervyn King, the Governor of the Bank of England [until 2013], used to have the nickname of 'Merv the Swerve' because he once changed his opinion about which way the interest rates should go from one meeting to the next. It took him a long time to live that down. But I just don't see that this is actually terribly useful information. You definitely need documentation on why the Board made the decision, and that has to be precise. But it's like a cabinet decision and I think it should be communicated like a cabinet decision. Basically the governor speaks and announces what it is and why they did it, and what exactly the Board members felt about it is something else. If you don't do that, you'll end up with people trying to work out what the decision will be by inviting the Board members along, giving them a good dinner, some good wine, hoping something might slip.

JL: Let's move from the institutional reforms of the 1990s to more recent times, namely the 2008 GFC shocks. Central banks responded with a lot of monetary stimuli, some of them lowering interest rates all the way to zero. Do you think that this was effective? And what are the 'unconventional' tools that central banks can use once interest rates are at zero?

AP: The studies that have been done on this monetary expansion and quantitative easing (QE) suggest that it actually has been quite effective. There have been quite a lot of studies done on the American QE2, some also on the Bank of England and on continental Europe. I think they all show QE did have a positive effect at the time, certainly upon output.

It seems to me that the question is not what monetary policy can do; monetary policy is never a strong instrument to work with. Its effects upon output and inflation are fairly weak; you need to make big monetary changes before you have effects. I think the zero-bound problem that we ran into shows that. What I mean is that even if you cut interest rates down towards zero, monetary policy may not have much of an effect. And therefore what we really need to think about is fiscal policy, it has much stronger effects. Continuing to think that there's one macroeconomic instrument out there, and that's the interest rate, is going to get us into a lot of trouble.

JL: Fiscal policy in fact seems to be much more potent in an environment where interest rates are at zero. We had the recent International Monetary Fund (IMF) confession that the fiscal multipliers they assumed in their 2008–10 models were much lower than what they probably should have been. So I agree with you that there may be a case for fiscal policy as a substitute or supplement to monetary policy. But let's go back to the quantitative easing you mentioned, what is it and what are the central banks trying to achieve?

AP: Quantitative easing is, on the broadest level, just changing the amount of liquidity (money) in the economy. But how you do it can vary a great deal. You actually have to go out in the market and buy some assets, and the question is what type of assets you buy. That's been one of the distinguishing features of the quantitative easing that's happened in the last few years, but there's been a huge variation in the way central banks have done this.

In some cases, they've bought bonds and in some cases they've even bought equity, which has different effects. Sometimes they've bought troubled assets, sometimes they've bought assets that aren't so troubled. But the ultimate effect, of course, is to increase liquidity and the money supply in order to lower long-term interest rates and stimulate economic activity. And one of the biggest problems with mainstream theory has been that there's been an awful lot of hoarding of liquidity and money. US companies, for example, have huge amounts of liquidity that they haven't actually spent, as you might have expected they would. So they've just exchanged one asset for another.

JL: The consequence of quantitative easing and 'unconventional monetary policy' has been several-fold increases in the central banks' balance sheets. Some people think QE is just printing money, which is obviously not quite accurate because much of the money hasn't really made its way into the economy. Most of it is just sitting on the commercial banks' accounts with the central bank. But will it eventually get in the real economy and be inflationary as some people fear?

AP: I think you have to realise that we have an enormous change in the money supply at the end of each year – and that's due to Christmas. Every Christmas, central banks go out there and buy assets supplying money to the banking sector and the public. The public use that to buy things for Christmas and then at the end of that period of time, the central bank goes back in and sells the assets again. So if you actually took a de-seasonalised measure of money supply in Australia, you'd see a huge rise in the last quarter of each year. Yet that doesn't cause any inflation.

So the added liquidity has to have an effect on expectations to make an impact. No one expects that money supply rising around Christmas is going to affect inflation. One reason is that it's a response to a demand that people are making, and the other reason is that they know this is going to be reversed within a month or two. I think that's the issue with the post-2008 liquidity: 'Does the central bank supplying this liquidity have credibility that when the time comes it will act quickly and responsibly in reining back liquidity?' One of the arguments for an independent central bank is that it is more likely to do that than one that isn't independent.

JL: I agree, and there's a lot of talk about the Fed's exit strategy, which is technical jargon for reducing this excess liquidity. In late 2008 the Fed was authorised by Congress to pay interest on the excess reserves that financial institutions hold with the Fed. So when the banks want to start releasing the money into the economy the Fed can always raise this interest on excess reserves to incentivise them not to do so, and gradually suck out all this excess liquidity. But such an exit strategy has never been tried before and there's doubt whether politically the Fed will have the courage to do that and impose negative effects on economic growth. Do you think the Fed can perform the exit successfully? The Christmas story is much easier to deal with than a several-fold increase in the balance sheet, right?

AP: I think that people can rein in liquidity fairly quickly. And I don't see it as an issue of having negative effects on growth, because if liquidity is causing demand to rise very strongly, then you would want to pull it back. That is one of the key things that a central bank has to look at all the time: what's happening to demand. And it then has to respond appropriately.

In 1994, the RBA was widely regarded as being rather weak on inflation. A few journalists actually wrote that the RBA was an extremely wimpy organisation. In 1994 when demand suddenly looked like it was taking off, the Bank put up interest rates 275 **basis points**, which stopped the demand in its tracks. Within the year, demand was back down to a reasonable growth rate and that, I think, gave the RBA a lot of credibility. It was the first test of them as an independent central bank, and they reacted to it appropriately.

I think that that could actually be done by the Fed as well; I don't see any reason why it wouldn't be done. So I'm not so concerned about all the liquidity that's out there. I think you can respond to it because you know what you're looking at. You can see the liquidity there, you can actually see the potential of very, very strong rises in demand and, because you see that, it's actually a lot easier to deal with. It's the things you don't see that you find very hard to deal with. Back to driving a car, the things that you can see happening ahead of you, you can respond to. The things that come in from the side or the things that you can't see in the blind spot in the rear vision mirror, they're the things that get you in the end.

JL: I would agree with you that the current liquidity measures are a lesser concern compared to the bigger issue of long-term fiscal sustainability. There is a large body of literature, starting with Sargent and Wallace's (1981) 'Unpleasant Monetarist Arithmetic', arguing that fiscal excesses eventually spill over and jeopardise the outcomes of monetary policy too. Do you think this is a longer-term danger?

AP: I think it certainly is a longer-term danger. Coordination of monetary and fiscal policy is really a tricky problem. In many ways you'd like an independent body manipulating some of the instruments of fiscal policy, in order to be able to stop public debt accumulation. I mean the business council some years ago suggested that the GST tax rate could be changed by 1 or 2 per cent by a body that was independent of the Treasurer, which would actually aim to stabilise the economy. Fiscal policy would be more flexible, and I think it would be good if we came up with more automatic ways of adjusting fiscal instruments.

JL: Don Brash, the former Governor of the RBNZ [Chapter 12], has made a similar suggestion in one of his speeches; he would use the taxes on petrol flexibly as an additional instrument of monetary policy. But, like with the GST, there may be some implementation issues.

AP: I think that's too narrow a tax, though. The GST is a good one to vary. For one reason, it's automated already into accounting systems so you could raise it from 10 to 12 per cent. Their suggestion wasn't that you could raise it from 10 to 50 per cent, it was plus or minus 2 per cent if I remember rightly. I think that was a good idea, but politicians are very reluctant to give up control over fiscal setting.

JL: I would like to ask you now about the lessons for monetary policy we can draw from the GFC experience.

AP: I think the lessons from the GFC are ones that policymakers learn every time we have a credit crunch. As I said, in 1974 we had a credit crunch, so economists then spent a lot of time looking at what was happening to credit and stresses on banks for almost a decade. But when that didn't happen again they decided to forget about it. The problem is that when you're doing monetary policy, you're always looking at the last war, and you've actually got the instruments to handle the last war, but the next war is going to be very different. One of the things I said in the review of the Bank of England's framework is that you should always be preparing for the next model. You shouldn't stick to one model. You've always got to have an eye out for the things that are going to threaten you in the future and you'd have to think about modelling to handle that.

Obviously what we see now is that all the models are adjusted to introduce financial factors into them and to look at a wide range of spreads. It's not that people didn't look at these in the old days, but they didn't look at them as closely as they do today. But that's probably not where the next crisis will come from.

JL: What about the future of inflation targeting? Should we modify the regime to target a broader measure of inflation than just consumer prices? For example, should central bankers take asset price inflation into account more explicitly?

AP: We look at consumer prices because they're the things which affect households and ultimately welfare. If the **consumer price index (CPI)** wasn't broad enough to do that, then you'd want to change it. But I think it's very difficult to change something like the CPI. I looked at this some years back and it is amazing how many contracts are indexed to it in law. It would be an enormous job.

A new price index might be better or worse for monetary policy depending on whether people could understand it or not, just because we'd have to go through all these legal changes. I'm not sure there'd be any real benefit from it in the long run. Think of the introduction of the ASX into Australian stock markets. We still see the All Ordinaries despite this other superior measure of stock prices. And I think we'd find that the CPI would just continue on and we'd end up with two indexes, and it wouldn't be clear which one we should in fact be looking at. So I'm in favour of just staying with the CPI.

JL: What about the idea of changing the inflation target at certain points in time? Some economists argue, especially in relation to the Eurozone because of its fixed exchange rates, that we should raise the inflation target post-GFC. The suggestion is from 2 to 4 or 5 per cent for several years in order to avoid deflationary pressures in countries like Spain, Greece and Ireland. Do you think that changing the inflation target in times of major economic weakness might be beneficial?

AP: Well maybe, but I'm not sure that's true in the case of Europe. If you think of Spain, for example, the problem is the long-term interest rates, not the short-term interest rates. It's the long rates which are actually creating all the trouble, and if you raise the inflation target, it will just get built into the long rates. I think it's the fiscal issues there that are really the problems rather than monetary policy issues. The European Central Bank was a little slow at providing stimulus but I do think now that they've actually pretty much got that in the right direction. I can't see any reason to raise the target inflation rate.

JL: What about the lessons from the GFC about macroprudential policy that strives to ensure the stability of the financial sector? Do you think the central bank should be involved in **banking regulation**? A handful of countries have a different institution for that – for example, APRA in Australia – but in most countries it's the central bank doing macroprudential polices. What do you think is the right model?

AP: I think it depends on the size of the country. In a large country, there's an argument for having monetary and macroprudential policies separated. In a small country there's less of an argument. If you have different organisations doing prudential and monetary policy the problem is how you do the coordination, and that's not an easy task. If there's going to be 'lender of last resort' arrangements, it's the central bank that's got the cheque book – the regulating body doesn't.

So you have to coordinate these policies, which is something we've done pretty well in Australia. Because of that, I would be in favour of a separation in Australia. In the Bank of England, for example, the supervisors are actually setting up a prudential committee, which is going to do things that the monetary policy committee may have done in the past. I think it's very difficult to cover all those things in one body, so it's a good idea to separate them out. But in very small countries it would just be too costly to do that.

JL: Reducing various costs was one of the reasons behind the creation of the Eurozone, and I would like to briefly ask you about your view on its future. Do you think that we're going to have a resolution of the Euro crisis any time soon? Do you think that the Euro will survive in its current form?

AP: I'm not really an expert on the Eurozone. I felt that Greece should have gone a long time ago, but I'm not so sure anymore. I think Eurozone leaders have invested a tremendous amount into keeping Greece in, and they have to follow through with it. So I think the Euro will survive.

JL: My last question before handing it over to the audience is about public policies that economics implies would improve overall wellbeing, but politicians have shied away from. Can you think of some in regards to monetary policy, or even more broadly?

AP: The policy I would most like to see changed is **negative gearing**. The ability to write off interest payments on property against labour income began in 1985. Before that one could only write them off against property income. In the 10 years from 2001 to 2010 we saw the tax deductions rise from $600 million to $13.2 billion (a 22-fold increase). This has created both fiscal and monetary headaches; the latter because it is hard not to think that a lot of the rise in existing house prices has been a product of it.

Audience member 1: Before the 2007 election, there was a bit of a debate about inflation in Australia between the two major parties in regards to bananas. One side said that inflation was caused predominately by bananas; the other said it wasn't and that interest rates were going to have to rise. How do you reflect on this? Do you think that bananas were the problem, and if so, do you think the removal of trade barriers could help with monetary stability by allowing banana imports from overseas?

AP: Well, it is quarantine regulations that prevent imports of bananas. So it is tricky because quarantine is not something you can vary according to monetary stability. I wasn't actually here in 2007 when this occurred, but you can see in the CPI if it's due to bananas. If it's due to bananas you know the price will go back down again, at least in a year's time, so it's not the type of thing that you would actually respond to. It's just like the GST. Inflation may have gone up, but it'll go back down again, and it therefore doesn't call for monetary action. Your question sounded like there was some doubt about whether inflation was caused by bananas or not, but that's just a matter of what the CPI says.

Audience member 1: I think the debate was more about the magnitude. Inflation was rising, and one party was saying it was predominately due to bananas, whereas the other party disagreed.

AP: Political parties are always going to choose the argument that most appeals to them. But one of the arguments for why Australia has a flexible inflation target is that you can run above this range that we normally operate – between 2 and 3 per cent – to accommodate things like banana price rises.

At that point in time in early 2007, the RBA was increasing interest rates and it was because there were other signs of inflation. Not so much the CPI as it was coming out in terms of wages. There was very strong wage growth in various sectors because demand was growing quite strongly, so you were naturally going to raise interest rates. I remember I was giving a talk at the Economic Society and I got asked: 'Why are interest rates so high?' And I said I thought raising interest rates at the time was a good thing because there were signs of wage growth that would lead to inflation. And subsequently of course when the GFC hit, the interest rates were quite high so they could be reduced a long way. And they could have quite a stimulatory impact on the Australian economy as a result.

Audience member 2: A question about defining a shock. A natural disaster will obviously be a shock, but in many cases it is not so clear. Say throughout the month you get all this data, retail sales for example, and if they are much above or below expectations do you attribute this to a shock?

AP: Well, I don't think the Board would seriously take too much notice of variations in a monthly series in employment, or credit, or virtually anything else. It has to be sustained for some time otherwise it is not really a shock. The sort of shocks I'm thinking of are things like the Asian Financial Crisis back in 1997–98. That was a shock because there was no real reason why it should happen. If you looked at exchange rates at the time, maybe they were 10 per cent overvalued in Thailand and neighbouring countries, but suddenly all the investors rushed to the doors and that was a clear shock – it was something that was totally unexpected and persistent. And there are lots of shocks like that. The variation in monthly statistics I don't think is a shock.

The best example from my time on the RBA Board was a huge drop in imports into Australia one month. A financial journalist wrote this up as evidence that the Australian economy was sinking, because imports were collapsing, and therefore demand must be going down. The RBA spent a lot of time looking at this and discovered that the reason was Easter falling in March that year. All the imports had come in, but all the people who write out the invoices to record them had gone off on Easter holidays so they didn't get recorded in March, they got recorded in April. So one month, imports went down; next month, they went up by a long way. That's the type of thing that happens with these monthly statistics all the time, and you don't call them shocks. You just think that something's peculiar, and trying to work it out is the key thing that the central bank does. It has a lot of people who are very good at this type of thing, far more than the private sector does.

This relates to one of the questions we touched on earlier: 'Should the central bank release all the information they have?' I don't think that there's much that they don't release. What they have is a lot of people analysing data that most of the private sector doesn't have and, because of that, they are actually much better equipped for analysing it. You also asked before the interview about the Secretary of the Treasury being on the RBA Board, and what the Secretary of the Treasury brings of course is all the Treasury's experience of analysing the data. It's data analysis that the Bank has, and that's not the sort of thing you can actually release. There would be reams and reams and reams of it! Lots of things get done that no one would ever want to read.

I work at the RBA every now and then and, when I go in, I have an account there with my emails that come in from people around the Bank, and there must be hundreds and hundreds since the last time I was in there. Lots of times they're little minutes about some data that someone's analysed, but you wouldn't want to release all that because most of it is just here today, gone tomorrow.

JL: You mentioned the Secretary of the Treasury being on the RBA Board, that's a bit of an anomaly in Australia, it is not the case in other countries. Some people worry that it might compromise the independence of the RBA.

AP: Well, the Secretary to the Treasury sits there as the Secretary to the Treasury, not as the representative of the Treasurer, and I think he takes that position very seriously. He effectively presents another view based on quite a lot of analysis that the Treasury's done. I think that it's been a very good thing. No one else on the Board has the same level of support, same level of information and capacity to analyse things as what the Secretary to the Treasury does. The academics who sit on the Board have to do it all by themselves. They don't get a big budget or a team of people. You might also think this arrangement would help with coordinating fiscal and monetary policies, but I don't think it's actually ever done that.

JL: Adrian, thank you very much for sharing your expertise with us, as well as for all your contributions to public policymaking and academic research!

9.3 Key economic insights and policy lessons

Economic insights	Implied policy lessons (for public officials and voters)
The legislated objectives of monetary policy in Australia dictate that the RBA stabilise both prices and employment – in attempt to enhance social welfare.	Policymakers should pursue their 'dual' mandate carefully since the goals of stabilising prices and employment may be inconsistent at times.
Monetary policy cannot reduce the long-term (natural) rate of unemployment, but it can reduce short-term fluctuations in unemployment.	Policymakers should not set a long-term unemployment target for monetary policy.
If monetary policy is carried out by the government, inflation tends to be higher than optimal (there is an 'inflation bias'). This is because of a time-inconsistency problem, a short-term political temptation to reduce unemployment below its natural level by excessively low interest rates.	Policymakers should delegate monetary policy to a central bank that is formally independent from the government in order to avoid the time-inconsistency problem and inflation bias.
The monetary regime of inflation targeting explicitly formulates price stability as achieving a numerical inflation target. In order to still allow flexibility for short-term employment stabilisation, the target only has to be achieved on average over the business cycle, not at every point in time.	Policymakers should not be 'inflation nutters', but pursue flexible inflation targeting. That consists of aiming to have inflation on target on average over the medium term.
If the central bank is made accountable for achieving the legislated inflation target, and required to make its decisions and processes transparent, it is more likely to have credibility.	Policymakers should make sure that central bank independence goes hand-in-hand with transparency and accountability of monetary policy – to be consistent with democratic principles.
A numerical inflation target tends to anchor inflation expectations, which makes it easier for policymakers to stabilise shocks. If expectations are not anchored, interest rates have to be changed more aggressively in order to offset both the shock and the change in expectations.	Policymakers should carefully communicate to ensure that their actions are understood and credible, which not only enhances their effectiveness but also reduces the public's cost of acquiring information. They should discard outdated theories that monetary policy must surprise people to have an effect.
Data show that a flexible inflation target can anchor expectation without making the central bank ignore the real economy, i.e. without increasing the fluctuations in output and unemployment.	Policymakers should explain to the public that flexible inflation targeting does not constitute a straightjacket on the real economy.
Inflation targets tend to be around 2 per cent growth in consumer price index (CPI) rather than 0. This is due to the 'CPI upward bias', the fear of deflation, and the 'grease effects' in the presence of inflexible wages.	Policymakers should advocate committing to a low inflation target rather than a zero inflation target. In normal times (absence of a major downturn) the exact target value – whether it be 2 or 3 per cent – seems unimportant as long as the commitment is credible.
There is a debate whether inflation targets should be specified in terms of a broader measure of inflation, also including credit and asset prices, rather than just the CPI.	Policymakers should explore the desirability of using a more comprehensive measure of inflation, but take into account the potential downside in terms of less clarity.

Economic insights	Implied policy lessons (for public officials and voters)
Up until the 1980s central banks did not even announce their interest rate decisions. In contrast, modern central banks are transparent, include and publish their models and forecasts. There is, however, no consensus in terms of the specific forecasts to publish.	Policymakers should carefully consider whether to publish forecasts (that go to the central bank board) with the existing interest rate fixed or forecasts with the future intended interest rate trajectory built in. Each serves a different purpose and is beneficial to a different audience.
A limited number of monetary policy aspects may be better kept unpublished; for example, voting of the individual central bank board members.	Policymakers should think twice before starting to publish voting records. This may put undue pressure on board members and compromise their independence.
Monetary policy affects aggregate demand and thus output and inflation through several channels. The direct effects of interest rate changes include consumption, investment, exchange rate and net exports. The indirect effects work through people's expectations and confidence.	Policymakers should carefully incorporate both direct and indirect 'transmission mechanisms' into their analysis, and include all relevant real as well as nominal variables such as credit growth.
Monetary policy affects the economy with a delay. An interest rate change takes roughly a year to have its maximum impact on output, and an additional year to fully feed through to inflation.	Policymakers should take the delays of monetary actions into account and respond pre-emptively. They should pursue 'inflation forecast targeting' in which policy actions ensure that forecasts of key variables are on their desired levels in several years' time.
Central bankers cannot effectively deal with supply-side shocks such as natural disasters and sudden changes in petrol prices or GST. This is because they cause inflation and output to move in opposite directions, and monetary policy can thus only stabilise one at the expense of the other.	Policymakers should generally not use monetary policy in offsetting supply-side shocks; central bankers should 'look through' these shocks, and explain to the public that this is to avoid the 'wage–price spiral'.
During the GFC, many central banks have lowered short-term interest rates to zero and then engaged in the 'unconventional' monetary policy of 'quantitative easing'. It consists of purchasing various financial assets from private financial institutions in an attempt to lower long-term returns in the economy and boost aggregate demand.	Policymakers should rigorously assess the existing evidence on the effectiveness of quantitative easing, and factor it into their future policy decisions in a liquidity-trap environment.
In some countries, macroprudential policy (ensuring financial stability) and monetary policy (ensuring price stability) are both done by the central bank. In some countries, these two polices are done by two different institutions, e.g., APRA and the RBA in Australia.	Policymakers should consider the pros and cons of separating macroprudential and monetary policies into two institutions, including the prerequisite that they can cooperate effectively.
Economic data are sometimes measured imprecisely, which is why frequent data revisions occur.	Policymakers should not take too much notice of a one-off swing in monthly economic series in order to avoid responding to inaccurate data.
The Secretary to the Treasury is a member of the RBA's Board, which is not the case in other countries. This could in principle compromise the Bank's independence, but it does not seem to have been the case in Australia since the introduction of inflation targeting.	Policymakers should carefully consider the advantages and disadvantages of having a government official on the central bank board.

9.4 Discussion questions

1   Using your own words, summarise the debate of Section 9.2 in three to five sentences.

2   Write down one idea discussed in the interview that you found new or interesting, or that you disagree with, and briefly explain why.

3   Write down one question on any topic covered in the interview that you would ask the speaker if you had a chance.

4   Consider the cartoon in Section 9.1, and explain the point to someone who has not read the section and does not have any knowledge of economics.

5   Examine Figure 9.1 from the perspective of a policymaker. Describe its key message to the public and explain what kind of policy improvement is implied by the data. Do the same for Figure 9.2.

6   Suppose you take part in a debating contest, in which the topic is the opening quote of the chapter by Milton Friedman:

> *Inflation is the one form of taxation that can be imposed without legislation.*

Prepare a speech you would give for the affirmative side. Then (you or your classmate) prepare a speech for the negative side. If possible, organise an audience and perform the debate.

7   What are the three monetary policy objectives legislated in the 1959 *Reserve Bank Act*? Why does Prof. Pagan assert that there needs to be more clarity around those objectives? Compare them to the monetary policy objectives of two other countries of your choice, and highlight the similarities and differences.

8   What is inflation targeting? Explain whether it is correct to infer from this term that central banks only focus on inflation and ignore all other economic variables. What is 'inflation forecast targeting' and why do central bankers pursue it in practice?

9   Download the one-page statement by the Governor of the RBA explaining the reasons for the most recent change in the cash rate target (all statements are available at **www.rba.gov.au/media-releases**). Summarise the reason for the change, and identify whether it is more from the demand or supply side of the economy. Explain the intended effect of the change on the main macroeconomic variables.

10 Why do central bankers usually 'look through' aggregate supply shocks? Discuss the two ways in which interest rates could be changed in response to such a shock, and explain why neither of them leads to satisfactory outcomes.

11 What does it mean for a central bank to be 'independent' and what are the advantages and disadvantages? The Secretary to the Treasury is a member of the Reserve Bank of Australia's Board. Does Prof. Pagan think this may compromise the RBA's independence? What is your view?

12 Why do central banks pay so much attention to inflation expectations? Why do they strive for expectations to be anchored? What role does a legislated numerical inflation target play in this respect? Find data on inflation expectations in Australia and assess whether the RBA has been successful in anchoring inflation expectations.

13 What does transparency mean in regards to monetary policy? (For a non-technical summary you can consult Libich, 2006.) Is there any aspect of the central banking operations that Prof. Pagan believes should not be made public? Explain his reasoning and outline your view on the issue.

14 Explain what 'quantitative easing' is and what it attempts to achieve. Based on some recent studies, try to assess the effectiveness of the quantitative easing pursued in the US in the post-GFC period.

15 What were the monetary policy lessons from the GFC? How does Prof. Pagan see the future of inflation targeting? What is your view?

16 What is macroprudential policy? Should central banks be involved in this policy, or should a different institution be in charge? Discuss the pros and cons of each alternative.

17 Outline Prof. Pagan's argument on 'negative gearing' and present your own view.

18 Propose a set of innovative policies that you think best promote price stability and ultimately people's wellbeing.

9.5 Where to find out more

Bank of England (1999), 'The Transmission Mechanism of Monetary Policy', The Monetary Policy Committee, available at **www.bankofengland.co.uk/publications/ Documents/other/monetary/montrans.pdf**

Batini, N., G. Callegari and J. Guerreiro (2011), 'An Analysis of U.S. Fiscal and Generational Imbalances: Who Will Pay and How?', International Monetary Fund Working Paper, WP/11/72.

Berg, C. (2000), 'Inflation Forecast Targeting: The Swedish Experience', in High-Level Seminar: Implementing Inflation Targets, International Monetary Fund.

Breusch, T. S. and A. R. Pagan (1979), 'A Simple Test for Heteroscedasticity and Random Coefficient Variation', *Econometrica*, Econometric Society, 47(5), pp. 1287–1294.

Czech National Bank (2014), 'Fan Chart for Consumer Price Inflation', *CNB Current Forecast*, 6 November, available at **www.cnb.cz/en/monetary_policy/forecast**

Dungey, M. and B. Hayward (2010), 'Data Surveys: Dating Changes in Monetary Policy in Australia', *The Australian Economic Review*, 33(3), pp. 281–285.

Greider, W. (1989), *Secrets of the Temple: How the Federal Reserve Runs the Country*, Simon and Schuster.

Hughes Hallett, A. and J. Libich (2012), 'Explicit Inflation Targets, Communication, and Central Bank Independence: Friends or Foes?', *Economic Change and Restructuring*, 45(4), pp. 271–297.

Hughes Hallett, A., J. Libich and P. Stehlík (2010), 'Macroprudential Policies and Financial Stability', *The Economic Record*, 87(277), pp. 318–335.

Krugman, P. (2014), 'Inflation Targets Reconsidered', draft paper for ECB Sintra conference, May, available at **https://2014. ecbforum.eu/up/artigos-bin_paper_pdf_ 0134658001400681089-957.pdf**

Lengwiler, Y. (2003), 'MOPOS: Excel Module Implementing Monetary Policy Simulation Game', *Statistical Software Components* X0305032, Boston College Department of Economics.

Libich, J. (2006), 'Should Monetary Policy be Transparent?', *Policy*, 22(1), Autumn, available at **http://www.cis.org.au/app/ uploads/2015/04/images/stories/policy- magazine/2006-autumn/2006-22-1-jan- libich.pdf**

Libich, J. (2009), 'A Note on the Anchoring Effect of Explicit Inflation Targets', *Macroeconomic Dynamics*, Cambridge University Press, 13(5), pp. 685–697.

Pagan, A. (2003), 'Report on Modelling and Forecasting at the Bank of England', *Quarterly Bulletin Economic Modelling*, Spring, Bank of England.

RBA (2013), 'Statement on the Conduct of Monetary Policy', The Treasurer and the Governor of the Reserve Bank, available at www.rba.gov.au/monetary-policy/framework/stmt-conduct-mp-6-24102013.html

Sargent, T. J. and N. Wallace (1981), 'Some Unpleasant Monetarist Arithmetic', *Federal Reserve Bank of Minneapolis Quarterly Review*, Fall, pp. 1–17.

10 Banking, financial markets and crises

When you combine ignorance and leverage, you get some pretty interesting results.

Warren Buffett, the world's most successful investor and philanthropist, date and source unknown.

Economic concepts discussed

Easy-to-understand explanations of all the concepts listed below appear in the glossary at the end of this book.

- AAA rating
- Basel III (the Third Basel Accord)
- Central bank
- Collateralised debt obligation (CDO)
- Consumption smoothing
- Credit crunch
- Credit default swap (CDS)
- Diversification
- Fiscal multiplier
- Fiscal stimulus

- Flight to safety
- Fractional reserve banking
- Game of chicken
- Government failure
- Government guarantee
- Hedging
- Leverage
- Liquid asset
- Liquidity trap
- Market failure
- Monetary base
- Money multiplier

- Money supply
- Moral hazard
- Mortgage-backed securities
- Mortgage securitisation
- Structured Investment Vehicle (SIV)
- Subprime mortgages
- Tier 1 capital
- Too-big-to-fail
- Zero-lower-bound on interest rates

10.1 Motivation and overview

The 2008 Global Financial Crisis (GFC) has focused the media on banks and other financial institutions. Gambling bankers, toxic mortgage securities, golden parachutes: 'What is the point of having a financial system?', many people ask. To give a short answer, the data shows that a well-functioning financial system increases the performance of the economy and prosperity of the people. But if it does not function well, the financial system can turn 'from hero to villain'.

This chapter, based on an interview with Michael Knox conducted on 31 October 2012, discusses both of these alter egos of the financial system. His wide range of expertise from both the private and public sectors offers unique insights into investment banking as well as the GFC and its main lessons. Mr Knox is currently Chief Economist and Director Strategy at RBS Morgans, one of Australia's top 10 investment banks, and past President of the Economic Society of Australia (Queensland branch). His experience with policymaking includes Australian Trade Commissioner in Saudi Arabia and Indonesia, Chairmanship of the Queensland Food Industry Strategy Committee and membership of the Ministerial Advisory Committee on Economic Development.[1]

To provide some background, the financial system has essentially two main functions. The first one is connecting savers and investors, and this linkage is not only from households to companies, allowing them to expand production capacity, but also within the lifecycle of each individual. In particular, the financial system enables people to engage in **consumption smoothing** over time by bringing their future earnings forward through mortgages and other types of loans.

The second important function of the financial system is a reduction of risks through 'diversification'. This is achieved by investing in different types of assets or 'hedging' against undesirable scenarios. For example, if you have all your savings in the form of gold or all in shares, you face the risk that its value will decline dramatically. But if you hold both gold and shares at the same time, the risk of loss is smaller because the returns to these two types of assets tend to be negatively correlated – when economic prospects are good the price of gold tends to go down and the price of shares up.

Economic data show that a well-functioning financial system can indeed be a 'hero' and have a positive effect on economic development. For example, a developed financial sector has been shown to lead to higher GDP per capita, higher productivity and a more equal distribution of income. The notion that only 'the rich' benefit from financial markets is therefore a myth.

However, the 'well-functioning' bit is crucial here, otherwise the financial system may turn out to be harmful. The GFC experience in the United States and Europe has shown how detrimental to people's wellbeing it may be when financial markets move away from their two key objectives described above, and start acting like a casino. A casino in which the players do not gamble with their own money, but rather with someone else's – the taxpayers' – money.

Mr Knox, however, stresses throughout the interview that in Australia the situation was very different, and the financial system did not engage in the risky financial innovation and opaque **mortgage securitisation** that almost brought Wall Street to its knees. He identifies two key differences responsible for widely different outcomes in the financial market: the quality of the Australian regulatory framework and political governance. He explains that:

> Both sides of the US Congress wanted the mortgage
> securitisation to happen because they wanted to gain more
> votes from lower-income voters. So I think this was a
> deliberate distortion of the regulatory framework resulting
> from the political process in the United States. It notably did
> not occur in Canada, it did not occur in Australia.[2]

---

1 The full video-interview is available at **https://youtu.be/sFFwQ0aPB5I**. For more details regarding Mr Knox, see **www.morgans.com.au/about-us/Our-People/Our-Research-Team/Michael-Knox**

2 As a demonstration of the resulting lax lending standards, journalist Michael Lewis wrote about a mortgage contract in regional California, in which 'a Mexican strawberry picker with an income of $14 000 and no English was lent every penny he needed to buy a house of $724 000' (Lewis, 2011).

Put differently, he sees the GFC in the US and Europe not so much as a result of a **market failure**, but predominantly as a consequence of **government failure**. The discussion then outlines how the trend towards **subprime mortgages** and their securitisation proceeded. This is highlighted in the cartoon below depicting a pre-2008 conversation between Fed Chairman Ben Bernanke and legendary investor Warren Buffett.

Concept by Jan Libich © 2015, drawing by Veronika Mojžišová. Used by permission.

Figure 10.1 reports relevant data on issuance of **mortgage-backed securities** in the United States: separately for the mortgage giants Fannie Mae, Freddie Mac and Ginnie Mae (the so-called 'Government Sponsored Enterprises', GSEs), and for other financial institutions. Both groups had seen a dramatic increase in the several years prior to the GFC.

Hand in hand with the mortgage securitisation process, the indebtedness of the financial sector had grown rapidly, much faster than the economy. For example, in the US and Europe it climbed from values around 50 per cent of GDP in 1995 to 110 per cent of GDP in 2007. The sum of banking assets in some countries exceeded their GDP by more than eight-fold. All this had a direct connection to both the internet (dotcom) bubble in the late 1990s and the subsequent housing bubble in the five years prior to 2008. Housing prices in real terms (i.e. adjusted for inflation) increased in many countries by 100 per cent between 1996 and 2006, with most of the increase recorded in the second half of this period.

The discussion then moves onto the dire consequences of this real estate bubble bursting, both for the financial markets and for real economies around the globe. Mr Knox describes the negative effect the crisis had on employees in the finance industry, and makes the following parallel: 'It's like the movie business, boom and bust. Some people

Figure 10.1: Mortgage-backed securities (MBS) issuance in the US between 1996 and 2014 (in USD billions). The GSE group includes Fannie Mae, Freddie Mac and Ginnie Mae

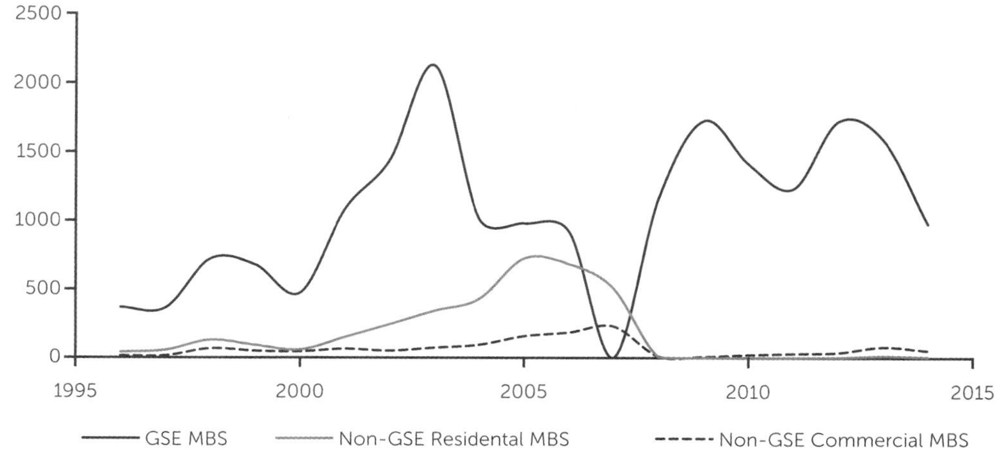

Source: Adapted from Sifma (2015).

make a lot of money, they get a lot of publicity, but you don't see the waiters getting interviewed – you only see the people who are successful.'

The issue of big bonuses paid to investment bankers is also discussed, where the situation is again very different in Australia and in the United States. As *The Wall Street Journal* reported in 2009, the nine largest US banks that were recipients of government bailout money paid out bonuses to their employees of nearly $33 billion in 2008:

> *including more than $1 million apiece to nearly 5000 employees – despite huge losses that plunged the US into economic turmoil.*

Mr Knox highlights one consequence of the asset bubble's bursting, namely banks in the US and Europe hoarding excess reserves in the post-GFC period. The left panel of Figure 10.2 shows that the US monetary base (currency + banks' reserves at the Fed) has been rising rapidly since 2008, whereas the money supply (currency + people's deposits with commercial banks) have increased much less. This resulted in the value of the US **money multiplier** dropping dramatically, similarly to the United Kingdom. The right panel of Figure 10.2, however, shows that the situation in Australia differed substantially.

The interview then discusses how the US and UK financial systems can be fixed, and in a sense transformed from villain back to hero. Mr Knox is in favour of the 'Teddy Roosevelt solution':

> *When former US President Teddy Roosevelt invented the anti-trust legislation at the beginning of the twentieth century, he broke up large oil and steel companies. Clearly some banks have now got to a point where they are too big and I think they need to be broken up as steel companies back then.*

Figure 10.2: Monetary aggregates (left axes) and money multipliers (right axes) in the United States (left) and Australia (right)

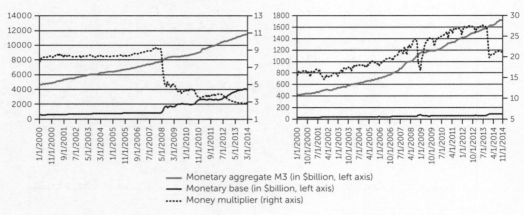

——— Monetary aggregate M3 (in $billion, left axis)
——— Monetary base (in $billion, left axis)
····· Money multiplier (right axis)

Source: Claeys et al. (2014).

This is to reduce the systemic risk in the financial system and avoid the '**too-big-to-fail**' problem. This term refers to the threat that the bankruptcy of a large financial company would cause havoc in the markets and bring even healthy institutions to a collapse. Such a threat is troublesome as it is associated with a '**moral hazard**' problem. It requires the government to offer (implicit) guarantees to such large financial institutions, which they may, however, abuse by acting in a reckless casino-type manner. This in turn adds unwelcome risk to the financial system and makes financial bankruptcies more likely, with the taxpayer footing the bill. Ireland provides an example of how costly it can be. Primarily due to bank bailouts, the gross public debt of Ireland increased from 25 per cent of GDP in 2008 to over 120 per cent of GDP within five years!

An alternative to the Teddy Roosevelt solution in making sure financial institutions do not grow too big is a suggestion by Nassim Taleb, author of the bestselling book *The Black Swan*. He argues that if a company grows large enough that it could threaten the financial system and require **government guarantees**, the salaries of its employees should be automatically reduced to the level paid in the public sector. Other influential proposals for fixing the financial system include a departure from the existing '**fractional reserve banking**' system back to '100 per cent reserve banking'; see, for example, Kumhof and Benes (2012).

The interview then touches on the **game of chicken** between the **central bank** and the government modelled in Hughes Hallett, Libich and Stehlík (2007). Mr Knox believes that the game:[3]

> is very much happening now … the government is hoping
> that this fiscal tightening will induce the RBA to reduce
> interest rates, which will decrease the cost of housing finance
> and indirectly increase the government's political popularity.

Economic data seem to support this conjecture, whereby the RBA reduced the cash rate target from 4.75 per cent to 2 per cent between the time the interview took place in October 2012 and mid–2015.

---

3 For more, see his federal budget lunch address, Knox (2012).

Many other questions are covered in the interview; for example: 'How to best eliminate excessive **leverage** of financial institutions through banking regulation?', 'Has the stock market boom since 2009 been justified or are we experiencing another global asset bubble?', 'Do economies need higher inflation in the aftermath of the GFC?', and 'What kind of **fiscal stimulus** is effective?'. Mr Knox concludes with a message he took away from the crisis:

> *We got to the US banking crisis on the road to good intentions –
> by trying to get lower-income people houses that they couldn't
> afford. In Europe it was the inclusion of poorer countries that
> should not have been in the Euro; for example, Greece. Both of
> these were driven by good intentions. So one lesson we can
> learn is that in terms of banking and other policy regulations,
> we should always be aware of good intentions.*

10.2 The debate

Dr Jan Libich (JL): When talking about financial markets and institutions one cannot but start with the difference between retail banking and investment banking. Could you summarise it for us, and suggest whether these two types of banking should be separated – as was the case in the United States between 1933 and 1999?

© Michael Knox. Used by permission.

< Michael Knox (MK): Retail banking is the place you go to get the services that you and I use to help us shop. You go to the branch, you make deposits, you make withdrawals, you get a mortgage loan for your house, you arrange a credit card; all those sorts of things that you need to facilitate day-to-day life. Investment banks are based on the idea of the US wholesale market. Back in the 1930s the US decided to break up branch banks. They had a 'brilliant' idea that if one branch in a bank failed, then all the other branches would fail too. They thought, with a towering level of intellect, that the problem to branches collapsing must be branch banking. So they outlawed it in 1933 in a piece of legislation called the *Glass–Steagall Act*.

And the result of that was that you needed a large capital market in the US for banks to trade bonds with each other, for capital to get around. So you had banks that specialised in the capital market and bond trading, and a very deep financial market grew out of that in the United States. With floating exchange rates that became a multinational thing, because to have a floating exchange rate you need to be able to swap bonds between one country and another. To do that you need investment banks. And they worked pretty well with retail banks. In Australia we need to raise money overseas in the wholesale investment banks and import it for our retail banks to provide it to the ordinary person.

JL: The separation of the two types of banking in the US lasted until 1999 when the *Glass–Steagall Act* you mentioned was repealed. What was the logic behind this move? And is it something we should blame the Global Financial Crisis (GFC) on?

MK: No, I don't think you should blame the GFC on this. I think the crisis came from a different area. This whole separation in the *Glass–Steagall Act* in the 1930s was really about branch banking, not necessarily about investment and retail banking. And when *Glass–Steagall* was repealed you had a process happening in the US which had already happened in British, Canadian, South African and Australian banks.

What you had in addition though was entirely new institutions that were unique to the US environment: Fannie Mae and Freddie Mac. They were supposed to support the wholesale mortgage market. We didn't need that in Australia or in the UK because we had branch banking. But you needed it in the US because of the absence of branch banking. And those mortgage originators seemed to be, over a period of 20 years or so, extremely safe. But at the end of the 1990s, both sides of US politics decided to distort the use of those mortgage originators by creating subprime loans …

JL: We should mention that these two giant mortgage companies have had implicit government guarantees, which is why they are referred to as 'Government Sponsored Enterprises' (GSEs). And they were set up to implement this 'affordable housing' idea of politicians, that as many people as possible should own their house. You mentioned that the GSEs were originally safe, why did that change in the lead-up to the GFC?

MK: Well, actually, in the late 1930s when Fannie Mae was set up, it was a government instrumentality. Then in the late 1960s under the Democratic administration, Lyndon Johnson took Fannie Mae off the government balance sheet in order to reduce the apparent accounting size of the US budget deficit. And then Freddie Mac, Fannie's little brother, came along in 1970 and just before that another trading intermediary called Ginnie Mae. It was around that time when the actual explicit government guarantee became an implicit guarantee.

And these functioned pretty well, including in the early 1980s when the Savings & Loans collapsed in the United States. It's due to the fact that the GSEs expanded their market share during this difficult period that people believed they were really rock solid. It's only in the late 1990s that the *Affordable Housing Act* was passed through Congress and this is the legislation that enables subprime loans. And then Fannie Mae and

Freddie Mac were put under pressure by both sides of US politics to try to advance these subprime loans.

The idea was that because US housing prices had been rising for 20 years, we can generate a new form of mortgage, subprime. People who can't afford housing at the moment because they don't have enough assets can still get immediate exposure to housing. And with the increase in their house price they will qualify for an ordinary mortgage in a few years' time, so the subprime loan is an entry level product into housing. In Australia we have a program called the First Home Buyer's Grant based on a similar idea. But subprime loans really only work if house prices continue to rise forever and the 'problem' was that they didn't.

JL: Regarding the poor lending standards, it was disappointing that the regulator allowed mortgage companies to offer various 'teaser' interest rates and 'no proof of income, no down payment' type loans. The numbers show the resulting rise in subprime mortgages. In the early 1990s they formed less than 5 per cent of the US mortgage market whereas in 2006 it was over 20 per cent. More than 80 per cent of these were securitised, mostly by Fannie Mae and Freddie Mac. And hand in hand with that the housing bubble was being inflated in the United States. In Australia one driver of rapidly rising house prices is the fact that people buy 'investment properties'. But we teach our students that the main thing about an investment is that it should be **liquid** – easily convertible into cash, which is certainly not the case with real estate. So how did we get into such an unsatisfactory state of affairs?

MK: Well, it's kind of history, if you have seen house prices going up for 20 years you think that they are going to continue to go up in future. But the peak in US house prices, which occurred in 2006, was about US$240 000 for a three-bedroom house, which is incredibly cheap in Australian terms. Prices then fell down to about US$160 000 in 2011 and now [October 2014] they are up to about US$180 000. So those house prices are really low relative to Australia. When you look at the data the problem is not so much that there was a boom in house prices, but that there was a boom in housing finance due to subprime loans and their securitisation.

Securitisation gave people the illusion that if you mixed up a whole lot of different mortgages together you could rate these mortgage-backed securities AAA – despite a high proportion of the underlying mortgages being subprime. Standard & Poor's actually went through a rating exercise with these securitised products. They found that as long as housing prices didn't fall by more than 10 per cent, the impact would be on the subprime section but not on the other sections, so it really had no effect on the value of the security. This is why they believed they could rate those mortgage-backed securities AAA. This is also why banks began to include them as part of the **Tier 1 capital** within the United States. And that seemed fine because they were **AAA-rated** by Standard & Poor's, but it wasn't fine in terms of the financial turmoil that happened later.

JL: This was, however, not the end of the financial magic, because these mortgage-backed securities were further securitised. And we did not just have plain vanilla **collateralised debt obligations (CDOs)** backed-up by the subprime mortgages, we had various 'mezzanine CDOs' and 'CDOs squared'. These were created from the risky part of the CDO and hence even riskier but their top tranches were still rated as (Senior) AAA. And they were insured through **credit default swaps (CDS)** and passed on like a hot potato. How come regulators allowed this mislabelling to be happening on a large scale? Has there been a regulatory failure in not imposing stringent rules and transparency in creating and labelling these complex financial products?

MK: I actually think there was a deliberate failure of regulation. There is a line that I love from Mark Twain that in the United States there is no organised criminal class except Congress. Both sides of the US Congress wanted the securitisation to happen because they wanted to gain more votes from lower-income voters. So I think this was a deliberate distortion of the regulatory framework resulting from the political process in the United States. It notably did not occur in Canada, it did not occur in Australia.

JL: So the common narrative of many people blaming bankers for the financial crisis is a misrepresentation of the facts in your view? How would you defend the financial industry?

MK: Well, if the US Congress investigates these matters it's likely to blame everybody except itself. But there are very good commentaries on the process, and the best is a book by Raghuram Rajan, who was Chief Economist at the International Monetary Fund during the 2003–06 period.

JL: *Fault Lines* I think it's called …

MK: *Fault Lines*, yes. Rajan spoke about this at the Jackson Hole symposium organised by the Federal Reserve in 2005. He forecast how these asset-backed securities that were held as Tier 1 capital by US banks would inevitably lead to a crisis. And Larry Summers, former US Treasury Secretary, said that Rajan was a roadblock in the way of financial progress.

JL: I guess the subsequent developments showed clearly who won the argument … But another problem that people have with the finance industry is this greed aspect. It is argued that investment bankers have a very short-term focus, and tend to jeopardise the long-term prosperity of their company and clients by excessively risky short-term focused investments to collect a high annual bonus. While I agree this is a serious problem, I am not sure about the difference between greed and self-interest, which we all seem to have. Can you perhaps shed some light on this?

MK: It's like chief executives' high salaries that people object to. If they weren't paid a lot of money they would be company owners in their own right. So rather than those people being successful operators of their own companies, large corporations pay them a lot of money to generate those kinds of gains for their companies.

In financial markets you are moving a large amount of capital, you have to move it very efficiently and very rapidly. The downside for the people who make losses in financial markets is enormous, they get fired. We've seen that kind of effect in JP Morgan. The person that was the head of risk in JP Morgan, an extremely competent person with a long background, got fired because of a failure in the British bank trading section of JP Morgan. So the rewards are enormous, the penalties for failure are immediate, and therefore the financial compensation is high.

JL: I think the problem is that some people and companies in the financial sector do not bear full responsibility for their actions, so the incentives are not quite right. Financial brokers don't have to give back their past bonuses even if these were earned by very risky short-term oriented investments that subsequently yield a huge cost to the company. And financial companies in trouble then turn to the government for a bailout arguing they are 'too-big-to-fail', so the taxpayer is on the hook ...

MK: Well, financial market compensation is good when it's good and terrible when it's bad. During the boom people got paid a lot of money but over the last four years job losses in finance have been dramatic, so we are seeing both sides of the industry now. Now it's really tough and companies are going broke, people are being fired. It's like the movie business, boom and bust. Some people make a lot of money, they get a lot of publicity, but you don't see the waiters getting interviewed – you only see the people who are successful.

JL: This reminds me of the joke popular in the post-financial crisis era: 'What's the difference between an investment banker and a pizza? Well, a pizza can still feed a family of four.'

MK: Yes, sure, maybe the investment banker is actually carrying the pizza ... But let me address the issue of 'too-big-to-fail' you raised. It's obvious that the amalgamation of banks led to a situation where some banks were beyond management, Citicorp would be the best example. It became the largest banking organisation in the world and then in the financial crisis it became insolvent. It only continued to exist because of the Troubled Asset

Relief Program (TARP) by the US Treasury, so clearly the company got too big. What is the best solution to that?

It's the original paradox in *Lombard Street*, the classic book by Bagehot that was written about central banking in the nineteenth century. To avoid the moral hazard problem you have to tell bankers that you will never provide them liquidity or bail them out. But when a crisis happens you renege on this promise in order to avoid panic and bank runs. So I subscribe to the Teddy Roosevelt solution. When former US President Teddy Roosevelt invented the anti-trust legislation at the beginning of the twentieth century, he broke up large oil and steel companies. Clearly some banks have now got to a point where they are too big and I think they need to be broken up as steel companies back then. In the US something like 20 smaller banks have gone broke without a bailout so far in 2012, but they haven't had any systemic effect on the finance industry.

We have banks in Australia which are much smaller than US and UK banks, but they operate effectively as international banks. US and British banks need to be broken down to the level of Australian banks to reduce the systemic risk. I think you have to support banks as part of central banking. You can't say you are not going to do it, and you can't effectively provide that kind of support only for banks above a certain size, so I think you should break up the banks as was the case with steel mills and oil companies at the beginning of the twentieth century.

JL: We saw first-hand in Ireland and Iceland what happens when banks grow too large, their banking assets amounted to roughly 10 times the size of the economy. The losses of banks in Iceland greatly exceeded the country's GDP, so even if the policymakers had wanted there was simply no way to bail out those institutions. A regulatory question related to that is: 'How do we eliminate excessive leverage?' Do policymakers need to impose regulation limiting indebtedness and specifying minimum capital requirements, such as the **Basel III Accord**, or will the market self-regulate and sort it out?

MK: Sure, of course we need to limit leverage, but it has always been regulated within banking legislation. It's just the level at which you should regulate leverage. But the problem before the financial crisis was that a lot of the risky asset-backed securities owned by US banks were actually parked off balance sheets in **Structured Investment Vehicles (SIV)** avoiding this regulation. So when you looked at the formal balance sheet of the US banks they were within the regulatory level and they had enough capital. And notionally the SIVs, which were subsidiaries of the banks, didn't affect the leverage (gearing) ratio of the parent company. But when the SIVs collapsed, the losses had to be taken onto the parent company's balance sheet.

So the regulatory structure always regulated the level of leverage that US banks could have, it's just that they were allowed to get around it by owning SIVs. I think there was a gross misunderstanding of asset-backed securities. I remember reading the speeches of former Fed Chairman Alan Greenspan, in which he did believe that a diversifying portfolio effect of having different asset-backed securities mixed together in the Collateralised Debt Obligation really reduced the risk and really allowed it to be rated AAA. So I think there was a financial innovation that was not understood at the time, which had vastly more risk because of its complexity, and the complexity shielded the understanding of the true level of risk.

JL: This misunderstanding had a major impact on the stock market. This is both in terms of the boom prior to the crisis, and the large decline following the September 2008 collapse of Lehman Brothers, the fourth-largest US investment bank at the time. But stock markets started recovering around March 2009, and have been booming since. What worries me is that when you look at the fundamentals in terms of the US and global economy and all the long-term problems on the horizon, it doesn't seem to me that such a stock market boom has been justified. And I am not alone, there are some prominent economists concerned that the recent boom could be another bubble. Others point to why the stock market started booming – suggesting that banks used the 2008/9 bailout money to buy stock at the bottom of the market and therefore made large profits. What is your view on such alleged unfair usage of taxpayers' money and more generally on the drivers of the US stock market?

MK: Well, I think that's a really great conspiracy theory that is supported by everything except the facts. The reason the US stock markets have recovered since 2009 has absolutely nothing to do with the banks. Bank earnings were, up until a year ago, very miserable I have to say. And the housing sector was still down until about a year ago, you have only seen some recovery this year, 2012. The stock of unsold houses has fallen down to a level that the inventory of unsold houses is, for the first time in five years, less than six months. So house prices have stopped falling in the United States, and the result of that is that mortgage lending has started to rise, meaning banks have started to make more money. But only now, after five years.

So why has the US stock market gone up since 2009? The stock market has gone up because the US has a dynamic economy and a whole lot of industries have boomed, which have nothing to do with banking, nothing to do with housing. We have seen a boom in two major US industries since about 2005, technology and energy. We've seen an enormous boom in technology investment. Technology investment in real terms year by year has been increasing in the last few years as rapidly as it was in the tech boom of the 1990s. But we have had a different sort of technology boom, we have had a consumer technology boom. In those days people were building the internet, now people are using the internet. So there has been an enormous boom of technology companies; for example, Apple has become the most profitable company in the United States. That wasn't true in 2006.

In addition to that, we have had a whole revolution in the production of energy in the United States since 2007, and that has been through shale gas. The price of shale gas relative to gasoline in the United States is one-sixth of what it was in 2002 because of the massive increase in the production of shale gas. This boom has produced enormous profits for energy companies and the technology boom has generated enormous profits for technology companies. So we think that stock markets in the US are about 200 points too cheap. They should be more than 15 per cent higher than they currently are; for example, the S&P 500 index around 1660 rather than 1410. That's because you have a broadly based dynamic US economy that has a lot more doing than just building houses and lending money to people to do it.

JL: That is true, but Keynesian economists would point to the poor employment record; unemployment is still much higher and labour force participation rates much lower than prior to the crisis. Anyway, let's now move from the causes of the crisis onto policy responses. Central banks have reduced interest rates to very low levels, many all the way to zero. Some economists, for example Warwick McKibbin [Chapter 11], a member of the Reserve Bank of Australia Board until last year, believe that once central banks reduce rates below about 3 per cent, capital misallocation is likely to occur. Are you worried that having zero interest rates for several years may lead to various imbalances in the future?

MK: There are a whole lot of issues in what you've just said but I will just cut to the chase. There is a very strong empirical relationship between the real (inflation-adjusted) Federal funds rate and US employment rate two and a half years later. So if you want to maximise year-on-year growth on payroll employment in the US what you've got to do is reduce the real Fed funds rate. The only way you can reduce the real Fed funds rate when the nominal rate is already zero per cent is by increasing inflation. And the only way you can do that is increasing the money base, i.e. print money. So my view is that if the Federal Reserve wants to increase employment it needs to be maintaining a higher level of inflation than the current 1.9 per cent, it needs to target an inflation rate between 3 and 4 per cent.

I think the insights of Hyman Minsky apply here in regards to low interest rates. He was the guy who invented the phrase 'credit crunch', which is what we went through in 2007–09, and he talked about what happens when you let your debt-to-GDP ratio get to very high levels.

If it can't be supported by the level of income, it can only be supported at very low levels of interest rate. So either you have extremely low real interest rates or you find this enormous public debt to crush the economy into deflation. So what do we want? Do we want to have deflation generating a 1930s Great Depression scenario or do we want a higher employment growth allowing us to grow out of the problems? This is why I don't think providing resources to employment growth is a misallocation of resources.

JL: I agree that a temporary increase in inflation would help, both on the employment front and on the public debt front. But it is still only a short-term fix. From a longer-term perspective what you want is that government debt doesn't reach high levels in the first place. And this brings us to fiscal policy and its responses to the crisis. We've seen a lot of fiscal stimuli in 2008 and beyond, have these packages been successful in averting a major disaster, or have they not really played an important role in countries like the US?

MK: The best individual study I have read on the US was by Mark Zandi and Alan Blinder, former Vice-Chairman of the Fed, who looked at the effects of two fiscal policy packages. The first was the October 2008 Troubled Asset Relief Program (TARP) attempting to re-capitalise banks by an injection of US$700 billion (later reduced to below US$500 billion). The second was the February 2009 Obama *Recovery Act*, which was around US$800 billion, aimed at creating jobs. The authors found that re-capitalising the banks and other industries was five times more effective than old-fashioned public spending, which had a **fiscal multiplier** lower than one.

So what I learnt from reading Blinder and Zandi was that if we want to do fiscal stimulus, what we should do is an entirely new form that wasn't done in the Great Depression of the 1930s. Rather than building schools or putting defective insulation in our ceilings, in Australia we should have been buying preference shares at the bottom of the stock market when the stock market was 50 per cent lower than it currently is. And that would have been a much better investment in terms of generating employment in Australia and as a return on taxpayers' money.

The old-fashioned fiscal stimulus worked really well when we all lived in closed economies, because the money went round and round so you had higher fiscal multipliers. Now we live in very open economies and many fiscal multipliers for European countries are 0.3 or 0.4. So for every Euro the government spends they get 30–40 cents in output, and in Australia we probably get 70 cents for a dollar the government spends. I think if you have to pay back $1 and you only get 70 cents to add to GDP, you're much better off not spending the money.

At the bottom of the GFC the RBA still had a 3 per cent interest rate, so we could have had a much bigger stimulatory effect on the Australian economy by cutting interest rates down to 0 per cent than by spending what turned out to be AU$200 billion in international debt. And we saw that the RBA had to turn around and tighten monetary policy to almost 5 per cent in 2011 to offset the stimulatory effect of the 2008–10 government spending. This actually turned out to generate a long-term growth recession in the Australian economy where retailing, house building, and all other industries except mining had to be stood on to reduce inflation, and inflation was too high because of the fiscal stimulus. So it seems to me that the cost we paid for the fiscal stimulus in Australia was much greater than the benefit that we received.

JL: In terms of the size of fiscal multipliers, there was a recent controversy featuring the International Monetary Fund (IMF). They openly conceded that in their post-2008 projections they were using a fiscal multiplier of around 0.5 based on past estimates, but they now believe that in the aftermath of a major financial crisis such as the GFC the fiscal multiplier is much higher, between 1 and 1.7. This is because interest rates hit the 'zero-lower-bound' and we are effectively in a 'liquidity trap' situation. Such a revised multiplier means that post-2008 fiscal stimuli would have probably been more effective than people had thought. And it also means that fiscal austerity that Europe and others have embarked on since 2010 may be a lot more damaging to the economy in the short term than anticipated.

MK: Like I say, Blinder and Zandi find that some parts of a fiscal stimulus might be amazingly effective, but the traditional fiscal stimulus done in the good ideological way of the 1930s may still have very low multipliers.

JL: You indicated that the RBA's interest rate decisions in 2010–11 were influenced by what the government did prior to that on the stimulus front, which points to an interaction between monetary and fiscal policy. In the past you kindly cited my research on this, so can you summarise your view on the policy interaction? How is it that even if the central bank is independent, its monetary policy is still somehow connected to what the government is doing with fiscal policy?

MK: Earlier this year, after the federal budget was announced, I gave a speech [Knox, 2012] on the same platform as the Australian federal Treasurer, Wayne Swan, and I quoted a previous article of yours on the relationship between central bankers and politicians. The IMF predicted there would be an enormous fiscal contraction in Australia, and in line with your analysis I thought the RBA might respond by cutting interest rates to offset that.

And Wayne Swan was enormously taken by that view and said that he might show my speech to the Governor of the RBA, so obviously he was playing the game that you modelled Jan. I was very happy to see that a theoretical game could actually be played out in practice. I do think, and I've said it on television interviews, that what is happening in practice is that the RBA is reacting to the fiscal tightening in Australia by cutting policy interest rates. And the government sees that very much as an advantage because it generates lower mortgage rates, leading to the government rising in the polls.

So there may be an additional feedback loop in the game Jan, which you could include in a further article. The Treasurer is not just responding to a threat from the central bank of what they might do with interest rates, he's responding to his own view of what he can get the central banker to do, and what that will then do to the Treasurer's political standing. And I think that is very much happening now. I think the government is hoping that this fiscal tightening will induce the RBA to reduce interest rates, which will decrease the cost of housing finance and indirectly increase the government's political popularity.

JL: You will be pleased to know that we have incorporated this feature in our analysis. In this 'game of chicken' we show that if the government is the leader (first mover) it has a lot more leverage over the central bank so it can force the RBA to cut interest rates. Not directly, but indirectly through the effect fiscal actions have on economic variables and expectations that the RBA responds to. And this monetary expansion, if sustained, can have some long-term consequences. For example, the Fed's balance sheet has more than tripled since 2008, and many people worry about this causing high inflation down the track. Do you think such concerns are justified?

MK: Well, it's a really good question because we have seen other big balance sheet expansions; for example, of the European Central Bank (but not of the RBA). And the Germans fear that it is going to cause a lot of inflation. The same is true of the libertarians within the US Republican Party. But we have seen a breakdown, a large decrease, in the 'money multiplier'. Time was when if you increased the **monetary base** then banks would lend more money, and that would increase the **money supply** and inflation. But in the GFC banks are not lending more money, the large increase in the monetary base has only led to a negligible increase in the money supply, and so there is no more inflation.

Sometime in the future we are going to see banks lending money again and the money multiplier working again at usual values. And I'm guessing that at around that time the Federal Reserve, the European Central Bank and others are going to reverse what they are doing on their balance sheets. But it hasn't happened yet and it's not going to happen next week.

JL: Let me add that the Fed has an 'exit strategy' for when that happens using the interest it pays to commercial banks on their reserves, but it is not obvious whether it will work. Another long-term challenge for the US and other economies is fiscal sustainability in the era of ageing populations. Some people are concerned that the problem will be solved through monetary means, by debasing the currency and creating high inflation. But if you look at long-term government bonds in the US and Japan, they have extremely low yields. Based on such low-risk premiums, economists such as Paul Krugman argue that there is no inflation on the horizon and we do not need to worry. On the other hand, economists such as Eric Leeper argue that low interest rates of major governments' bonds may not really imply much about long-term inflation expectations; they may just indicate a '**flight to safety**', and that could quickly change. So what are your views on long-term yields, prospects of future inflation and long-term fiscal sustainability?

MK: There is an influential paper on this by Ken Rogoff and Carmen Reinhart. It shows that once countries get their net debt-to-GDP ratio over 90 per cent, then there is a rapidly increasing probability of some kind of fiscal crisis. So even though interest rates may be low, and interest rates are low because inflation is low, it doesn't mean that countries like the United States, Japan and the UK can't be in situations of having big collapses in their bond market when their debt-to-GDP ratio gets too high. If we look at the IMF forecasts for the United States, their net debt-to-GDP ratio should be about 90 per cent within five years, which is the same as Ireland currently has. So US politicians will have to do something about the budget deficits, or they have to learn a lot of good Irish jokes between now and then.

JL: You mentioned the debt-to-GDP ratio, and politicians do tend to focus on this statistic. But it doesn't seem to show the full scale of the fiscal problem as it does not include a lot of government future liabilities such as promised public pensions. And we see it in Europe where, for example, Spain has had a lower debt-to-GDP level than France but it is facing a debt crisis whereas France is not. So expectations about the future seem very important and they are not reflected in the official debt numbers ...

MK: I think there is also a demographic aspect. If you look at the Japanese economy, the population is much older and older people tend to save more. Therefore you can support higher levels of debt-to-GDP, whereas in Spain the population is much younger so their savings rate tends to be lower. So to me there is a major demographic effect too, as well as the net debt-to-GDP ratio, as to whether a country is going to fall into a fiscal crisis.

JL: Let me ask a final question about the key lesson we should learn from the crisis. I am primarily interested in lessons that policymakers seem to have ignored.

MK: You mentioned the Basel III financial regulation and I think it is faulty. Setting a single set of rules for all banks is a lot harder than it seems to be. I asked Raghuram Rajan what was the signal to him that the financial crisis was going to happen, and it was when asset-backed securities were engaged in Tier 1 capital. In Europe it was the reverse, it was the inclusion of sovereign debt in Tier 1 capital that caused the banking panic.

So, how did we get here? We got to the US banking crisis on the road to good intentions – by trying to get lower-income people houses that they couldn't afford. In Europe it was the inclusion of poorer countries that should not have been in the Euro; for example, Greece. Both of these were driven by good intentions. So one lesson we can learn is that in terms of banking and other policy regulations, we should always be aware of good intentions.

JL: That's worthy of a last remark. Thank you very much Michael for sharing your expertise and all the best for the future.

10.3 Key economic insights and policy lessons

Economic insights	Implied policy lessons (for public officials and voters)
Even well-intentioned public policies sometimes turn out to reduce rather than enhance social welfare.	Policymakers should pay careful attention to the substance of each policy, even if it is not immediately 'marketable' to the public.
Financial regulation pursued by governments tends to be pro-cyclical rather than counter-cyclical, i.e. it usually magnifies the costly cycles in the financial market.	Policymakers should resist the political pressure of loosening financial regulation when markets boom and tightening it in the aftermath of a financial crisis. Doing the opposite would reduce fluctuation of financial and economic variables.
Political interference in the housing market in order to deliver 'affordable housing' can lead to large swings in house prices with major negative consequences.	Policymakers should not attempt to artificially increase the number of people owning their house as the resulting market distortion can backfire by inflating a real estate bubble.
Governments provide implicit guarantees of a bailout to large financial institutions they consider systemically important – 'too-big-to-fail'. This gives these institutions a number of advantages over their smaller competitors.	Policymakers should not advantage some institutions over others as this unfairly distorts competition. If government guarantees are seen as desirable, they should be explicit, and the protected institutions should pay for the public protection.
While government guarantees may avert short-term panic, they lead to a moral hazard problem. Financial institutions have an incentive to take on excessive risk which increases the likelihood of financial collapses and bailouts.	Policymakers should carefully weigh the short-term benefits of government guarantees and their long-term costs.

Economic insights	Implied policy lessons (for public officials and voters)
There exist several ways to alleviate the 'too-big-to-fail' problem and reduce long-term risk in the financial system; for example, not letting financial companies grow excessively large.	Policymakers should examine regulatory ways of incentivising financial companies not to grow too large and threaten the stability of the financial system. They should consider breaking up existing financial giants, following the Teddy Roosevelt example.
The US mortgage ('government sponsored') companies, Fannie Mae and Freddie Mac, had subprime mortgage targets set by the government, which induced them to engage in subprime mortgage securitisation between 2003 and 2007 and led to the subsequent fiasco.	Policymakers should carefully monitor and regulate financial innovation such as mortgage securitisation and make sure the process is transparent.
The incentive structure of investment banker bonuses may be inappropriate in some countries, encouraging excessively risky behaviour narrowly focused on short-term profits.	Policymakers should study carefully the link between reimbursement schemes in the financial sector and risk, and if a market failure occurs there they should address it through regulation.
Pre-2008 regulation of leverage was ineffective because financial companies were allowed to avoid it – by parking asset-backed securities off balance sheet in 'Structured Investment Vehicles'.	Policymakers should ensure that their regulation is properly enforced, otherwise it may become counter-productive.
Major central banks have expanded their balance sheets dramatically post-2008 (some by several hundred per cent) in an effort to rescue the financial system and stimulate their underperforming economies.	Policymakers should carefully devise 'exit strategies' through which they will reduce their balance sheets to normal levels (when appropriate), and thus prevent their stimulatory actions causing excessive inflation.
In the post-2008 period, financial companies have been hoarding cash in their accounts with the central bank rather than lending the money to businesses. This means that while the monetary base has ballooned, the money supply has not changed much, which has manifested as a 'breakdown' (large decrease) in the money multiplier.	Policymakers should re-examine the analysis of money creation and money multipliers in a liquidity trap environment in which the zero-lower-bound on interest rates is binding.
Economists' views on the 2009–14 stock market boom in the US (and elsewhere) differ. Some believe they have been justified by solid economic prospects, some argue it has been a bubble blown by loose monetary policy (pointing to the near-perfect positive correlation between US stock indices and US monetary base).	Policymakers should pay extremely close attention to the developments in asset markets in the post-GFC period. This is to avoid the mistakes of the pre-GFC period in which excessively low interest rates fuelled housing and stock market bubbles.
If 'flight to safety' occurs, very low long-term interest on government bonds may not unambiguously imply that long-term inflation expectations are well-contained and markets do not fear higher inflation down the track.	Policymakers should not be complacent about the markets' assessment of future inflation, and should use a number of measures of inflation expectations.
The specific type of fiscal stimulus matters for its effectiveness. While fiscal multipliers are known to be higher for government expenditures than taxes, the government's buying of preference shares, sending people cheques in the mail, or paying for insulation may have dramatically different stimulatory impacts.	Policymakers should amass more evidence regarding the effectiveness of various fiscal measures, and implement mechanisms for a swift introduction of the most effective ones when a major adverse shock such as the GFC strikes.

Economic insights	Implied policy lessons (for public officials and voters)
The expansionary stance of the RBA's monetary policy since 2011 seems to have been influenced by the federal government's fiscal behaviour – offsetting the contractionary budgets.	Policymakers should coordinate their actions across various macroeconomic instruments.
Financial crises are very costly for the economy, also because they reduce the neutral levels of employment and output and thus make the subsequent recession longer and deeper.	Policymakers should be cautious in comparing a recession induced by a financial crisis with one induced by a non-financial shock. This is so as not to overestimate the neutral levels of employment and output, which would lead them to implement excessively aggressive monetary/fiscal responses.

10.4 Discussion questions

1   Using your own words, summarise the debate of Section 10.2 in three to five sentences.
2   Write down one idea discussed in the interview that you found new or interesting, or that you disagree with, and briefly explain why.
3   Write down one question on any topic covered in the interview that you would ask the speaker if you had a chance.
4   Consider the cartoon in Section 10.1, and explain the point to someone who has not read the section and does not have any knowledge of economics.
5   Examine Figure 10.1 from the perspective of a policymaker. Describe its key message to the public and explain what kind of policy improvement is implied by the data. Do the same for Figure 10.2.
6   Suppose you take part in a debating contest, in which the topic is the opening quote of the chapter by Warren Buffett:

> When you combine ignorance and leverage, you get some pretty interesting results.

Prepare a speech you would give for the affirmative side. Then (you or your classmate) prepare a speech for the negative side. If possible, organise an audience and perform the debate.
7   Explain in your own words the difference between retail and investment banking. How did the separation of the two systems come about in the United States, and how did it cease to exist? Based on your research, do you think this separation is a good idea?
8   Watch the 10-minute animation at **http://crisisofcredit.com**. Summarise its narrative of the crisis and identify the mistakes of all the parties involved.
9   Explain the difference between prime and subprime mortgages. Explain the difference between a Collaterised Debt Obligation (CDO) and a Credit Default Swap (CDS).

10 Outline the process of mortgage securitisation (more background information can be found in Gorton, 2009). What was the main 'glitch' in this process? What do you think are the implications for government regulation?

11 Outline how the corporate credit rating process works and its rationale. Can you identify any problems, both prior to and post 2008?

12 In relation to the role of US politicians in the lead-up to the GFC, Mr Knox reproduces Mark Twain's quote that: 'There is no organised criminal class except Congress.' Explain whether you agree or disagree, and why.

13 Investment bankers' bonuses and 'golden parachutes' are often subject to a heated debate. Provide some relevant data for the US and Australia, then summarise Mr Knox's view on this and relate it to your own. Try to suggest a reimbursement scheme that would incentivise investment bankers to take a long-term perspective, and avoid excessively risky short-term oriented investments.

14 Outline existing global regulations regarding adequate capital requirements of financial institutions. Do you think they are sufficient in ensuring prudent behaviour?

15 What is Mr Knox's view regarding the post-2009 boom of the US stock market, is he worried about an asset bubble? What is your view, also taking into account the strong positive correlation between US stock indices and the US monetary base?

16 Discuss the two different ways of providing a fiscal stimulus Mr Knox mentions. Which one was primarily used in Australia in response to the GFC? Describe its main features, and summarise the main pros and cons.

17 Consider one of the widely discussed proposed reforms of the financial system, the Chicago Plan. It argues for a return to 100 per cent reserve banking (for more, see Kumhof and Benes, 2012, or for a summary, Kumhof, 2013). Discuss the advantages and disadvantages of the proposal.

18 Propose a set of policies that you think best promote the stability of the banking sector and ultimately people's wellbeing.

10.5 Where to find out more

Bagehot, W. (1873), *Lombard Street: A Description of the Money Market*, New York: Charles Scribner's Sons.

Blinder, A. and M. Zandi (2010), 'How the Great Recession Was Brought to an End', Moody's Analytics, available at www.economy.com/mark-zandi/documents/End-of-Great-Recession.pdf

Buera, F. J., J. P. Kaboski and Y. Shin (2011), 'Finance and Development: A Tale of Two Sectors', *American Economic Review*, No. 101(5), pp. 1964–2002.

Claeys, G., Z. Darvas, S. Merler and B. G. Wolff (2014), 'Addressing Weak Inflation: The European Central Bank's Shopping List', *Bruegel Policy Contributions*, issue 2014/05.

Filer, R. K., J. Hanousek and N. F. Campos (2000), 'Do Stock Markets Promote Economic Growth?', CERGE-EI Working Paper Series No. 151, available at http://papers.ssrn.com/sol3/papers.cfm?abstract_id=1535900

Gorton, G. (2009), 'The Subprime Panic', *European Financial Management*, European Financial Management Association, 15(1), pp. 10–46.

Herndon, T., M. Ash and R. Pollin (2014), 'Does High Public Debt Consistently Stifle Economic Growth? A Critique of Reinhart and Rogoff', *Cambridge Journal of Economics*, 38(2), pp. 257–79.

Hughes Hallett, A., J. Libich and P. Stehlík (2007), 'Monetary and Fiscal Policy Interaction with Various Degrees of Commitment', CAMA

Working Papers 2007–21, published in 2014 in the *Czech Journal of Economics and Finance*, 64(1), pp. 2–29.

Jahan, S. and B. McDonald (2011), 'A Bigger Slice of a Growing Pie', *Finance & Development*, 48(3).

Knox, M. (2012), 'Economic Strategy: Overview Address by Michael Knox at the CEDA Federal Budget Lunch with The Hon. Wayne Swan MP, Deputy Prime Minister and Treasurer', Sofitel, Brisbane, Friday 11 May, available at **www.janlibich.com/ per_michael_knox_budget_speech.pdf**

Knox, M. (2015), Michael Knox Economic Strategy Reports, available at **https:// my.morgans.com.au/index.cfm?objectid= D136624B-A48C-7F8D-40DB987BA5626308**

Kumhof, M. (2013), 'We Should Seriously Consider Revisiting "The Chicago Plan" of the 1930s Which Separates the Monetary and Credit Functions of the Banking System', The London School of Economics and Political Science, 25 November, available at **http:// blogs.lse.ac.uk/usappblog/2013/11/25/ chicago-plan-revisited/**

Kumhof, M. and J. Benes (2012), 'The Chicago Plan Revisited', IMF Working Papers, issue WP/12/202.

Leeper, E. M. (2010), 'Monetary Science, Fiscal Alchemy', Proceedings – Economic Policy Symposium – Jackson Hole, Federal Reserve Bank of Kansas City, pp. 361–434.

Lewis, M. (2011), *The Big Short: Inside the Doomsday Machine*, W. W. Norton.

Minsky, H. (1992), 'The Financial Instability Hypothesis', Levy Economics Institute of Bard College, working paper no. 74, available at **www.levyinstitute.org/pubs/wp74.pdf**.

Rajan, R. (2005), 'Has Financial Development Made the World Riskier?', Proceedings – Economic Policy Symposium – Jackson Hole, Federal Reserve Bank of Kansas City, issue August, pp. 313–369.

Rajan, R. (2010), *Fault Lines: How Hidden Fractures Still Threaten the World Economy*, Princeton University Press.

Reinhart, C. M. and K. S. Rogoff (2010), 'Growth in a Time of Debt', *American Economic Review*, 100(2), pp. 573–78.

Reinhart, C. M. and K. S. Rogoff (2014), 'Recovery from Financial Crises: Evidence from 100 Episodes', *American Economic Review*, 104(5), pp. 50–55.

Sifma (2015), 'US Mortgage-Related Issuance and Outstanding', updated 2/3/15, available at **www.sifma.org/research/statistics.aspx**, accessed 17 February 2015.

Taleb, N. (2007), *The Black Swan: The Impact of the Highly Improbable*, Random House.

Wall Street Journal (2009), 'Bank Bonus Tab: $33 Billion', 31 July, available at **www.wsj.com/ news/interactive/BONUSES090730? ref=SB124896891815094085**

11 The 2008 global financial turmoil: an inside-policy view

When written in Chinese, the word 'crisis' is composed of two characters. One represents danger and the other represents opportunity.

John F. Kennedy, the 35th President of the United States, 12 April 1959, in a speech in Indianapolis.

Economic concepts discussed

Easy-to-understand explanations of all the concepts listed below appear in the glossary at the end of this book.

- Asian crisis of 1997–98
- Austerity
- Australian Prudential Regulation Authority (APRA)
- Bailout
- Basel III (the Third Basel Accord)
- Capital flight
- Central bank
- *Community Reinvestment Act*
- Credit freeze
- Crowding out

- Current account
- Deleveraging
- Dotcom bubble
- Exchange rate
- Expansionary/contractionary monetary policy
- Federal Reserve (Fed)
- Fiscal cliff
- *Glass–Steagall Act*
- Global saving glut
- Hyperinflation
- Inflation targeting
- Leverage (gearing)

- Lifecycle hypothesis
- Liquidity trap
- Moral hazard
- Mortgage securitisation
- Mundell–Fleming model
- Nominal income targeting
- Productivity
- Quantitative easing
- Seigniorage
- Subprime mortgage
- Taylor rule
- Too-big-to-fail
- Total dependency ratio

11.1 Motivation and overview

Since 2008, the word 'crisis' has been one of the most frequently used economic terms. The problems that first transpired in the US real estate market spread to the rest of the world like an avalanche, causing substantial damage to people's lives on its journey.

In the ruins, the Global Financial Crisis (GFC) left behind a number of questions economists have been trying to answer ever since: 'What were its main causes?', 'How did the crisis propagate from the US housing market to the financial system?', 'Why did the problems spill over to the real economy – virtually everywhere in the world?', 'Were the observed responses of monetary and fiscal policies the right way of dealing with the crisis?', 'Why has leaving zero interest rates for several years not led to a full recovery in the US and Europe?', 'Will such a policy of easy money eventually lead to high inflation?', 'What are the key lessons for policymakers about optimal regulation and institutional setting?'.

In this chapter, based on an interview conducted on 26 October 2012, Professor Warwick McKibbin from the Australian National University offers answers to these and many other questions in his insightful summary of the GFC. He is well positioned to do so given his influential academic research and a wealth of experience with real-world policymaking. His policy roles have included the Congressional Budget Office in the United States, member of the Australian Prime Minister's Science, Engineering and Innovation Council, as well as membership of the Board of the Reserve Bank of Australia (RBA). During the latter 2001–11 appointment, he was directly involved in dealing with the crisis through monetary policy. The fact that Australia got through the crisis virtually 'unharmed' – the only high-income country that avoided a recession post 2008 – gives credence to Prof. McKibbin's views.[1]

The discussion starts with Prof. McKibbin's narrative of the causes of the GFC. He traces one of its roots as far back as the **Asian Crisis of 1997–98**. The large movement of capital away from that region ('**capital flight**') searching for a good return on investment was one of the driving forces behind the build-up of the **dotcom bubble** in the United States. Its bursting then induced the **Federal Reserve (Fed)**, the US **central bank**, to substantially ease monetary policy during 2001–05. Many economists, Prof. McKibbin included, believe that the Fed's monetary stimulus over this period was 'too much for too long', and the RBA did not follow in the Fed's footsteps. Figure 11.1 compares the Fed's and RBA's policy interest rate and shows the former to have been substantially lower than the latter over this period.

Together with global demographic factors, such **expansionary monetary policy** of the Fed resulted in interest rates at very low levels during the 2001–05 period; not just in the US but globally. These contributed to the creation of another bubble, this time in the real estate markets. This bubble, which saw house prices in many countries double in real terms (adjusted for inflation) in the decade prior to the GFC, was further fuelled by financial innovation. Many investors wrongly believed that the securitisation of mortgages was a perpetuum mobile for converting risky mortgages into safe, AAA-rated assets.

The actions of credit rating agencies in this process also played an important role. And so did the push by politicians for 'affordable housing', which led to a drop in lending standards and to a large increase in the risky '**subprime**' segment of the mortgage market. In the list of potential causes one cannot leave out government guarantees to large financial institutions, those considered '**too-big-to-fail**'. These guarantees created an incentive for financial institutions to take on excessive risk, and led to a substantial increase in **leverage** (indebtedness) and systemic risk of the financial sector. This undesirable behavioural response is known as the **moral hazard** problem.

---

[1] The full video-interview is available at **https://youtu.be/ksWPSTNqFGM**. For more details regarding Prof. McKibbin and his research, see **https://crawford.anu.edu.au/people/academic/warwick-mckibbin**

Figure 11.1: Monthly averages of the short-term monetary policy interest rates in the US (Effective Federal Funds rate) and Australia (the cash rate target)

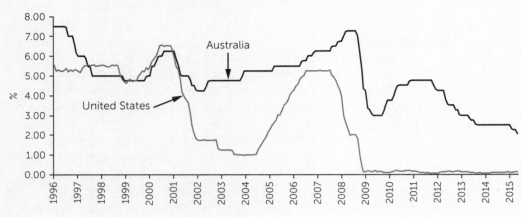

Sources: Adapted from RBA (2015) and Fred (2015).

Prof. McKibbin explains that on top of all this we saw a 'big structural transformation of the global economy'. This included trends in the quality of US education and the skills of its workforce, changes in **productivity** across countries, divergence in the prices of manufacturing goods relative to the prices of energy and raw materials, and many other developments. Given these myriad contributing factors Prof. McKibbin is critical of attempts to point to a single cause of the GFC and advocate a silver bullet solution. He argues that '… the world is far more complicated than that'.

The debate then moves from the causes of the crisis to its propagation. Prof. McKibbin outlines why it spread, like some infectious disease, from the US and European real estate markets throughout the financial systems, and why the damage to the banking sector was so great. Importantly, the discussion implies how the troubles spilled over to the real side of the economy, and caused major increases in unemployment and disruption of economic activity worldwide.

This is followed by Prof. McKibbin describing the responses of monetary and fiscal policies to the crisis, assessing their effectiveness, and considering likely future developments. In doing so, the possible inflationary consequences of the ballooning of the Fed's balance sheet, essentially a five-fold increase in its size between 2007 and 2014 (see Figure 11.2) that has occurred primarily as part of the **quantitative easing** process, are discussed. The figure shows that while the UK and Japan have experienced similar increases in the monetary base, Australia's situation is different.

Many other themes are touched on in the interview. Prof. McKibbin discusses the desirability of **inflation targeting** vis-à-vis **nominal income targeting**, long-term fiscal sustainability, and the effect of the common currency Euro on its member countries. While the level of discussion is slightly more advanced than in other chapters of the book, most of the content will be accessible to a typical first-year student of

Figure 11.2: Expansion of selected central banks' balance sheets during the GFC. The vertical axis shows an index, which is set to 100 on 1 June 2006.

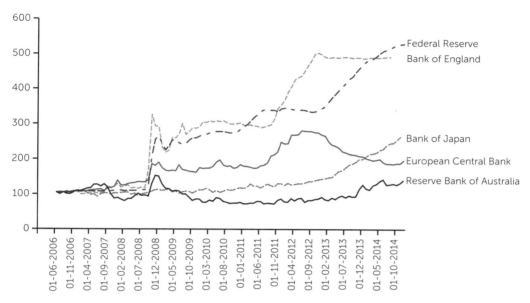

Source: Claeys et al. (2014).

macroeconomics. This includes Prof. McKibbin's summary of the lessons from the GFC, and his suggestions for policy reforms that would decrease the likelihood of similar crises in the future.

One issue not discussed but worth mentioning is the fact that an economic downturn may have a 'silver lining', namely positive effects on some people's health. The research of economists Ulf Gerdtham and Christopher Ruhm shows that a (mild) recession may, as a consequence of reductions in people's incomes and workloads, reduce mortality. They report that an increase in unemployment by 1 percentage point tends to lead, on average in OECD countries, to a fall in mortality by 0.4 per cent; that is, four saved lives from a thousand existing deaths. This fall, which is due to fewer deaths from liver and cardiovascular diseases as well as from fewer car accidents, is larger than the rise in suicides during recessions.[2] However, Gerdtham and Ruhm (2006) stress that:

> Evidence that health deteriorates when the economy improves
> is not an argument for inducing recessions, which have
> overwhelmingly negative consequences even if worse physical
> health is not one of them.

This is depicted in the cartoon on the following page.

---

[2] More details can be found in Gerdtham and Ruhm (2006) and Ruhm (2005).

Concept by Jan Libich © 2015, drawing by Veronika Mojžišová. Used by permission.

11.2 The debate

Dr Jan Libich (JL): Let's start with the causes of the Global Financial Crisis (GFC), what's your narrative?

© Warwick McKibbin. Used by permission.

< Prof. Warwick McKibbin (WM): Firstly, I don't think there was a single cause of the crisis and I don't think there was a single way to avoid what happened. There's been a whole range of different factors impacting on the global economy over many years. I'd probably go back to the Asian Financial Crisis of 1997–98. We saw what happened when investors lost confidence and pulled their money out of the Asian economies such as Thailand and Indonesia.

JL: Was this sudden withdrawal of capital from these countries justified?

WM: Well, ex post it was, because the economies went into a deep recession. But I think there was bad policy being put in place. There were bubbles in the banking industry, in Thailand for example. Investors really didn't have enough information to know which countries were exposed to which sort of problems. They saw countries that looked similar to each other, and when Thailand went into crisis, they figured the others were probably going to have a crisis too. The capital that left Asia flowed mainly into the equity markets in the United States, and also into Europe and Australia. And I think it was creating the next round of problems because it bid up the price of dotcom stocks. And from the dotcom stocks crashing we had a recession in 2001 in the United States, and also in Europe.

Then there were policy mistakes. A large amount of capital was flowing around the world; from excess savings in China and other developing countries. There were also very large relative price shocks, coming out of Asia in particular. That is, the prices of manufactured goods were falling, and the prices of energy and mining were rising. These relative price shocks, the liquidity shock and the interest rate changes were impacting the US economy at roughly the same time. There was the build-up of a structural shock and then when the US went into recession in 2001, the Federal Reserve (Fed) cut interest rates to 1 per cent, which at the time was seen to be a very low interest rate. Today, that looks rather high. Because inflation didn't take off, the Fed sat on 1 per cent interest rates for a very long time.

JL: How come such an expansionary monetary policy stance was not inflationary?

WM: My view as to why that didn't lead to an instantaneous shift in prices was because of the relative price shocks – the prices of manufactured goods exported to the US from China were falling. But there were a number of other things happening, with the key to it being this big structural transformation of the global economy. All the economies in the world were being impacted by this, including Australia and Europe. When the Fed responded initially in 2001, there was too much liquidity for too long. Through many countries pegging to the US dollar, this very loose monetary policy spread throughout Asia and the rest of the world. That increased aggregate demand in these economies, and that accentuated the relative price shock.

JL: Let's consider the Fed's behaviour in the early 2000s you described. Are you implying that the Fed deviated from the policy prescription known as the **Taylor rule** by leaving interest rates too low for an extended period of time? As an important aside, it should in fact be called the Henderson–McKibbin–Taylor rule, because in the 1993 Carnegie-Rochester conference volume, in which John Taylor formulated his famous monetary policy rule, you actually proposed an almost identical rule with your co-author, right?

WM: Well actually, Henderson and I wrote a survey paper for a Brookings conference a year before that. The conference asked modellers to model these interest rate rules, John Taylor modelled the rule and we did too, so neither of us should be credited with that rule. It came from Ralph Bryant,

Cathy Mann and Peter Hooper. But yes, it is true we presented it at the same conference in 1993. Ours was a more general rule. What John Taylor did was actually calibrate it to US monetary policy to see if he could explain how the Fed had been behaving. What he did was clever.

JL: And did the Fed actually deviate during 2001–05 from the original prescription of the rule to respond to inflation and output deviations with equal weights? There is some research showing that they substantially increased the emphasis on output stabilisation relative to inflation stabilisation – compared to Taylor's original weights.

WM: Well, you've got to be careful because the original weights that came from Taylor were the ones that replicated what the US Fed had been doing over the historical period. I actually had another paper in the same Brookings volume which was a more fundamental examination of the key issues. It looked at what were the optimal feedback rules. Not 'What was the Fed doing?' but 'What should the Fed do?'. The answer turns out to be very model-specific, so the response coefficients on inflation and output can move around a great deal depending on the structure of your model and the way consumer and firm behaviour is modelled.

Coming back to the question, yes, the Fed was deviating from the rule that John Taylor had written down that replicated the behaviour of the 1980s and 1990s. And in my view of someone actually sitting on the Board of a central bank looking at what the Fed was doing, I was very concerned. You can't have 1 per cent interest rates in an economy that has pretty reasonable growth prospects for very long without a massive misallocation of capital. My concern was that with 1 per cent interest rates you start getting bubbles in various asset markets.

JL: I actually remember you were talking about this danger long before other people had come to realise that the Fed had been too expansionary for too long in the early 2000s. But let's go to the other issue you identified, which Bernanke called the 'global saving glut'. It was the fact that there was too much saving floating around, partly also due to demographic trends. The total dependency ratio, which is the proportion of the population aged above 65 or below 15 relative to the rest of the population, reached a trough in the early 2000s in high-income countries. This meant that the number of workers – who save – relative to the dependent population – who dis-save – was the highest. How big a factor do you think this was pre-GFC? Was it more important than the Fed's mistake?

WM: Well, the demographics component is a part of this key issue of savings and investment. So if savings double and investments don't double, then the real interest rate will fall. The interesting question wasn't: 'Why is there so much savings?' It was: 'Why is investment so weak relative to the amount of savings available?'

The second issue was that this distribution of savings and investment was very asymmetric. China and other large developing countries – and Germany – were running very high savings rates relative to their investments. The US was experiencing very high investment (or consumption) relative to its savings, and this imbalance showed up as very large **current account** (and trade) deficits in the US and very large surpluses in other countries. So the savings and investment imbalance phenomenon was represented twice: through the interest rate imbalances and through the current account imbalances. Both of those played a role in the policy adjustment in the United States.

Fiscal policy is a key part of the story. When you ask: 'Did the Fed get it wrong?', it has to be in the context of what choices they had, given what was happening with fiscal policy. And that is extremely relevant today. But back in the 2000s in the US, I think both monetary and fiscal policies were too loose. As a central banker looking at what this meant, the Fed was essentially pushing through the global economy a series of asset price bubbles. As well as potentially down the track, very high inflation, which Australia would have to deal with as a small, open economy. With an inflation-targeting central bank, it is very hard to keep your inflation rate separate from the world inflation rate.

JL: We will certainly talk about monetary and fiscal responses to the crisis. Before doing so let's look at how the low interest rates affected the US housing market, which is considered to be the trigger of the crisis. The pre-crisis housing boom started around the time of the Asian crisis and was unprecedented. Between 1998 and 2006 house prices in real terms (i.e. adjusted for inflation) increased in the US by 80 per cent, and by an even greater percentage in many other countries such as the United Kingdom, Ireland, France, Spain, South Africa and Australia. Why is it that housing markets experience such large swings or even 'bubbles'?

WM: Well, you've got to be careful, because there are two sides to the market. There's supply and there's demand. In the Australian case there is actually quite an undersupply of housing. That's to do with planning and state government regulations and local councils.

JL: But that's quite unique to Australia, right?

WM: It is. But when you have enormous liquidity in the system, you have people buying assets because they're trying to get a rate of return on these assets. And when they expect prices to rise, they will continue to buy until the price stops rising. In some of the countries you mentioned I would regard the developments as bubbles. But in some of them it was part of an economic transformation. Remember that during this period there was a large debate about how the world had changed and that we were in a new world order. A new period of stability.

JL: With higher productivity?

WM: With high productivity and low inflation. The story was that central banks of the world had done their jobs and now we were in an age of great prosperity. If you're in an age of great prosperity – and this is particularly true for the Australian debate – what should you do? Well, you should increase your consumption, borrow against those future income gains. Take that consumption, and don't necessarily consume it all today, but create assets that give you a higher flow of consumption over time. Housing is such an asset. In the debates we were having at the Reserve Bank of Australia, the question was: 'Is the demand in housing coming from a bubble or is it actually driven by fundamentals?' The potential income of Australians had jumped so much because of the China boom, so this may be quite a rational allocation of resources.

JL: Do you have in mind a jump to a new equilibrium in terms of lifetime income and consumption, and therefore house prices? This could in principle rationalise the observed housing booms, without resorting to a bubble equilibrium such as Robert Shiller's irrational exuberance story ...

WM: That's right. If you believe that consumers are consuming based on their expected future income, and you change the growth rate of income by just a small amount, then the increase in the present value of the future is a very big number. Wealth rises. Thus it was difficult to say ex-ante in the period up to 2009 that there was definitely a bubble in the housing market in Australia. You could only say: 'Well, let's look at other factors and see if the fundamentals are consistent.' It is important to also look at valuations of other types of asset classes. Was there a misallocation of resources? My view in the Australian situation was we couldn't see a bubble in the housing market; except perhaps in 2006–07 when I was very concerned that housing prices were rising too quickly. And you'll notice that when the Reserve Bank did raise interest rates, the housing price market just levelled off for a number of years.

The Fed, in contrast, just kept low interest rates and prices of housing and equities kept rising and rising and rising. The argument in the US was that this was just a new era of productivity. But the lower prices we were observing were really driven by productivity boosts in China, and not much by productivity boosts in the United States, so I think that was the fundamental mistake. Also, the combination of rising prices and large over-construction was a fatal mix.

JL: Some people would argue that a part of this story was a push by politicians for 'affordable housing'. We certainly saw that a lot in the United States, where it was done through the government-sponsored enterprises (GSEs), Fannie Mae and Freddie Mac. They played a key role in the **mortgage securitisation** fiasco. These mortgage giants have implicit government guarantees, and are required to extend their mortgage assistance to medium- and low-income earners in the legislation called the *Community Reinvestment Act*. What is your view on the contribution of this political aspect of the crisis?

WM: I think all this played a role, and this demonstrates the problem with trying to politically influence the housing market. But everyone always wants to point to a single cause because if you can find a single cause you can then advocate a silver bullet solution. Politicians in particular like to be able to say: 'This is how you fix the problem.' My view is that the world is far more complicated than that. To fix this problem, you needed to not only change the way in which the financial industry was allocating capital, but you had to change interest rates.

And again, this comes back to this fundamental question: 'Is it sensible to have nominal interest rates at 1 per cent and negative real interest rates in an economy with reasonably low unemployment and very good growth prospects?' The answer is 'no'. The overall policy setting was wrong. That's the problem with the debate in the media which focuses on what the central bank will do at the next meeting. The commentators are often not focusing on the level of interest rates; they're focusing on the change. And they say: 'Should rates go up or down?' My view is always to ask first: 'What should the interest rate in Australia be today, given the state of the economy?'

And if where the interest rate is currently is a long way from where the interest rate should be, the fact that we might've got a bit of data in the opposite direction should really not be the driving factor for changing interest rates. It's how far they have deviated from what would be a sensible policy. And right now, if you came from outer space, you would say interest rates in Australia look remarkably low compared to any sort of natural equilibrium where capital is being allocated efficiently.

JL: I agree it is hard to pin down the relative contributions of low interest rates versus the political push for affordable housing. This is also because the start of the housing boom in the US in the second half of the 1990s coincided not only with the inflow of cheap capital you discussed, but also with stricter government targets to GSEs regarding 'subprime' mortgages. The minimum proportion of their mortgage loans to low- and moderate-income households was increased from 30 per cent to 42 per cent over 1996–97 (and by 2006 the legislation required 56 per cent of all GSEs' mortgages to be held by people with below-average incomes).

WM: Well again, there are so many factors. If you had closed that channel down, if you could repeat history and not implement that piece of legislation, or that policy, you would have probably ended up in the same sort of situation given the fundamental shifts in the global economy. The trigger might have been different. And that's the key – you can't predict that there's going to be some particular trigger. But if you're in the middle of a very high-fuel situation and someone drops a match, everything is there to ignite. And that's what happened in this case.

And you could also point to the securitisation issue: that there were lots of assets being bundled and people were misrepresenting the risk by creating all these new assets. Why were these assets being created? It was partly because of the search for yield due to interest rates being so low. So there were so many things that were happening simultaneously.

As an aside, this is where institutional structures and good policy makes a big difference. You don't know how good or bad a policy is until you push against it. Once you get these big shifts in either relative prices or interest rates or **exchange rates**, that's when you can tell whether or not you've designed an economic structure that's robust. We're seeing this today in Australia with the mining tax. A system can be designed that might work in a particular world but when China stops booming and there's no revenue, the tax revenue is zero. A serious problem arises if the government has allocated all the revenue already. That's really bad policy design because it assumes the policy you are designing is going to work the way you plan it.

JL: The government's implicit guarantees to 'too-big-to-fail' financial institutions such as banks and insurance companies also turned out to be a problematic policy when pushed against. What role did these play in your view?

WM: That was a serious problem because it led to a set of incentives amongst managers of these corporations to behave in a particular way – assuming the government would bail them out. When Lehman Brothers went down, that was really a trigger because it sent the signal that the government may not save these big institutions. My view is that these institutions shouldn't have been allowed to grow as big as they did. The breaking of the US *Glass–Steagall Act* in 1999 was really one of the key mistakes that was made, amongst many. I think having these very large institutions led to systemic risk we didn't necessarily have to have. But it's easy to say that now. The question is to act before this becomes a problem. That's the big issue for policymakers around the world today.

JL: Many countries including Australia have never had this separation of investment and retail banking that was ensured in the US between 1933 and 1999 by the *Glass–Steagall Act*. But their financial and banking system seemed to be working fine; Australian banks didn't run into these kinds of problems.

WM: We have a different regulatory framework. The work that the **Australian Prudential Regulation Authority (APRA)** does in Australia is a very different sort of regulatory intervention to what the equivalents do in the United States. Australia is a smaller economy. The US is on a much larger scale and it's much harder to do the regulatory framework in an efficient way. But even if we'd not had that particular financial system in the United States, we would still have had the sort of problems we've experienced. We see that in parts of Europe and in other parts of the world where you experience a global trade shock, or push down world interest rates, and all of a sudden all the fragilities in those economies start to stand out.

JL: You mentioned regulation so let's talk about excessive leverage, which many people see as a major contributor to the crisis. What kind of regulation should we have in this respect? Is the 2011 **Basel III** international agreement on bank capital adequacy going in the right direction? Is it sufficient to alleviate these problems?

WM: A lot of these international agreements are driven too much by politics. So, for example, there is a debate about European countries in particular wanting government debt to be included as a risk-free asset in the calculation of risk for Basel III. Now, they want that because they need the demand for government debt to rise – a lot of these countries are producing too much government debt and they therefore need to create an artificial demand for that debt. In Australia, we couldn't reach the proposed Basel III levels that the Europeans want on the balance sheets of our financial entities because we do not have enough government debt. So again, the principles of why you want to do this are good principles. But the implementation is ultimately driven by politics in these international negotiations. That is a bit of a concern.

JL: If you could design a regulatory framework dealing with excessive leverage from scratch, based on good economics, what would it look like?

WM: Firstly, the question arises: 'Is it excessive leverage?' Go back to the earlier story about a new world where inflation has been eliminated, 2 to 3 billion people are entering the global labour market, and a massive global transformation is occurring. In such a world, if you're an individual consumer you should be leveraging because your future wealth will be much higher than your current wealth. So you should bring that forward. What I am saying is that you've got to identify what the fundamentals might be and then what's excessive. That's the first issue.

The second issue is then to say: 'What sort of policies can you use to slow down this accumulation of leverage?' One way is to regulate the lending of institutions; another way is to use interest rates from the central bank – a pretty heavy tool – to get people to pull back. There's a whole variety of different techniques but the key issue here is how much is excess and how much is not excess. For example, take the terms of trade shock that Australia has been experiencing. It was always going to eventually level out – not disappear necessarily but come down. In that environment, it did pay for the Australian private sector to probably be a little bit less leveraged, and for the government to be a lot less leveraged. It seemed desirable to have a sovereign wealth fund, so that we could push offshore some of the benefits in case we needed them later. That sort of risk management I think is the best way to design policy.

JL: I agree with you that individuals can leverage against their future income; as Modigliani's **lifecycle hypothesis** states. But is it a good system in which banks leverage so much that, in effect, they play roulette with the financial system and gamble with taxpayers' money? The key is that they have, in addition to implicit government guarantees, limited liability, so they do not bear the full responsibility for their actions.

WM: Well again, the question there is, are they doing too much? Capitalism works because of leverage; someone is willing to take a risk and invest in some activity. Some of the investments will pay off and some of them won't.

JL: But you can do this with no leverage, right?

WM: You can, but if you leverage up, then in a world with all sorts of productivity improvements, the payoff can be enormous. Think about taking risks like Microsoft or Apple or one of these success stories. I don't have any problem with leverage per se. I think the problem arises if you create a system where people taking risks get the private benefit but the government takes the public cost. Then you create a very dangerous system. So it's not the leveraging that's the problem; it's making sure that if someone takes a leveraged position, they're the ones that pay the price, or the lender shares in the pain if it goes wrong. But we've created a system where people could take risks with other people's money, often not even knowing where that pool of securitised assets have come from. And in the system the lenders themselves don't take a 'haircut' when things go bad. That to me is more important.

JL: How do we change the system and incentives to stop this? You mentioned that one way is not letting financial companies grow too big to threaten the stability of the financial system. Don Brash, the former Governor of the Reserve Bank of New Zealand [Chapter 12], once made an alternative suggestion. The government should make the guarantees explicit rather than implicit, and formally acknowledge which financial institutions are 'too-big-to-fail'. They would then need to ex-ante compensate the taxpayer for the guarantee of a potential **bailout**. And the government would commit to not bailing out the other institutions that are not too-big-to-fail. Would that be a feasible solution?

WM: That would be a very feasible situation. It's not just the 'too-big-to-fail' institutions, the banks that have implicit government guarantees are getting funds cheaper than would otherwise be the case, competing with smaller financial institutions that don't have that implicit guarantee. That distortion needs to be rectified and they need to pay a premium to the government for the fact that they're getting this sort of overarching guarantee – implicit or explicit.

JL: Let's now move from the causes of the crisis into how it propagated. We discussed the reasons for rapid growth in debt, both at the level of individuals and companies, as well as mortgage securitisation. In the US the proportion of subprime mortgages that were securitised increased from 31 to 81 per cent between 1994 and 2006. All of this contributed to a rise in the overall risk of the financial system. How did the problems spread from the housing markets in the US and Europe to the rest of the financial markets and then the real economy virtually everywhere in the world? What was the mechanism?

WM: Well, in 2006 Andy Stoeckel and I wrote a paper called 'The Collapse of the US Housing Market'. We took one of our models and we examined what would happen if the bubble that was in the US housing market collapsed. What we found in that analysis was that the US would go into a recession, but the rest of the world would just have a mild downturn. And the capital reallocation effect that we had observed in Asia in 1997 and 1998 would also occur for the United States, with this capital flowing to the rest of the world.

What was wrong with that analysis? The real effects we captured, but we didn't capture the financial impacts, especially people changing their perception of risk. So in subsequent work, published in 2009, we've thrown into the model what we observed in different financial markets in terms of changes in levels of risk. And we found that if you increase the risk premium in the consumer's mind or in a corporation's investment strategy, a small change in risk means that the present value of the future returns from your investment will drop dramatically.

Thus, those wealth effects and those investment effects are actually very negative for the real economy. Another issue was that we had no idea what the linkages among financial institutions in 2007 and 2008 were, and even sitting on the board of a central bank, we had no confidence that we knew what was happening in terms of who owed what. That seizing up of the financial system was an additional shock which meant that there was no financing for anything, so banks at some point weren't even lending to banks, the so-called **credit freeze**. Now once you do a shock like that in our sort of models it brings the entire financial system down.

Then there's a series of subsequent shocks. The most persistent shock – which we're still experiencing – comes back to your original point that a lot of individuals and corporations had leveraged a lot. And because of this new world order with higher risk, the leverage ratios were too high. People had to deleverage, and once you start **deleveraging** and everybody's selling their assets, then the values of these assets are collapsing. So the third-round wealth effect of the deleveraging is large and very persistent. Right now the key policy prescription is to keep nominal GDP growth as high as possible in these economies. And that might mean, due to low real GDP, getting inflation up. Because if you don't have that, if you have deflation, the real value of all these debts will be escalating and that's a recipe for a Great Depression.

JL: This is in line with the argument of Paul Krugman, the 2008 Nobel Prize laureate. He's been saying that if the private sector is deleveraging, we need the government and/or the central bank to step in and offset that by a fiscal or monetary expansion. Obviously the problem is that if a country is already in a very difficult fiscal situation and has interest rates at zero, it cannot do much. This brings us to the policy responses to the GFC. Let's start with monetary policy, given your position on the RBA Board until 2011. What were the actions of central banks during the crisis and what's your assessment of their effectiveness?

WM: There have been very different responses in different countries. In Australia we did not follow the US with interest rates going to zero, despite a lot of people saying we should. I had a very strong opinion that once you get away from an interest rate around 3 to 4 per cent, you're misallocating capital. Secondly, the shock we were experiencing is a very different shock to the shock that was being experienced in Washington and in London. The big problem was that all of the policymakers were meeting in these places that were going through a financial crisis, and coming up with solutions suitable for them. They wanted the rest of the world to stimulate their economies as well to help carry them out of the slump.

So the analogy would be, if we'd gone to Jakarta or Bangkok in 1997–98, the policymakers there would've been advocating a totally different set of policies than what the International Monetary Fund (IMF) was advocating, because these countries' self-interest was to have the whole world stimulate them. And it's currently the case for the US and Europe, and the IMF is part of this. The Fund wanted countries around the world who weren't even in crisis to stimulate their economies because we know fiscal policy alone doesn't have much of an effect in an open economy. If you do a fiscal stimulus, you get a stronger exchange rate, you get a higher interest rate, and you get a **crowding out** of exports and investment.

And so, in the **Mundell–Fleming model**, you get very little effects of fiscal policy in a flexible exchange rate regime. But if the whole world has a fiscal expansion together, you eliminate the exchange rate effect and so you can actually stimulate the global economy if all countries stimulate together. Now that's still Keynesian economics, but that's in a real Mundell–Fleming world with capital mobility. And I think it was a mistake that countries stimulated everywhere and then all of a sudden they didn't have a mechanism – except in one or two places – to get the future debt-to-GDP ratio back down to reasonable levels.

We see that in the US, we just had a budget deficit of 10 to 11 per cent of GDP with no credible policy on how to bring that back in the future. Once you have that problem, investors get worried about future tax liabilities and future debt and don't invest, individuals don't save. So there's a real problem, the lack of a future strategic policy position meant that the fiscal expansions really damaged the global economy in the medium term. What you can do with monetary policy in that case is very little, because monetary policy doesn't create real things and ultimately taxes destroy things.

JL: Well, the central bank can print money …

WM: What printing money does is to shift demand from one period to another or from one country to another. If you print money today you bring spending from the future to the present. But very few people believe that monetary policy actually permanently creates real activity. It can help smooth business cycles but it doesn't create a whole new world where everybody is better off. And this is the fallacy that too many countries don't understand.

JL: Well, being the devil's advocate, some people would use the fact that the global economy, and especially the US economy, is so weak as a counter argument. They would argue that fiscal policy wasn't strong enough. If we compare post-2008 employment in the United States with previous recessions, the adverse effect lasted much longer and was much deeper. Based on this some people say: 'We need more fiscal stimulus to get out of the slump.' They would also point to the fact that while there was fiscal stimulus in the US at the federal level, at the state and local levels we have seen the opposite, **austerity**, with a large number of public sector jobs cut and other reductions in public expenditures.

WM: The problem is the American economists who make this argument only ever look at the United States. One of the advantages of living outside of the US is that you know that there are 240 other examples of different countries that do things differently. The UK did a massive fiscal stimulus, did they end up any different? Not in the near term. So, to me it's not the scale of the fiscal stimulus. This is reflecting that from the mid-1990s right through to 2007 the US should have been following some fairly substantial structural adjustment policies. Low-skilled, white males, mostly, should've been losing their jobs. Instead, the government was continuously trying to pump up the economy so that the building industry survived, so that the motor vehicle industry survived, even when they could not compete with China, India and Latin America. So this structural problem was getting bigger and bigger.

When the confidence effects hit, the structural problem was there. You don't fix the structural problem by pumping in government spending. You have to invest in a whole long-run retraining; you have to have efficient industries created. You have to let the economy be more mobile and flexible. Real wages have to fall in some sectors of the economy. That's what should have been happening. Throwing fiscal policy on top of that when it's not a demand problem, it only creates a lot of debt, a lot of uncertainty, a lot of political friction. And in the case of Europe, if you have a fixed exchange rate as well, it creates a really, really seriously flawed economic system. It has social ramifications and nothing to do with fiscal policy.

I think the US did enough fiscal stimulus, but they didn't have a plan for the recovery so the future debt liabilities were not controlled. That's what's overhanging the world now and it's the same in parts of Europe. In Australia, we did it the right way in the sense that Treasury managed to put on the table a policy of a stimulus with a very clear profile of reduction. The only problem I had was the stimulus was far too big. We could have done half the stimulus with the same phase out and right now we wouldn't be having the debate about having to run a budget surplus by 2012–13. Australia was probably the best of all the countries but still didn't get it quite right.

JL: There is a lot of evidence for what you're saying about the United States; for example, about their long-term fiscal outlook looking bleak and the quality of their education getting worse. In terms of the employment comparison, I agree that comparing the GFC with previous recessions in the US is wrong as they were of a very different nature, they were not induced by a financial crisis. As Reinhart and Rogoff argue in their 2009 book, if post-2008 US employment is compared to other high-income countries that had experienced a financial crisis over the past few decades, the current situation actually doesn't look so bad.

WM: I agree with that. And the US is actually doing quite well at the moment. There are some issues; for example, demographic factors that are disguising what's happening in the US economy, particularly where it involves participation rates. That's having some impact. Japan is a clearer example of that, anything you put up of Japan should always be in per-capita terms. If people use total output instead, they say there are two lost decades in Japan starting from the 1991 banking crash. Actually, there's only one lost decade, because in per-capita terms Japan has been growing faster than most of the other industrial countries in the twenty-first century. But their population is ageing fast so their labour force has been falling very quickly. It implies that you've got to be very careful in these cross-country comparisons. To come back to your point, the US is a middle ground. In Europe they have a series of other structural problems, largely related to the fixed exchange rate system and the lack of any institutions to support that. This is going to make the situation, in southern Europe in particular, far worse than the United States.

JL: Let's look in more detail at some of the challenges facing policymakers, starting with the central banks' balance sheets. For example, the balance sheet of the Fed has more than tripled between 2008 and 2012 as a consequence of their response to the crisis. How is the monetary base going to be reduced back, and do you think this may be inflationary as some people fear?

WM: I point to the increase in the Fed's balance sheet in many of my presentations too. We have no example of a central bank turning around such a balance sheet expansion in the way that's required. My view of this situation is that it's probably do-able, but 'why is this not causing inflation now?' is the first question. And that is because even though central banks have expanded the supply of money dramatically, the demand for money also increased dramatically. People don't want to hold certain assets, they're just holding money because they're worried about a big crash.

They can do that now; holding money is okay when you have low inflation. But as soon as you start getting some information that would suggest inflation is on the rise, people will start to dump their money balances. They'll get into real assets, they'll get into gold. When that happens the Fed and the other central banks that have done this have to be ready to contract their balance sheets. Because if they don't, if the demand for money crashes and the supply of money is extremely large, that would be very inflationary.

I don't think this would be **hyperinflation**. I'm not saying we're going to have 50 per cent inflation. But realistically, the Fed should have announced an inflation target of 5 or 6 per cent. If they had announced an inflation target that was credible and started buying up the government securities at the time, people would say: 'These guys are acting like they're trying to have inflation, maybe they are going to have inflation.' Real interest rates would have fallen far more than they did because people were unsure what the Fed was doing, what the policy was. I think they made the same mistake as the Japanese made. The Japanese should have increased inflation as quickly as possible, got their currency to collapse, and that would have stimulated the economy. And that's what the US should have done very early on.

JL: Are you saying this would have been more effective than the quantitative easing and other unconventional policies that they've pursued?

WM: I think you needed some quantitative easing. But the way you did that was to announce an inflation target, a reasonably high one. I wrote about this quite a few years ago. You needed to get inflation to rise. What you wanted to avoid was people thinking inflation was going to go negative, because then the real interest rate is positive even with a zero nominal interest rate. That was the problem and I don't think the Fed has done it in a way which is credible.

JL: The situation you described with zero nominal interest rates and high real rates due to expected deflation is called 'liquidity trap'. And your suggested solution reminds me of the Eggertsson and Woodford story. These prominent economists argue the Fed should 'commit to being irresponsible' and promise to leave nominal interest rates at zero even after the economy starts recovering.

WM: It's quite interesting, because I was heavily involved in the Japanese debate, working with the Japanese Prime Minister's office for a while back in the 1990s. All the American economists that came through the door were saying to the Bank of Japan: 'You should announce a high inflation target, you should debase your currency, it's easy to debase your currency, you just print as much money as you need to.' The Japanese were saying: 'No, we don't want inflation to get out of control'. Now the Americans are saying the same thing and it's got to be mostly politics.

JL: It certainly seems so. Ben Bernanke was a big proponent of inflation targeting before he became Chairman of the Fed. And everyone expected he would push for an announcement of a numerical inflation target, but there must be some political constraints because he did not do that. In relation to the political side of things, let's consider the long-term fiscal outlook you mentioned. Projections by the Congressional Budget Office show the debt-to-GDP ratio in the United States on a substantial upward trend. How long will it take before the markets start realising that there may be a serious fiscal sustainability problem in the US?

WM: I actually worked at the Congressional Budget Office for a while and I'm still involved with them. The US not consolidating its public finances and getting under fiscal pressure is a real worry, and actually this feeds back into this inflation issue. US liabilities to the rest of the world are all in US dollars. If you look at how much government debt there is, and who's holding it, the simplest thing for the US to close its budget deficit is not to raise taxes, because of the politics, not to cut spending, because of the politics. It is to create high inflation, which has solved many fiscal problems for many countries over the centuries.

So the US has the incentive to have high inflation. The Fed should have taken that into account and announced a higher inflation target or in fact a high nominal income growth target which implies higher inflation. Not very high, but enough to get the economy moving. This is a real problem and I don't see it being resolved when the presidential election is held the week after next. It's not going to go away and there's a **fiscal cliff** coming in January which actually is quite a dangerous thing for the world economy.

JL: As our final topic before turning to the audience for questions, can you summarise other lessons implied by the crisis? I am primarily interested in policies that economic research shows would be beneficial, but policymakers seem to shy away from.

WM: The first thing goes back to the 1993 paper Henderson and I wrote, which compared various monetary rules. Nominal income targeting in that empirical analysis was better than inflation targeting, and the crisis seems to have confirmed that finding. So my view is that central banks should be targeting nominal income growth, not inflation. If you get a shock like we're observing now, even if real output falls people are confident that the inflation rate will rise and that'll avoid the debt deflation dynamic. So there are a lot of reasons to switch our arguments on monetary policy.

JL: But inflation expectations will become less well anchored, which was one of the main benefits of inflation targeting, and which would favour your alternative suggestion of announcing a 5–6 per cent inflation target temporarily …

WM: De-anchoring of inflation expectations is the usual argument against nominal income targeting. But which is easier to forecast, nominal income growth or inflation? I've had students doing PhDs on this and the evidence for the US says you can get a better forecasting rule on nominal GDP growth than you do on inflation. Therefore, I disagree with the argument of losing the anchor. The anchor on nominal GDP is just as real as an anchor on inflation. In fact, nominal GDP is something you measure, while inflation is an index that you create by putting together a whole range of data. So desirability of nominal income targeting is to me the first major lesson.

The second lesson is to be very careful what policies you put in place. For example, think about policies on climate change. If you don't look at what they mean for these other shocks coming through the system, that's a big oversight because some policies change the propagation mechanism. And pushing up against it can create very negative impacts if you haven't got the policy right.

The third lesson is that institutions matter a lot. You've got to design your political institutions to stop politicians from making major judgement errors. And economic institutions, such as central banks, independent budget offices, and Productivity Commission-type institutions that evaluate alternative policies; all those should be set up in the good times. So when the bad times come, you don't get irresponsible policy by governments.

JL: I think the situation in Europe now shows that reforms done under pressure may be problematic.

WM: It's the worst time to do it.

Audience member 1: In almost every interview post-GFC, the question comes up about regulation. I was wondering what you think; is there a case for more regulation in the financial industry at the moment or less?

WM: I think better. Markets unfettered do not work very well, but bad regulation is probably even worse. And so the question should always be: 'What's the best way to design the regulations so that the incentives of everybody in the market place are aligned to the social good?' That's the principle. It's easy to say that, it's harder to work out how to do it in specific cases. But there are some glaring holes in the United States. You can see the incentives in the financial system were really poorly structured and the regulatory frameworks just couldn't deal with them.

JL: To follow up on that, there seem to be these two camps, especially in the United States. One says that the GFC was primarily a market failure and that's why we need more regulation. The other camp says it was mainly a government failure and we need less regulation …

WM: Well, my problem, Jan, is I think that simplistic idea comes out of 30-second grabs in the media. It's just too simplistic, it's wrong. The world is complicated. We're talking about mostly people's behaviour, psychology. We're talking about how people interact in markets, et cetera. I just think those simple conclusions are too simple. You have to sit down and carefully look at the evidence and that's where I think behavioural economics is teaching us a lot of things: 'How do you structure models to capture the real behaviour that we observe, and design policies accordingly that can evolve over time?'

And the other idea I think is wrong is that: 'We know everything now and this is what we do.' It's again coming back to the climate change debate where the usual argument is: 'We know the science, we know that we've got to stop this thing.' I think that's completely the wrong way to think about climate change. What we should be dealing with is: 'How do we manage the risk?' The risk of the policies, the risk of the climate change on the society and so on. It's a risk-management question and that requires very clever and adaptable policy as we get new information.

JL: I should add that you take the complexities of the real world very seriously. I remember a decade ago when I was starting my PhD I came across one of your big models, which many institutions including the Fed use. And when I saw it had what, 6000 equations …?

WM: 15 000 actually.

JL: There you go! Well, I remember it really gave me goose bumps about economics being way too complicated for me to absorb. But that model can really capture at least big chunks of that complexity.

WM: Well, it's very simple compared to the real world. The only reason that it's so big is that each little bit we think we understand, we model. Then, when we put it all together, the interaction of all the bits is too hard to do in your head. Although my co-author, Jeff Sachs, who was with me the very first time we built one of these models, he seems to be able to do it in his head. But no one else can, and so given that he's not running the world, you need to build one of these models so that policymakers can understand all these linkages, because it's very complicated.

Audience member 2: You spoke about the US potentially inflating themselves out of the fiscal problem. How do you think China's going to react if America starts printing off money at a large scale and monetising their debt? Are they just going to get rid of all the US government bonds they own?

WM: Well, there are two sets of questions. The first set of questions is answered by what we observed from 2001. As the US was expanding liquidity, the Chinese were worried about losing competitiveness, and they also pegged their exchange rate to the US dollar. This meant effectively that the Chinese also expanded domestic liquidity to maintain that peg. That's why I think an inflation impulse from the US would feed through very, very quickly. Not just to China, but all of Asia and Latin America would peg to the US dollar not to lose competitiveness. So while the inflation surge may start outside the US, it would be quickly transmitted to the United States.

The other aspect of your question is that the Chinese are holding a lot of the US securities. If there's high inflation, they're going to lose value, and we've already seen many central banks change their portfolio allocation. It's not that they're dumping US dollars, but they're diversifying; they're now holding more Australian dollars, more Swiss francs, more Japanese yen. And they're keeping their US dollar holdings roughly constant, so the share is falling. But if people do get concerned that the US is going to go down the road of inflation, you will have this problem of dumping the US dollar.

We modelled this scenario for the World Bank last year for the G20. We took one of our global models and asked: 'What if China all of a sudden sells all their holdings of US securities?' In a model, you can do that. What

this does is to drive up real interest rates in the US by about
4–5 percentage points. It causes about an 8 per cent decline in the
US economy in that year, really large effects. This is because we are
talking about trillions and trillions of dollars, and it's not just paper, it's
actually real assets. Thus, when you dump assets, the prices fall and the
interest rates go up.

We can only hope we don't see that scenario. It's a very dangerous
situation for the US to contemplate because they're not a big closed
economy any more. They're less than 20 per cent of the world whereas
they used to be 50 per cent. So they're playing in a game that Australia
plays in; a medium-sized economy that is open to the world and whose
outcomes depend on what happens in countries like China and Brazil and
India. This reality is dawning on America now, but it's also a serious
problem for some of the economic models. You know, Jan, that many of
the models that people use for monetary and fiscal policy are closed
economy models. Well, that's crazy. There's no closed economy in the
world except North Korea.

JL: Cuba perhaps?

WM: Well, yes, there are a few. But it's a dangerous mindset because
you're working in an analytical space that's not actually mapped onto the
real world. And sometimes the exchange rate matters and sometimes oil
prices set outside the US matter. And people tend to get it wrong because
they can't see that in their model. And that's why I think the Fed got it
wrong in the early 2000s, because they didn't see the relative price shock
and the low manufactured goods' prices coming out of China as anything
relevant for the US economy.

JL: You have an interesting suggestion in relation to the trend you
mentioned – that other central banks are buying Australian dollars for
their portfolios, which tends to appreciate the Australian dollar and hurt
our exports. You suggest that the RBA should be selling our dollars to
them directly rather than going through the markets. Can you just outline
the reasoning behind it?

WM: Yes, this actually created a lot of problems. I had union leaders coming
out and saying that they agreed with my proposition, but I wasn't saying that
we should control the exchange rate at all. I was saying that if another
central bank wants to hold Australian dollars, we know that's a shock
because they've announced it. And if we can take that shock out of the
market, we should. So we should print the Australian dollars they want, sell
it to them directly, and therefore the exchange rate won't move. They'll get
their preference, we'll get the **seigniorage** from them holding our currency.

Now that's very different to: 'Should we intervene in the foreign
exchange market to peg the currency like the Swiss do?' And I don't think

we should, because the flexible exchange rate is such an important part of our success. Jeff Sachs and I wrote a number of papers in the 1980s about optimal degrees of exchange rate intervention. If you can identify the shock, you should hit the shock rather than offset it in another market. Pure floating exchange rates without ever dealing with a particular shock are actually not optimal if you know what the shock is. If you don't know the shock, then let the market sort it out for you.

JL: We have a lot of recent evidence that flexible exchange rates are very beneficial; for example, Iceland's speedy recovery from its recent banking crisis. Many European countries like Spain and Ireland are now learning the hard way that being in a common currency area such as the Euro and losing the exchange rate adjustment mechanism is very costly.

Audience member 3: Do you think that the US will be able to work their way out of the situation and retain their role of a global economic leader?

WM: That's a very good question. The economics of the US solution is pretty sound in my view. They need to be willing to deal with their fiscal problems by cutting some spending and raising some taxes, and by having higher inflation for a short period. Americans are incredibly productive, a lot of innovation goes on in the United States, it is a very flexible economy. You give people the right incentive, and it will generate what we observe around us in terms of most of the technology on the planet. So, I'm an optimist. I think in fact the US is in a great situation because they are at the frontier of most technology.

But the politics is where the problem is. And this bifurcation between the extreme Republicans and the extreme Democrats, and the fact that there is no consensus in the middle means that inevitably you're not going to get the spending and tax changes. You're going to end up with some inflation and you're going to end up with someone having to deal with the structural adjustment problems.

The fact is bailing out General Motors doesn't fix the problem that the US can't compete in terms of automobiles. This whole idea that you want to take all the manufacturing low-skilled workers and turn them into builders in Florida – that's not a policy solution. So education is a big deal, they've got to deal with the educational problems in the United States. At the very elite levels their education is fantastic. But two of my kids went through US schools and while junior education was fantastic too, high school was a disaster. So there are some real flaws in the system and it comes back to the role of government and the role of the private sector. I think what you need is a couple of states to have experiments, whether it be Massachusetts or others, to show how certain types of strategies work. And then use that as an experimental design for the whole country.

But I'm very optimistic on the US if they can get through the political divide in the Congress. This election is going to be very interesting. If President Obama wins, he's got some incentive for not preventing the fiscal cliff. Because someone has to hit Congress with a major shock and I think if the Republicans create the fiscal cliff they're going to pay dearly for it in the future – it would cause a severe recession in the United States. Obama has got more incentives fixing it that way than I think any other way, but it's complicated.

JL: I am glad we finished on a more positive note. Warwick, I would like to thank you very much for sharing your interesting insights with us and for your contribution to public policymaking over the years. We'll be following your views and interest rate predictions very closely now that you're on the RBA Shadow Board.[3]

11.3 Key economic insights and policy lessons

Economic insights	Implied policy lessons (for public officials and voters)
The GFC was caused by a number of interconnected developments, none of which would have been a sufficient cause by itself.	Policymakers should attempt to better understand the interconnections between various segments of the economy and their linkages to policy.
The 1997–98 capital flight from Asian countries dramatically increased an inflow of finances into the US stock market. This fuelled both the dotcom bubble of the late 1990s and the subsequent housing bubble of the 2000s, which was exacerbated by global demographic trends (low total-dependency ratios).	Policymakers should pay attention to global capital flows, and make sure their policies do not contribute to a build-up of economic imbalances.
The 'global saving glut' of the 2000s resulted in a 'search for yield' and contributed to the rise of mortgage securitisation and the asset bubbles prior to 2008.	Policymakers should monitor the effect of global factors on asset returns and financial innovation.
The Fed's lowering of interest rates in response to the dotcom bubble bursting in 2001, and keeping them at excessively low levels for several years, further inflated the US asset bubbles. Such 'cheap money' policy was exported to the rest of the world through currencies fixed to the US dollar.	Policymakers should carefully consider the rationale for sustained major deviations from historical patterns of monetary responses (as captured, for example, in the traditional Taylor rule weight between inflation and output). This means policies should not contribute to misallocation of capital and deviations from fundamentals.
The period prior to the GFC saw large relative price shocks; the price of manufactured goods imported from Asia to high-income countries was falling while energy prices were rising.	Policymakers should look beyond basic indicators such as the consumer price index in identifying inflationary and deflationary pressures.

---

3 The RBA Shadow Board coordinated by the Centre for Applied Macroeconomic Analysis at the Australian National University consists of 10 distinguished macroeconomists who provide their own recommendation regarding interest rates the day before the official RBA decision; details are available at **https://cama.crawford. anu.edu.au/rba-shadow-board**

Economic insights	Implied policy lessons (for public officials and voters)
In the three decades prior to the GFC the global economy has been experiencing a big structural transformation.	Policymakers should not ignore changing global productivity patterns, nor sweep them under the rug by subsidising uncompetitive industries.
A temporary period of rapid growth in house and stock prices may not be a bubble; it may be due to a domestic productivity increase. In smoothing consumption, people then borrow against their future (higher) incomes, and asset prices jump to a new equilibrium.	Policymakers should carefully analyse productivity trends in order to recognise whether asset prices are being driven by fundamentals or whether a bubble is being inflated. In doing so they should avoid mistakenly considering productivity growth abroad as their own.
The economy is affected primarily by the level of (real) interest rates, not so much by the direction of the recent policy change(s).	Policymakers should focus on assessing and communicating the monetary policy stance in terms of whether the level of the interest rate is below/above/at the neutral level. Several subsequent interest rate increases are not sufficient to conclude that policy is contractionary; the interest rate must actually be above neutral.
The quality of institutional design and robustness of policies can sometimes only be evaluated when challenged by an adverse shock.	Policymakers should not prematurely assess a policy as successful without it being confronted by adverse economic developments. They should design policies that are robust in light of such developments.
Debt (leverage) is not a problem per se; capital accumulation and innovation require investment and thus borrowing. Debt only becomes problematic when risk-takers enjoy the gains of their investments, but the government (taxpayer) covers the losses.	Policymakers should design systems in which risk-takers (especially in the financial sector) do not free ride on the rest of the society.
The role of the financial system is crucial in the transmission of various shocks throughout the economy, and in the magnitude of their impact on key variables.	Policymakers should use modelling frameworks that better capture the role and effects of the financial system.
Nominal income targeting has some advantages over inflation targeting, especially in a downturn.	Policymakers should carefully explore the monetary regime of nominal income targeting, in which a decline in real GDP automatically translates into a proportionate rise in the inflation target and thus lowers the threat of a deflationary spiral.
Monetary and fiscal policies work through the aggregate demand side of the economy. They are incapable of dealing with supply-side issues such as labour force skill mismatch and low productivity.	Policymakers should generally engage macroeconomic policies only in tackling aggregate demand-side fluctuations.
It is in the interest of a country hit by a crisis to have other countries implementing expansionary policies that stimulate it. But it may not be in the interest of the other countries.	Policymakers should carefully judge to what extent their country is affected by adverse developments rather than engage in 'herd behaviour' unsupported by facts.
In an open economy with floating exchange rates, fiscal policy does not have much expansionary effect as it results in an exchange rate appreciation reducing net exports. In contrast, monetary policy's expansion leads to exchange rate depreciation reinforcing the stimulatory effect of fiscal policy under floating exchange rates.	Policymakers should, especially in small open economies with flexible exchange rates, favour monetary policy to provide an economic stimulus. This is unless interest rates are already at zero and/or the adverse shock is very large.

Economic insights	Implied policy lessons (for public officials and voters)
The effectiveness of a fiscal stimulus may depend on whether the government has a credible strategy to subsequently eliminate the resulting debt. If households are credit-constrained such strategy boosts the short-term stimulatory effects.	Policymakers should take into account the nature of the public's expectations in packaging a fiscal stimulus and a subsequent debt reduction.
Printing money via monetary policy shifts spending and investment (and hence unemployment and output) from one period to another; it generally does not lead to a change in their overall level. That is, the long-term aggregate supply and the long-term Philips curve are commonly vertical.	Policymakers should carefully distinguish between the long-term and short-term effects of monetary policy on real economic variables such as investment, unemployment and output.
Demographic trends of ageing populations imply that overall statistics for the population as a whole may be misleading.	Policymakers should always consider changes in the demographic structure of the population in interpreting economic data, e.g. look at labour-force participation rates for individual age cohorts rather than the total.
Viability of various policies partly depends on the timing of their implementation.	Policymakers should generally introduce (unpopular but necessary) regulatory and policy changes in good times to maximise their public support and chances of success.
If China and other emerging market countries were to sell their holding of US dollars on a large scale, it would bring about a major recession in the US and the rest of the world.	Policymakers should make sure they do not contribute to imbalances that make their economies overly exposed to the economic and political will of other countries.
If central banks want to diversify their portfolio of foreign currency holdings, they may purchase these directly from the relevant central bank rather than the market so as not to affect the exchange rate unnecessarily.	Policymakers should attempt to disentangle various shocks, and respond to those they can identify (such as portfolio rebalancing of foreign central banks), rather than offsetting them in another market.

11.4 Discussion questions

1   Using your own words, summarise the debate of Section 11.2 in three to five sentences.
2   Write down one idea discussed in the interview that you found new or interesting, or that you disagree with, and briefly explain why.
3   Write down one question on any topic covered in the interview that you would ask the speaker if you had a chance.
4   Consider the cartoon in Section 11.1, and explain the point to someone who has not read the section and does not have any knowledge of economics.
5   Examine Figure 11.1 from the perspective of a policymaker. Describe its key message to the public and explain what kind of policy improvement is implied by the data. Do the same for Figure 11.2.

6   Suppose you take part in a debating contest, in which the topic is the opening quote of the chapter by John F. Kennedy:

> *When written in Chinese, the word 'crisis' is composed of two characters. One represents danger and the other represents opportunity.*

Prepare a speech you would give for the affirmative side. Then (you or your classmate) prepare a speech for the negative side. If possible, organise an audience and perform the debate.

7   What is the relationship between the nominal and real interest rate? What is the relationship between inflation and expected inflation? What is the relationship between interest rates and (expected) inflation?

8   What does the term 'asset bubble' refer to? Describe its effect, both prior and post its bursting. Can you think of ways in which policymakers can identify bubbles? How should they respond?

9   Based on Prof. McKibbin's account, explain the difference between some of the 'shocks' prior to the GFC: a relative price shock, a terms of trade shock, a liquidity shock and various structural developments in the labour market. How did these impact upon the events leading up to the GFC?

10 Prof. McKibbin states that: 'You don't know how bad policy is until you push against it.' Describe the example he gives and offer other examples in relation to the GFC or in other policy areas.

11 What is the Basel III Accord? Based on your research, attempt to summarise its strengths and weaknesses, and identify how it could be improved to prevent excessive leverage.

12 Explain the meaning of 'too-big-to-fail'. Highlight the problem and propose some solutions.

13 Summarise Prof. McKibbin's narrative in terms of monetary and fiscal policy responses to the GFC, and his view on their effectiveness. Contrast them to your own views, informed by some relevant studies.

14 Prof. McKibbin argues that 'fiscal policy alone doesn't have much of an effect in an open economy'. What is the gist of his argument? Based on your reading of Mundell (1963) or subsequent work, describe the effectiveness of monetary and fiscal policies under fixed and flexible exchange rates.

15 What lessons from the GFC does Prof. McKibbin draw, particularly regarding policies that economic research shows would be beneficial but have not been implemented? Express your view on his suggestions.

16 Prof. McKibbin states that the solution to the problems of the US economy is 'pretty sound'. What is the rationale for his claim? What are your own thoughts on this?

17 Propose a set of policies that you think best avoids economic crises and thus promotes people's wellbeing.

11.5 Where to find out more

Bernanke, B. S., T. Laubach, F. S. Mishkin and A. S. Posen (2001), *Inflation Targeting: Lessons from the International Experience*, Princeton University Press.

Claeys, G., Z. Darvas, S. Merler and B. G. Wolff (2014), 'Addressing Weak Inflation: The European Central Bank's Shopping List', Bruegel Policy Contributions, issue 2014/05.

Eggertsson, G. B. and P. Krugman (2012), 'Debt, Deleveraging, and the Liquidity Trap: A Fisher-Minsky-Koo Approach', *The Quarterly Journal of Economics*, 127(3), pp. 1469–1513.

Eggertsson, G. B. and M. Woodford (2004), 'Policy Options in a Liquidity Trap', *American Economic Review*, 94(2), pp. 76–79.

Fleming, J. M. (1962), 'Domestic Financial Policies Under Fixed and Floating Exchange Rates', IMF Staff Papers, 9, pp. 369–379.

Fred (2015), 'Effective Federal Funds Rate', Fred Economic Data, St. Louis Fed, available at **https://research.stlouisfed.org/fred2/series/DFF/downloaddata?cid=118**

Gerdtham, U. G. and C. J. Ruhm (2006), 'Deaths Rise in Good Economic Times: Evidence from the OECD', *Economics & Human Biology*, 4(3), pp. 298–316.

Henderson, D. W. and W. J. McKibbin (1993), 'A Comparison of Some Basic Monetary Policy Regimes for Open Economies: Implications of Different Degrees of Instrument Adjustment and Wage Persistence', *Carnegie-Rochester Conference Series on Public Policy*, 39(1), pp. 221–318.

McKibbin W. J. and J. Sachs (1991), 'Global Linkages: Macroeconomic Interdependence and Co-operation in the World Economy', Brookings Institution.

McKibbin, W. J. and A. Stoeckel (2006), 'The Collapse of the US Housing Market', available at **www.economicscenarios.com/files%5Cissue14.pdf**

McKibbin, W. J. and A. Stoeckel (2009), 'Modelling the Global Financial Crisis', *Oxford Review of Economic Policy*, 25(4), pp. 501–607.

McKibbin W. J. and P. Wilcoxen (1999), 'The Theoretical and Empirical Structure of the G-Cubed Model', *Economic Modelling*, 16(1), pp. 123–148.

Modigliani, F. (1986), 'Life Cycle, Individual Thrift, and the Wealth of Nations', *American Economic Review*, 76(3), pp. 297–313.

Mundell, R. A. (1963), 'Capital Mobility and Stabilization Policy under Fixed and Flexible Exchange Rates', *Canadian Journal of Economic and Political Science*, 29(4), pp. 475–485.

RBA (2015), 'Interest Rates and Yields – Money Market – Daily', Reserve Bank of Australia, available at **www.rba.gov.au/statistics/historical-data.html#interest-rates**

Reinhart, C. and K. Rogoff (2009), *This Time Is Different: Eight Centuries of Financial Folly*, Princeton University Press.

Ruhm, C. J. (2005), 'Healthy Living in Hard Times', *Journal of Health Economics*, 24(2), pp. 341–363.

Shiller, R. J. (2000), *Irrational Exuberance*, Princeton University Press.

Stonecash, R., J. Libich, J. Gans, S. King, M. Byford and G. Mankiw (2014), *Principles of Macroeconomics*, Australian Edition, 6th Edition, Cengage Learning Australia, Chapter 17: The global financial crisis of 2008.

Taylor, J. B. (1993), 'Discretion Versus Policy Rules in Practice', *Carnegie-Rochester Conference Series on Public Policy*, 39(1), pp. 195–214.

12 Central banks and governments: cooperation or conflict?

Permit me to issue and control the money of a nation,
and I care not who makes its laws!

Attributed to Mayer Amschel Rothschild, German banker and the founder of the
Rothschild banking dynasty, date and source unknown.

Economic concepts discussed

Easy-to-understand explanations of all the concepts listed below appear in the glossary
at the end of this book.

- Asset bubble
- Budget deficit/surplus
- Cash rate
- Central bank
- Central bank transparency
- Commitment

- Credibility
- Deflation
- Disinflation
- Fiscal gap
- Game of chicken
- Global saving glut

- Inflation targeting
- Monetary Conditions Index
- Phillips curve
- Quantitative easing
- Time-inconsistency problem

12.1 Motivation and overview

The ability to print money is a powerful tool and it is therefore not surprising that it has
always attracted the attention of politicians. They have often been tempted to use it for
their political agenda, similarly to what they sometimes do with fiscal policy. All high-
inflation episodes of the past can be largely attributed to politicians 'inducing' their
country's **central bank** to print money excessively to finance **budget deficits**.

A fair amount of economic research of the late 1970s and 1980s was devoted to
identifying the main reasons for the surge in inflation in the 1960s and 1970s.[1] The main
conclusion was that countries need to separate monetary and fiscal policy; they need to
make the central bank formally independent from the government in order to avoid
political interference in interest rate setting. And then the pioneering 1989 *Reserve Bank of
New Zealand (RBNZ) Act* came along. This piece of legislation took the idea of central bank
independence to a whole new level, and the resulting **inflation targeting** regime was so
successful that it was subsequently adopted by almost all advanced countries.

---

1 See, for example, Kydland and Prescott (1977) or Barro and Gordon (1983).

Dr Don Brash, the Governor of the RBNZ during 1988–2002, was a key figure in both the implementation of the RBNZ Act and the global popularisation of inflation targeting. This chapter, based on an interview recorded on 26 May 2011, offers unique insights into the logic behind the major reforms of monetary policy over the past two and a half decades (including behind-the-scenes discussions with other central bank governors, such as the Fed's Alan Greenspan and the Bank of England's Mervin King). Importantly, the debate sheds light on the topical issue of the interactions between monetary policy (performed by the central bank) and fiscal policy (performed by the government). Dr Brash is well placed to offer such insights as he's had the highest-level experience with both of these macroeconomic policies. After completing nearly three terms as RBNZ Governor, he entered politics and soon become leader of the New Zealand National Party.[2]

The discussion starts with the background of the 1989 RBNZ Act, which single-handedly transformed global central banking as we know it. Dr Brash explains that:

> New Zealand had a very bad inflation record over the
> previous 20 years … Not only was inflation quite high but its
> cycles bore a curious resemblance to the political cycle.

The aim of the RBNZ Act could therefore be summarised in one word: **commitment**. The same way that a person addicted to alcohol needs to commit to 'kicking the habit', the central banking reforms sought a commitment strategy ensuring that, as Dr Brash puts it: 'politicians could not manipulate monetary policy for their short-term political gain'. Figure 12.1, which reports history's biggest recorded hyperinflations, shows that politicisation of monetary policy can have some dire consequences. In some cases prices doubled every day! It is not hard to imagine how destructive this is for economic activity and people's wellbeing.

There were three key features of the RBNZ legislation attempting to separate monetary and fiscal policy. First, the central bank was made formally independent from the government, similar to ensuring that the alcohol-prone patient would not be allowed to buy a bottle in the liquor store. Second, the objective of monetary policy was made crystal clear, and price stability was specified as its only goal. This was implemented as a numerical inflation target, which amounted to specifying an explicit blood alcohol concentration limit to the patient. Third, the Governor of the RBNZ was made personally accountable for achieving the inflation target. He or she could lose the job if they failed to do so, similar to a pre-specified punishment to the patient for breaching the given alcohol limit.

The transparency of the inflation objective and other communication aspects (such as publishing models and economic forecasts) aimed to ensure that any breach of the arrangement would be clearly visible to the public. The attached accountability was then all about getting the incentives right. Dr Brash recalls his surprise when being told that the contract was between the Finance Minister and himself as Governor, not the Reserve Bank as such. The Minister explained: 'We can't fire the whole central bank, we can't even fire the central bank board, but we sure as hell can fire you!' (for more, see Brash, 2013). So, in a way, the government did not only exclude itself from going to the bar,

---

2 Upon leaving politics Dr Brash also worked as Adjunct Professor in the School of Economics and Finance, La Trobe University, thanks to which (and his Australian National University PhD) we are able to include him among 'Australian economists'. The full video-interview is available at http://youtu.be/Nq99Wm4b920; for more details regarding Dr Brash, see www.donbrash.com

Figure 12.1: Episodes of major hyperinflations and their characteristics

Location	Start Date	End Date	Highest Monthly Inflation Rate	Equivalent Daily Inflation Rate	Time Required for Prices to Double
Hungary	Aug. 1945	Jul. 1946	$4.19 \times 10^{16}\%$	207%	15.0 hours
Zimbabwe	Mar. 2007	Mid-Nov. 2008	$7.96 \times 10^{10}\%$	98.0%	24.7 hours
Yugoslavia	Apr. 1992	Jan. 1994	313 000 000%	64.6%	1.41 days
Republika Srpska	Apr. 1992	Jan. 1994	297 000 000%	64.3%	1.41 days
Germany	Aug. 1922	Dec. 1923	29 500%	20.9%	3.70 days
Greece	May 1941	Dec. 1945	13 800%	17.9%	4.27 days
China	Oct. 1947	Mid-May 1949	5 070%	14.1%	5.34 days
Free City of Danzig	Aug. 1922	Mid-Oct. 1923	2 440%	11.4%	6.52 days
Armenia	Oct. 1993	Dec. 1994	438%	5.77%	12.5 days
Turkmenistan	Jan. 1992	Nov. 1993	429%	5.71%	12.7 days
Taiwan	Aug. 1945	Sep. 1945	399%	5.50%	13.1 days
Peru	Jul. 1990	Aug. 1990	397%	5.49%	13.1 days
Bosnia and Herzegovina	Apr. 1992	Jun. 1993	322%	4.92%	14.6 days
France	May 1795	Nov. 1796	304%	4.77%	15.1 days
China	Jul. 1943	Aug. 1945	302%	4.75%	15.2 days
Ukraine	Jan. 1992	Nov. 1994	285%	4.60%	15.6 days
Poland	Jan. 1923	Jan. 1924	275%	4.50%	16.0 days
Nicaragua	Jun. 1986	Mar. 1991	261%	4.37%	16.4 days
Congo (Zaire)	Nov. 1993	Sep. 1994	250%	4.26%	16.8 days
Russia	Jan. 1992	Jan. 1992	245%	4.22%	17.0 days
Bulgaria	Feb. 1997	Feb. 1997	242%	4.19%	17.1 days

Source: Hanke and Krus (2012). Used by permission.

it also tied the hands of the bartender in case the government broke in and demanded to be served.

The debate then highlights an interesting and unexpected side-effect of this institutional arrangement between the government and the central bank. It turned out that a stronger central bank commitment helped to discipline not only monetary actions but also fiscal actions – it seems to have improved the outcomes of both policies. Figure 12.2 shows that within three years of legislating an inflation target in the early 1990s, governments in New Zealand, Australia, the UK, Canada, Sweden and other countries started ameliorating their budgets and reducing the size of their debt. And this fiscal consolidation effort was sustained over many subsequent governments up until the Global Financial Crisis (GFC).

This experience made it apparent that it is not just the government affecting the central bank, but indirectly, the effect can go in the opposite direction too. How does it work? The interaction between the central bank and government can be depicted as the

Figure 12.2: Evolution of public debt-to-GDP ratio (in %, de-meaned) in early inflation-targeting countries. A rise means that the budget deficit is larger than the economy's GDP growth rate; a fall means the opposite. The regime's adoption is indicated by the start of the shaded area.

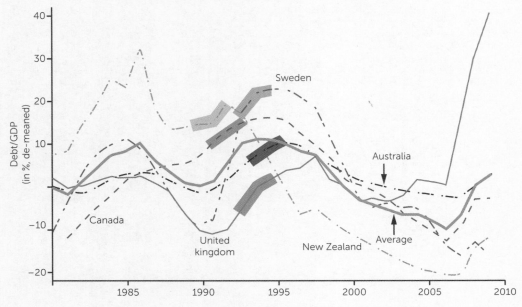

Source: Republished with permission of John Wiley & Sons, Inc., from Franta et al. (2011). Permission conveyed through Copyright Clearance Center, Inc.

'game of chicken'.[3] Suppose, realistically, that there is a rapidly growing public debt, largely due to the demographic trend of ageing populations (for more, see Chapters 6 and 7). There are essentially two ways in which this problem can be dealt with and government default avoided: a fiscal solution and a monetary solution.

The fiscal solution consists primarily of conceptual reforms of the public pension and healthcare systems that will align government expenditures and revenues over the long term. The monetary solution, only available to countries with their own currency, is to 'monetise' the debt. By printing money excessively and creating inflation the central bank can reduce the real value of the debt burden, i.e. it can pay it back in watered-down dollars.

The problem is, however, that neither the central bank nor the government may be keen to solve the sustainability problem of public finances. Both tend to prefer the other institution to do so. Why is that? It is because the central bank does not like high inflation, and the government does not like to lose votes by doing unpopular (albeit necessary) fiscal reforms. This begs a natural question, depicted in the cartoon opposite: 'Which institution will give in and become the chicken?'

---

3 The game of chicken is famously shown in the 1955 Hollywood movie *Rebel without a Cause*, in which two young men compete for the attention of a girl. They drive two stolen cars towards a cliff, having agreed that jumping out first makes one a chicken (coward). This chapter focuses on policy interaction of a long-term nature. The monetary–fiscal game of chicken in relation to short-term stabilisation (such as the post-GFC period) is discussed in Chapter 10; for more, see Libich and Nguyen (2015).

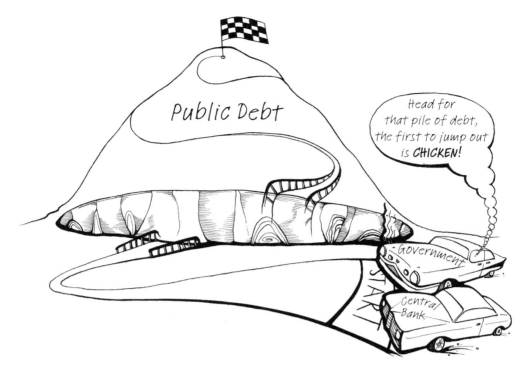

Concept by Jan Libich © 2015, drawing by Veronika Mojžišová. Used by permission.

Dr Brash's account of the New Zealand experience, as well as the data in Figure 12.2, suggest that a legislated inflation target may give the central bank an upper hand in the game of chicken, and induce fiscal reforms. This is because the government knows that if it tried to buy elections by excessive spending, such a committed central bank would 'send voters the bill in the form of higher mortgage rates' (see Dr Brash's case study in Hughes Hallet et al., 2014). Specifically in New Zealand, the fiscal consolidation was further advanced by the 1994 adoption of the *Fiscal Responsibility Act*, which may have been partly induced by the new monetary policy regime. Together, these institutional improvements moved New Zealand from a long succession of budget deficits to 15 years of **budget surpluses**, brought to an end only by the GFC and the Christchurch earthquakes.

The interview looks at many other topical policy questions, some of which were touched on in previous chapters as well: 'Why is price stability defined as an inflation target around 2 per cent rather than 0 per cent?', 'Is a numerical inflation target a "straightjacket" on the real economy leading to inferior unemployment outcomes?', 'How should policymakers respond to large price rises (possible "bubbles") in the housing and stock markets?', 'Is the unconventional monetary policy of **quantitative easing** a good idea?', 'What is the **time-inconsistency problem** of policymaking and why is it harmful to people's wellbeing?', 'Why do central bankers strive for inflation expectations of the public to be anchored?'. Importantly, Dr Brash also contemplates the future of central banking and discusses how the inflation-targeting regime could be improved.

12.2 The debate

Dr Jan Libich (JL): My first question relates to the *Reserve Bank of New Zealand Act* of 1989. It was quite an innovative piece of central banking legislation, a revolutionary change in fact. Can you please outline what it was about?

Courtesy of Southlight, Wellington. Used by permission.

< Dr Don Brash (DB): I think the background was that New Zealand had had a very bad inflation record over the previous 20 years, quite high inflation by developed nation standards – in the double digits over a period of time. Not only was inflation quite high but inflation cycles bore a curious resemblance to the political cycle. And we had, as indeed most countries had at that time, a central bank which was totally under the control of the government. The central bank provided advice on monetary policy to the government but the decisions were made by the Minister of Finance, and that meant that monetary policy was very much driven by the political needs of the government rather than by the need to keep inflation under control.

And we'd had a National Party government under Prime Minister Robert Muldoon where the inflation record was particularly bad. When the Labour government came to office in 1984 under Prime Minister David Lange, the Finance Minister Roger Douglas told the Treasury and the Reserve Bank of New Zealand (RBNZ): 'Find a way of Robert Muldoon-proofing monetary policy. Try to find a way in which politicians could not manipulate monetary policy for their short-term political gain.'

JL: Is this what's sometimes called 'institutionalising' good policy?

DB: That's exactly right. I was not involved in the RBNZ at the time, but the Bank sent several people around the world talking to a number of central bankers and academics and asked: 'What's the best way of dealing with that?' Now bear in mind that prior to that period there were really two models of central banking in the world. There was what I call the old Bank of England model, as we had in New Zealand, where the government made the decisions and the central bank simply implemented those decisions. And we had the other model of total central bank independence. The Bundesbank in Germany, the Swiss National Bank, the Federal Reserve Board of the United States; there was a very small number of countries where the central bank was at least in principle totally separate from the political process.

The *RBNZ Act* in 1989 was an attempt to find a third approach to central banking and I think it's been very successful. It basically said: 'Let's recognise that monetary policy does have an impact on inflation. It does not have an impact on economic growth or employment in the long term (unlike in the short term) so the best thing monetary policy can do for long-term growth and employment is to keep inflation low and stable.' This is why the 1989 *RBNZ Act* says that monetary policy must be focused on 'achieving and maintaining stability in the general level of prices'. There's no reference to employment, no reference to growth, no reference to balance of payments, no reference to motherhood, it's straight price stability.

JL: How is this designed to actually keep inflation under control? What's the institutional improvement?

DB: Prior to the 1990s, monetary policy in New Zealand, Australia and other countries had to achieve a whole series of objectives. This reflected the academic opinion of the 1960s and 1970s that monetary policy actually could sustainably achieve higher rates of employment or faster rates of economic growth. But the more modern thinking is that, in the long term, monetary policy only affects inflation rates, and this drove the focus on keeping prices stable.

The second unusual feature of the RBNZ framework was that it required the government of the day, the Minister of Finance on behalf of the government, to reach a formal written agreement with the Governor defining what stability in the general level of prices will be during the Governor's term of office. And originally that was 0–2 per cent measured by the consumer price index (CPI), with the formal agreement ensuring that there's a political input into the goal.

The third feature was the Governor's complete operational independence to deliver the agreed inflation target. But with the independence, of course, came accountability. I well recall talking with the Minister before the Bill was finalised. I expressed surprise that the contract was to be between the Minister and Governor, not between the Minister and the Reserve Bank. And he said: 'Ah yes, we can't fire the whole central bank, we can't even fire the central bank board, but we sure as hell can fire you!' It was designed to make it clear that while the Governor had independence to run monetary policy, the quid pro quo was the Governor being personally accountable for delivering the target.

The last feature I should mention, mandatory **central bank transparency**, is in some ways the most important single part of the framework (along with accountability). The form of the agreement between the Minister and the Governor is transparent to the public. Any change in that contract has to be public. The central bank has to disclose on a quarterly basis how it sees the economy, how it sees the inflation outlook, and right through the whole process it is very transparent. That in a sense locks both parties into prudent policy. You can't easily depart from that as everyone knows what the game plan is. This is why it's worked very well.

JL: You touched on the issue of interactions between monetary and fiscal policy, which has become very topical during the Global Financial Crisis. I remember vividly our first meeting, back in 2006 in the New Zealand Parliament, where you kindly agreed to meet me to discuss this issue. I had written a theoretical paper showing that a stronger commitment of monetary policy may improve discipline of not only monetary policy but also of fiscal policy; i.e. that an inflation target can induce the government's budgetary discipline. I recall my excitement when your reaction was: 'This is exactly what happened in New Zealand.' Can you recount what happened there in the early 1990s?

DB: That's exactly right. The first actual agreement between me and the Minister of Finance was signed at the beginning of 1990 and I was required to deliver an inflation rate of between 0 and 2 per cent by 1992; at that point it was higher than that by quite a margin. There was a general election coming up at the end of 1990 and the government eased fiscal policy aggressively in the mid-year budget. And the question was: 'What does the central bank do in the face of a major easing of fiscal policy and an inflation target which the government and the Reserve Bank have agreed?' In order to prevent overshooting our target, we had no choice but to tighten monetary policy.

And that had a very substantial impact on thinking about monetary and fiscal policy in New Zealand. The opposition National Party campaigned that if they won the election they would get interest rates down, not by leaning on the central bank but by tightening fiscal policy and liberalising the labour market. They said: 'If we tighten fiscal policy and liberalise the labour market you'll be able to ease monetary policy and still reach the agreed target.' So there is no question that the 1989 *RBNZ Act* had a major positive impact on the government's incentives.

Five or six years later when the National Party government was in office and running a big surplus, they said: 'We want to reduce tax rates but we can only do that if a) the budget is still in surplus, b) the government's debt target is still met, and c) the central bank confirms that they can accommodate such easing of fiscal policy without markedly tightening monetary policy.' And they formally wrote to me saying: 'Do you think if we cut income tax rates like this you could still keep your inflation on target without an aggressive tightening of monetary policy?' And we said: 'Yes'. So there is no question at all that a tightly specified and agreed inflation target between the central bank and government does have an impact on fiscal policy prudence.

JL: We've done more research on this since 2006, and found this 'disciplining' effect of committed monetary policy on fiscal policy seems to have been in force in all of the early inflation targeters. But you mentioned managing expectations as one of the benefits of transparency. Central bankers sometimes talk about 'anchoring expectations', did that actually occur in New Zealand?

DB: When we first introduced the 0–2 per cent inflation target in New Zealand a number of people thought we were absolutely out of our minds. We had had high inflation for quite a long time. Most people thought with a bit of hard work we might get it down to about 5, but the idea of getting it below 2 was regarded, even in the central bank itself, as preposterous. I well recall the head of our trade union movement in New Zealand writing an article in the newspaper saying this single-minded focus on getting inflation under control is nuts: 'It's very bad news for workers, it's very bad news for employers. But unfortunately this madman in the central bank is absolutely committed to doing it so we really have no choice than to adjust wage and salary demands in line with that objective.'

And in fact I recall having a meeting with him and the Prime Minister in which I said: 'Unemployment is going to go up if you guys keep on insisting on wage demands markedly higher than the inflation target we and the government have agreed. Because if the prices are going up at this modest rate but your wages are going up at two or three times that rate, the thing which gives is the employment rate.' He absolutely understood that unemployment would go up. And for a number of months the head of the union movement went around the countryside campaigning for modest wage demands.

I must say I am not well type-cast for this role, Jan, because I'm a nice, gentle kind of guy. You need to be seen as a hard-nosed, miserable so-and-so because you have to convince people that you are absolutely committed to the low inflation target. Once people believe that, and start behaving in line with that, the social costs of getting to the lower inflation target disappear. They only occur if people don't really think the central bank means it so they behave in ways that are conditioned by the high inflation of the past rather than by the new inflation target.

JL: Good to know union officials understand the mechanics of the short-term **Phillips curve** we teach first-year students. Can you explain the logic a bit more?

DB: I recall having a discussion with Michael Cullen who became the Labour Party finance spokesman. We were talking about employment and inflation and I explained it as follows. When you reduce inflation from, say, 10 per cent to 2 per cent, unemployment almost always goes up. Why? Because when inflation is 10 per cent people demand wage increases geared to that expectation. Firms price things on that expectation. The general assumption is that this is going to continue, but as monetary policy squeezes down inflation to 2 per cent per annum, all of a sudden businesses find they can't pass on 10 per cent wage increases. They need to lay off staff, some businesses collapse, unemployment goes up and it stays up until inflation expectations decrease; that is, until the short-run Phillips curve decreases. Then price and wage-setting behaviour adjusts to whatever the new inflation rate is, and unemployment returns to its long-term rate level.

Conversely, of course, if inflation has been trucking along at 2 per cent and you wind the inflation rate up to say 6 or 8 per cent, in the short term unemployment goes down. Why? Because real wages have gone down so it is cheaper for firms to produce. But workers realise they have been taken for a ride and start demanding higher wages to compensate for the higher prices. Then unemployment again returns to where it was previously. Michael Cullen said: 'I guess you get a bigger increase in unemployment when you are winding inflation down than you get a reduction in unemployment when you are cranking inflation up, because given our history it's so much harder to reduce inflation expectations than it is to increase inflation expectations'. He was absolutely right.

JL: Yes, there is a lot of evidence that wages are more rigid downwards than upwards. You raised the issue of **credibility** which largely determines the cost of a **disinflation**, and I recall a nice analogy by Mervyn King, Governor of the Bank of England. A credible central bank is like a good referee in soccer. The mere fact that it is there and can give a red card (send players off) makes the players behave in the desired way. If the central bank had perfect credibility it wouldn't have to change the interest rate at all; like a good referee does not have to blow the whistle much. The central bank would only make an announcement and economic agents would adjust their behaviour accordingly. It would say, for example: 'The economy is overheating so unless aggregate demand slows down we will have to raise interest rates.' And households and firms would respond to this announcement by spending and investing less, making the interest rate rise no longer necessary. Has the credibility of the RBNZ improved in this direction under inflation targeting?

DB: Absolutely, I agree with Mervyn King. Funnily enough, that's true not only of the economy more generally but also true of financial markets. During the first decade of my being Governor, we did not have an official **cash rate** as is common now. We modified the total amount of settlement cash across all the settlement banks in their accounts with the Reserve Bank and we basically ran the system on a very tiny base of settlement cash. And the principle was that when we wanted to ease monetary policy we would increase that slightly, if we wanted to tighten we would reduce it slightly. But one of the things which astounded me was that over a period of years we didn't change it at all.

Why not? Because we just had to say: 'Ahem, we are a bit unhappy about the inflation rate', and all of a sudden conditions in the economy would tighten. It was the ultimate 'no hands' central banking. Occasionally, of course, you had to do something because you had to make the financial markets know that you were actually serious and that you were able to tighten or loosen conditions. But for the most part we barely touched the levers at all. All we had to do was publish a forecast for the inflation rate and say we were happy or unhappy. So it worked very well.

JL: Given the benefit of inflation targeting in terms of increased credibility and expectations anchoring, why do you think that some countries have not adopted a numerical inflation target? The United States is a prime example, especially because Ben Bernanke was a big proponent of the regime before he became Chairman of the Fed. Can you see any reasons why he did not push more strongly for the adoption of a numerical inflation target after his appointment?

DB: I think you're right, it is surprising, because most developed countries now have a formal numerical inflation target. The United States is the major exception to that and Bernanke wrote a book on inflation targeting. I don't know the answer, but I suspect it may be that in the legislation the Fed is obliged to focus not just on inflation but also on employment. Bernanke, like Greenspan before him, may be absolutely convinced that the only thing monetary policy can do for long-term employment is to keep price increases low and stable, but if the legislation is such that he is in theory also responsible for employment, he may feel unable to adopt a framework so explicitly focused on inflation. I can't think of any other good reason.

It may also mean that there are some people who don't understand inflation targeting. They simply don't understand it's not the rigid straightjacket that some people try to portray it as. American economist Joseph Stiglitz, for example, has said something like: 'I pity all the countries with inflation targets because it's such a rigid straightjacket that it crucifies people.' Every inflation-targeting central bank that I'm aware of does specifically allow for exogenous shocks. If you get a doubling of the international oil price, for the sake of argument, you are not required to tighten monetary policy so that every other price falls and offsets the rise in the oil price. If it's a genuinely exogenous shock, such as a change in oil prices or in the GST rates, most inflation-targeting central banks look through that. But that may not be fully understood by the critics.

JL: Former Fed Chairman Alan Greenspan, too, opposed inflation targeting for fear of a straightjacket. But, in line with what you said, there is a lot of evidence that inflation-targeting central banks do not ignore the real economy, they are not 'inflation nutters'. For example, the variability of unemployment or output has not increased after the introduction of inflation targeting, in fact it decreased somewhat relative to non-targeters.

DB: I'm not sure whether Greenspan really believed that because he understood better than anyone that monetary policy does not have a long-term effect on unemployment. I've spoken to audiences in Jackson Hole, Wyoming, at a central bankers' junket at the end of August from time to time and I talked to Greenspan about the fact that we only have a single focus for monetary policy. He was green with envy and said something like: 'I wish we had that in the United States.'

JL: Let's now look at the recent Global Financial Crisis and consider the lessons for monetary policy. One of the issues that is often suggested is that central banks should target a broader measure of inflation than just consumer prices; perhaps also including asset prices and/or some monetary measures. What's your view on this?

DB: You mentioned Mervyn King earlier, Governor for the Bank of England. I asked him that question myself a couple of years ago, whether he still believed in inflation targeting. And he said: 'Yes I do, I think inflation targeting is a good system but it's not sufficient. It's necessary but not sufficient.' And he was, at that point at least, ready to say we do have to keep an eye on some of the other prices in the community such as asset prices.

And he quoted some relevant numbers in a speech he gave at the beginning of last year. Over the five years to 2007, when CPI inflation in the UK had averaged close to the 2 per cent target, the balance sheets of UK banks had trebled in size. He was saying that this credit boom clearly was a major factor feeding huge increases in property prices, and when that bubble burst all hell broke out. So he was I think inclined to say: 'Yes, inflation targeting is good, but we probably do need to think of some kind of macroprudential instrument which will restrain the growth of credit to avoid **asset bubbles**.'

There's a very interesting article in the annual report of the Federal Reserve Bank of Cleveland in 1998. It's widely assumed to have been written by its (then) President Jerry Jordan who was also a member of the Federal Reserve Board's Federal Open Market Committee at the time. He didn't feel able to write about the 1990s so he pretended he was writing about the 1920s, but the relevance to the 1990s was pretty obvious. In the 1920s we had high productivity growth and very well-controlled CPI inflation, a massive increase in credit and money and assets prices and, of course, that all came horribly unstuck in 1929, starting the Great Depression. And he was really saying to Greenspan and anyone else who would listen: 'The 1990s is the 1920s again – high productivity growth, well-controlled CPI inflation, a very sharp increase in money and credit, a big asset price bubble in the high tech stocks and this is going to end in tears.' And of course, that's exactly what happened.

JL: This narrative also resembles the mid-2000s with low interest rates inflating a housing bubble, the bursting of which marked the start of the Global Financial Crisis ...

DB: You point to very low American interest rates, but I think we will come to recognise in due course that China's decision to anchor its currency to the US dollar at an artificially low level was another major source of the current difficulties. China exported vast amounts of goods to the United States, keeping inflation pressures low, which made the Fed keep its policy interest rate instrument low. The argument was: 'Inflation is low, why should we tighten?' China of course accumulated vast foreign exchange reserves, invested them in US treasuries, thereby keeping longer-term interest rates low also.

That seemed fantastic for the US, low inflation, low interest rates, rising property prices, everybody was happy. It was good for China too in the short term, because China had access to the largest consumer market – it could employ lots of people coming from the countryside. But it was a kind of 'Faustian bargain', because while it was very nice for the short term it backfired badly in the longer term and both sides are now angry. We have seen the implosion of the property bubble in the United States. Americans no longer feel grateful for imports from China, they feel upset about them. China feels angry because the foreign exchange reserves invested in US treasuries are going down in value. So both sides feel angry with the outcome and I think when we look back at the Global Financial Crisis we will say that that is one major factor driving it. There are many others as well but I think it's too easy to blame the financial crisis on greedy bankers. There are greedy bankers without a doubt but that is only one of the factors which caused the crisis.

JL: You touched on what Ben Bernanke called the '**global saving glut**'. Due to global demographic and productivity trends, there was an excess of saving in the financial markets which pushed interest rates to really low levels. For example, the proportion of people aged below 15 or above 65 – relative to the working age population – was at low levels in high-income countries in the early 2000s; below 50 per cent compared to 60 per cent in the 1960s. More relevant for the future is the fact that, due to the ageing population trend, the forecast for 2040 is 70 per cent and rising. What is your view on the fiscal implications?

DB: Well, it's a serious issue, not least because most developed countries start this process in very weak fiscal positions with government debt at very high levels. The worst case I guess is Japan where the government debt-to-GDP ratio is now over 200 per cent on a gross basis. But the United States, the UK, in fact all the G7 countries have government debt-to-GDP ratios approaching 100 per cent – that's before the baby boomers reach 65, so it's a serious position I think and you're absolutely right to highlight it.

One of the worrying things also is that the savings glut which you talked about coming out of Asia will also disappear because China's demography is changing. China's policy of one child per family means that China will quite quickly face an ageing problem, very much like developed countries. So the world as a whole is going to face a situation where a relatively larger and larger share of the total population will be over 65. That has implications for pensions and health spending, because most spending on healthcare occurs in the last few years of life. So we are going to have a big increase in those costs as more and more people go into that older age range.

The question is: 'What do you do about it?' For the individual it makes sense to save more. What is not clear though is how the world as a whole deals with that. Because at the end of the day, you save more and the assumption is that you can draw down on someone else's resources to supplement your own in retirement. But if all developed countries and China and Japan and Korea are in the same situation, you can't draw down from those countries. You can't draw down on Mars; you have to draw down on something else. And my hunch is the only real solution will be people working longer, retiring later and contributing to tax revenues longer than has been the case in the past. Politically that's quite tough. I see that in France the Socialist Party officials are recommending reducing the age of eligibility for the pension from 62 to 60. I don't know whether they can't count, but it's depressing that political parties can make proposals of that kind and be taken seriously.

JL: Given the political realities that also occur in the US and elsewhere, do you think that it's all going to end up badly? Should we be preparing for sovereign defaults on a large scale? Or should we expect an alternative 'solution' to the debt problem whereby central banks print money excessively and monetise the debt? Do you think such a high inflation scenario is a reason for concern?

DB: It certainly is a reason for concern, I agree with that. Governments in democratic countries find it very difficult to confront voters with reality. And I guess that's never clearer than right now in the United States. You don't have to look very far ahead to realise the US is in serious fiscal trouble. I read an article by a Professor of Economics at Boston University last year which argued that to stabilise the American fiscal position in the long term, given their promises on social security and healthcare, the federal tax revenues have to roughly double; from 15 per cent to roughly 30 per cent of GDP.

Now you've got an American congressional situation which makes that very hard to achieve. If fiscal policy can't fix the problem, are we faced with a possibility that central banks allow inflation to erode the level of debt? I profoundly hope that's not the case, and so far at least central banks around the world appear to be quite firmly committed to keeping inflation under control. But there is clearly a collision coming between those spending commitments and the countries' willingness to fund them.

JL: I believe Larry Kotlikoff was the Boston University economist you mentioned. He's been instrumental in arguing that we really need to look at budgets in an intergenerational-type perspective. He convincingly shows that the widely used debt-to-GDP indicator is meaningless, because it does not include many public liabilities; for example, promised pensions. Last month's study by the International Monetary Fund (Batini et al., 2011) gives the most recent estimate of a comprehensive debt measure, the 'fiscal gap'. It finds that in the United States: 'a full elimination of the fiscal and generational imbalances would require all taxes to go up and all transfers to be cut immediately and permanently by 35 per cent'.

DB: Yes, the magnitude of the problem is a real worry.

JL: Let me ask one last question before turning to the audience. Can you think of some long-term macroeconomic policies we have not yet mentioned that would likely improve economic outcomes and people's wellbeing, but which politicians have shied away from?

DB: There are plenty of long-term challenges, and we've talked about some of them – the ageing of the population and the fiscal implications of that being arguably the most important of these. Most democratic governments have a hard time dealing with this challenge because the political pain is immediate and the benefits of any change come well into the future.

Audience member 1: What do you find more dangerous in the long run: government default or high inflation? For example, in Europe the choice is letting some countries default or the European Central Bank monetising the debts through inflation.

DB: I think there are two options in the European Monetary Union. One is that Greece and some other 'periphery' countries leave the Euro and then they can presumably inflate some of their debts away. Alternatively, they stay with the European Monetary Union and renegotiate their debt. It's hard to see how else they could do that. I suspect that it's less disruptive to renegotiate their debt than to leave the Euro but it's a tough choice.

Audience member 2: In 2008 you gave a speech entitled 'Big Ideas to Super-Size the New Zealand Economy'. One of your suggestions was to give the Reserve Bank of New Zealand an additional instrument to tackle inflationary pressures, namely a 'constrained authority to vary the excise tax on fuel'. Was that ever implemented?

DB: No. The proposal was motivated by a concern of the export sector in New Zealand that floating currencies' fluctuations are quite substantial. If you look at the New Zealand dollar over the last 20 years, the largest appreciation from the trough to the peak, on a trade-weighted basis in real terms, was about 50 per cent. And you'd think: 'That's a heck of a large appreciation to deal with for an exporter.' And I looked around the world and that is characteristic of most floating currencies, including the Australian dollar.

So I was looking for a way of reducing the amplitude of those fluctuations by finding some instrument we could give the central bank to supplement the official cash rate. Not to replace it, just something that would mean the central bank didn't have to move the interest rate quite so aggressively. Some economists, for example Larry Ball, suggested varying tax rates generally, but I think that is totally impractical. You can't simply kick income tax rates or the GST rates around as much as you'd like to, but the excise tax on fuel is collected from a very small number of points.

The public are accustomed to the price of fuel going up and down like a yo-yo because demand for it is inelastic, at least in the short term. The effect of the excise tax on petrol on other spending is very similar to the effect of changing interest rates. So I believed it was a useful way of giving an additional instrument to the central bank. I think it was a pity that no one has taken the proposal seriously in New Zealand or anywhere else.

Audience member 3: You mentioned that your initial inflation target was between 0 and 2 per cent. Personally, what target do you feel most comfortable with, because as you are heading close to 0 per cent you play with the possibility of **deflation** and a liquidity trap? So do you think it's better to target the higher end of the inflation intervals?

DB: The 0–2 per cent target was rationalised by my central bank colleagues as being 1 per cent plus or minus 1. And 1 per cent was chosen because according to estimates a 1 per cent increase in the CPI is probably equivalent to genuine price stability due to its upward measurement bias – not allowing properly for quality changes and substitution to cheaper products. The origin of the number is actually much cruder politically. When inflation, which had been very high in New Zealand, came below 10 per cent the then Minister of Finance Roger Douglas was asked on television: 'Aren't you satisfied now that the inflation rate is only 9?' And Roger Douglas said: 'No, I want price stability like 0–2 per cent.' And that sort of stuck, even though at the point he announced it he'd done no analysis of the correct target at all.

Subsequently, we changed the target from 0–2 per cent to 0–3 per cent. The logic was that, particularly in a very small country, you get a lot of shocks which have an impact on the CPI and tend to get smoothed out in a much larger economy. So we said: 'Rather than constantly explaining why you are outside this 2 per cent point range, widen the range to 0–3 per cent'. Then in 2002 the target range was changed again to 1–3 per cent and that's where it is now. This was the reason you mentioned, most central banks are keen to avoid getting too close to 0 per cent for fear of deflation.

I must say I'm not totally persuaded by that myself. Yes, the zero-lower-bound on interest rates is an issue for a large economy, but in a small open economy like New Zealand and Australia, easing of the exchange rate can have quite a profound impact on monetary conditions. If you drop the Australian interest rate to 0 per cent you will almost certainly get some weakening of the Aussie dollar and that would provide a stimulus which may not be so obviously true in the case of the United States.

JL: Let me add that this question was motivated by the student's experience with a monetary policy simulation game we played throughout the semester. It was designed by Swiss economist Yvan Lengwiler. It gives you an opportunity to act as a Reserve Bank Governor: analyse incoming economic data and respond by changing the interest rate in order to stabilise inflation and the economy. The inflation target in that game is set at 1.5 per cent and the observation students made was that targeting a higher level, say 2.5 per cent, would be easier. Staying further away from deflation would allow them to achieve a more stable inflation rate, because they would not have to respond so aggressively when inflation is below the target. So I am surprised you did not find the 1 per cent target mid-point an issue, but you are right that in a small open economy the exchange rate provides an extra channel.

DB: I think that's a crucial point, and the bigger the tradable sector is, the more relevant the exchange rate becomes. Incidentally, one of the things we have not talked about is our use of the **Monetary Conditions Index** for two years in the second half of the 1990s. We adopted it from Canada, and the idea was that in a small open economy the exchange rate has a very profound effect on inflation both directly through price effects and indirectly through shifting production. Therefore, the question for central banks is: 'How do you calibrate interest rate movements for what's happening to the exchange rate?'

And at that point we didn't have an interest rate instrument per se at all, we just had a view of what the inflation target should be. But we knew that both interest rates and the exchange rate had an effect on the inflation rate, so we decided to determine a formula trying to work out what effect a 1 per cent movement in the official interest rate would have on inflation compared with a movement in the exchange rate. We determined a ratio of those two and then ran monetary policy by saying we wanted the Monetary Conditions Index in a certain interval over the next quarter.

We didn't try to determine whether that was the interest rate movement or the exchange rate movement, but we told the market what the conversion rate between the exchange rate and interest rate was. So if the exchange rate fell very sharply, other things being equal, we would expect interest rates to rise in order to deliver the monetary conditions we wanted. This regime didn't succeed in New Zealand mainly because we didn't get our head around how big those movements in the MCI should be. We didn't move the MCI nearly enough through the Asian Crisis of 1997–98.

JL: Are you talking about the relative weight on interest rates versus the exchange rate?

DB: It wasn't necessarily the relativity of the two as the index number as such. We defined the index as being 1000 for the monetary conditions in the December quarter of 1996. And we were easing policy reflecting the Asian Crisis and the impact of that on the New Zealand inflation rate. But we weren't dropping the index nearly far enough. If we had had a longer history of the MCI we would have seen we needed to drop it by much more. As a consequence we had conditions too tight.

JL: I am afraid we are out of time. I would like to ask everyone to join me in thanking Don for his very interesting views and for his major contributions to public policymaking over the years.

12.3 Key economic insights and policy lessons

Economic insights	Implied policy lessons (for public officials and voters)
If the workers' (union's) wage demands are excessive, there is a surplus of labour supply over demand leading to a rise in unemployment.	Policymakers should communicate with the public and unions to make sure wage increases are in line with (expected) inflation and productivity growth.
If wages, prices and expectations do not adjust flexibly, then a deviation of inflation from its expected level leads to a deviation of unemployment from its natural level. Since wages are more 'rigid' downwards than upwards, the off-equilibrium increases in unemployment tend to be larger and longer than its declines.	Policymakers should explore mechanisms of reducing the rigidity of wage setting while taking into account the effects on equity.

Economic insights	Implied policy lessons (for public officials and voters)
The inflation-targeting regime performed by an independent central bank was a model initially adopted by countries with a track record of high inflation in the 1970s – as a way to restore monetary policy credibility. This may be why the US and Germany never adopted the regime.	Policymakers should consider using the commitment effect of inflation targeting, especially following an inflationary episode.
A mere announcement of policy intentions by a credible central bank may be sufficient to change the behaviour of economic agents – without having to actually change the interest rate policy setting.	Policymakers should, through a solid track record, aim to improve their credibility in order to be able to pursue a 'hands-off' approach to monetary policy.
In order to avoid political interference, the central bank must have formal instrument-independence from the government; i.e. freedom regarding interest rate setting. But it is not necessary for the bank to also have goal-independence.	Policymakers should generally not enable the central bank to choose its own goals, because this can lead to a 'democratic deficit' – a powerful institution with neither a political mandate nor accountability.
Even if the central bank has formal instrument-independence, monetary and fiscal policies are still closely interrelated, because each policy affects a number of economic variables (and expectations) to which the other policy responds.	Policymakers should attempt to better understand the various channels through which monetary and fiscal policies interact, both directly and indirectly.
The preferences of the central bank and government over inflation and unemployment outcomes tend to differ, especially in the presence of a large fiscal gap. This may lead to a strategic policy conflict (the 'game of chicken').	Policymakers should design the institutional setting of monetary and fiscal policies to avoid a conflict between the central bank and government. This is both in relation to the short term (regarding shock stabilisation) and long term (regarding persistent budgetary shortfalls).
If the government accumulates debt, fiscal excesses tend to spill over to monetary policy and lead to higher and/or more variable inflation.	Policymakers should design mechanisms to make sure that irresponsible fiscal policy does not jeopardise optimal monetary policy outcomes.
If the government has to reach a formal written agreement with the central bank regarding monetary policy goals and the level of the inflation target, the scope for a mis-coordination and conflict between fiscal and monetary policies seems to be reduced.	Policymakers should coordinate monetary and fiscal policies in a way that is transparent and predictable, which includes the formalisation of monetary policy goals. Only then is monetary–fiscal coordination not seen as compromising central bank independence.
A formal commitment to a numerical inflation target seems to give the central bank more ammunition in the 'game of chicken' against the government, and may therefore lead to an improvement in both monetary and fiscal policy outcomes.	Policymakers should explore the possible 'disciplining effect' of explicit inflation targets on fiscal policy, as it may provide the government with a mechanism for enhancing the political chances of electorally unpopular fiscal reforms.
In a small open economy such as Australia's the exchange rate has a profound effect on monetary conditions, and therefore the zero-lower-bound on interest rate is less of a problem than in a large economy such as the United States and Eurozone.	Policymakers should carefully consider the exchange rate channel in setting monetary policy, especially in a small open economy.
If a country anchors its currency to another currency at an artificially low exchange rate level, various problematic imbalances usually build up.	Policymakers should beware of consistently manipulating their exchange rate to gain competitiveness.
Varying some type of taxes (e.g. GST or excise tax on fuel) may in principle serve as an additional monetary policy instrument.	Policymakers should examine the pros and cons of central banks using certain types of taxes for the purposes of macroeconomic stabilisation.

12.4 Discussion questions

1   Using your own words, summarise the debate of Section 12.2 in three to five sentences.

2   Write down one idea discussed in the interview that you found new or interesting, or that you disagree with, and briefly explain why.

3   Write down one question on any topic covered in the interview that you would ask the speaker if you had a chance.

4   Consider the cartoon in Section 12.1, and explain the point to someone who has not read the section and does not have any knowledge of economics.

5   Examine Figure 12.1 from the perspective of a policymaker. Describe its key message to the public and explain what kind of policy improvement is implied by the data. Do the same for Figure 12.2.

6   Suppose you take part in a debating contest, in which the topic is the opening quote of the chapter attributed to Mayer Amschel Rothschild:

> *Permit me to issue and control the money of a nation, and I*
> *care not who makes its laws!*

  Prepare a speech you would give for the affirmative side. Then (you or your classmate) prepare a speech for the negative side. If possible, organise an audience and perform the debate.

7   What does 'institutionalising' good policy mean? Why was there a feeling in the late 1970s and 1980s, in New Zealand and other countries, that a central banking reform was necessary?

8   Describe the three main institutional features of inflation targeting: instrument independence, transparency and accountability. What are their main benefits? Why do you think all three are necessary for inflation targeting to work effectively? In your view, should central banks have goal-independence, i.e. ability to choose their own goals?

9   Using available data, assess Joseph Stiglitz's argument that inflation targeting acts as a rigid straightjacket for the economy (for more on his view, see Stiglitz, 2008).

10 What is Dr Brash's view on the effect of ageing populations on fiscal sustainability and on the financial markets? Explain his reasoning.

11 Outline Dr Brash's suggestion on using excise taxes as an additional instrument of monetary policy. Consider its benefits and potential drawbacks.

12 In the late 1990s New Zealand experimented with a Monetary Conditions Index. Explain what it is and why it was abandoned.

13 Even if the central bank is formally independent from the government, there is still an interaction between fiscal and monetary policy. Describe the various macroeconomic channels through which the two policies affect each other (for a non-technical summary, you can consult Libich and Savage, 2010, or watch the interview with Professor Eric Leeper from Indiana University, the world's leading scholar in the area of monetary-fiscal policy interactions: **http://youtu.be/ sEe56ctdShg).**

14 In the presence of a large fiscal gap, a 'game of chicken' type conflict may arise between the central bank and government. Describe the reasons for the strategic conflict, the possible ways in which it can be resolved and the resulting monetary and fiscal policy outcomes (for a non-technical summary, you can consult Franta et al., 2011).

15 Propose a set of policies that you think best avoid a conflict between the central bank and government and thus promote people's wellbeing.

12.5 Where to find out more

Barro, R. J. and D. B. Gordon (1983), 'Rules, Discretion and Reputation in a Model of Monetary Policy', *Journal of Monetary Economics*, Elsevier, 12(1), pp. 101–121.

Batini, N., G. Callegari and J. Guerreiro (2011), 'An Analysis of U.S. Fiscal and Generational Imbalances: Who Will Pay and How?', International Monetary Fund Working Paper, WP/11/72.

Brash, D. (2011), 'Monetary and Fiscal Policy: How an Agreed Inflation Target Affects Fiscal Policy', *Economic Papers*, 30(1), 15–17.

Brash, D. (2013), 'Open Bank Resolution – Better than Bank Closure or Government Bailout', New Zealand Centre for Political Research, 31 March, available at **www.nzcpr.com/ open-bank-resolution-better-than-bank-closure-or-government-bailout**

Brash, D. (2014), *Incredible Luck*, Troika Books Limited.

Evans, R. W., L. J. Kotlikoff and K. L. Phillips (2012), 'Game Over: Simulating Unsustainable Fiscal Policy', in: *Fiscal Policy after the Financial Crisis*, National Bureau of Economic Research, pp. 177–202.

Franta, M., J. Libich and P. Stehlík (2011), 'The Big Picture of Monetary–Fiscal Interactions', *Economic Papers*, 30(1), pp. 6–14.

FRBC (1998), 'Beyond price stability: A reconsideration of monetary policy in a period of low inflation', *Annual Report*, The Federal Reserve Bank of Cleveland.

Hanke, S. H. and N. E. Krus (2012), 'World Hyperinflations', CATO working paper, no. 8, 5 August.

Hughes Hallett, A., J. Libich and P. Stehlík (2014), 'Monetary and Fiscal Policy Interaction with Various Degrees of Commitment', *Czech Journal of Economics and Finance*, 64(1), pp. 2–29.

Kydland, F. E. and E. C. Prescott (1977), 'Rules Rather than Discretion: The Inconsistency of Optimal Plans', *Journal of Political Economy*, 85(3), pp. 473–491.

Leeper, E. M. (1991), 'Equilibria under "Active" and "Passive" Monetary and Fiscal Policies', *Journal of Monetary Economics*, 27(1), pp. 129–147.

Leeper, E. M. (2011), 'Monetary–Fiscal Interactions: Prof. Eric Leeper Interviewed by Dr Jan Libich', 8 July 2011, La Trobe University, available at **http://youtu.be/ sEe56ctdShg**.

Libich, J. (2011), 'Inflation Nutters? Modelling the Flexibility of Inflation Targeting', *The B.E. Journal of Macroeconomics*, 11(1), Article 17.

Libich, J. and D. Nguyen (2015), 'Strategic Monetary–Fiscal Interactions in a Downturn', *Economic Record*, 91(293), pp. 172–190.

Libich, J. and J. Savage (2010), 'Tethering the Fiscal Sow: Monetary Policy that Keeps Pork in the Sty', *Policy*, 26(3), Spring, pp. 14–19, available at **http://www.cis.org.au/app/ uploads/2015/04/images/stories/policy-magazine/2010-spring/26-3-10-james-savage-jan-libich.pdf**

Stiglitz, J. (2008), 'The Failure of Inflation Targeting', Project Syndicate, available at **www.project-syndicate.org/commentary/ the-failure-of-inflation-targeting**

13 The European currency union: will the Euro survive?

There is no example in history of a lasting monetary union that was not linked to one State.

Otmar Issing, former Chief Economist of the European Central Bank, 1991, source unknown.

Economic concepts discussed

Easy-to-understand explanations of all the concepts listed below appear in the glossary at the end of this book.

- Austerity
- Basis points
- Counter-cyclical mechanism
- Currency union
- Deutsche Mark

- Euro
- European Monetary Union
- European Union
- Exchange rate
- Fiscal gap
- Fiscal union

- Free-riding problem
- Government bonds
- Optimum currency area
- Risk premium
- Time-inconsistency problem

13.1 Motivation and overview

Have you ever imagined how much easier overseas travel would be if the Australian dollar was used everywhere? Buying tickets to the Louvre in Paris to see the *Mona Lisa*, getting entry to the ancient site of Acropolis in Greece, paying for a seat at the Nou Camp to see Barcelona play the 'real' football, all hassle free. No foreign ATM withdrawal charges, no need to worry about the **exchange rate** going up and down. Well, such a traveller's dream has come true for the 19 countries (as of 2015) that have adopted the **Euro** currency since its inception (in 1999 in electronic form, and 2002 in physical form).

Making travellers happy was obviously not the main reason behind Europe embarking on the common currency. In this chapter, two La Trobe University academics consider other advantages of such a monetary union as well as its disadvantages, and the implications of the Euro for policymakers in the aftermath of the Global Financial Crisis (GFC). Associate Professor Stefan Auer from the History and Politics department, and Jean Monnet Chair in European Union Interdisciplinary Studies (currently at the

University of Hong Kong), invited me, an economist, to the recording studio on 6 April 2011 to talk to his students. Being from different disciplines, the debate is multi-faceted and the economic angle is also placed within the broader political context.[1]

The discussion touches on a number of policy-relevant questions such as: 'Is a **fiscal union** a prerequisite for a well-functioning **currency union**?', 'To what extent is the Euro responsible for the Eurozone's current debt and banking problems?', 'What are the reasons behind most countries violating the rules specified in the **European Union**'s Growth and Stability Pact?', 'Is an Europe-wide government desirable?', 'Will Greece go bankrupt and/or exit the common currency?', and 'Should additional countries join the Euro?'.

The interview starts by Prof. Auer asking a seemingly straightforward question: 'Was that a good idea to have a common currency in Europe?' I first offer a summary of the pros, such as promoting trade between the member countries, establishing a common labour market, pooling risk across the nations and eliminating the costs of exchange rate fluctuations. There are, however, some cons: for example, the initial cost of adopting a new currency, the loss of national sovereignty and, most importantly, the loss of flexibility in macroeconomic management. It is explained that:

> By giving up its own currency a country loses two important adjustment mechanisms, namely the floating exchange rate and autonomous monetary policy.

In order to outline the latter, recall the analogy from Chapter 9, in which conducting monetary policy is compared to driving a car. The central bank behind the wheel attempts to maintain the economy's optimal speed by stepping either on the accelerator (lowering interest rates if the economy underperforms) or on the brake (increasing interest rates if the economy is overheating). In a monetary union the same logic applies, and there is generally no problem if the business cycles of the member countries are synchronised. If all member countries are subject to similar shocks, and all experience downturns as well as recoveries at the same time, then the common central bank's response in the driver's seat is appropriate for all countries.

If, however, the member countries do not form an '**optimum currency area**' (see Mundell, 1961), and go through different ups and downs, there is a problem. The common central bank cannot step on the accelerator and the brake at the same time in order to stimulate some member economies while halting others. In such a case, the common central bank tends to leave the monetary policy setting unchanged, which is inappropriate for both the countries needing to slow down and those needing to go faster. Such a problem is known as the 'one-size-fits-none' problem, and it is depicted in the cartoon below (the car is replaced with a bus to fit the Eurozone members in and for German Chancellor Angela Merkel and European Central Bank Governor Mario Draghi behind the wheel to be recognisable).

---

1 The full video-interview is available at http://youtu.be/RL9EapixPmc. For more details regarding Prof. Auer and Dr Libich, see www.europe.hku.hk/staff/SAuer.html and www.janlibich.com

Concept by Jan Libich © 2015, drawing by Veronika Mojžišová. Used by permission.

Absence of the exchange rate mechanism after the adoption of a common currency is equally problematic:

> If a country with its own currency is hit by some economic
> shock, as we have seen recently with Iceland's collapsing
> banking system, its exchange rate depreciates (weakens).
> This makes the country's exports more competitive and such
> increased external demand helps domestic firms recover,
> leading to a milder downturn and lower fluctuations in the
> economy in general. If you give up your own currency you no
> longer have this counter-cyclical mechanism.

While it is impossible to make a conclusion with certainty, the run-up to the GFC as well as its aftermath both suggest that the Eurozone is not an optimum currency area, unlike the United States. Therefore, such a broad adoption of the Euro may not have been warranted. Figure 13.1 reports estimates of the European Central Bank's (ECB's) monetary policy stance for three groups of countries: 'the core' (Austria, Germany, Finland, Luxembourg, the Netherlands), 'the coreiphery' (France, Italy, Belgium) and 'the periphery'

Figure 13.1: ECB's policy interest rate in % less year-on-year nominal GDP growth by Eurozone country grouping (the zero 0% line indicates appropriate policy, neither too tight nor too loose)

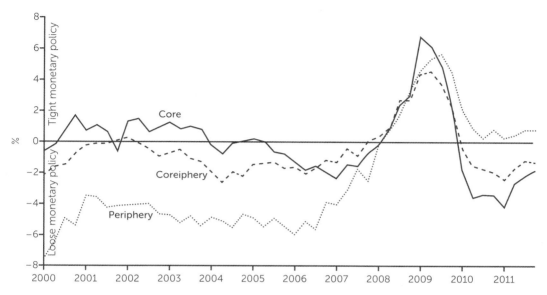

Core: Germany, the Netherlands, Luxembourg, Austria, Finland.
Coreiphery: France, Belgium, Italy.
Periphery: Spain, Portugal, Ireland, Greece.

Source: McCallum and Moretti (2012). Used by permission.

(Greece, Ireland, Portugal, Spain). It shows that during the 2001–04 period, interest rates were only appropriate (i.e. close to the 0% line) for the coreiphery, whereas they were too high for the core and too low for the periphery. During the 2005–07 period, monetary policy became too loose for all three regions; and, for example, interest rates in the periphery should have been higher by a whopping 5 percentage points (500 **basis points**).

As Libich (2015) explains: 'Such loose monetary policy led to higher wage and price inflation on the periphery, which in turn led to their loss of competitiveness against Germany and the rest of the European Union core … What was worse, such low interest rates significantly contributed to the creation of bubbles in the banking, real estate and stock markets in the periphery countries …'

Their bursting in 2008 had severe negative consequences, many of which are discussed in the interview. Just to name a few: the GDP of Greece declined by 15 per cent over the 2008–13 period with the country's stock market plunging by 80 per cent; Spanish unemployment more than tripled to 26 per cent; Irish house prices halved in inflation-adjusted terms (see *The Economist*, 2015), and the country's gross debt increased from 25 to 120 per cent of GDP. And as the post-2008 period in Figure 13.1 shows, speedy recovery in the periphery is unlikely since the ECB's monetary policy setting has been too tight for those countries (and too loose for the rest of the Eurozone since 2010).

A major problem in Europe at the time of the interview was the interconnectedness in the ownership of debt, where most of the periphery countries' public debt was owned by banks in the EU core countries, as is apparent in Figure 13.2. This created a strong link between the probability of fiscal crises and banking crises going in both directions; in fact,

Figure 13.2: Debt linkages between the EU periphery countries and the EU core in the run-up to the debt crisis (at the end of 2009, the amounts are in billions of US dollars). The debtors are governments and the creditors are the countries' banks. The size of each circle and arrow reflects the amounts

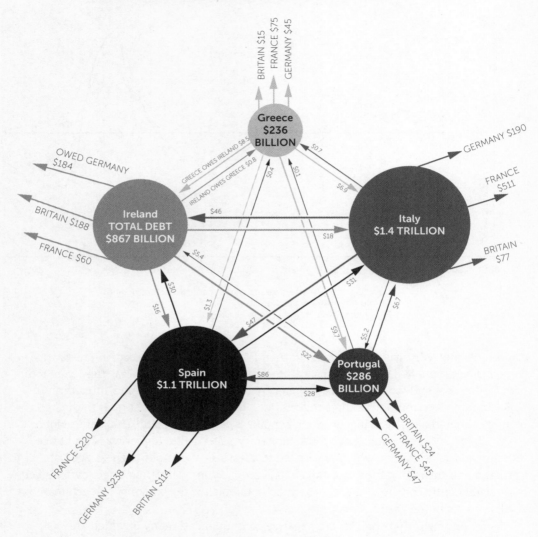

a vicious circle. Government solvency problems reduce the value of their bonds, and hence the value of the banks' assets. This may in turn require government funds to be used to prop up banks and honour deposit insurance, making their fiscal outlook worse.

Many other policy-relevant questions are discussed in the interview: for example, two types of a moral hazard (**free-riding problem**) that occur once a country joins a monetary union, the appropriateness of fiscal **austerity** and the future of Greece. In answering the question 'Do you think it would have been better to let Greece fail?', I made a prediction:

> *I think eventually, one way or another, it will happen. It's not going to be called 'letting Greece fail', it's not going to be called*

'bankruptcy', it's going to be called 'debt restructuring' … The size and the extent of the problem are such that all these Greek bailouts just seem to be pushing away the inevitable, I think.

Not all predictions by economists turn out to be correct, but this one did. Within a year and a half of the interview, Greek sovereign bonds held by private investors, worth over 100 per cent of the country's GDP, were virtually eliminated, with investors getting a major 'haircut' (for details, see Zettelmeyer et al., 2013). And unfortunately this is not the end with the fiscal troubles, social unrest and a possible 'Grexit' (Greece leaving the Euro) making the headlines in 2015.

13.2 The debate

© Dr Stefan Auer. Used by permission.

< Dr Stefan Auer (SA): To start with, let me ask you a blunt question: was that a good idea to have a common currency in Europe? I was in Dublin when the currency was introduced and I attended lectures presented by distinguished economists on the topic. They were able to marshal evidence in favour of the common currency as well as against it, and I wasn't quite sure who was right then. Now we know better …

< Dr Jan Libich (JL): Well, the answer is still disputed; there is no consensus among economists and politicians. What economic research identified prior to the creation of the **European Monetary Union** was a number of advantages and disadvantages, and people disagreed about their relative importance. This discussion still continues and is far from being 100 per cent settled – despite having a lot more data than we did in the late 1990s, most of it highlighting the disadvantages.

The main advantage of adopting a common currency is that it promotes trade. It improves the trade linkages between countries, it gets rid of the exchange rate risk and of the cost associated with exchanging currencies. A monetary union also enables pooling of risk. If you combine different countries that have different risks then you might be able to better insure against those risks. Obviously once you join through a common currency that also enables a free flow of labour. And to me, having a common labour market is a great achievement of the European Union (EU), both economically and socially. So there are some strong general arguments in favour of a currency union. The United States is an example of a currency union, and most people would agree that in its case the advantages more than outweigh the disadvantages.

SA: There are strong economic arguments in favour of the common currency, but there are also important political arguments in its favour. Would you like to explain that?

JL: I would like to focus on the economics of the EMU, but the key political drivers were evident. It was already in 1988 that Jacques Delors, one of the architects of the European monetary model, predicted that 'within 10 years 80 per cent of economic legislation, and perhaps also fiscal and social legislation, would be of EC/EU origin'. So there were many political ambitions at play, the arguments have not been purely economic.

SA: Well, I expect that's true not only for many European leaders but also for some national leaders like Francois Mitterrand in France and Helmut Kohl in Germany. The idea was that the project of a common currency would bring the nations of Europe closer together. That is something tangible that they can experience, right?

JL: Yes, for some people that was certainly another advantage of European monetary integration. But the fact that countries lose some national sovereignty was perceived as a disadvantage by others. Everybody becomes more European but also less Czech and less Slovak and less Spanish. And some people felt that this was a bad thing because they wanted to preserve their national identity.

SA: And what are the economic disadvantages of the common currency?

JL: There are some relatively minor issues such as the one-off cost of the adoption and the temporary psychological cost of people getting used to the new common currency. But the important disadvantages relate to the loss of flexibility in macroeconomic management. By giving up its own currency a country loses two important adjustment mechanisms, namely the exchange rate and autonomous monetary policy. If a country with its own currency is hit by some economic shock, as we have seen recently with Iceland's collapsing banking system, its exchange rate depreciates (weakens). This makes the country's exports more competitive and such increased external demand helps domestic firms recover, leading to a milder downturn and lower fluctuations in the economy in general. If you give up your own currency you no longer have this **counter-cyclical mechanism**.

Giving up autonomous monetary policy when joining a common currency can be even more problematic, as many countries at the EU periphery have learnt the hard way. Like the exchange rate, monetary policy also helps reduce the fluctuations of the economy, and it works through interest rates and the amount of money in the economy. In a nutshell, when the economy grows too fast and tends to overheat, which is accompanied by inflationary pressures, the central bank raises the interest rate and takes the heat out of the economy. A higher interest rate basically means people don't go out and consume as much but instead they save more, and firms defer investments because it is more costly to borrow. This reduces aggregate demand and slows economic growth to some natural level.

But if you join a common currency you cannot really use this adjustment channel because there is just one monetary policy interest rate for the currency area as a whole, and it is set based on the considerations of the whole union rather than any individual country. So if the member countries' shocks and business cycles are not synchronised, with some being in a downturn whereas others are booming, then the common monetary policy may be inappropriate for all individual countries. This is called the 'one-size-fits-none' problem.

SA: So the member states don't just lose their currency as a source of national identity. For the Germans, for example, it was an important part of their German identity; the German philosopher Jürgen Habermas spoke about the German **Deutsche Mark** nationalism. But I think that the basic problem with the common currency was that the EU leaders, including the national politicians that were part of the project, expected more political unification than really occurred; for example, more harmonisation of fiscal policies. So in some ways could we say that the cart was put before the horse? For the common currency to work, much closer political integration is required, and the question is whether this is the most plausible response for EU leaders and national politicians to take right now …

JL: It is true that many economists had argued a fiscal union is a prerequisite for a well-functioning monetary union. They point to the fact that in an independent country like the US or Australia there is active fiscal redistribution from the well-performing regions to less successful ones. But in terms of the EU, I don't think making spending and tax decisions at the European rather than the national level is feasible or necessary …

SA: These decisions are very political, aren't they? This is the key question of democratic politics: who gets what, when, how, from whom?

JL: Exactly, but I don't think you need a Europe-wide government for that. What you do need is for the individual member countries to maintain fiscal discipline. And this relates to another disadvantage of a monetary union that people have not thought through enough; the fact that there is a moral hazard problem when a country joins the European Monetary Union. Let me explain what it is and why it is likely to lead to fiscal neglect. If an independent country lives beyond its means and accumulates debt, financial markets tend to punish it relatively quickly. Assessing its fiscal policy as unsustainable leads to a sharp increase in the **risk premium** on the country's debt. So the country can no longer borrow easily and there is pressure on the political leadership to reform their fiscal policy.

In contrast, if a country became part of the European Monetary Union in the early 2000s, like Greece did, it got sheltered from such market pressures. All of a sudden, it faced a much lower borrowing cost because markets believed that if something goes wrong Greece would be bailed out by the other countries – even though it was in breach of EU legislation. So it was easy for a country like Greece to become complacent. Rather than putting fiscal policy on a more sustainable path, EMU membership encouraged profligacy; there was no longer the whip on politicians to behave responsibly.

SA: But now the whip is back with a vengeance. I was looking at a textbook that was published two years ago in Germany describing in great detail the accomplishments of the European Monetary Union. And one of them was the fact that government bond yields quickly converged, even before the common currency was introduced, so countries like Greece, Portugal, Spain and Italy paid as little interest as the Germans. Now the spread between those bonds has expanded and the market notices something is not right with these countries. But what is the way out of it? There is the Growth and Stability Pact with the Maastricht criteria, but most countries violated these basic fiscal rules prior to the crisis.

JL: That's true, there is certainly need for better in-built mechanisms to ensure long-term fiscal reforms and discipline. In terms of a possible solution to the current short-term economic weakness via greater monetary stimulus, we need to factor in the limitations imposed by the common currency. I mentioned the 'one-size-fits-none' problem, which means countries are likely to disagree on how much the ECB needs to do now.

The periphery countries need more stimulus, but since Germany is doing well, the ECB is not too keen. So the situation is exactly the opposite of what it was in the several years prior to the crisis. Spain, Ireland and other EU periphery countries were booming and performing better than the EU core. But due to the stagnation of Germany and France, the ECB left interest rates at a low level. Such cheap credit largely contributed to the overheating of the periphery economies, loss of their competitiveness due to higher inflation, and a creation of bubbles in their housing, banking and stock markets.

The bursting of these bubbles was really costly. House prices fell dramatically, and so did stock prices. GDP dived, unemployment increased dramatically. Banks have gone bankrupt; for example, the International Monetary Fund estimates that Ireland's implicit liabilities for their banking sector are in the order of 200 per cent of GDP.

SA: I wonder what you think as an economist about country bailouts. When Greece was bailed out more than a year ago, German voters were told that this step was necessary to pre-empt other countries facing similar difficulties. And then almost a year later Ireland found itself in the same situation and many people predict that Portugal will need a bailout too.

Even Spain is sometimes mentioned, or Belgium at the very heart of Europe. So the bailout strategy didn't work, did it?

JL: From a short-term perspective the answer is not obvious, because bailouts may have (at least in theory) averted major turmoil in the financial markets. But from a long-term perspective it is certainly a bad strategy, and the reason is again the moral hazard problem. If a country or a financial institution knows they are implicitly covered in case something goes wrong, they tend to misbehave; for example, take on too much debt, which increases the overall level of risk.

There is a related concept in economics called the **'time-inconsistency' problem**. In good times there is an incentive to say: 'We are not going to bail anyone out!' This is both in terms of the EU to member governments, and these governments to their large banks. The problem is that if these authorities find themselves staring bankruptcies in the face they are going to renege and go ahead with a bailout. Because of that, the 'no-bailout' announcement is not credible from the outset, even if it is legislated. This is why in the early 2000s the markets considered Greece under the umbrella of the EU core and did not require a risk premium on Greek **government bonds**, despite legislation prohibiting country bailouts.

SA: Well, the markets are no longer so confident about that umbrella, and that is why the umbrella had to be reinforced very recently with the Euro Plus Pact.

JL: The Pact attempts to strengthen fiscal discipline as well as the competitiveness of EU countries. The motivation is in the right direction because we do need to change the incentives of individual governments, and implement transparent, enforceable rules on fiscal policy. The Maastricht criteria have tried to do that, but they were mere recommendations and they were not enforced.

A major problem with these sorts of rules in Europe (and elsewhere) is that they use the wrong measure of indebtedness, usually the debt-to-GDP ratio rather than a more comprehensive **fiscal gap**. They therefore tend to focus too much on the short term rather than solving the main problem of unsustainable pension and healthcare systems implied by ageing populations. The problems Europe is facing now are nothing compared to what is waiting in the pipeline when baby boomers start retiring.

We need to explain to the voters that the long-term budgetary situation is really serious and reforms need to be adopted. Only then will the politicians have the courage to stand up and implement them. Unfortunately, the political clock is ticking, because the greater the number of elderly people, the harder it is to push through pension and healthcare reforms. There is a 2002 study by two German professors

[Sinn and Uebelmesser, 2002], who examine how the changing age profile of the population affects the voting on the necessary reform of the German pension system. Their analysis finds that: 'Until 2016, a reform can be democratically enforced. After 2016, Germany will be a gerontocracy.'

SA: But could you say that voters in many EU countries feel rightly betrayed? Voters in Greece feel betrayed because they will endure measures that will not get their country out of trouble anyway. Germans feel betrayed because the rules on the rescue mechanisms were violated repeatedly. Irish voters feel betrayed because of the bank bailouts. Some people see them as socialism for the rich, because the banking losses are nationalised and paid by Irish citizens while bank managers remain unharmed. One Irish economist argued that: 'to have capitalism without bankruptcy is like having Catholicism without hell'.

JL: ... And they say economists are a boring bunch with no sense of humour ... But seriously, the short-term reasons for bailouts of big financial institutions, those that are 'too-big-to-fail', are similar to the reasons for country bailouts we discussed. And the long-term reasons against bailouts are also the same, namely the moral hazard problem. One solution to this dilemma is never letting financial institutions grow too large so that their bankruptcy endangers the health of the financial system.

Regarding the frustration you mention, it should be said that some people are more justified to feel that way than others. Ireland's problems, related to its oversized banking system, were partly driven by global investment flows, and thus very different from Greece's poor governance and fiscal excesses. In pre-crisis Greece the proportion of average pay in the public sector relative to the average pay in the private sector was 2.5, whereas for many countries including Australia it is below 1. The number of teachers per student in Greece prior to the GFC was four times what it is in Finland, which has one of the best educational systems. For example, a Greek school made the headlines for only having 10 students, but 40 full-time teaching staff on the books. You can continue on and on with examples of fiscal indiscipline in Greece. In contrast to that, Ireland ran budget surpluses prior to the crisis.

SA: For me the most worrying part is that the Greek government's incompetence has become a European problem. In other words, if Greece had done what it did outside the Eurozone it would have been mostly a Greek problem, and there would not have been any strong reasons for the Germans to feel upset about it or for the Greeks to feel exploited by the Germans. The same applies to the Irish and the Portuguese ...

JL: That's true, but it should be mentioned that even a country outside the Euro may be a problem if major Eurozone banks hold a lot of its government bonds. This is an important reason why core EU countries do not want to let Greece fall; it could get some of their banks into trouble. For example, based on data from a year ago, French banks held almost a third of Greek government debt, over 75 billion Euros. As if this was not enough of a threat, they also held over €150 billion of Spanish debt and a whopping €350 billion worth of Italian government debt. German and British banks follow suit with slightly smaller numbers but a heavy exposure to Ireland's debt.

Another relevant point is the synchronisation of member countries' shocks and business cycles, which is a prerequisite of a functioning currency union. It was believed that binding the countries through a common currency would lead to economic convergence and ensure better synchronisation across them. But the fiscal excesses and other imbalances in many countries actually led to a divergence. It is likely that the Eurozone will now monitor more closely who they let in.

SA: But should countries actually want to join the Euro? Is it in the interest of one of the recent EU members to enter the Eurozone now – considering all the problems?

JL: You can certainly find examples of countries that would benefit from EU membership from a short-term point of view. One is Iceland, as the Euro would have probably sheltered the country from some of the recent financial turmoil. But again, that's only one part of the story. On the other hand, losing the exchange rate channel would likely reduce the speed of Iceland's subsequent recovery.

So I think it would be wise for countries to wait and reassess the situation in a few years' time. I'm certainly not a Euro-sceptic who would think that the Euro can never work; in principle a common currency can be beneficial. But unless major structural and governance reforms in Europe are undertaken and economic cycles synchronised, I would advise governments not to join in.

Audience member 1: You were speaking about some financial companies being 'too-big-to-fail'. But if you do let them fail would that not mean that in the future financial companies would behave more responsibly?

JL: That's very true. The issue with politicians is, however, that they tend to have a very short optimising horizon. Many of them, if not most, seem to only see to the next election, which is a problem because the benefits of what you are suggesting are long term whereas the cost of a financial turbulence with a lot of people losing jobs and savings would be felt immediately. This discourages politicians from letting banks fail. And because of that, implementing a credible commitment to never bail out banks is very hard.

Audience member 2: In relation to country bailouts, do you think it would have been better to let Greece fail?

JL: I try to avoid speculation and there are many things that go into this equation. But I think eventually, one way or another, it will happen. It's not going to be called 'letting Greece fail', it's not going to be called 'bankruptcy', it's going to be called 'debt restructuring'. I'm sure people in charge are going to come up with nice labels. The size and the extent of the problem are such that all these Greek bailouts just seem to be pushing away the inevitable, I think.

Audience member 3: Last year French President Sarkozy proposed a common European economic government for all the Eurozone countries with its own administration, and Germany opposed that. What would such a project look like in Europe?

JL: The idea behind the proposal is to more closely coordinate policies, including regulation and fiscal decisions. Think about the relationship of the federal government and state governments in Australia. One of the advantages would be that an EU-wide government could better monitor the spending discipline and prevent some of the excesses we have seen in many countries. If they can be trusted.

SA: But 'if they can be trusted' is an important qualification. The German elite had a different idea about how to manage the economy from the one that the French represented. The French lean more towards the government and regulation. The Germans, partly due to the success of the post-war reconstruction, are more committed to the markets and classical liberal ideas. Is that right?

JL: Yes, but one thing is the intention and another is the final outcome. One could rightly worry that this proposal would add yet another layer of bureaucrats to what is already a somewhat bureaucratic institution with a myriad of absurd regulations and directives. Did you know bananas mustn't be smaller than 14 centimetres in length nor too bendy. Or how about the costly frequent travel of European Parliament members between Brussels and Strasbourg? And apparently there is insufficient evidence that water hydrates you, which is why this message cannot appear on bottled water in the EU ...

SA: So you would not advocate an EU-wide economic governance?

JL: No, my preference would be to implement transparent and enforceable rules, but keeping a fair amount of autonomy across EU countries.

SA: Jan, thank you for your contribution.

13.3 Key economic insights and policy lessons

Economic insights	Implied policy lessons (for public officials and voters)
Becoming a member of a currency union has several advantages such as mitigating exchange rate risk and costs, promoting trade and facilitating free flow of labour. The main disadvantage is the loss of two adjustment mechanisms: the exchange rate and autonomous monetary policy.	Policymakers should carefully examine the available evidence on the pros and cons of adopting a common currency, and they should not downplay this evidence even if it is inconsistent with their political ambitions.
The loss of the exchange rate and monetary policy mechanisms is particularly problematic if the member countries are subject to different shocks. An important prerequisite for a common currency is therefore that the members' economic cycles are synchronised.	Policymakers should realistically assess whether a set of countries form an 'optimal currency area' before proceeding with adoption of a common currency.
Similarly to a car that cannot accelerate and slow down at the same time, the common central bank in a currency union cannot jointly provide a monetary expansion to some member countries and a monetary contraction to others.	Policymakers should acknowledge that common monetary policy in a currency union is incapable of dealing with idiosyncratic shocks, and use alternative policy tools to address them.
One way to partly alleviate the 'one-size-fits-none' problem of monetary policy in a currency union may be to temporarily raise the inflation target in a major downturn such as the GFC. This helps the affected countries to avoid deflation during the necessary process of internal devaluation.	Policymakers should be mindful of the costs of internal devaluation and the threat of a deflationary spiral in some monetary union members. They should consider increasing the inflation target as a temporary measure, especially if the affected countries feature highly rigid wage setting.
To achieve greater economic convergence it seems important to first achieve greater political integration. It is not clear whether a fiscal union is necessary, but legislated and effectively enforced fiscal rules are.	Policymakers should deepen political integration before embarking on a common currency project, which includes implementation and enforcement of fiscal rules.
There exist two types of moral hazard (free-riding) in a currency union, which may manifest in fiscal profligacy. One is associated with the (implicit) guarantee of a bailout by other members, the other with the inability of the common central bank to effectively punish the misbehaving country with higher interest rates.	Policymakers should take into account the perverse incentives created by accession to a monetary union, and put in place mechanisms to minimise them.
To reduce the moral hazard problems a currency union should not be a one-way arrangement; it should clearly specify 'exit' procedures for countries to leave the common currency.	Policymakers should explore ways of implementing exit rules, which would reduce uncertainty in the markets and improve incentives of member governments.

13.4 Discussion questions

1   Using your own words, summarise the debate of Section 13.2 in three to five sentences.
2   Write down one idea discussed in the interview that you found new or interesting, or that you disagree with, and briefly explain why.
3   Write down one question on any topic covered in the interview that you would ask the speaker if you had a chance.
4   Consider the cartoon in Section 13.1, and explain the point to someone who has not read the section and does not have any knowledge of economics.
5   Examine Figure 13.1 from the perspective of a policymaker. Describe its key message to the public and explain what kind of policy improvement is implied by the data. Do the same for Figure 13.2.
6   Suppose you take part in a debating contest, in which the topic is the opening quote of the chapter by Otmar Issing:

> There is no example in history of a lasting monetary union
> that was not linked to one State.

Prepare a speech you would give for the affirmative side. Then (you or your classmate) prepare a speech for the negative side. If possible, organise an audience and perform the debate.
7   What are the economic arguments for and against the adoption of a common currency? Rank them in order of importance according to your own perspective, taking the Eurozone's experience during the crisis into account.
8   What were the political arguments in favour of the Euro, and how important do you think they are compared to the economic arguments? Find some literature on the impact of Euro adoption on national identity; do you think this should be taken into account?
9   As a disadvantage of membership in a monetary union the interview discusses 'loss of flexibility in macroeconomic management'. One relevant channel is losing the exchange rate as a stabilisation mechanism. Outline the reasoning behind this.
10 In your own words explain the 'one-size-fits-none' problem and give examples of countries that have fallen victim to it – both prior to and post 2008. Find one esteemed economist that considers it a serious problem (and is therefore against the Euro), and one that does not think it is a major issue (and is therefore supportive of the Euro).
11 Why do you think fiscal rules postulated as part of the Growth and Stability Pact failed in the European Union? Do you think a fiscal union would have avoided the fiscal excesses we saw prior to 2008? Find some information on the post-2008 modifications of the EU fiscal rules, and assess whether they are likely to succeed.
12 What does the economic future hold for Greece in your view? How do you think other EU countries should proceed in relation to Greece? How should Greece proceed in relation to the Eurozone and its creditors?
13 Based on some research, describe and evaluate the monetary policy actions of the ECB since 2008, both conventional (interest rate decisions) and unconventional

(quantitative easing). Highlight possible policy errors and suggest a better course of action.

14 Find data on the amount of banking assets in proportion to GDP for EU countries. Assess this in light of the 'too-big-to-fail' problem and government deposit insurance, identifying any possible threats. In your answer also consider the changes in some countries' debt (most notably Ireland) as a consequence of bank bailouts.

15 The banking crises and fiscal crises may be closely linked. Explain how and discuss the potential risks in relation to Europe, using relevant data.

16 Suppose you are a policymaker in charge of a country that is a part of the EU but has not yet adopted the Euro. Summarise your argument on whether or not to join the common currency.

17 Do you think some member countries should be allowed (or forced) to exit the Euro? Try to suggest a mechanism through which this could occur without causing major havoc in the financial markets. You may want to consider arguments that Germany rather than Greece and other periphery countries should leave the Euro, see e.g. Khan (2015).

18 Present your view on the economic future of Europe (for one possible narrative, you can consult Libich, 2015).

19 Propose a set of policies that you think best promote economic outcomes in a monetary union and ultimately people's wellbeing.

13.5 Where to find out more

Friedman, M. (1997), 'The Euro: Monetary Unity To Political Disunity?', available at **www.project-syndicate.org/commentary/the-euro--monetary-unity-to-political-disunity**

Khan, M. (2015), 'Why it's Time for Germany to Leave the Eurozone', *The Telegraph*, 21 July 2015, available at **www.telegraph.co.uk/finance/economics/11752954/Why-its-time-for-Germany-to-leave-the-eurozone.html**

Libich, J. (2015), 'The Economic Future of Europe: Change of Diet or Premature Death?', *World Economics*, 15(4).

Libich, J., P. Stehlík and J. Savage (2010), 'Fiscal Neglect in a Monetary Union', *Economic Papers*, 29(3), pp. 301–309.

McCallum, J. and G. Moretti (2012), 'One Size Fits None', *Economist Insights*, UBS Asset Management, 10 April, available at **www.ubs.com/global/en/asset_ management/research/economist-insights/2012.html**

Mundell, R. A. (1961), 'A Theory of Optimum Currency Areas', *American Economic Review*, 51(4), pp 657–665.

Sinn, H. W. and S. Uebelmesser (2002), 'Pensions and the Path to Gerontocracy in Germany', *European Journal of Political Economy*, Vol. 19, pp. 153–158.

The Economist (2015), 'Global House Prices: Location, Location, Location', available at **www.economist.com/blogs/dailychart/2011/11/global-house-prices**

The New York Times (2010), 'Europe's Web of Debt', 1 May, available at **www.nytimes.com/interactive/2010/05/02/weekinreview/02marsh.html?_r=0**

Zettelmeyer, J., C. Trebesch and M. Gulati (2013), 'The Greek Debt Restructuring: An Autopsy', *Economic Policy*, 28(75), pp. 513–563.

14 Save or spend? On managing personal finances

'Keeping up with the Joneses': Spending money you don't have for things you don't need to impress people you don't like.

Actor Walter Slezak's version of 'Keeping up with the Joneses', *Look Magazine*, volume 21, issues 14–26, p. 8. Published by Cowles Media, 1957.

Economic concepts discussed

Easy-to-understand explanations of all the concepts listed below appear in the glossary at the end of this book.

- Aggregate demand
- Delayed gratification
- Deleveraging
- Diversification
- Foreign exchange market
- Human capital
- Index funds
- Nature vs nurture debate
- Paradox of thrift
- Passive investing
- Speculation
- Stock market

14.1 Motivation and overview

The 2008 crisis brought to the fore the importance of financial literacy. The media have been full of sad stories of people taking on excessive amounts of debt or speculating in the **stock market**, and losing their houses or savings. Can economics help us manage our personal finances better? Can it offer advice on how to minimise the risk of financial stress and personal bankruptcy?

This chapter, based on an interview I was invited to do for the 'Real' series on Australian TV Channel 31 in October 2012, suggests that the answers are affirmative.[1] The debate, hosted by Anthony Ziella, touches on many other topical questions such as: 'Is investing in the stock market a good idea or is it like gambling in a casino?', 'How can we best reduce risk through **diversification**?', 'Can marshmallows signal future success of a child?', 'Is buying a luxury yacht needless spending?', and 'Why are many people experiencing the **paradox of thrift** in the aftermath of the Global Financial Crisis (GFC)?'.

The discussion starts with the main mistakes people make while managing their personal finances. 'Putting all eggs in one basket' is a common example. I explain why it is a good idea to reduce risk by spreading ('diversifying') investments into various

---

1 The full interview is available at http://youtu.be/okOhm-QjKys. All episodes of the 'Real' series are available at www.thereallab.com/real-series.html

assets. And why it is not advisable to hold all our savings in the shares of the company we work for.

Attempting to outsmart the market and invest in stocks for short-term gain is another common mistake. Economic research, starting with Burton Malkiel's 1973 classic book *A Random Walk Down Wall Street*, has shown convincingly that short-term **speculation** in the stock and **foreign exchange markets** is unlikely to bring sustained success. Malkiel's conjecture was that since all publicly available information gets quickly incorporated in the prices of assets:

> *a blindfolded monkey throwing darts at a newspaper's*
> *financial pages could select a portfolio that would do just as*
> *well as one carefully selected by experts.*

His conjecture that financial 'experts' engaging in active asset management does not tend to generate higher returns – depicted in the cartoon below – has since been confirmed by a number of studies.

Concept by Jan Libich © 2015, drawing by Veronika Mojžišová. Used by permission.

Therefore, I explain in the interview that attempting to beat the market by buying stocks or foreign currency low and selling high is comparable to playing roulette in a casino:

> *By putting your money on red you may win or lose in*
> *individual rounds, but on average you are expected to lose.*

*The odds are against you because of the green zero, which
reduces the probability of red below 50 per cent, whereas the
win is exactly double the bet. The same is true about
speculation in the financial markets where transaction costs
paid to financial intermediaries play the same role as the zero
in roulette.*

All this implies that **passive investment** into **index funds** that 'buy and hold' all listed companies is generally a much better option than trying to 'pick winners'. This is also because a passive investor does not have to pay fees for frequent portfolio changes.[2]

The interview also mentions conventional gambling, and many people do not realise that this is a major social problem in Australia. Figure 14.1 shows that Australians are the biggest gamblers in the world, with a greater loss per capita than New Zealanders (ranked fourth) and Americans (ranked fifth) combined! Based on the data from the Australian government (Problem Gambling, 2015): 'Up to 500 000 Australians are at risk of becoming, or are, problem gamblers'. As a problem gambler's annual losses average over $20 000, and he or she negatively impacts the lives of five to 10 other people according to the government's estimates, the social burden of gambling is enormous.

Figure 14.1: Average gambling loss (in $) in 2013 per resident adult (i.e. not just for gamblers). It combines casino, gaming machines, betting, lotteries and interactive gaming (computer, mobile and TV).

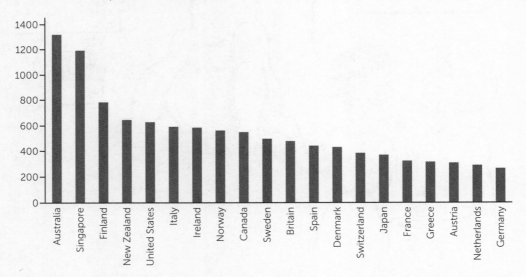

Source: *Today Online* (2014). Used by permission.

Wishful thinking is another common mistake people make in regards to their finances. They tend to be overly optimistic about their future income, and take on

---

2 A funny summary of this idea (for mature audiences only) is offered by Matthew McConaughey to Leonardo DiCaprio in the restaurant scene of the 2013 movie *The Wolf of Wall Street*.

excessive debt that they struggle to repay. One example is the post-GFC period featuring very low interest rates, which many new mortgage holders hope will continue. But both economic theory and past data imply that mortgage rates are likely to increase sooner or later, depending on many factors such as the strength of the global recovery from the crisis. To document, between the adoption of inflation targeting in 1993 and the collapse of Lehman Brothers in September 2008, the average mortgage rate in Australia was 7.31 per cent. While various demographic and technological factors may alter this number going forward, it would be a mistake to assume that the current low interest rates (and low repayments) will last for the whole duration of one's mortgage loan!

Taking on excessive debt is often driven by the 'keeping up with the Joneses' mindset, whereby our 'status-seeking' among our peers starts to dominate what we do and how we feel. The following joke sums it up nicely. A person prays: 'Dear God, my neighbour has a cow and it gives him a lot of milk.' God interrupts him and asks kindly: 'And you would also like a cow like this, right?' The person, however, replies: 'No, I just wish his cow would die'.[3]

The 'keeping up with the Joneses' discussion connects to the next topic, which is the perspective of economists on what may seem 'needless' spending. Is there such a thing? Who is to decide which spending is needless and which is not? Unfortunately, economics cannot help much in this respect; all it can do is provide good arguments for why the benefit from consumption of a certain product can be neither fully measured nor objectively compared across different individuals. Economics can also shed light on the common (and incorrect) criticism of the market economy system that excessive spending is necessary to fuel economic growth.

This links to the 'paradox of thrift', a surprising phenomenon observed in many countries in the aftermath of the GFC. Imagine you decide to spend less in order to increase the amount of your savings. But if many other people decide to do the same, there is a large short-term reduction in demand, businesses see their revenues drop and they are forced to cut wages or even dismiss some workers. This means that your savings may actually decrease rather than increase, leading to a vicious economic circle of dropping consumption, weak **aggregate demand**, rising unemployment, and yet lower income. Such logic seems to be a partial explanation for the poor economic performance in the United States and Europe in the aftermath of the 2008 financial crisis, whereby '**deleveraging**' (reducing debt) is conducted not only by households, but also by businesses, financial companies and governments. See Figure 14.2 for the deleveraging trend in the US.

The debate then explores the role of early childhood in a person's development. Research by psychologists from Stanford University has shown that being patient and able to 'delay gratification' (consumption of a marshmallow) is a strong predictor of good results at school and achievements in life more generally. This includes better decisions related to personal finances. As a demonstration of the negative effects of impatience, we discuss crime and some striking statistics regarding imprisonment of young males who do not finish high school. Anthony's lesson: 'Kids, stay in school or you are going to jail!' is probably taking it too far, but the research evidence of the positive effect of quality education, especially early on in life, is overwhelming.

---

3 A portrayal of this sort of thinking and its adverse consequences is captured in the 2009 movie *The Joneses*, starring Demi Moore and David Duchovny.

Figure 14.2: The percentage difference between actual debt and equilibrium debt calculated from an economic model using US data. Observations above zero represent excessive debt. The credit bubble is apparent from 2002 with the main credit boom occurring especially between 2005 and early 2008; deleveraging is apparent from late 2008.

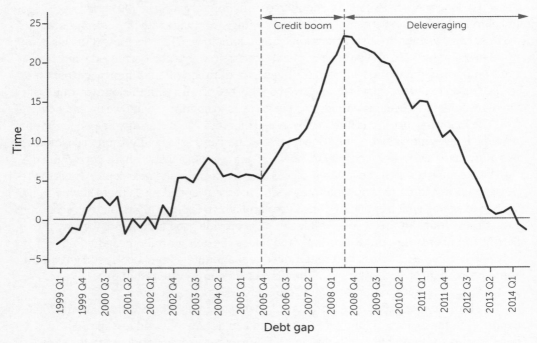

Source: Albuquerque et al. (2014).

14.2 The debate

Anthony Ziella (AZ): We are here with Dr Jan Libich, who is hopefully going to give us an insight into how we can create a more sustainable future for ourselves. We will also look at our spending and splurging and all things in between. What are the biggest mistakes people make with regard to their finances?

< Dr Jan Libich (JL): One of the major problems is that they put all their eggs in one basket. They don't reduce risk by having different types of investments, what finance calls 'diversification'. One example is having all your savings invested in the stock of the company you work for. If the company goes bankrupt, not only do you lose your job and income, but you also lose your savings. In contrast, having your savings invested in other companies, ideally from different industries, and in other types of financial and real assets, is much safer.

AZ: So what you're saying is: 'Don't take all your money and put it on black?'

JL: That's exactly right.

AZ: Got it. Folks, put it on red.

JL: Well, not quite.

AZ: That's not really diversifying my portfolio, is it, if I play roulette and blackjack?

JL: Gambling is another common mistake people make. And I mean both conventional casino-type gambling and gambling in asset markets. Many people try to outsmart the market; they think they are going to make money in the stock or foreign exchange market by buying low and selling high. But economics teaches us that it is exactly like gambling in the casino. By putting your money on red you may win or lose in individual rounds, but on average you are expected to lose – the odds are against you because of the green zero, which reduces the probability of red below 50 per cent, whereas the win is exactly double the bet. The same is true about speculation in the financial markets where transaction costs paid to financial intermediaries play the same role as the zero in roulette.

AZ: Is that always a bad thing to buy foreign currency and expect it to go up in value?

JL: If you are gambling on the short-term gains you may get lucky, but due to the fees, on average you are going to make a loss relative to alternative passive investments. So ex-ante such speculation is a bad idea. If investors purchase foreign currencies as part of their medium-term portfolio diversification rather than short-term speculation, it may however be a good thing; one currency may lose value, not all will. This may reduce investors' risk without lowering their return much.

AZ: What advice would you give to young people who are starting out in life with regard to managing their accounts?

JL: Diversification would be one thing. Another piece of advice is to leave a bit more of a buffer. Many people seem to be overly optimistic and engage in wishful thinking regarding their future prospects. For example, they get a mortgage that is too high and then struggle to make ends meet every month. The resulting stress is unnecessary. So I would advise people not to go for the dream house or car but for the slightly smaller versions – just to be on the safe side. And a broader message is not to fall into the 'keeping up with the Joneses' trap. Constantly comparing yourself with your classmate or neighbour, and always wanting to have what they have, is a recipe for feeling miserable. This is even if you are actually 'successful' in life on commonly accepted measures.

AZ: What should we be spending our money on?

JL: Things that you enjoy, things that you feel help you grow in the direction you want to grow, which is very individual. For some people this might be travelling, for some bungee jumping, for some playing board games with their kids and for some studying astrophysics in their spare time or helping the disadvantaged. So there's no universal answer to that question.

AZ: Do something that makes you happy, not just because Mr Jones next door does it. I know what you're saying. In my parents' house there are three big flat-screen TVs, is that too many?

JL: Again, there is no clear answer. One of the basic theories in economics tells you that you can't compare satisfaction across different people. Basic needs are a bit of an exception; if you are starving that's obviously a bad thing objectively. But the satisfaction derived from most things beyond basic needs is very subjective. By the same token, one cannot say objectively that for a multi-millionaire another luxury car is needless or that for a family three plasma TVs are too many. You simply have no way of objectively measuring how important it is to them. We may have a view on that, I personally don't have a fancy TV or the latest mobile phone, but that is my personal preference and it would be wrong for me to impose it on others. You see people doing all sorts of things you may find crazy ...

AZ: Like Felix Baumgartner taking a balloon into outer space and then free-falling ...

JL: Exactly. And the fact that people do it and risk their lives reveals that it must have a very high value to them, while to other people it may have no value at all. So again, it would be wrong to say that having a big yacht is necessarily needless spending.

AZ: How important is it to instil good saving habits into children, especially younger children?

JL: More important than most people realise. There's an ongoing debate in biology and other disciplines about the relative importance of **nature vs nurture**: 'Are we formed more by our genes or by our upbringing and education?' My reading of the literature is that both are important, but the early childhood influences seem slightly more influential. For example, a 2010 paper found, using the differences between identical and fraternal twins, that 'approximately 25% of individual variation in portfolio risk is due to genetic variation' [Cesarini et al., 2010].

One early piece of evidence was the Stanford marshmallow experiment. Psychologists took four-year-old kids and gave them a marshmallow, saying: 'You can eat it now, but if you save it for later you will get another marshmallow.' What they were testing was the theory of '**delayed gratification**'; whether the kids were patient enough to postpone their consumption and able to resist temptation. And we know that many adults struggle with that; as Oscar Wilde once put it: 'I can resist anything except temptation.'

The researchers were tracking the same kids over time and what they found was fascinating. Being patient and able to delay the consumption of the marshmallow at that early age was a great predictor of success later on, including better high school grades and graduate income. So it seems that if you have small kids, patience is one of the virtues you should nurture in them, ideally through your own example. Patience is important in life because to be good at something we need to 'save' some of our time and effort and 'invest' them into acquiring the relevant skills and knowledge. We need to accumulate what economists call **human capital**.

AZ: That's interesting. I think they did the same thing with monkeys once.

JL: Monkeys don't like marshmallows though. But seriously, some animals seem better at delaying gratification than many humans.

AZ: It's good to see that we have progressed from studying monkeys and we are now onto humans with the same tests. Sooner or later, there might be some results, scientists?!

JL: People's attitude towards the future has a really big impact on the society as a whole. Think about crime, which is very much about whether people can delay gratification. Even in the absence of moral reasons, patient people are less likely to steal because they put greater weight onto the future threat of going to jail compared to the immediate benefit of the loot. Let me share a very interesting statistic that relates to this. Think about the United States, and specifically the group of African American males who dropped out of high school. What proportion of these men do you think will have been in prison by their mid-30s?

AZ: Probably a big number.

JL: Yes, two-thirds, two out of three. And the social cost of crime is huge. In addition to the harm done to the victims, it is very expensive to get someone to jail in terms of the police, lawyers and judges. It is even more expensive to keep someone in jail, I think the estimates in Australia are A$300 a day per person. And then there is the indirect cost of these people not working, not contributing to the society, and their skills deteriorating. And all that could perhaps be avoided by nurturing the child's ability to delay gratification.

AZ: So kids, stay in school or you are going to jail! But going back to needless spending, is there really no way of telling what is needless spending and what is not?

JL: If you compare yourself to people a few decades ago, most of our current spending is needless in a way. They didn't have mobile phones, they didn't have the things we now take for granted. But if you compare yourself to your classmate or friend it seems that all these things are absolutely necessary, you just have to have them.

AZ: But doesn't that kind of needless spending fuel our economy in a way?

JL: It is true that the more people spend, the greater the demand for goods and services, so firms respond by producing more and the official economic statistics like the gross domestic product (GDP) increases. But if people spend less they have more money to invest, either in future productive capacity or in their personal development, both of which are likely to bear fruit in the future.

AZ: But it seems that the best thing for our economy is to spend your money as soon as you get it – on something you don't really need like a better TV or car.

JL: That's the short-term view often put forward by politicians focused on official statistics like the GDP. It is based on the fact that if all people decide to save more and spend less, especially in an economic downturn such as the GFC, it is going to have a short-term negative effect on the economy. Businesses see demand for their products drop and therefore reduce production, wages and possibly lay off some workers. Overall income in the economy falls too and this further reduces consumption, production and people's savings – contrary to their initial intention to increase their savings.

Such a 'paradox of thrift' is occurring currently in Europe and the United States, where people, companies, as well as governments have been attempting to reduce their indebtedness after the GFC. You may have heard the term 'deleveraging'. But from a long-term perspective the economic system is not dependent on excessive spending. If people become less consumption-prone the economy may not grow as fast in the short term, but people's wellbeing may be unaffected or even increase; they will simply enjoy more leisure or invest in their future.

AZ: It's very interesting and we could be here for days talking about this. Thanks so much for coming in today and sharing your knowledge. There are a lot of people that need this kind of advice, and all our viewers will agree you have certainly given us a lot to think about.

14.3 Key economic insights and policy lessons

Economic insights	Implied policy lessons (for public officials and voters)
Some people expose themselves to an excessive level of risk by putting all their wealth into one type of financial or real asset. The risks are even greater if this asset is linked to the person's employment.	Policymakers should raise awareness of the benefits of (low-cost) risk diversification options.
Attempting to make a short-term gain in the stock or exchange rate market by buying low and selling high is similar to playing roulette in a casino; on average a person is expected to lose compared to less risky passive investment options.	Policymakers should, together with financial literacy educators, help people correctly assess the likely financial consequences of their actions and make better financial choices.

Economic insights	Implied policy lessons (for public officials and voters)
Many households are unreasonably optimistic about their future income and take on too much debt.	Policymakers should abandon policies (e.g. in the housing market) that encourage people to leverage excessively.
There is no objective way to compare satisfaction derived from some product or service across people. The term 'needless spending' therefore has a rather subjective connotation.	Policymakers should respect people's spending choices – upon first setting rules that correct for possible externalities and market failures, and upon educating the public about these issues.
Early childhood influences are important in forming a person's saving and spending habits. Ability to delay gratification at a preschool age is a strong predictor for good academic performance and future income.	Policymakers should support educational activities that help children foster their patience.
Violent as well as non-violent crime is extremely costly for society, and it can be linked to people's inability to delay gratification.	Policymakers should pursue educational strategies that develop personal qualities known to minimise the likelihood of dropping out of high school and possibly future criminal activity.
'Paradox of thrift' is not a theoretic construct but a pressing problem in the aftermath of the GFC.	Policymakers should consider the post-2008 deleveraging process at the household and firm level, and if possible attempt to offset its short-term contractionary effects by a monetary or fiscal expansion.

14.4 Discussion questions

1   Using your own words, summarise the debate of Section 14.2 in three to five sentences.
2   Write down one idea discussed in the interview that you found new or interesting, or that you disagree with, and briefly explain why.
3   Write down one question on any topic covered in the interview that you would ask the speaker if you had a chance.
4   Consider the cartoon in Section 14.1, and explain the point to someone who has not read the section and does not have any knowledge of economics.
5   Examine Figure 14.1 from the perspective of a policymaker. Describe its key message to the public and explain what kind of policy improvement is implied by the data. Do the same for Figure 14.2.
6   Suppose you take part in a debating contest, in which the topic is the opening quote of the chapter attributed to Walter Slezak:

> Too many people spend money they haven't earned, to buy
> things they don't want, to impress people they don't like.

Prepare a speech you would give for the affirmative side. Then (you or your classmate) prepare a speech for the negative side. If possible, organise an audience and perform the debate.

7   In your own words outline what 'diversification' is in relation to financial investments. Discuss its advantages and disadvantages.

8   What argument is offered against casino gambling, and how does it relate to 'gambling' on the stock or foreign exchange market? What does economic research says about an investor's ability of consistently beating the market? Explain the reasoning and find some experiments that confirm or refute the theory.

9   What is passive investment and what do index funds have to do with it? Using online sources, give one or more examples of successful passive investors and explain their strategies and results.

10 Do you think that some spending can be described as needless? If so, should such spending be discouraged or even prohibited in your view? How?

11 The desire to 'keep up with the Joneses' is an age-old problem and one which usually negatively impacts an individual's situation, both financially and mentally. Think about some ways in which the problem can be alleviated, both at the level of the family and in society more broadly.

12 What is your personal philosophy in terms of spending your money? Do you think you manage your finances appropriately? Try to suggest ways in which you could improve on your current practices.

13 Think about the Stanford University marshmallow experiment as it would apply to Australians. Give examples of the type of expenditure that requires delayed gratification for better long-term personal outcomes. What does the Stanford experiment imply about the effects of such expenditure?

14 Outline the discussion around crime and delayed gratification. What are the various costs of crime, both financial and non-financial? Refer to the internet for data, including recent trends in crime. Suggest some strategies for reducing crime in Australia.

15 Explain the effect of spending and saving on (short- and long-term) GDP; is one preferable to the other? Can you think of situations in which policymakers should encourage spending over saving, and vice versa?

16 Explain the 'paradox of thrift' as it relates to the GFC. What negative and positive outcomes has the post-2008 deleveraging created? (For more information, see Huo and Rios-Rull, 2012.)

17 Propose a set of policies that you think best promote financial literacy of children as well as adults, and ultimately people's wellbeing.

14.5 Where to find out more

Albuquerque, B., U. Baumann and G. Krustev (2014), 'US Household Deleveraging Following the Great Recession – a Model-based Estimate of Equilibrium Debt', *The B.E. Journal of Macroeconomics*, 15(1), pp. 255–307.

Cesarini, D., M. Johannesson, P. Lichtenstein, Ö. Sandewall and B. Wallace (2010), 'Genetic Variation in Financial Decision-Making', *Journal of Finance*, 65(5), pp. 1725–1754.

Huo, Z. and J.-V. Rios-Rull (2012), 'Engineering a Paradox of Thrift Recession', *Staff Report 478*, Federal Reserve Bank of Minneapolis, available at **www.minneapolisfed.org/research/sr/sr478.pdf**

Malkiel, B. (1973), *A Random Walk Down Wall Street*, W. W. Norton & Company, Inc., USA.

Mischel, W., E. B. Ebbesen and A. Raskoff Zeiss (1972), 'Cognitive and Attentional Mechanisms in Delay of Gratification', *Journal of Personality and Social Psychology*, 21(2), pp. 204–218.

Mischel, W., Y. Shoda and M. Rodriguez (1989), 'Delay of Gratification in Children', *Science*, 244, pp. 933–938.

Problem Gambling (2015), 'The Facts: Gambling in Australia' in *The Facts*, Australian government, available at **www.problemgambling.gov.au/facts**

The Joneses (2009), Echo Lake Entertainment, 96 minutes, details available at **www.imdb.com/title/tt1285309**

The Wolf of Wall Street (2013), Paramount pictures, 180 minutes, details available at **www.imdb.com/title/tt0993846**

Today Online (2014), 'S'poreans Remain Second-biggest Gamblers in the World', *Today Online*, 6 February, available at **www.todayonline.com/singapore/sporeans-remain-second-biggest-gamblers-world**

Glossary

AAA rating The highest rating of credit-worthiness awarded to a company or country by credit rating agencies.

Active/passive asset management Portfolio strategies whereby the investor either tries to actively outperform the market by frequent buying and selling of financial assets, or passively achieve a return in line with the market's average using the 'buy and hold' approach.

Adaptation policies Adjustment steps taking advantage of opportunities in a changing system or coping with its undesirable consequences (e.g. global warming).

Adverse selection A situation in which one party of a transaction (for example a second-hand car seller) has better information about the object of the transaction (the condition of his car) than the other party (the car buyer). Such informational asymmetry leads to inefficient outcomes, possibly even disappearance of the market.

Age dependency ratio The proportion of people above a certain age (usually 65) relative to the working age population (usually 15–64). The ratio has implications for the structure and sustainability of public finances.

Ageing population The demographic trend observed in most high-income countries whereby fertility declines, life expectancy increases, and thus the median age in the population rises.

Aggregate demand The total amount of final goods and services bought at different price levels within an economy.

Anchoring fiscal expectations Making people's beliefs about future public debt developments more stable – through greater clarity about planned government budgetary policies.

Annuitisation A mechanism that converts some person's accumulated benefits into a stream of periodic (monthly) payments to that person.

Annuity payment An ongoing payment of a fixed annual amount.

Appreciation/depreciation of the exchange rate An increase/decrease in the value of a country's currency in relation to one or more other currencies.

Aptitude distribution Ordering of some group of people (e.g. teachers) based on their relative capabilities.

Asian Crisis of 1997–98 A financial crisis which erupted in July 1997 in Thailand and spread quickly to other East Asian countries, especially South Korea and Indonesia. It saw a capital flight from these countries, large drops in the value of their currencies, major falls in GDP and increases in public debt.

Asset bubble A situation in which prices of stocks, housing or other assets become overvalued compared to their fundamental value; usually due to exaggerated expectations of their future price growth.

Asset meltdown hypothesis A theory predicting a large drop in asset returns as baby boomer generations leave the labour force and start selling their assets to finance retirement – to a decreasing number of workers.

Atmospheric concentrations A measure of the chemical make-up of the atmosphere.

Austerity Government's fiscal policies used to reduce budget deficits and public debt, e.g. expenditure cuts.

Australian Prudential Regulation Authority (APRA) A public institution set up by the Australian government in 1998 in order to regulate and oversee the financial sector.

Australia Post disease The use of pricing for one product to either subsidise another product or to subsidise other consumers of that product.

Baby bonus A payment to parents of a newborn to assist with the cost of raising the child.

Bailout Financial support commonly provided by the government to a company facing serious financial trouble, such as bankruptcy.

Balanced budget rule A law requiring that the government cannot spend more than its income in any given year.

Banking regulation Government rules aimed at ensuring soundness of the banking sector.

Basel III (the Third Basel Accord) A voluntary international banking standard aimed at ensuring the good health of financial institutions, e.g. through minimum capital requirements.

Basis points A unit of measure that is equal to one-hundredth of a percentage point. In smoothing interest rates, central banks tend to change them by 25 basis points at a time.

Beggar-thy-neighbour A policy of solving a country's economic problems in a way that has undesirable consequences for other countries;

for example, a deliberate weakening of its exchange rate to gain a competitive advantage.

Budget deficit/surplus A budgetary imbalance whereby government expenditures are higher/lower than its tax revenues.

Business cycle fluctuations Increases and decreases of GDP and other variables occurring over time around a long-run trend.

Capital flight A large exodus of money or other assets from a country, often following a period of economic or political instability.

Carbon tax A levy on the amount of carbon dioxide emissions an entity produces, designed to incentivise firms to switch to less carbon-intensive fuels.

Cash rate The rate of interest for which financial institutions borrow and lend 'overnight' money in the money market, and which the RBA influences in conducting monetary policy.

Central bank A public institution that has the monopoly on printing currency; its main role is the conduct of monetary policy.

Central bank transparency A set of institutional arrangements that make information regarding the strategy and procedures of the central bank publicly available.

Charter of Budget Honesty A piece of Australian legislation adopted in 1998 outlining principles of transparent and sustainable fiscal policy, but not specifying any quantitative fiscal rules.

Climate change A change in the mean and/or variability of climate systems over a prolonged period of time.

Cognitive decline The decreasing ability to use one's mental capabilities, such as learning new tasks.

Collateralised debt obligation (CDO) A tradeable financial product that packages a range of different loans such as credit card debt and mortgages. They are 'collateralised' because the value of the CDO stems from the promised repayment value of the underlying loans.

Commitment A promise to fulfil an action.

Community Reinvestment Act A piece of legislation in the United States inducing private financial institutions to extend their loans to households with below-average incomes in pursuit of 'affordable housing'.

Comparative advantage Ability to produce a good at a lower marginal cost (including opportunity cost) than others.

Confidence interval A term from statistics denoting a range of values within which a certain parameter appears with a given probability, most commonly 95 per cent. It is estimated from the data.

Congestion pricing A mechanism in which the fee charged to consumers varies over time in order to balance supply and demand more effectively. Common examples include road or parking levies which increase during peak hours in order to reduce traffic congestion.

Consumer price index (CPI) An indicator measuring changes in the price of a basket of goods and services purchased by an average consumer.

Consumption hardship Financial strain experienced by an individual or family, usually due to loss of income or excessive debt repayments.

Consumption smoothing The process of balancing borrowing, saving and spending over time in order to achieve the highest possible standard of living, while minimising differences in consumption from one period to the next.

Convex preferences A situation where a person prefers a combination of two different types of a good in a bundle over two identical goods.

Counter-cyclical mechanism A stabilisation program attempting to reduce economic fluctuations, i.e. ensure that variables such as GDP and unemployment return fast to their optimal (neutral) level.

Creative destruction The economy's constant transformation during which innovative products and processes replace old ones.

Credibility A quality of being trustworthy or believable.

Credit crunch A substantial reduction in available investment capital that drives up the cost of borrowing.

Credit default swap (CDS) An insurance-type financial contract where the seller of a CDS compensates the buyer if the underlying asset (such as a CDO) does not provide the expected stream of income.

Credit freeze A major interruption of borrowing and lending activity in financial markets due to fears of insolvencies on a large scale.

Credit rating A formal forward-looking assessment of one's ability to repay debt, performed by an external institution.

Crowding out A reduction of private investment as a consequence of the government's borrowing to finance a fiscal expansion. It occurs because this borrowing drives up the market real interest rate, which makes it more expensive for businesses to acquire investment funding.

Currency union A group of countries that has replaced their national currencies by a common one.

Current account One of the two main components of a country's balance of payments, it includes the trade balance (exports minus imports), net foreign income and net current transfers.

Data aggregation problem The inaccuracies that may arise when 'micro-level' data for individuals are combined into 'macro-level' data for the whole group.

De-accumulation of pension saving The process of drawing down the amount of savings in one's pension fund.

Default A situation where a borrower is unwilling or unable to meet their required debt repayments.

Defined-benefit system A pension system in which an individual is promised (by government and/or employer) a regular payment upon retirement, commonly dependent on years of service and past salary.

Defined-contribution system A pension system in which an employer, employee or both make regular contributions, commonly a pre-specified proportion of salary, to a private retirement fund or the public purse.

Deflation Negative inflation, i.e. a potentially dangerous situation of an economy experiencing a decline in the price level.

Delayed gratification Capacity to be patient enough to defer some instantaneous reward with the view of receiving a greater reward in the future.

Deleveraging The process of reducing one's level of debt.

Deutsche Mark The official currency of West Germany and the unified Germany until the common currency Euro was born (in 1999 in electronic form and 2002 in physical form).

Diminishing returns A reduction in the additional output generated through adding one production input (for example, physical capital) while keeping the other inputs unchanged.

Discount rate The extent (expressed in percentages) with which an individual puts lower weight on future utility compared to present utility. The term is also used for the interest rate the central bank charges financial institutions for borrowing money.

Discouraged worker Someone that is able and willing to work but not actively seeking a job as they have given up hope of finding one; usually due to a long spell of unemployment.

Disinflation A process of decreases in the rate of inflation, designed to bring inflation to optimally low levels.

Diversification A risk-management approach that chooses a number of diverse investments for one's portfolio to protect it from a decline in value of any one particular type of asset.

Dividend imputation A tax arrangement where businesses can pay tax on all or part of an investment dividend, and shareholders are then not required to pay tax on the same dividend.

Dotcom bubble A dramatic speculative increase in stock prices between 1997 and 2000 driven by internet-related companies.

Dutch Disease The causal relationship between an increase in natural resource production and a decline of the manufacturing and agricultural sectors. This occurs because a resource boom appreciates a country's currency, making its exports relatively more expensive and imports cheaper.

Earned-income tax credits A refundable portion of the tax aimed at low-income workers.

Econometrics A set of quantitative techniques used to analyse data for economic and social purposes.

Economic growth The percentage increase in economic output (commonly measured as the Gross Domestic Product, GDP) over a certain period (commonly one year).

Economies of scale A situation where increasing the size or number of inputs of some economic subject is beneficial because it decreases the per-unit fixed costs.

Emissions trading scheme A system in which a central authority sets a limit of emissions that can be produced, and provides firms with an allocation of emissions that can be traded on the market.

Enterprise bargaining The process of negotiating the terms and conditions of employment between an employer, employee and their representatives.

Euro The common currency of the Eurozone used by the majority of European Union countries.

European Monetary Union A group of European countries that have formed the common currency area and adopted the Euro.

European Union An organisation established to advance the political and economic objectives of the member countries, such as free movement of labour. The Union is represented by a number of supranational institutions, e.g. the European Commission and European Central Bank.

Exchange rate The relative value of two currencies as traded in the market.

Expansionary/contractionary monetary policy The easing/tightening of monetary conditions, conventionally done by the central bank reducing/increasing short-term interest rates through open market operations.

Fallacy of sunk cost A sunk cost is an expense that cannot be recovered, which is why incorporating it in one's decision is fallacious and irrational.

Fan chart A line graph that shows estimates of multiple possible future scenarios and the associated probabilities.

Federal Reserve (Fed) America's central bank, responsible for the conduct of monetary policy.

Fertility The ability to produce offspring. It is commonly quantified as the fertility rate, which is the average number of children per woman.

Fiscal cliff A major tightening of US fiscal policy on 1 January 2013 as a consequence of several enacted laws automatically expiring, leading to higher taxes and lower government spending.

Fiscal Commission An (independent) institution consisting of experts set up to advise public institutions on fiscal matters and produce intergenerational reports, as well as monitor and enforce quantitative fiscal rules.

Fiscal crisis A situation where a government either cannot afford to pay for its regular expenditures, such as defence and welfare, or is feared not to be able to do so in the future. It tends to start with a major increase in the risk premium on the government's bonds.

Fiscal gap The difference between the present value of all future government spending and revenues implied by the existing legislation.

Fiscal multiplier An indicator expressing the impact of a change in government spending or taxation on the country's GDP. An expenditure multiplier greater than one means that GDP increases by more than one dollar for every dollar of additional government spending.

Fiscal policy Government spending and taxation measures that aim to alter economic conditions in order to reduce the fluctuations in unemployment and production.

Fiscal stimulus An attempt to boost economic activity by increasing the level of government spending or by lowering taxes.

Fiscal sustainability The long-term solvency of public finances whereby a government's planned stream of revenue does not fall short of its expenditure.

Fiscal union A group of countries that cooperate on how the governments spend and raise revenue, and engage in fiscal redistribution across the countries based on economic conditions.

Fixed/floating exchange rate The rate at which one currency can be changed for another is determined by their supply and demand (floating regime), or set officially by the authorities and maintained through foreign exchange interventions (fixed regime).

Flight to safety A sudden increase in preference for highly liquid, low-risk investments compared with more risky options, leading to rapid asset movements out of a country or industry.

Forecast An estimate of future outcomes based on historical data and/or a theoretic model.

Foreign exchange market A decentralised international platform for currency trading.

Forward looking Type of behaviour that takes into account for the future possible scenarios in making a decision.

Fractional reserve banking A system in which banks lend out more money than they receive from depositors, i.e. less than 100 per cent of deposits are kept as cash reserves.

Free-riding problem A moral-hazard type of situation whereby a member of a certain group behaves irresponsibly at the expense of other members.

Friedman's k-per cent rule A theoretic prescription for monetary policy arguing that central banks should increase money supply by a certain percentage annually, which is the sum of economic growth and the desired level of inflation.

Game of chicken A strategic interaction between two parties (such as the government and central bank) featuring both a coordination problem and conflict. Each party prefers a different outcome, but if they engage in a tug-of-war the resulting outcome is even worse than coordinating on the opponent's preferred outcome.

Garnaut Review A federal government-commissioned report published in 2008 by

Professor Ross Garnaut (with an update in 2011), which studied the impacts of climate change on the Australian and global economy and society.

Gender pay discrimination Existence of a difference (gap) between earnings of equally skilled males and females for identical jobs.

Glass–Steagall Act US legislation adopted in 1933 separating investment and retail banking. It was repealed in 1999, which is considered one of the contributing factors to the housing bubble and the 2008 financial crisis.

Global saving glut The situation during 2003–07 when international financial markets were experiencing an excess of saving due to demographic factors as well as to international capital flows. This led to very low global interest rates and a 'search for yield'.

Global warming The observed systemic change to the Earth's climate, namely unprecedented rapid global temperature increases threatening natural and economic systems.

Government bonds An interest-bearing financial instrument issued by the government in order to raise funds to pay for its spending.

Government failure Public policies resulting in a decline of society's welfare.

Government guarantee A promise requiring the government to pay for an outstanding amount in the event of some institution's insolvency.

Grease effects In the presence of inflexible adjustment of nominal wages, inflation of around 2–4 per cent can 'grease the wheels' of the economy by reducing the real wage.

Great Depression A severe global economic downturn of the 1930s, which saw a dramatic worsening of all economic variables including a massive rise in unemployment.

Greenhouse gases A group of gases such as CO_2 and methane that trap heat in the Earth's atmosphere, and thus contribute to the greenhouse effect and the planet's warming.

Gross Domestic Product (GDP) The most widely-used measure of economic performance, which expresses the amount of products and services produced within an economy over some period (commonly one year).

Growth and Stability Pact A set of rules for countries within the European Union that aim to deliver fiscal discipline and economic convergence of members.

Happiness The experience of positive wellbeing and contentment. It combines the experience of joy with a deeper notion of purpose or meaning.

HECS The Higher Education Contribution Scheme is a publicly-run system of tertiary education student fees combined with government loans. The loan repayment is income-contingent as it constitutes a certain percentage of the graduate's income, not a fixed amount.

Hedging Making an investment that offsets the potential loss of another investment.

Housing affordability People's ability to purchase their own house and make regular mortgage repayments without experiencing financial stress.

Human capital The sum of people's skills and knowledge that can be used effectively in the economic process.

Hyperinflation A very rapid and accelerating growth in the price level of more than 50 per cent per month.

Hysteresis A feature of an economic variable (such as unemployment) whereby past developments have a persistent effect on the variable's future path.

Income-contingent loan A type of loan where the borrower's repayments each period are a certain percentage of their wage rather than a prearranged amount.

Income tax A government levy on earned income such as wages and unearned income such as dividends.

Indexation An automatic adjustment of payments or numerical thresholds over time to take into account changes in some relevant variable such as the price level or life expectancy.

Index funds An investment option designed to track the performance of some market by holding all the stocks of that index – proportionately to the index.

Inequality A measure of the (un)evenness of the distribution of income and wealth across individuals or countries.

Inflation Percentage increase in the general level of prices in the economy.

Inflation forecast targeting A forward-looking variant of the inflation-targeting regime whereby the central bank interest rate setting is pre-emptive. Due to policy lags it attempts to ensure that its inflation forecast two to three years down the track is on target.

Inflation targeting A legislated monetary policy regime characterised by a high degree of instrument-independence, transparency and accountability, including a numerical target for the inflation rate over the medium term.

Insurance A contract whereby an individual or business entity receives a financial repayment in the event of an agreed future incident; for example, the theft of one's property. In return, they pay a financial sum for the protection they receive.

Intellectual property rights A legal term assigning ownership over one's innovations and creations through patents, copyright and trademarks.

Intergovernmental Panel on Climate Change (IPCC) A scientific body set up by the United Nations and the World Meteorological Organization to provide objective information on climate change and its expected effects.

Kyoto Protocol An international treaty set up in 1997 that (unsuccessfully) attempted to address the climate change problem and reduce greenhouse gases.

Labour force participation rate The percentage of working-age persons who actively take part in the labour market by either working or seeking work, i.e. the proportion of the adult population classified as employed or unemployed.

Labour market A market where workers search for paid employment and employers search for the service of employees. The intersection of these two groups determines the wage level.

Legal Aid Free or inexpensive legal advice provided for people unable to afford an attorney.

Lender of last resort A public entity, usually the central bank, that provides emergency funds for struggling financial institutions considered too-big-to-fail.

Leverage (gearing) Acquiring large amounts of assets through borrowing in the hope that their value will increase.

Lifecycle hypothesis A theory postulating that individuals' consumption is driven by expected lifetime income rather than their income at that point in time.

Life expectancy An estimate of how long a person may live, based on age, gender and other demographic factors.

Liquid asset An asset able to be converted into a means of payment quickly, with little or no cost.

Liquidity In finance theory, it is the ease with which an asset can be converted into cash. The term is also used as a synonym of money.

Liquidity trap A problematic situation in which the central bank's attempts to increase the amount of money in the economy and stimulate aggregate demand are ineffective. This may happen in a zero interest rate environment where cash and bonds become perfect substitutes and economic subjects hoard cash.

Look through a shock Not to respond to an economic disturbance, usually the central bank ignoring those on the supply side of the economy.

Maastricht Criteria A set of five conditions for key economic variables grounded in the Growth and Stability Pact that a country must meet to be able to be a part of the Euro currency.

Macroprudential policies Targeted rules and regulations aimed at reducing instability in financial markets, e.g. minimum capital requirements.

Market concentration A measure of the number of firms within a market and their respective shares of total production.

Market failure A situation where the market alone does not result in an efficient allocation of resources.

Medicare The public healthcare scheme in Australia through which residents have access to healthcare services.

Medicare levy A payment (2 per cent of taxable income as of mid-2015) that contributes towards Australia's public healthcare funding. Individuals with higher incomes are also subject to the Medicare levy surcharge, an extra 1–1.5 per cent payment.

Minimum wage An amount stipulated in the legislation as the lowest remuneration an employer is allowed to pay for a given job.

Mining boom A substantial increase in economic activity related to the extraction of a country's natural resources.

Mitigation Measures to eliminate or reduce the potential impact of a threat such as climate change.

Monetary aggregates Measures of the money supply in the economy based on the financial assets' liquidity.

Monetary base A measure of 'high-powered' money, consisting of currency plus the reserves private banks hold at the central bank.

Monetary Conditions Index An indicator used for the conduct of monetary policy in New Zealand during the 1997–99 period, combining the effect of a change in the interest rate and exchange rate in a certain proportion.

Monetary policy The process carried out by the country's central bank, usually consisting of interest rate changes to affect money supply, inflation and (in the short-term also) production.

Monetary transmission mechanism The various channels through which interest rate changes made by the central bank affect the key macroeconomic variables.

Money A good that serves as a medium of exchange, a unit of account and store of value. It derives its value from being declared legal tender by the government.

Money multiplier An indicator expressing the extent to which an injection of funds into the economy (such as a bank deposit from a foreign country) leads to an expansion of the money supply. The size of the multiplier largely depends on the commercial banks' reserve ratio.

Money supply Measure of the amount of money in the economy, namely currency plus current deposits.

Moral hazard A scenario in which an individual or entity (agent) has incentives to engage in behaviour that is deemed undesirable by another party in a transaction (principal), arising from the principal's inability to perfectly monitor the agent's behaviour.

Mortgage-backed securities Debt obligations that are claims to the cash flows of mortgage loans.

Mortgage securitisation The process of bundling mortgages and converting them into financial instruments such as collaterised debt obligations.

Mundell–Fleming model A framework relating an economy's exchange rate, interest rate and aggregate output. It assesses the effectiveness of monetary and fiscal policies under fixed as well as flexible exchange rates.

Myopic agents Individual or business entities whose decisions concentrate on the short-term perspective (benefits) while ignoring the long-term perspective (possible costs).

National Broadband Network (NBN) Australia-wide data network aiming to provide better fixed-line phone and wireless broadband connection to all Australians, including those in rural areas.

Natural monopoly An industry where a single firm can supply the whole market at a lower price than two or more firms due to the fixed cost being large in proportion to the variable costs.

Nature vs nurture debate The scientific discussion regarding the extent to which a person's characteristics are developed from genes (nature) or constitute learned behaviour (nurture).

Negative externality An activity that has an adverse economic impact on a third party without due compensation.

Negative gearing A situation of an investor borrowing money to invest with the income generated from the investment being less than the cost of servicing the loan. For example, if a house is bought as an investment and the rental income is less than the amount of interest paid on the loan, the asset is negatively geared.

Nominal income targeting A monetary policy regime that attempts to achieve a pre-specified level of nominal GDP, which implies that a drop in economic activity automatically raises the targeted level of inflation.

Nominal/real interest rate The nominal interest rate is the level quoted in loan and deposit agreements. The real interest rate is the nominal rate adjusted for the effect of a (expected) change in prices. For example, if the nominal rate is 5 per cent and the inflation rate is 2 per cent, then the real interest rate is approximately $5 - 2 = 3$ per cent.

Notional Defined Contribution (NDC) system A government-run pension system whereby an individual's contributions to the public purse are calculated as if they had been paid to the person's individual superannuation account. The scheme is commonly a reform step between pay-as-you-go and pre-funded systems.

Oligopolistic market An industry that is characterised by a small number of competing firms, featuring prices that are lower than in the case of monopoly but higher than under perfect competition.

Open market operations A central bank procedure that involves buying and selling government securities in order to manipulate the money supply and conduct monetary policy.

Opportunity cost The loss of potential benefit from other alternatives when one alternative is chosen. It is calculated as the value of the best alternative forgone net of its associated costs.

Optimum currency area A geographic region in which the economic cycles of the countries are synchronised, and therefore the benefits of a single currency more than outweigh its costs.

Paid parental leave An employee benefit that provides paid time off work to care for a newborn child.

Paradox of thrift A scenario in which people's attempt to save more during an economic downturn has the counterproductive effect of lowering people's saving. This is because it leads to a drop in aggregate demand, higher unemployment and lower wages.

Parts per million A measure of very small concentrations in a much larger body of mass, e.g. carbon dioxide in the atmosphere.

Passive investment A strategy focused on the long-term performance of a portfolio, achieved by the 'buy and hold' approach instead of frequent buying and selling of financial assets.

Patent The government's award of exclusive rights for production and sale of an innovation.

Pay-as-you-go financing A public accounting scheme (for example, in the pensions area) whereby revenues from one year are used to pay expenditures in the same year; there is no pre-accumulation of funds.

Payroll taxes Payments by employees and employers to the government tax office, calculated as some proportion of the worker's wage.

Pension pillars A multi-faceted approach to saving for retirement, including a public pay-as-you-go first pillar, an employer-based third pillar and possibly also a pre-funded private second pillar such as the superannuation scheme in Australia.

Pension system A scheme designed to ensure that elderly people have sufficient financial resources after their retirement.

Percentile A statistical term expressing a certain value below which a given percentage of the sample appears.

Phillips curve The observed inverse relationship between inflation and unemployment in the short run.

Policy lag The time it takes for a policy instrument to affect the target variables.

Ponzi scheme A deceitful investment system in which the returns of a member are paid from money new members bring in rather than from the investment profits.

Population ageing A demographic trend whereby the median age of a nation is rising over time due to increases in life expectancy and/or decreases in fertility.

Positive externality An unintentional benefit to a third party arising from an economic action. For example, it is beneficial to a beekeeper to be located near a fruit farm as it provides a free source of nectar helping to maximise honey production.

Postage stamp pricing Charging the same price to groups of customers irrespective of the different associated costs.

Poverty The condition where one's basic necessities such as food, shelter and clothing are not met.

Prediction markets Platforms in which participants place bets on various economic and political outcomes. The bets jointly imply the market's assessment of the probability of those events, which can be their useful predictor.

Price discrimination The act of selling a good at different prices to different customers (whose demand sensitivity to prices differ) in order to maximise profits.

Prisoner's dilemma A strategic situation in which 'rational' parties do not cooperate in attempting to secure an additional benefit for themselves, which paradoxically leads to poorer outcomes for all of them.

Privatisation Transfer of ownership from the public sector to the private sector in exchange for a financial payment to the government.

Productivity An indicator expressing the efficiency of an economic system; i.e. how effectively inputs are converted into outputs.

Progressive taxation A scheme whereby the percentage of income paid as tax increases with income so that high-income earners pay a greater proportion than low-income earners.

Public debt (gross/net) The amount of money owed by the government. If reported in net terms, adjustment is made by subtracting money owed to the government and some of its other assets that could be used to repay the debt.

Quantitative easing Unconventional type of monetary policy whereby the central bank buys large amounts of various financial instruments from private institutions in order to lower long-term yields and stimulate the economy.

Regressive system A scheme that redistributes money from low- to high-income earners, which contradicts the principle of solidarity and is therefore seen as undesirable.

Regulation A legislated norm aiming to alleviate some market imperfection and ensure socially desirable economic outcomes. This is usually by changing the incentives and actions of market participants.

Regulatory capture A form of political corruption where a body, set up to act in the public interest, advances special groups' interests rather than the social good.

Reserve Bank of Australia (RBA) Australia's central bank, the main functions of which are issuing the currency and conducting monetary policy.

Resource Rent Tax A tax on profit generated from the extraction of natural resources.

Retention rate The percentage of customers kept; for example, the proportion of first-year undergraduate students continuing to second year.

Reverse mortgages A loan through which home owners can borrow money against the value of their property.

Ricardian equivalence A theory stating that a debt-financed fiscal expansion is incapable of stimulating aggregate demand, because in anticipation of future tax increases (to pay off the debt) people save the stimulus rather than spend it.

Risk averse A preference of most people for reducing the probability of various undesirable future scenarios, even if this implies a decrease in the person's expected monetary payoff.

Risk pooling Reducing risk by distributing it more evenly across a large number of individuals and/or firms, commonly seen in the insurance sector.

Risk premium The added incentive (such as a higher nominal interest rate) an investor requires to undergo the risk involved in an investment.

School productivity The incremental academic achievement of the school's students per dollar of expenditure.

Seigniorage A country's profit from printing money.

Skill mismatch The gap between workers' skills and the skills the labour market requires.

Sovereign default A government's insolvency or bankruptcy, a failure to pay back their debt in full.

Speculation Risky financial actions attempting to gain from the short-term swings in the markets by buying low and selling high.

Stern Review A 2006 report funded by the British government written by Professor Nicholas Stern on climate change.

Stock market A network of buyers and sellers that trade shares, most commonly through a stock exchange.

Structured Investment Vehicle (SIV) A smaller credit-spread-focused financial institution used (prior to the GFC) by banks to 'offload' some of their assets and make their balance sheet satisfy regulatory requirements.

Subprime mortgage A loan for financing the purchase of real estate by a person with problematic credit history and/or low income.

Subsidy An economic benefit provided by the government to a sector or group of individuals. It should only be provided in justified cases with the goal of improving economic or social policy.

Superannuation The Australian pension system whereby people (with the contribution of employers) save up for their retirement, and subsequently receive benefits from their accumulated funds.

Supply/demand shocks A sudden event that changes the amount of aggregate supply/demand and thus output and prices.

Tariff A tax applied to imported goods and services – the most common barrier to trade.

Tax break An instance of the government agreeing to lower (or zero) tax being imposed.

Tax churning A process in which an individual pays taxes and receives welfare benefits in the same period, which commonly leads to unnecessary administrative burden and social losses.

Taylor rule A prescription for monetary policy stating how the central bank should alter its interest rate instrument in response to deviations of inflation from the target and output from its potential level.

Technological progress A measure of the speed and extent of the innovative process.

Tier 1 capital A classification of a company's own financial resources indicating its solvency and ability to withstand unexpected losses.

Time-inconsistency problem A (predictable) change in a decision-maker's preferred action over time in a way that conflicts with the original preferred action.

Too-big-to-fail A large financial institution covered by an implicit government guarantee of a rescue (bailout). This is because its bankruptcy is deemed too dangerous for the financial system as a whole.

Total dependency ratio A measure of the non-working demographic group (children and the elderly) relative to the working age (generally between 15 and 64 years old).

Trade balance/surplus/deficit The zero/positive/negative difference between the value of a country's exports and imports in a given period.

Uncertainty A situation in which a credible degree of probability cannot be assigned to an outcome.

Unconscionable conduct An act that is judged highly unfair – against conscience and society's norms.

Unemployment The situation whereby an agent of working age is actively looking for a job, but is unable to find one.

Use it or lose it rules A policy that requires users to relinquish a benefit after a stated period of time. For example, health insurance policies commonly offer benefits that have to be used within 12 months.

Wage–price spiral A feedback loop (vicious circle) where an increase in wages to keep up with growing price levels contributes to further increases in the price level and wages.

Wage rigidity Inadequate and/or slow adjustment of nominal wages to changes in economic conditions, which leads to inappropriate real wages, deviations from natural levels of output and unemployment, and a surge in economic cycles.

Zero-lower-bound on interest rates The inability of central banks to reduce interest rates (substantially) below zero, even if the state of the economy warrants such a reduction.

Index